W9-BNB-273

THE CHOPSTICKS-FORK PRINCIPLE x 2
A BILINGUAL READER

筷子叉子 双管齐下
双语课本

FOR ADVANCING

THE TEACHING & LEARNING OF

教 & 学
ENGLISH & CHINESE

英 & 汉
LANGUAGE & CULTURE

语言 & 文化

THE CHOPSTICKS-FORK PRINCIPLE x 2
A BILINGUAL READER

筷了叉子 双管齐下
双语课本

CATHY BAO BEAN 包圭漪

DONGDONG CHEN 陈东东

HOMA & SEKEY BOOKS

PARAMUS, NEW JERSEY

FIRST EDITION

Copyright © 2009 by Cathy Bao Bean

All rights reserved. No part of this book may be reproduced, stored in a retrieval system, or transmitted in any form, or by any means, electronic, mechanical, photocopying, recording or otherwise, without prior permission from the publisher.

Library of Congress Cataloging-in-Publication Data

Bean, Cathy Bao, 1942-
  The chopsticks-fork principle x 2, a bilingual reader / Cathy Bao Bean, Dongdong Chen. -- 1st ed.
      p. cm.
Chinese and English.
Includes bibliographical references.
ISBN 978-1-931907-51-4 (pbk.)
1. Chinese language--Textbooks for foreign speakers--English. I. Chen, Dongdong. II. Title.
PL1129.E5B43 2009
495.1'82421--dc22

                          2008039022

Published by Homa & Sekey Books
3rd Floor, North Tower
Mack-Cali Center III
140 E. Ridgewood Ave.
Paramus, NJ 07652

Tel: 201-261-8810; 800-870-HOMA
Fax: 201-261-8890; 201-384-6055
Email: info@homabooks.com
Website: www.homabooks.com

Printed in U.S.A.
1 3 5 7 9 10 8 6 4 2

DEDICATION

TO MY PARENTS, SISTERS AND HUSBAND

献给我父母、姐妹和先生

— Dongdong Chen

TO ALL WHO LIVED THESE STORIES WITH ME

献给我故事中的每一个人

— Cathy Bao Bean

ACKNOWLEDGEMENTS
特此鸣谢

BENNETT BEAN

陈衍

CHENGZHI CHU 储诚志

NANDOR FORGACH 傅南地

BOSHUO HAO 郝博硕

WAYNE HE 何文潮

WEIJIA HUANG 黄伟嘉

DI LUO 罗荻

GLENN NORDIN

TERRY RUSSELL

沈三山

JOYCE WANG 王训愉

王亚娜

TAO-CHUNG YAO 姚道中

MEI ZHAO 赵梅

赵一飞

CONTACT AUTHORS OR PUBLISHER

FOR SUPPLEMENTAL MATERIAL PERTAINING TO THIS BOOK

CATHY BAO BEAN: cathy@cathybaobean.com

DONGDONG CHEN: chendong@shu.edu

HOMA & SEKEY BOOKS: info@homabooks.com

TABLE OF CONTENTS

PART ONE
A DIFFERENT PASSPORT FOR A NEW JOURNEY WITH A CHINESE-AMERICAN GUIDE

PART TWO
TOURING THE WORLD FOR POSSIBILITIES AND TECHNIQUES TO UNDERSTAND CULTURAL DIVERSITY

PART THREE
SHAPING A LIFE WITH THE POSSIBILITIES AND TECHNIQUES

目录

第一辑：走南闯北的"护照"——美籍华人的心路历程

第二辑：周游列国、开阔眼界、欣赏多元文化

第三辑：塑造多姿多彩的生活

TO THE READER

"Culture hides much more than it reveals, and strangely what it hides,
it hides most effectively from its own participants."
— Edward Hall, *The Silent Language*

DEAR READER:

We have developed a unique, bilingual, cross-cultural reader composed of personal, often humorous, stories followed by innovative as well as more standard exercises to help you become more proficient in your second *language and culture* while better understanding your first.

The goal of foreign language education according to the (American) Modern Language Association's *Ad Hoc* Committee on Foreign Languages (as published in *Perspectives*) is to raise "translingual and transcultural competence." We achieve this through *The Chopsticks-Fork Principle* in that "familiar" events—like traveling, the first day at school and birthdays—are seen through "foreign" lenses tinted with good humor. In the process, both CFL and EFL learners can appreciate both the target and native culture. To this end, stories from Cathy Bao Bean's Chinese-American life and book, *The Chopsticks-Fork Principle, A Memoir and Manual,* are presented in English even as they are interpreted and *re*-presented in Chinese by Dongdong Chen whose linguistic training and teaching expertise pedagogically enrich the narrative. By revealing the text and context in two languages and cultural settings, the impact of the "5 Cs"—**C**ommunication, **C**ulture, **C**onnections, **C**omparisons and **C**ommunities—are *at least* doubled.

Understanding how Cathy Bao Bean learned to talk, analyze, laugh and cry about being *bi*cultural will prepare you, as it did her, to travel in a *multi*cultural world. By acquiring these techniques, it is our hope that you will also learn how to talk, analyze, laugh and cry about your own experiences.

Sincerely,

CATHY BAO BEAN and DONGDONG CHEN

致读者

"文化掩盖的东西比揭示的多，奇怪的是，它最有效地隐瞒了本文化的人"。

—选自爱德华·霍尔的著作《沉默的语言》

(Edward Hall, *The Silent Language*）

亲爱的读者：

　　我们编写了这本独特的双语、跨文化读物。其中不乏风趣的真实故事和具创意的练习。希望您通过阅读本书能使自己的外语语言和文化运用技能变得更加娴熟；同时也能进一步提高母语语言和文化修养。

　　美国现代语言协会外诰特设委员会提出外语学习要培养学生的跨语言和跨文化的能力。我们用筷子-叉子原则实现这一外语教学的最高境界。习以为常的事件，诸如旅行、开学第一天仪式、生日聚会用"外国人的"角度和幽默的色彩一一剖析，使以英语和汉语为外语的学习者可以更好地欣赏外语和母语文化。为此，包圭漪（Cathy Bao Bean）根据其美籍华人的生活阅历及英文著作 *The Chopsticks-Fork Principle, A Memoir and Manual* 编写了一个故事，陈东东（Dongdong Chen）根据其语言学训练和教学经验用中文重现这些轶事哲理。这种用双语揭示文化的方法极大地体现了五大外语教学目标：沟通、文化、贯连、对比、社区。

　　了解包圭漪对双元文化的喜怒哀乐将帮助您驰骋于多元文化世界。我们希望，通过学习这些技能，您也能更好地驾驭您的双元文化经历。

真诚地，

包圭漪，陈东东

Notes About The Text

1. Understanding humor is probably the best way to gauge how well you understand a culture. Therefore, we punctuate with three exclamation marks **!!!** where you should smile in one or both languages. If you don't get the joke, find someone who can explain—this is a great way to start a good conversation.

2. We emphasize the connection between written and spoken communication by using, in addition to regular quotation marks " ", a second kind " " in the English text when the vocal intonation suggests a non-literal meaning and/or ironic tone.

3. "Four-Character Word" (FCW) is used to include the Chinese *chéngyǔ* expressions which have four characters, and those which are not *chéngyǔ*, given that the structure of four-character words is unique and productive in Chinese. Not to be confused with the English "four-letter words," these FCWs are used by all members of Chinese society **!!!**

4. Footnotes contain culturally relevant information so please read them before continuing.

5. Stylistically, the text is written in the informal voice of Cathy Bao Bean—so expect some linguistic variety!

6. For pinyin orthography, we follow *Dúsù Rules for Hanyu Pinyin Orthography,* and *Xiàndài Hànyǔ Guīfàn Cídiǎn.*

7. The following list of abbreviations are used:

abbr.	=	abbreviation
adj.	=	adjective
adj. p.	=	adjectival phrase
adv.	=	adverb
conj.	=	conjunction
f.c.w.	=	four-character word
m (n)	=	nominal measure word
m (v)	=	verbal measure word
n.	=	noun
n.p.	=	noun phrase
p.n.	=	proper noun
p.p.	=	prepositional phrase
prep.	=	preposition
pron.	=	pronoun
r. f.	=	reduplicated form
v.	=	verb
v (c)	=	verb-complement
v.o.	=	verb-object
v.p.	=	verb phrase

体例说明

1. 理解幽默也许是衡量您对某一文化了解程度的最佳途径。因此，我们特地在英语或汉语或两者有趣的地方用三个感叹号来提醒您 。假如您未理解，请找人解释。这是用外语开始精彩会话的第一步。

2. 我们强调书面语和口语的联系。为此在英语课文中，除了使用正规的双引号" "以外，我们还使用 " " 这一符号以表示该处带有非字面或讽刺语气。

3. 我们用"四字词"涵盖四个字的成语和非成语的四字词组。由于汉语独特的构词结构，以中文为母语的本族语者使用大量的"四字词"。请勿与英语中"四字母词"相混淆!!!

4. 每章的脚注提供了许多文化背景知识。请先读脚注，再继续阅读课文。

5. 英语课文采用的是包圭漪的非正规语体，请留意不同的语言风格。

6. 汉语拼音的拼写规范以《汉语拼音正词法基本规则》和《现代汉语规范词典》为准则。

7. 以下是本书使用的缩写词：

abbr.	=	缩写词
adj.	–	形容词
adj. p.	=	形容词短语
adv.	=	副词
conj.	=	连词
f.c.w.	=	四字词
m (n)	=	名量词
m (v)	=	动量词
n.	=	名词
n.p.	=	名词短语
p.n.	=	专有名词
p.p.	=	介词短语
prep.	=	介词
pron.	=	代词
r. f.	=	重叠形式
v.	=	动词
v (c)	=	动词-补语
v.o.	=	动词-宾语
v.p.	=	动词短语

PART ONE

A DIFFERENT PASSPORT

FOR

A NEW JOURNEY

CHINESE-AMERICAN GUIDE

第一辑

走南闯北的"护照"——美籍华人的心路历程

CHAPTER ONE

*E*MIGRATIONS, *IM*MIGRATIONS AND *INTER*GRATIONS

Because this book uses personal stories, it would help to know more about the characters. The following introduction to them is written in the first-person in the voice of the author, Cathy Bao Bean, chronicling:

- Her *e*migration from China

- Her *im*migration to the United States

- Her *e*migration from being a suburban "Banana"

- Her *inter*gration into a "Chinese-American" who happily lives on the hyphen.

Although facts may be hard, the brain doesn't have to be **!!!** In other words, one set of (physical) *circumstances* can produce different (human) *situations*. By evaluating how our lives are changed by age, travel, education, jobs, and relationships, we hope:

- Facts can become more or less relevant because what happens later can change the meaning of what happened earlier.

- People, including yourself, can become more complex, more multicultural, and more interesting.

THE FACTS

- In Ānhuī, when my mother's young feet were bound so each would be mangled into a three-inch "golden lotus," she rebelled and freed herself of the bindings. Probably my grandmother looked at my mother's size five—a little over nine inches—with the same horror that my mother felt decades later when she wore pointy-toed spike heels but saw me wearing clunky Birkenstock sandals. This was as close as I would get to walking in my mother's footsteps **!!!**

2

第一章

离开中国、移居美国、融汇东西

本书采用真人真事，所以了解故事"人物"对阅读本书有很大帮助。下面以作者包圭漪（Cathy Bao Bean）为第一人称，按时间顺序从四个方面来介绍：

- 离开中国

- 移居美国

- 从郊区的"香蕉"脱颖而出

- 游刃了东西文化的"美籍华人"

这些也许是"铁的"事实，但是人脑不需要那么"坚硬"**!!!** 换句话说，同样的物质环境，不同的人会有不同的解释。年龄、旅行、教育、工作、人际关系会改变我们的生活。我们希望通过评估这些因素：

- 往事或多或少会变得前后相关，因为后来发生的事能改变先前发生的事的意义；

- 人们，包括你自己，会变得更为成熟、更具多元化、更加丰富多彩。

人生轨迹

- 在安徽，当我母亲那双嫩脚被布裹着以致有朝一日变成"三寸金莲"时，她奋力反抗，最后解放了双脚。当初我外祖母也许惊讶、恐怖地看着我母亲那五号大（九英寸多）的脚。几十年后，当我母亲自己穿着尖尖的高跟鞋时，也用同样可怕的眼光看着我那笨拙的勃肯牌（Birkenstock）凉鞋。我几乎是踩着母亲的脚印在走路**!!!**

- 与此同时，在天津，当我父亲因逃学而被抓时，他那气愤的父亲把他揍了一顿，然后重新给他起了一个名字，叫"新第"，希望这调皮的孩子能痛改前

3

- Meanwhile, in Tientsin (Tiānjīn), when my father was caught playing hooky, his irate father beat him then renamed him "Xīndì," hoping a drubbing and dubbing would teach the mischievous child to walk a narrower, more traditional path. My father did learn a lesson, which is why he never laid a hand on me and always smiled when calling me by my nickname "Xiǎo Tǔfěi" or "Little Bandit."

- I was born as Bao Kwei-yee (Bāo Guìyí), a native of Ningpo (Níngbō) by virtue of my father's ancestry, in the Year of the Water Horse, during the 77th or 78th Cycle (depending on which book you consult).

- Four years later, my parents, older sister, Bette, and I arrived in Brooklyn, New York. As a result, I became "Cathy Bao," born in Kweilin/Kuei-lin/Guilín (depending on which atlas you consult) on August 27, 1942. In the process, I also became a Virgo and Dodgers[1] baseball fan.

- One day later, Bette and I were enrolled in Public School No. 8. I spoke no English. Bette could say "Lucky Strike" and "Shut up." The Principal let her skip two grades and made me do kindergarten twice **!!!**

- In 1949, we moved to New Jersey. I started to think in English and forget in Chinese.[2]

- In 1960, I went to college where I majored in History, Government. And screaming **!!!** The screaming didn't get me the lead role in *The Diary of Anne Frank* because the Director didn't think a Chinese could play a Jew from Amsterdam but it did get me on the Tufts cheerleading squad[3] and, from there, onto a full page of *Sports Illustrated*…clothed **!!!**

---

[1] 1947 年黑人球星吉克·罗宾逊（Jackie Robinson）进入大联盟队（major league team）打棒球，首次打破了种族歧视。对于许多移民来说，这表明美国是一个富有机会的国家。

[2] 虽然现在我能说中文，但我只能用英文思考问题。假如记忆是用某种特殊语言储存于大脑的话，这就是为什么我现在对我孩提时的记忆一点也没有了的缘故，因为那时我所感受的一切都借助于中文。然而，有时候我跟其他人一样仍然习惯用母语来描述自己的感情生活。

[3] 那个时候，有色人种很少在美国公共场所露面。比如，直到二十世纪的最后三十年由白人扮演亚洲人的做法才在好莱坞的电影中逐渐消失。当时不成文的规则是，不同种族的男女演员在屏幕上不能有身体接触。同样，那时候，大学每年招收的非白人和犹太人学生也限制在少数几个。我觉得，Bette 和我是白人学校里第一批有色人种的拉拉队员。

非，走上一条更狭窄、更传统的道路。我父亲的确从中吸取了教训——这就是他从未碰过我一个手指，而且每次叫我"小土匪"的绰号时也总是笑嘻嘻的原因。

- 我叫包圭漪，[1] 祖籍宁波，[2] 生在第 77 或第 78 轮的水马年 [3]（看以哪本书为依据）。

- 我 1942 年 8 月 27 日生于桂林（"桂林"的拼音有 Kweilin、Kwei-lin、Guilín，看你查哪本地图集），四年后，我父母、姐姐包柏漪（Bette）和我来到了纽约的布鲁克林（Brooklyn）。于是，我成了"Cathy Bao"，有了处女座星座，并成了布鲁克林道奇（Dodgers）棒球队的"粉丝"。

- 第二天，我和 Bette 在第八公立学校注册。由于我不会说英文，而 Bette 会说"Lucky Strike"和"Shut up"，校长让她跳了两级，却让我上了两次幼儿园!!!

- 1949 年，我们搬到新泽西州（New Jersey）。从此我开始用英语思考问题，同时也忘了所有跟中文有关的记忆。[4]

- 1960 年，我进塔夫茨大学（Tufts University）读书，主修历史和政治学，还有叫喊!!! 虽然我的叫喊技能没有使我赢得《安妮少女日记》（The Diary of Anne Frank）剧中的女主角，因为导演认为中国人演不好一个来自阿姆斯特丹（Amsterdam）的犹太人，但是却让我进了学校的拉拉队。我做拉拉队员的一张照片后来还被登在著名的《体育画报》（Sports Illustrated）杂志上......当然是穿着衣服的呵!!!

---

[1] It used to be that siblings shared a common component in their two-syllable first names. In our case, it was the "yee" of "Kwei-yee". My parents also gave us English names that sounded like the Chinese ones.

[2] When asked, "Where are you from?" the Chinese answer would cite the paternal family home.

[3] This refers to one of the possible combinations of twelve animals and five elements that add up to the sixty years of one Chinese cycle. The nature of the animals and elements is supposed to describe personality traits as well as what kind year to expect.

[4] Although I can still speak Chinese, I now only think in English. So, if memories are stored in our brains in a particular language, then this is the reason I have no memories of my childhood when I experienced everything "in Chinese." Nevertheless, I, and many others, sometimes describe our emotional life in our first language, the language of family feelings.

- In 1962, I heard Malcolm X tell my roommate she was no longer a Negro, she was a Black Woman.

- In 1963, debutante Hope Cooke married the Crown Prince of Sikkim. She was dropped from the *Social Register*. That same year, my sister married Winston Lord. He too was dropped from the *Social Register*. In those days, marrying an Asian, even if she were the Empress Dowager, was an automatic disqualifier for social elitism. By 1986, Bette had written three world-wide best-sellers and Winston was the American ambassador to China.

- In 1964, I went to graduate school in California and learned how to Philosophize and be my own Matchmaker.

- One month later, I met Bennett Bean, a Caucasian male who didn't wear socks and wanted to make art. He thought I was Japanese.

- Two days after he found out I wasn't, he was declared psychologically unfit to serve in the army.

- Two weeks later, he proposed. I accepted.

- In 1965, I went to the University of California in Berkeley. There I met several of Bennett's friends. Mostly they lived in communes and/or nudist colonies. I became a Democrat **!!!**

- The next year, Bennett started teaching at a private college. After he shaved his beard and cut his hair, we got married. My mother said the word "sex" to me for the first time.

- In 1967, the Whitney Museum bought Bennett's sculpture even though it was upside down, and I was accused of being a prostitute in a big New York hotel because the concierge didn't know that women with long Chinese hair might prefer using their brains for a living.

- The next year, I started teaching at a state college for less money than I made as a waitress **!!!**

- One year later, we were both fired. The students protested and we were both re-hired.

- 1962 年，我听马尔科姆 X（Malcolm X） 说我的室友再也不是黑鬼了，而是黑人妇女。

- 1963 年，当初出茅庐的霍普·库克（Hope Cooke）嫁给了锡金国王之后，她被《社会名流录》（Social Register）除了名。同年，温斯顿·洛德（Winston Lord）娶了我姐姐，他的名字也从《社会名流录》中消失了。在那个年代，谁要是与亚洲人通婚，即使她是什么豪门贵妇，也会被社会名流所不容!!! 到 1986 年，我姐姐出了三本全球畅销书，温斯顿当了美国驻中国大使。

- 1964 年，我去加利福尼亚的一个研究生院读书，研究怎样从哲学角度看问题，以及怎样为自己做红娘。

- 一个月以后，我遇见班尼特·比恩（Bennett Bean）， 一个不穿袜子却想做艺术的白人男子。他以为我是日本人。

- 后来班尼特发现我不是日本人。两天后他被诊断为心理上不宜服兵役。

- 两个星期后，班尼特向我求婚，我接受了。

- 1965 年，我去加州大学伯克利（Berkeley）分校读书，在那儿我遇见了班尼特的几位朋友。他们大多群居在一起，过着共产主义或裸体主义或两者皆有的生活。从此我变成了一个自由主义者，赞同民主党的思想和观点。

- 第二年，班尼特开始在一所私立大学任教。他剃了胡须、剪了头发后我们结了婚。这时我母亲第一次跟我提起"性"这个字。

- 1967 年，纽约惠特尼艺术博物馆（Whitney Museum ）购买了班尼特的雕塑作品，并把雕塑倒放着。同年我在纽约的一家大旅馆被指控为妓女，因为大堂经理不知道留有长发的中国女人会凭借大脑谋生。

- 接下来的那一年，我开始在一所州立大学教书，薪水比餐馆服务员挣的还少。

- In 1970, we met Billie Burke, the actress. Once the Good Witch Glinda in *The Wizard of Oz* movie, she had since become a Real Estate agent **!!!** She pointed us toward the east coast equivalent of Kansas, northwestern New Jersey, where we bought an old farmhouse. The neighbors thought I was the maid.

- One year later, I got tenure. When the Chairperson asked me to make curtains for the office, I became a feminist before I was a Chinese-American.

- In 1973, I became a United States citizen—that's when the mayor asked me to be a Lenape Indian in the town's Bicentennial Parade. To this day I am still not sure which error in judgment led him to make this request **!!!**

- In early 1974, our son, William, was born.

- In 1986, I turned 44 and didn't stop smoking because the hypnotist couldn't find my subconscious **!!!** So I opened up an aerobics studio. My mother was not happy that the daughter she brought from China and educated at great expense would spend hours per week:

  1) Going up and down a fake step at the rate of 4.1 miles per hour, sweating to the beat of some of the most dreadful music available to humankind, then

  2) Developing and stretching muscles in ways that could be training for football or the *Kama Sutra*, or both **!!!**

- Around this time, my college roommate became an African-American.

- Soon thereafter, William and I entered The Warring States Period. We argued about everything. I was sure he needed my motherly advice about dating, grades, clothes, haircuts, driving, even how to walk. My son was equally sure I could benefit by a change in temperature—as in "chill." Happily, I remembered that Confucius had never heard about hormones **!!!** In other words, our warring state was not due to his lack of filial piety or my loss of parental moral rigor, but was the result of putting an adolescent son and menopausal mother under the same roof.

- In 1990, William got his first tattoo.

- 一年以后，我和班尼特同时被解雇。因学生的抗议，我们又重新受聘回校工作。

- 1970 年，我们遇见女演员比利·伯克（Billie Burke）。曾在电影《绿野仙踪》（The Wizard of Oz）中扮演好巫婆葛琳达的比利现在成了一个房地产经纪人，她为我们介绍了相当于东部堪萨斯（Kansas）的新泽西州西北部，在那儿我们购置了一个旧农房。邻居以为我是家中的女佣。

- 一年以后，我拿到了大学的终身教职。当系主任要我为办公室缝制窗帘时，我成了一个女权主义者（辞掉了工作）。

- 1973 年，我成为了美国公民。那年，我们的镇长要我在镇二百周年大游行中扮演德拉瓦族印第安人（Lenape Indian）。我全今仍不明白究竟是什么错误判断使得那位镇长向我提出这样的要求。

- 1974 年初，我们的儿子，威廉（William），出生了。

- 1986 年，我 44 岁时还在抽烟，因为施行催眠术的心理学家找不到我的潜意识可以帮我戒烟!!! 于是我开了一个健身房。为此我母亲很不高兴，因为她从中国带到美国，并用昂贵学费培养出来的女儿居然每周花去人量时间从事以下两项活动：

  （1） 在一个人工的台阶上以每小时 4.1 英里的速度、伴着最糟糕的音乐节奏跑上跑下直到汗流浃背；

  （2） 用训练足球运动员或性爱高于或者训练两者的方法来锻炼肌肉!!!

- 大约这个时候，我大学的室友成了非裔-美国人。

- 不久，威廉和我进入"战国时期"（Warring States Period）。我们为一切而争吵。我深信，儿子在很多方面都需要我这个当母亲的指导，比如，谈情说爱、学习成绩、穿着打扮、发型、开车，甚至怎么走路。而我儿子也同样坚信，如果我的脾气改一改，比如冷静一点，那将对我大有裨益。幸运的是我

- One year after that, I slept next to some of my teeth **!!!** and started to write my memoir. William got a second tattoo.

- Ten years later, William married Lisa, an ABC.

- By the twenty-first century, both my parents had died and I, at fifty-eight, was no longer a Chinese "child."

- In 2002, once again the Year of the Water Horse, I began the second cycle of my life as an elder, teaching people to live and laugh by the Chopsticks-Fork Principle.

In doing so, I realized that *everyone* except hermits is *at least* bicultural. When we leave our home, the language spoken by our family may be technically the same one used with friends, teachers, colleagues, neighbors, bosses, priests, and government officials but the words and style of conversation can vary greatly. The cultural norms are often determined by ethnicity as "Chinese-American," "African-American," and "Irish-American,"[4] but there is also cultural identity based on gender, generation, sexual orientation, place, minority and majority status. Often, the latter simply think they are "normal" and everyone else is "different."

None of us automatically knows how to talk about our several cultural selves because Edward Hall was correct when he wrote in his book, *The Silent Language*, "Culture hides much more than it reveals, and strangely what it hides, it hides most effectively from its own participants."

This book will try to make our several selves and cultures unhidden at the same time it provides a means to view our facts retrospectively as well as be more linguistically competent through translation and interpretation.

---

[4] 为了避免不当的措辞，当我使用"American"时，我指居住在美国的人民。但是请不要忘记该术语也泛指北美洲人和南美洲人。

记得孔夫子从未听说过荷尔蒙**!!!** 换句话说，我发现，我和儿子之所以有战争既不是因为他不孝顺，也不是因为我管教不严，而是青春期的儿子和更年期的母亲生活在同一屋檐下的结果。

- 1990 年，威廉有了第一个纹身。

- 一年以后，我和我的牙齿一起睡觉（我戴起了假牙）**!!!** 这时我开始写回忆录，而威廉也有了第二个纹身。

- 十年以后，威廉娶了丽莎，一个生在美国的华人女孩。

- 在二十一世纪来临之前，我的父母都已过世。五十八岁的我再也不是中国人的"孩子"了。

- 2002 年，又一个水马年。作为长者的我开始传授筷子-叉子原则，指导人们如何嬉笑生活，以此展开我人生的第二轮。

回首往事，我发现除了隐士以外，每个人都会涉及到至少两种不同的文化。当我们来到社会，和朋友、老师、同事、邻居、上司、牧师以及政府官员交谈所使用的语言与我们在家同家人所用的语言理论上是一个，然而，我们在会话时的用辞和风格却大不相同。人们经常从种族的角度把文化分为"华裔-美国人的"、"非裔-美国人的"、"爱尔兰裔-美国人的"，[5] 等等。但是，生活里还有另一种文化认同，那是由性别、代沟、性爱倾向、地区、少数族群和多数族群的身份而决定的。属于多数族群的人常常以为他们是"正常的"，而别人都是"不正常的"。

没有人不假思索就知道怎样谈论几种不同的文化自我，因为爱德华 霍尔（Edward Hall） 在他《沉默的语言》（The Silent Language）一书中曾经这么说过："文化掩盖的东西比揭示的多，奇怪的是，它最有效地隐瞒了本文化的人"。

本书试图展现多种自我和文化，同时为您提供一个回顾往事的机会，并以翻译和解释为手段使您提高语言能力。

---

[5] To avoid some awkward phrasing, when I use the term "American," I am referring to people residing in the U.S.A. Nevertheless, please do not forget that there are both North and South Americans.

VOCABULARY

emigration	n.	leaving one country to live in another.	移居出去	yíjū chūqù
immigration	n.	moving into a country after leaving another.	移居进来	yíjū jìnlái
**inter****gration**	n.	this word is original to this book and created to suggest journeying between two equally important cultures and not "integration" when different racial groups co-exist peacefully as legal and social equals.	融汇	rónghuì
chronicle	v.	to write a chronological record of events, history, annals.	把…… 载入编年 史，记述	bǎ…zǎirù biān-niánshǐ, jìshù
live on the hyphen	v.p.	during the 1980s, it became customary (first among the non-White population in the U.S.) to describe their racial or ethnic heritage by placing a hyphen between it and "American." The phrase was popularized in 1994 with the publication of _Life On the Hyphen: The Cuban-American Way_ by Gustavo Perez Firmat. By the 2000 census, this practice was formally acknowledged so that people could choose more than one category such that there were 63 possible combinations. Also – "living _in_ the hyphen" to indicate overlapping heritages.	生活在双 元文化中	shēnghuó zài shuāngyuán wénhuà zhōng
"Banana"	p.n.	during the 1950s, even though 38% of Teaneck, New Jersey was Jewish, the dominant culture was "WASP" or **W**hite **A**nglo-**S**axon **P**rotestant. New terms like **"Banana"** to describe Asians (yellow on the outside, white on the inside) and **"Oreo"** (a cookie that is black on the outside, white on the inside) to describe African-Americans came into use as People of Color became conscious of how much they were influenced by the WASP values and attitudes—even to the extent they were prejudiced about their own cultures.	指具有英 国后裔白 人价值观 的黄种人 指具有英 国后裔白 人价值观 的黑人	zhǐ jùyǒu Yīng-guó hòuyì báirén jiàz-híguān de huángzhǒngrén zhǐ jùyǒu Yīng-guó hòuyì báirén jiàzhí guān de hēirén
hard facts	n.p.	since facts are presumed to be true state-	铁的事实	tiě de shìshí

生词

移居	移居	yíjū	v.o.	emigrate
真人真事	真人真事	zhēnrén-zhēnshì	f.c.w.	actual person and event
阅读	閱讀	yuèdú	v.	read
本书	本書	běnshū	n.	this book
包圭漪	包圭漪	Bāo Guīyí	p.n.	the Chinese name for Cathy Bao Bean
第一人称	第一人稱	dì-yī rénchēng	n.p.	the first person
香蕉	香蕉	xiāngjiāo	n.	Banana (refers to an Asian-American who is "yellow" on the outside but "white" on the inside)
脱颖而出	脫穎而出	tuōyǐng'érchū	f.c.w.	blossom, develop
游刃于	游刃于	yóurènyú	v.p.	be highly competent in
文化	文化	wénhuà	n.	culture
美籍华人	美籍華人	Měijí Huárén	p.n.	Chinese-American, Americanized Chinese
人脑	人腦	rénnǎo	n.	human brain
坚硬	堅硬	jiānyìng	adj.	hard
换句话说	換句話說	huànjùhuàshuō	conj.	in other words
解释	解釋	jiěshì	n./v.	interpretation, interpret
人际关系	人際關係	rénjì guānxì	n.p.	human or interpersonal relationships
往事	往事	wǎngshì	n.	past events
或多或少	或多或少	huòduō-huòshǎo	f.c.w.	more or less
包括……在内	包括……在内	bāokuò…zàinei	v.p.	include sth.
多元化	多元化	duōyuánhuà	adj.	diversified
丰富多彩	豐富多彩	fēngfù-duōcǎi	f.c.w.	interesting, rich and colorful
轨迹	軌跡	guǐjì	n.	track, path along which a person goes through his or her life
安徽	安徽	Ānhuī	p.n.	Anhui (province)
以致	以致	yǐzhì	conj.	so…that…
有朝一日	有朝一日	yǒuzhāoyīrì	f.c.w.	some day in the future
三寸金莲	三寸金蓮	sāncùn jīnlián	n.	golden lotus
奋力	奮力	fènlì	v.	exert oneself to the utmost, do all one can
双脚	雙腳	shuāngjiǎo	n.	one's two foot
英寸	英寸	yīngcùn	m(n)	(English) inch
尖尖	尖尖	jiānjiān	adj.	pointy-toed
高跟鞋	高跟鞋	gāogēnxié	n.	high-heeled shoes
笨拙	笨拙	bènzhuō	adj.	clunky, clumsy, awkward
勃肯牌	勃肯牌	Bókěnpái	p.n.	the Birkenstock brand
凉鞋	涼鞋	liángxié	n.	sandals

		ments, describing them as "hard" suggests they are immutable. Also – being realistic, however difficult, as in "facing the cold truth."		
in retrospect	p.p.	different from "hindsight" when new information would have resulted in making a better prediction, this process is to look back and *think about* what happened.	回顾	huígù
mangle	v.	to disfigure, ruin, crush. Also – n. a machine for squeezing excess water from laundry.	碾压	niǎnyā
spike heels	n.p.	women's footwear with the vamp tapering to a point, and high heels, sometimes 3-5 inches long, tapering to a narrow base of less than ½ inch diameter.	女子高跟鞋	nǚzǐ gāogēnxié
clunky	adj.	not refined or delicate, awkward-looking.	笨拙	bènzhuō
Birkenstock	n.p.	a German-made shoe popularized in the 1960s by the "hippies" and "flower children" that is characterized by a solid, not delicate, thick sole.	勃肯牌	Bókěnpái
sandals	n.	flat, open shoes that generally have straps on top.	凉鞋	liángxié
play hooky	v.p.	not attend (school) when one should.	逃学	táoxué
drubbing	n.	corporal punishment; a beating or thrashing.	殴打	ōudǎ
dubbing	n.	the act of naming or conferring knighthood.	命名	mìngmíng
walk a narrow path	v.p.	from the phrase "the straight and narrow," meaning the morally proper way to behave implying a strict adherence to rules and/or (severe) limitations.	走小路	zǒu xiǎolù
lay a hand on sb.	v.p.	to use physical force with the intention of forcing or imposing one's will on another.	动手打人	dòngshǒu dǎrén
Year of the Water Horse	p.n.	this refers to one of the possible combinations of twelve animals and five elements that add up to the sixty years of one Chinese cycle. The nature of the animals and elements is supposed to describe personality traits as well as what kind of year to expect.	水马年	Shuǐmǎ'nián
Virgo	p.n.	this refers to one of twelve astrological	处女座星	Chùnǚzuò

与此同时	與此同時	yǔcǐ-tóngshí	f.c.w.	at the same time, meanwhile
逃学	逃學	táoxué	v.o.	play hooky
揍一顿	揍一顿	zòuyīdùn	v.p.	beat, hit, strike
痛改前非	痛改前非	tònggǎi-qiánfēi	f.c.w.	sincerely mend one's ways
狭窄	狹窄	xiázhǎi	adj.	contracted, cramped, narrow; limited
从未	從未	cóngwèi	adv.	never
笑嘻嘻	笑嘻嘻	xiàoxīxī	r.f.	grinning, smiling broadly
绰号	綽號	chuòhào	n.	nickname
土匪	土匪	tǔfěi	n.	bandit, brigand
祖籍	祖籍	zǔjí	n.	original family home, ancestral home
宁波	寧波	Níngbō	p.n.	Ningbo (city in Zhejiang Province)
水马年	水馬年	Shuǐmǎnián	p.n.	Year of Water Horse
布鲁克林	布魯克林	Bùlǔkèlín	p.n.	Brooklyn
生于	生於	shēngyú	v.p.	be born in
桂林	桂林	Guìlín	p.n.	Guilin (Guangxi)
拼音	拼音	pīnyīn	n.	spelling
地图集	地圖集	dìtújí	n.	atlas
处女座星座	處女座星座	Chùnǚzuò Xīng-zuò	p.n.	Virgo (constellation)
粉丝	粉絲	fěnsī	n.	fans (also, vermicelli made from bean starch)
公立学校	公立學校	gōnglì xuéxiào	n.p.	public schools
新泽西州	新澤西州	Xīnzéxīzhōu	p.n.	New Jersey
主修	主修	zhǔxiū	v.	major in
叫喊	叫喊	jiàohǎn	v.	scream
安妮	安妮	Ānnī	p.n.	Anne Frank
剧	劇	jù	n.	play
女主角	女主角	nǚ zhǔjué	n.p.	female lead
阿姆斯特丹	阿姆斯特丹	Āmǔsītèdān	p.n.	Amsterdam
犹太人	猶太人	Yóutàirén	p.n.	Jew
塔夫茨大学	塔大茨大學	Tǎfūcí Dàxué	p.n.	Tufts University
拉拉队	拉拉隊	lālāduì	n.	cheer leading squad
马尔科姆 X	馬尔科姆 X	Mǎ'ěrkēmǔ X	p.n.	Malcolm X
室友	室友	shìyǒu	n.	roommate
黑人	黑人	hēirén	n.	person with black skin
初出茅庐	初出茅廬	chūchū-máolú	f.c.w.	debutante
霍普•库克	霍普•庫克	Huòpǔ Kùkè	p.n.	Hope Cooke
锡金	錫金	Xíjīn	p.n.	Sikkim
名流	名流	míngliú	n.	elite, person distinguished by society
同年	同年	tóngnián	n.	same year
温斯顿•洛德	溫斯頓•洛德	Wēnsīdùn Luòdé	p.n.	Winston Lord

		signs of the Western Zodiac. The character of each is supposed to describe personality traits and is associated with one of twelve periods of one solar year.	座	Xīngzuò
Lucky Strike	p.n.	this was a popular brand of American cigarettes.	好彩牌香烟	Hǎocǎipái Xiāngyān
skip	v.	to pass to a higher grade, point or place without stopping at the intervening grade, point or place; to omit or not attend. *Also – walking fast, lightly leaping, dancing, or advancing by putting one foot forward and then hopping on it once before doing the same with the other.*	跳级	tiào jí
Diary of Anne Frank		this very important play, translated into 67 languages, was based on the personal record written by a 13-year old Jewish girl who hid from the Nazis for 25 months. The climax occurs when she screams at seeing the police.	《安妮少女日记》	《Ānnī Shàonǚ Rìjì》
Sports Illustrated		since 1964, this magazine has annually featured a "swimsuit" issue that is known for photographs of females wearing swimsuits that have, over the years, needed less and less material to make **!!!**	《体育画报》	《Tǐyù Huàbào》
debutante	n.	a young woman who "comes out" or is formally introduced to society as was the custom among daughters of those in the *Social Register* [see below].	初进社交界的女子	chū jìn shèjiāojiè de nǚzǐ
Social Register		or "Blue Book." Started at the end of the 19th century, this book listed the social "upper crust." Like the *New York Times* wedding announcements, inclusion was limited to the "high society" of "WASPs" to the exclusion of others, including Catholic Whites. Being "dropped" used to be reported in national newspapers!	《社会名流录》	《Shèhuì Míngliú Lù》
Empress Dowager	n.	an (elderly) woman who holds (high) rank, office, or position by virtue of being a surviving widow. In China, this term usually refers to Cíxǐ Tàihòu.	豪门贵妇 慈禧太后	háomén guìfù Cíxǐ Tàihòu
disqualifier	n.	an intentional misuse of the verb "disqualify"—to render unfit or ineligible to com-	被……取	bèi…qǔxiāo

亚洲人	亞洲人	Yàzhōurén	p.n.	Asians
通婚	通婚	tōnghūn	v.o.	intermarry
即使	即使	jíshǐ	conj.	even if
豪门贵妇	豪門貴婦	háomén guìfù	n.p.	Empress Dowager
不容	不容	bùróng	v.	not approved of
畅销书	暢銷書	chàngxiāoshū	n.	best-seller
红娘	紅娘	hóngniáng	n.	match-maker
班尼特·比恩	班尼特·比恩	Bānnítè Bǐˈēn	p.n.	Bennett Bean
白人	白人	Báirén	p.n.	Caucasian, White man or woman
服兵役	服兵役	fúbīngyì	v.p.	serve in military
求婚	求婚	qiúhūn	v.o.	propose marriage
加州大学	加州大學	Jiāzhōu Dàxué	p.n.	University of California
伯克利	伯克利	Bókèlì	p.n.	Berkeley
分校	分校	fēnxiào	n.	one of the school campuses
群居	羣居	qúnjū	v.	live in commune
共产主义	共產主義	gòngchǎn zhǔyì	n.	communism
裸体主义	裸體主義	luǒtǐ zhǔyì	n.	nudism
自由主义	自由主義	zìyóu zhǔyì	n.	liberalism
两者皆有	兩者皆有	liǎngzhě jiēyǒu	f.c.w.	both
者	者	zhě	n.	person (who does sth.)
民主党	民主黨	Mínzhǔdǎng	p.n.	Democratic party
赞同	贊同	zàntóng	v.	approve of, agree with
私立大学	私立大學	sīlì dàxué	n.p.	private university
任教	仕教	rènjiào	v.o.	teach
剃	剃	tì	v.	shave
胡须	鬍鬚	húxū	n.	beard, moustache
雕塑	雕塑	diāosù	n.	sculpture
倒放	倒放	dàofàng	v.p.	be placed upside
指控	指控	zhǐkòng	v.	accuse
妓女	妓女	jìnǚ	n.	prostitute, whore
大堂经理	大堂經理	dàtáng jīnglǐ	n.	concierge, hotel manager
留有	留有	liúyǒu	v.	wear
长发	長髮	chángfà	n.	long hair
凭借	憑借	píngjiè	v.	rely on, use
谋生	謀生	móushēng	v.o.	earn a living
接下来	接下來	jiēxiàlái	adj.	then, the following
州立大学	州立大學	zhōulì dàxué	n.p.	(public, not private) state university
薪水	薪水	xīnshuǐ	n.	salary, wage, emolument
餐馆	餐館	cānguǎn	n.	restaurant
服务员	服務員	fúwùyuán	n.	waitress, waiter

		pete, enter, join, etc.	消资格者	zīgézhě
social elitism	n.p.	the idea or practice that a (small) group of people are more desirable, privileged. See *Social Register*.	社会精英论	shèhuì jīngyīnglùn
Berkeley	p.n.	the University of California in Berkeley was, like San Francisco, the birthplace of the "Hippie," "Flower Children," anti-Vietnam and anti-establishment movements—those who felt that no (government) agency could be trusted to honor individual freedom to be different from those in the mainstream or (WASP) norm.	伯克利，加利福尼亚大学伯克利分校 反-权力	Bókèlì, Jiālìfúníyà Dàxué Bókèlì Fēnxiào fǎn-quánlì
concierge	n.	French term for a hotel employee in charge of welcoming guests and providing special services.	大堂经理	dàtáng jīnglǐ
nudist	n.	someone who prefers to be naked, to wear no clothing.	裸体主义者	luǒtǐzhǔyìzhě
The Wizard of Oz		a (still popular) 1939 musical film about a girl from rural Kansas who, literally and figuratively, finds herself in a magical kingdom, trying to return home and to her "real" self. The theme and characters are often used as metaphors and archetypes for a wide variety of human conditions.	电影《绿野仙踪》	diànyǐng 《Lǜyě xiānzōng》
feminist	n.	a term that succeeded "suffragette" to describe those who believe in equal opportunity and rights for women as for men.	女权主义者	nǚquánzhǔyìzhě
Lenape Indian	p.n.	a member of a tribe inhabiting an area near the Delaware and Hudson rivers.	德拉瓦族印第安人	Délāwǎzú Yìndì'ānrén
hypnotist	n.	Sigmund Freud, a 19th-century thinker, is considered the "father of psychoanalysis." As a result of his approach to understanding human behavior and the importance of sex, Westernized cultures tend to believe a person's identity consists of a conscious, subconscious, ego, superego, id, etc. Being hypnotized or put into a trance-like state allows access to the "subconscious" self which is often "hidden" from the conscious mind.	施行催眠术的心理学家	shīxíng cuīmiánshù de xīnlǐxuéjiā
Kama Sutra		this 2,000 year-old book contains lessons	《爱经》	《Àijīng》

解雇	解僱	jiěgù	v.	fire, discharge
受聘	受聘	shòupìn	v.o.	be employed by
绿野仙踪	綠野仙蹤	Lǜyěxiānzōng		The Wizard of Oz (a movie)
巫婆	巫婆	wūpó	n.	wItch
葛琳达	葛琳達	Gělíndá	p.n.	Glinda
经纪人	經紀人	jīngjìrén	n.	broker, middleman, agent
相当于	相當于	xiāngdāngyú	v.p.	be equivalent of
堪萨斯	堪薩斯	Kānsàsī	p.n.	Kansas
购置	購置	gòuzhì	v.	purchase, buy
女佣	女傭	nǚyōng	n.	maid
教职	教職	jiàozhí	n.	teaching job
缝制	縫製	féngzhì	v.	sew
女权主义	女權主義	nǚquán zhǔyì	n.	feminism
镇长	鎮長	zhènzhǎng	n.	mayor
游行	游行	yóuxíng	n.	parade
印第安人	印第安人	Yìndì'ānrén	p.n.	(American) Indian
年初	年初	niánchū	n.	beginning of the year
威廉	威廉	Wēilián	p.n.	William
戒烟	戒煙	jièyān	v.o.	give up smoking
施行	施行	shīxíng	v.	apply
催眠术	催眠術	cuīmiánshù	n.	hypnotism
心理学家	心理學家	xīnlǐxuéjiā	n.	psychologist
潜意识	潛意識	qiányìshí	n.	the subconscious
健身房	健身房	jiànshēnfáng	n.	aerobics studio
昂贵	昂貴	ángguì	adj.	expensive, costly
台阶	臺階	táijiē	n.	step
英里	英里	yīnglǐ	m(n)	mile
汗流浃背	汗流浃背	hànliú-jiābèi	f.c.w.	sweat, perspire
性爱	性愛	xìngài	n.	love between the sexes, sexual love
高手	高手	gāoshǒu	n.	master, expert
两者	两者	liǎngzhě	n.	both
非裔	非裔	Fēiyì	p.n.	African descendent
战国时期	戰國時期	Zhànguó Shíqī	p.n	Warring States Period
争吵	爭吵	zhēngchǎo	v.	quarrel
深信	深信	shēnxìn	v.	firmly believe
在很多方面	在很多方面	zài hěnduō fāng-miàn	p.p.	in many ways
谈情说爱	談情說愛	tánqíng-shuō'ài	f.c.w.	romantic dating
穿着	穿着	chuānzhuó	n.	the way to be dressed
发型	髮型	fàxíng	n.	hair style

		and descriptions for human sexual intercourse hence its name in Sanskrit— "sensuous love" and "formula."		
Warring States Period		around 221 B.C.E. in China, the Qín managed to overwhelm the Chǔ , Hàn, Qí, Wèi, Yàn, and Zhào states.	战国时期	Zhànguó Shíqī
chill	v.	*Slang* - like "be cool," the idea is to calm down, not get upset.	冷静	lěngjìng
rigor	n.	strict, austere, extreme, harsh, scrupulous.	严格，严峻	yángé, yánjùn
menopausal	adj.	referring to the time when women cease to menstruate, usually between 45-50 years old.	更年期的	gēngniánqī de
ABC	abbr.	**A**merican **B**orn **C**hinese.	生在美国的华人	shēng zài Měiguó de Huárén
hermit	n.	sb. who lives alone, apart from society (often for religious reasons).	隐士	yǐnshì
ethnicity	n.	the customs, religion, language, appearance, etc. that characterize a people.	种族	zhǒngzú

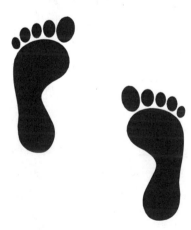

脾气	脾气	píqì	n.	temper
大有裨益	大有脾益	dàyǒu bìyì	f.c.w.	be of great benefit
孔夫子	孔夫子	Kǒngfūzǐ	p.n.	Confucius
荷尔蒙	荷爾蒙	hé'ěrméng	n.	hormone
孝顺	孝顺	xiàoshùn	v.	filial piety
管教	管教	guǎnjiào	v.	control, teach, or discipline sb.
青春期	青春期	qīngchūnqī	n.	adolescence, puberty
更年期	更年期	gēngniánqī	n.	menopause
屋檐	屋簷	wūyán	n.	roof, eaves
纹身	紋身	wénshēn	n.	tattoo
回忆录	回憶錄	huíyìlù	n.	memoir
丽莎	麗莎	Lìshā	p.n.	Lisa
过世	過世	guòshì	v.o.	die, pass away
长者	長者	zhǎngzhě	n.	elder, senior
传授	传授	chuánshòu	v.	teach
叉子	叉子	chāzi	n.	fork
嬉笑	嬉笑	xīxiào	v.	laugh and play
回首	回首	huíshǒu	v.o.	look back
隐士	隱士	yǐnshì	n.	hermit
上司	上司	shàngsī	n.	boss, supervisor
牧师	牧师	mùshī	n.	priest
政府官员	政府官員	zhèngfǔ guānyuán	n.p.	government official
用辞	用辭	yòngcí	n.	wording
大不相同	大不相同	dàbùxiāngtóng	f.c.w.	vary greatly
种族	種族	zhǒngzú	n.	race (of people)
华裔	華裔	Huáyì	p.n.	Chinese descent
爱尔兰裔	愛爾蘭裔	Ài'ěrlányì	p.n.	Irish descent
代沟	代溝	dàigōu	n	generation gap
性爱定向	性爱定向	xìng'ài dìngxiàng	n.	sexual orientation
少数族群	少數族羣	shǎoshùzúqún	n.	minority
不假思索	不假思索	bùjiǎ-sīsuǒ	f.c.w.	not think deeply
爱德华•霍尔	愛德華•霍爾	Àidéhuá Huòěr	p.n.	Edward Hall
揭示	揭示	jiēshì	v.	reveal, bring to light
隐瞒	隱瞞	yǐnmán	v.	hide
回顾	回顧	huígù	v.	review, look back

第一章

離開中國、移居美國、融匯東西

本書采用真人真事，所以了解故事"人物"對閱讀本書有很大幫助。下面以作者包圭漪（Cathy Bao Bean）為第一人稱，按時間順序從四個方面來介紹：

- 離開中國

- 移居美國

- 從郊區的"香蕉"脫穎而出

- 游刃于東西文化的"美籍華人"

這些也許是"鐵的"事實，但是人腦不需要那么"堅硬"!!! 換句話説，同樣的物質環境，不同的人會有不同的解釋。年齡、旅行、教育、工作、人際關系會改變我們的生活。我們希望通過評估這些因素：

- 往事或多或少會變得前后相關，因為后來發生的事能改變先前發生的事的意義；

- 人們，包括你自己，會變得更為成熟、更具多元化、更加豐富多彩。

人生軌迹

- 在安徽，當我母親那雙嫩腳被布裹着以致有朝一日變成"三寸金蓮"時，她奮力反抗，最后解放了雙腳。當初我外祖母也許驚訝、恐怖地看着我母親那五號大（九英寸多）的腳。幾十年后，當我母親自己穿着尖尖的高跟鞋時，也用同樣可怕的眼光看着我那笨拙的勃肯牌（Birkenstock）涼鞋。我幾乎是踩着母親的腳印在走路!!!

- 與此同時，在天津，當我父親因逃學而被抓時，他那氣憤的父親把他揍了一頓，然后重新給他起了一個名字，叫"新第"，希望這調皮的孩子能痛改前非，走上一條更狹窄、更傳統的道路。我父親的確從中吸取了教訓——這就是他從未碰過我一個手指，而且每次叫我"小土匪"的綽號時也總是笑嘻嘻的原因。

- 我叫包圭漪，[1] 祖籍寧波，[2] 生在第 77 或第 78 輪的水馬年 [3]（看以哪本書為依據）。

- 我 1942 年 8 月 27 日生于桂林（"桂林"的拼音有 Kweilin、Kwei-lin、Guilín，看你查哪本地圖集），四年后，我父母、姐姐包柏漪（Bette）和我來到了紐約的布魯克林（Brooklyn）。于是，我成了"Cathy Bao"，有了處女座星座，并成了布魯克林道奇（Dodgers）棒球隊的"粉絲"。

- 第二天，我和 Bette 在第八公立學校注冊。由于我不會說英文，而 Bette 會說"Lucky Strike"和"Shut up"，校長讓她跳了兩級，卻讓我上了兩次幼兒園!!!

- 1949 年，我們搬到新澤西州（New Jersey）。從此我開始用英語思考問題，同時也忘了所有跟中文有關的記憶。[4]

- 1960 年，我進塔夫茨大學（Tufts University）讀書，主修歷史和政治學，還有叫喊!!! 雖然我的叫喊技能沒有使我贏得《安妮少女日記》（The Diary of Anne Frank）劇中的女主角，因為導演認為中國人演不好一個來自阿姆斯特丹（Amsterdam）的猶太人，但是卻讓我進了學校的拉拉隊。我做拉拉隊員的一

---

[1] It used to be that siblings shared a common component in their two-syllable first names. In our case, it was the "yee" of "Kwei-yee". My parents also gave us English names that sounded like the Chinese ones.

[2] When asked, "Where are you from?" the Chinese answer would cite the paternal family home.

[3] This refers to one of the possible combinations of twelve animals and five elements that add up to the sixty years of one Chinese cycle. The nature of the animals and elements is supposed to describe personality traits as well as what kind year to expect.

[4] Although I can still speak Chinese, I now only think in English. So, if memories are stored in our brains in a particular language, then this is the reason I have no memories of my childhood when I experienced everything "in Chinese." Nevertheless, I, and many others, sometimes describe our emotional life in our first language, the language of family feelings.

張照片后來還被登在著名的《體育畫報》（Sports Illustrated）雜志上…… 當然是穿着衣服的呵!!!

- 1962 年，我聽馬爾科姆 X（Malcolm X） 説我的室友再也不是黑鬼了，而是黑人婦女。

- 1963 年，當初出茅廬的霍普 · 庫克（Hope Cooke）嫁給了錫金國王之后，她被《社會名流錄》（Social Register）除了名。同年，溫斯頓 · 洛德（Winston Lord）娶了我姐姐，他的名字也從《社會名流錄》中消失了。在那個年代，誰要是與亞洲人通婚，即使她是什么豪門貴婦，也會被社會名流所不容!!! 到 1986 年，我姐姐出了三本全球暢銷書，溫斯頓當了美國駐中國大使。

- 1964 年，我去加利福尼亞的一個研究生院讀書，研究怎樣從哲學角度看問題，以及怎樣為自己做紅娘。

- 一個月以后，我遇見班尼特 · 比恩（Bennett Bean），一個不穿襪子卻想做藝術的白人男子。他以為我是日本人。

- 后來班尼特發現我不是日本人。兩天后他被診斷為心理上不宜服兵役。

- 兩個星期后，班尼特向我求婚，我接受了。

- 1965 年，我去加州大學伯克利（Berkely）分校讀書，在那兒我遇見了班尼特的幾位朋友。他們大多群居在一起，過着共產主義或裸體主義或兩者皆有的生活。從此我變成了一個自由主義者，贊同民主黨的思想和觀點。

- 第二年，班尼特開始在一所私立大學任教。他剃了胡須、剪了頭發后我們結了婚。這時我母親第一次跟我提起"性"這個字。

- 1967 年，紐約惠特尼藝術博物館（Whitney Museum）購買了班尼特的雕塑作品，并把雕塑倒放着。同年我在紐約的一家大旅館被指控為妓女，因為大堂經理不知道留有長發的中國女人會憑借大腦謀生。

- 接下來的那一年，我開始在一所州立大學教書，薪水比餐館服務員掙的還少。

- 一年以后，我和班尼特同時被解雇。因學生的抗議，我們又重新受聘回校工作。

- 1970 年，我們遇見女演員比利 · 伯克（Billie Burke）。曾在電影《綠野仙踪》（The Wizard of Oz）中扮演好巫婆葛琳達的比利現在成了一個房地產經紀人，她為我們介紹了相當于東部堪薩斯（Kansas）的新澤西州西北部，在那兒我們購置了一個舊農房。鄰居以為我是家中的女傭。

- 一年以后，我拿到了大學的終身教職。當系主任要我為辦公室縫制窗簾時，我成了一個女權主義者（辭掉了工作）。

- 1973 年，我成為了美國公民。那年，我們的鎮長要我在鎮二百周年大游行中扮演德拉瓦族印第安人（Lenape Indian）。我至今仍不明白究竟是什么錯誤判斷使得那位鎮長向我提出這樣的要求。

- 1974 年初，我們的兒子，威廉（William），出生了。

- 1986 年，我 44 歲時還在抽烟，因為施行催眠術的心理學家找不到我的潛意識可以幫我戒烟!!! 于是我開了一個健身房。為此我母親很不高興，因為她從中國帶到美國、并用昂貴學費培養出來的女兒居然每周花去大量時間從事以下兩項活動：

  （1）在一個人工的臺階上以每小時 4.1 英里的速度、伴着最糟糕的音樂節奏跑上跑下直到汗流浹背；

  （2）用訓練足球運動員或性愛高手或者訓練兩者的方法來鍛煉肌肉!!!

- 大約這個時候，我大學的室友成了非裔-美國人。

- 不久，威廉和我進入"戰國時期"（Warring States Period）。我們為一切而爭吵。我深信，兒子在很多方面都需要我這個當母親的指導，比如，談情説愛、學習成績、穿着打扮、發型、開車，甚至怎么走路。而我兒子也同樣堅信，如果我的脾氣改一改，比如冷靜一點，那將對我大有裨益。幸運的是我記得孔大子從未聽説過荷爾蒙!!! 換句話説，我發現，我和兒子之所以有戰爭既不是因為他不孝順，也不是因為我管教不嚴，而是青春期的兒子和更年期的母親生活在同一屋檐下的結果。

- 1990 年，威廉有了第一個紋身。

- 一年以后，我和我的牙齒一起睡覺（我戴起了假牙）!!! 這時我開始寫回憶錄，而威廉也有了第二個紋身。

- 十年以后，威廉娶了麗莎，一個生在美國的華人女孩。

- 在二十一世紀來臨之前，我的父母都已過世。五十八歲的我再也不是中國人的"孩子"了。

- 2002 年，又一個水馬年。作為長者的我開始傳授筷子-叉子原則，指導人們如何嬉笑生活，以此展開我人生的第二輪。

回首往事，我發現除了隱士以外，每個人都會涉及到至少兩種不同的文化。當我們來到社會，和朋友、老師、同事、鄰居、上司、牧師以及政府官員交談所使用的語言與我們在家同家人所用的語言理論上是一個，然而，我們在會話時的用辭和風格卻大不相同。人們經常從種族的角度把文化分為"華裔-美國人的"、"非裔-美國人的"、"愛爾蘭裔-美國人的"，[5] 等等。但是，生活里還有另一種文化認同，那是由性別、代溝、性愛傾向、地區、少數族群和多數族群的身份而決定的。屬于多數族群的人常常以為他們是"正常的"，而別人都是"不正常的"。

沒有人不假思索就知道怎樣談論幾種不同的文化自我，因為愛德華 · 霍爾（Edward Hall）在他《沉默的語言》（The Silent Language）一書中曾經這麼説過："文化掩蓋的東西比揭示的多，奇怪的是，它最有效地隱瞞了本文化的人"。

本書試圖展現多種自我和文化，同時為您提供一個回顧往事的機會，并以翻譯和解釋為手段使您提高語言能力。

---

[5] To avoid some awkward phrasing, when I use the term "American," I am referring to people residing in the U.S.A. Nevertheless, please do not forget that there are both North and South Americans.

练习 EXERCISES

I. 思考和课堂讨论 FOOD FOR THOUGHT

A. PERSONAL 个人的

列出你的人生往事或里程碑，然后描述其重要意义。

Decide what are the facts or milestones of your life, then explain their significance to someone who is not like you by ethnicity, gender, age, etc.

B. GENERAL 普遍的

Some idiomatic words, abbreviations, or phrases are popular, useful, and thought-provoking. After reading the following explanation and sample sentence, discuss the question posed.

某些习惯用语、缩写词语或短语很流行、很有用，而且引人深思。阅读以下英语注释和例句，然后讨论问题。

> **expat** is derived from the Latin *expatria* (*ex* = "out of"; *patria* = "country").
>
> **comment:** There is usually a large **expat** community living wherever there are many global corporations with offices because they often employ people from many countries.
>
> **question:** What is the difference, if any, between an "expat" and an "immigrant"?

C. CROSS-CULTURAL 跨文化的

阅读以下短文，并用中文对所提出的问题进行讨论。

After reading the following, discuss in Chinese how or why being polite has changed.

> Sir Walter Raleigh—a writer and explorer—was dubbed a knight by Queen Elizabeth I of England. Thought to have laid his cloak on the ground so the queen could walk on it instead of step into a puddle, his name is synonymous with courtly manners. Since that time and for various reasons, polite men were expected to do certain things with respect to women:
>
> - Stand when a woman entered the room.
> - Open and hold the door for her.
> - Pay for the movies, dinner, etc. when going out together.
> - Walk on the side nearest the street.
> - Hold a coat from the back to help her put it on or take it off.

II. 配对 MATCHMAKER

A. VOCABULARY 词汇

找出以下两列中的对应词，并在其间划线。

Draw a connecting line between the word and its correct definition.

a.	移居出去	1.	play hooky
b.	回顾	2.	ethnicity
c.	严格，严峻	3.	emigrate
d.	出生在美国的人	4.	live on the hyphen
e.	施行催眠术的心理学家	5.	in retrospect
f.	命名	6.	chill
g.	种族	7.	feminist
h.	逃学	8.	Banana
i.	具有英国后裔白人价值观的黄种人	9.	immigrate
j.	冷静	10.	dub
k.	女权主义者	11.	hypnotist
l.	生活在双元文化中	12.	rigor
m.	移居进来	13.	ABC

a.	earn a living	1.	美籍华人
b.	culture	2.	殴打
c.	concierge	3.	从未
d.	inter-marry	4.	或多或少
e.	sandals	5.	大堂经理
f.	atlas	6.	高跟鞋
g.	social elitism	7.	文化
h.	drubbing	8.	社会精英论
i.	more or less	9.	地图集
j.	Chinese-American	10.	通婚
k.	skip	11.	跳级
l.	high-heeled shoes	12.	凉鞋
m.	never	13.	谋生

B. ANTONYMS & ALTERNATES 反义词和多义词

First draw a connecting line between the words or phrases in the left-hand column with the best possible <u>antonym</u> listed in the middle column, then draw a line between the antonym and an alternate meaning of the antonym listed in the right-hand column. <u>Be forewarned</u> that the part of speech may change from one column to the next and that slang terms may be used. E.g.,

"hit" ——————————— *"miss"* ——————— *"honorific for unmarried female"*

"warm" ——————————— *"cool"* ——————— *"excellent"*

首先在第二列中找出与第一列相对应的反义词，然后在第三列中找出与第一列相关的多义词。注意：词性会有变化。

		ANTONYMS		ALTERNATE MEANING
a.	kind and generous	1. **gifted**	i.	effortless, fluent
b.	unsuitable, ill-matched	2. **fancy**	ii.	prepared for
c.	calm down, soothe	3. **easy**	iii.	defeat
d.	particular, specific	4. **rosy**	iv.	*slang* sexually active
e.	tired and exhausted	5. **fresh**	v.	military officer
f.	without energy	6. **fitted for**	vi.	intend
g.	plain and unadorned	7. **frisky**	vii.	prefer, like
h.	difficult	8. **upset**	viii.	*informal* impudent, bold
i.	disinherited	9. **mean**	ix.	talented
j.	wan, pale	10. **general**	x.	optimistic

III. 解字/词、构字/词 DECONSTRUCTION & CONSTRUCTION

A. 将以下汉字分解成最小的构字部件，然后用每个部件构成三个汉字。例如"鸣"可以分解成"甲"和"鸟"两个部件。"甲"能构成"押"，"岬"，"钾"；"鸟"可以构成以"鸡"，"鸦"，"鸣"。请借助字典完成练习。

Deconstruct the following characters into the smallest components, then form 3 new characters using each component.

脱_____ 际_____ 安_____

华_____ 薪_____ 催_____

B. Using only the letters of the word "**EMIGRATION**," form English words that are not proper nouns, abbreviations, or acronyms and that consist of 4 or more letters. A letter can only be used again if it appears in the given word more than once. E.g., "gyrate" is unacceptable because there is no "y" and "moon" is not because there is only one "o." Like many Olympic

sports, weight categories mark performance. We filled in a few cells to get you started. Fill in the rest to achieve the highest category. If you think up more than 88, you beat the authors!

用"EMIGRATION"中的字母构词。新构建的词不能是专有名词、缩写词、或首字母缩略词。每个单词必须至少含有四个字母，但不能重复使用同一字母，除非该字母在"EMIGRATION"中出现两次。

CHAMPION STATUS						
FLY 13	BANTAM 26	FEATHER 39	LIGHT 52	WELTER 65	MIDDLE 78	HEAVY 88
emit	mite	gate	time			
emir	mate	grate	timer			

C. 用"真人真事"中的每个汉字组成不同的词。看看最多能组多少个词。

Use each of the characters in "真人真事" to form as many words (of 2-4 characters) as you can.

D. Pair any two of the following 12 words to form at least 8 different, unhyphenated words.

在下列十二个词中配对、组词，新组的词只能含有两个单词，中间没有连字号。请至少组出八个词。

wife wagon fly width house band butter worm grass inch love crab

IV. 阅读理解 READING QUIZ

根据课文，选择准确答案。Based on the text, choose the best answer.

1. 作者生于哪一个城市？

   a. 中国的桂林。

   b. 中国的宁波。

    c.   中国的天津。

    d.   美国的纽约。

2.   成为大学拉拉队一员需要什么技能？

    a.   会叫喊。

    b.   会表演。

    c.   会说英语。

    d.   会说中文。

3.   为什么惠特尼艺术博物馆把班尼特的雕塑作品倒放着？

    a. 因为博物馆的工作人员不懂艺术。

    b. 因为博物馆的工作人员不清楚。

    c. 因为博物馆的工作人员不合格。

    d. 作者没有解释。

4.   大约什么时候起黑人妇女在美国被称为非裔-美国妇女？

    a.   1962 年。

    b.   1973 年。

    c.   1974 年。

    d.   1986 年。

5.   为什么作者和威廉有一段"战国时期"的经历？

    a.   因为威廉不懂事，作者管教不严。

    b.   因为威廉不孝顺，作者指导不妥。

    c.   因为威廉不听话，作者脾气不好。

    d   因为威廉处于青春期，而作者处于更年期。

6.   阅读本书会有哪些收获？

    a.   学习中国文化。

    b.   学习美国文化。

    c   提高中文能力。

    d.   提高英文能力。

    e.   以上都对。

V. 填空 FILL IN THE BLANK

A. 选择正确答案。Choose the correct answer.

1. 我几乎是踩着母亲的_____在走路。

    a. 脚跟   b. 脚背   c. 脚步

2. 我父亲小时候不好好读书，经常_____在外。

    a. 逃课   b. 逃夜   c. 逃婚

3. 我会说中文，但我习惯用英文_____问题。

    a. 思想   b. 思维   c. 思考

4. 人们经常从种族这个_____来看文化。

    a. 角度   b. 态度   c. 程度

5. 上个世纪九十年代初, 我开始写_____。

    a. 备忘录   b. 回忆录   c. 同学录

B. Using your target language, write a word or phrase from the vocabulary lists and/or dictionary that means the <u>same</u> or is a <u>synonym</u> for the italicized word or phrase. Keep in mind that the part of speech and/or tense may have been adjusted to achieve grammatically correct results.

在以下段落中找出与斜体词意义相近的同义词。如果你所学的外语是中文，找出相应的中文词或短语。如果你所学的外语是英语，找出相应的英语词或短语。注意：词性或时态会有变化。

> Because the student liked to *skip classes*_____, his absences were *the reason for no longer being eligible* _____ to qualify for the *exclusivity* _____ associated with the school his royal mother had attended so, when he returned home for vacation, his mother insisted on *strict discipline* _____ when it came to his study schedule.

VI. 翻译 TRANSLATION

A. 将以下句子翻译成英文。Translate the following sentences into English.

1. 与此同时，在天津，当我父亲因逃学而被抓时，他那气愤的父亲把他揍了一顿，然后重新给他起了一个名字，叫"新第"，希望这调皮的孩子能痛改前非，走上一条更狭窄、更传统的道路。

2. 在那个年代，谁要是与亚洲人通婚，即使她是什么豪门贵妇，也会被社会名流所不容!!!

3. 同年我在纽约的一家大旅馆被指控为妓女，因为大堂经理不知道留有长发的中国女人会凭借大脑谋生。

B. Translate the following sentences into Chinese. 将以下句子翻译成中文。

1. In 1964, I went to graduate school in California and learned how to Philosophize and be my own Matchmaker.

2. The next year, I started teaching at a state college for less money than I made as a waitress.

3. None of us automatically knows how to talk about our several cultural selves because Edward Hall was correct when he wrote in his book *The Silent Language*, "Culture hides much more than it reveals, and strangely what it hides, it hides most effectively from its own participants."

VII. 完型填充　CLOZE TEST

A. 在以下短文的每一空格处填入一个汉字，如有可能，给出相应的英语单词。

Fill in a Chinese character that retains the original meaning or intent of the text, then write an English equivalent, if any.

在安徽，当我母亲_____双嫩脚被布裹_____以致有朝一日_____成"三寸金莲"时，_____奋力反抗，最后_____放了双脚。当初_____外祖母也许惊_____、恐怖地看着我_____亲那五号大（九_____寸多）的脚。几十_____后，当我母亲自_____穿着尖尖的高_____鞋时，也用同样_____怕的眼光看着_____那笨拙的勃肯_____凉鞋。

B. Fill in an English word or phrase that retains the original meaning or intent of the text, then write a Chinese equivalent, if any.

在以下短文的每一空格处填入一个英语单词，如有可能，给出相应的汉字或词。

In Ānhuī, when my mother's young feet _____ bound so each would be mangled into _____ three-inch "golden lotus," she rebelled and freed _____ of the bindings. Probably my grandmother looked _____ my mother's size five （a little over _____ inches）with the same horror that my _____ felt decades later when she wore pointy-toed _____ heels but saw me wearing clunky Birkenstock _____. This was as close as I would _____ to walking in my mother's footsteps **!!!** Meanwhile, _____ Tientsin (Tiānjīn), when my father was caught _____ hooky, his irate father beat him then _____ him "Xīndì," hoping a drubbing and dubbing _____ teach the mischievous child to walk a _____, more traditional, path.

VIII. 身体部位　BODY PARTS

A. There are many useful idioms which contain "body parts." Choose the most appropriate to fill in the blank based on your best guess of what the idiom means.

英语中的许多习惯用语含有表示"身体部位"的单词。在下面三个习惯用语中选择最恰当的填空。

     1. elbow grease   **2.** elbowroom   **3.** rub elbows with

He was a social climber who bought a big house that required much of his own _____ to clean and maintain. In this way, he could _____ celebrities while providing them with sufficient _____ to be seen and admired from across the room.

B. 将以下短文翻译成中文。注意：划线的词或短语与以上含有"身体部位"的习惯用语相对应。

Translate the following into Chinese taking note that the underlined words or phrases correspond to the meaning of the above "body parts."

The mother was proud that her daughter was going to <u>be in the same room with</u> so many important CEOs after only two weeks at her new job. After the CEO reception, the daughter reported that the room was so crowded that there was hardly any <u>room to breathe</u>, let alone have a conversation. In other words, she was telling her mother that simply standing near powerful people was no substitute for a lot of <u>hard work.</u>

C. Using your target language, create sentence(s) containing the following three English idioms or their Chinese equivalents.

用以下短语分别造句。如果你所学的外语是中文，请用中文来做这个练习。如果你所学的外语是英语，请用英语来做这个练习。

1. at one's elbow = 近在身边，伸手可及

2. out at the elbows = 穿得很破烂，衣衫褴褛，捉襟见肘，穷困潦倒

3. up to one's elbows = 忙死了，忙于（工作）

IX. 写作 PRÉCIS

用所学的外语总结课文。如果你用中文来写，请至少使用 450 个汉字，并用电脑打出摘要。如果你用英文来写，请不超过 450 个词。

Write a summary of this chapter in your target language. If writing in Chinese, use <u>more</u> than 450 characters; if writing in English, use <u>no more</u> than 450 words.

PART TWO

TOURING THE WORLD

FOR

POSSIBILITIES AND TECHNIQUES

TO UNDERSTAND CULTURAL DIVERSITY

第二辑

周游列国、开阔眼界、欣赏多元文化

CHAPTER TWO

SEEING THE DUCK-RABBITS IN THAILAND

 Is it a duck? A rabbit? A radish? A fish?[5]

If you concentrate, one or the other comes into view. Or something no one else has seen. But no matter how many you perceive, no matter how quickly you can switch from the "duck" to the "rabbit" and back again, the drawing can only be one thing at a time. This is what it's like to be *at least* bicultural—I am Chinese, then I am North American. I can't be both simultaneously but I can get faster at switching from one to the other. Like a good basketball player, you can also be more comfortable with the switching—one second you play offensively, the next you switch to a defensive mode. The game or circumstance is the same but you see the court and your options differently. You may be ethnically "North American" but you probably dress, talk, think, maybe even believe differently depending on whether you are at grandmother's, the bowling alley, work, or school. Switching en route from one place or frame of mind to another is a more accurate description of the bicultural experience than "melting pot" because it does not automatically suggest that becoming "Americanized" means destroying the distinctive character of the home culture. Furthermore, "switching" is itself a learning experience if you pay good attention to what's happening.

This switching happened when we visited Thailand in 1993. Spending a few days in Krabi, we stayed at an inexpensive place where young backpackers, mostly German, liked to stop. Although we shared our small palm hut with cockroaches the size of my thumb !!! and had electricity for just two hours each day, the view of the Andaman Sea from the fine white sand beach was divine. After dinner, we remained seated at our tables. On a wooden deck, it was the only area with lights. After the first night, we knew that the manager would eventually provide "entertainment"—Sylvester Stallone

---

[5]1985 年 3 月 22-24 日纽约大学石溪分校举行了 "On *In A Different Voice*" 学术研讨会。会上 Carol Gilligan 将鸭子-兔子的背景-前景图比喻成不同的观点。

36

第二章

在泰国的鸭子-兔子秀

 那是一只鸭子？一只兔子？一个红萝卜？一条鱼？[6]

如果你全神贯注地看这幅画，你可能会把它看成生活中不同的东西，也可能会把它看成人们从未见过的东西。 但是不管你看到了多少东西，也不管你怎么把一只鸭子看成一只兔子，然后又把兔子看成鸭子，如此来来去去、反反复复，这幅画在一个特定的时间里只可能表示一个东西。这就是所谓双元文化的意思所在。我先是中国人，然后是美国人。虽然我不可能在同一瞬间既当中国人又当美国人，但是我能在两者中间迅速变换角色，而且，我对这种角色的转换比较轻松自如。就像一个好的篮球运动员，一会儿防守，一会儿进攻。同一场球，你在不同的场地位置，就会扮演不同的角色。从人种上说，你是个美国人，但是你在奶奶或姥姥家、在保龄球馆、在公司、在学校，你的穿着、言语、思维、信仰可能会跟其他美国人不同。能够随时随地从一个地方或一种心态转换到另一个地方或另一种心态，这比用"熔炉"来描述什么是双元文化的经验更为准确，因为"转换"没有暗示如果"美国化了"就必须消除自己母语文化的特征。另外，假如你能仔细观察，"转换"本身也是一种学习经验。

1993 年我们在泰国旅游的时候就遇到过类似这样的转换。我们在卡拉比（Krabi）一个比较便宜的旅游胜地住了几天，很多徒步旅行者喜欢住在那里，他们大多是从德国来的。一间棕榈树的小木屋住着我和我先生，还有跟我拇指一样大的蟑螂!!!而且每天供电只有两个小时。然而，站在精细的白沙滩上遥望安达曼海（Andaman Sea）时，那景观在

---

[6] At the "On *In A Different Voice*" conference, State University of New York at Stony Brook, March 22-4, 1985, Carol Gilligan likened the background-foreground duck-rabbit drawing to the phenomenon of having different "voices" or basic outlooks.

on VHS. The "Rocky" movies were in stark contrast with the peaceful setting but that was all he could afford and not a bad choice since everybody but us were students. Our third evening, a quartet of young women arrived from Finland. Newcomers, they didn't know that Sylvester would soon appear on the TV screen. Seeing everyone just sitting at their tables, the four started singing in harmony. Their voices were sweet and clear—perfect accompaniment to the moonlight on the water. When we were all still savoring the last note, the quiet magic was suddenly destroyed by loud rock 'n roll music. People turned to look at the manager standing by a boom box. In response, he smiled until he saw how angry the guests were. He was bewildered.

He didn't understand. He had gone to Tourism School where he learned that it is a manager's duty to provide entertainment. When he heard the singing, he thought it was the singers' way of telling him that he had failed to respect their need for entertainment in a timely fashion. When the guests heard the raucous music, they jumped to the conclusion that the manager was rude and disrespectful. Meanwhile, his father, the owner of the resort, sensed something was wrong and was ready to blame his son who was losing his face as thoroughly as Michael Jackson had been losing his **!!!** to the song's refrain of "I'm Bad, I'm Bad, you know it!" [6]

The manager spoke Thai, a little French but no Chinese. His father spoke Chinese and Thai but no English. None of the other tourists spoke Thai, French or Chinese but they all knew German. Most knew some English. I spoke English, some Chinese, a bit of French, about 10 words of German—mostly about eating milk and bread **!!!**—and no Finnish. Trying to explain the misunderstanding caused by the "duck-rabbit" situation got so complicated that I gave up and started disco dancing with my husband. This dramatic, non-linguistic, solution by two elders made everybody laugh at no one's expense.

---

[6]这是美国歌星迈克尔·杰克逊唱的一首名为《坏》的歌中的一句歌词。

人间是罕见的。第二天晚上，我们吃了晚饭，坐在外面木头平台上的餐桌旁，唯一一个有灯光照明的地方，我们知道旅馆经理一会儿要给大家提供一点儿娱乐——放西尔维斯特·史泰龙（Sylvester Stallone）的电影录像。平和温柔的夜晚跟那血腥残暴的《洛奇》(Rocky)电影形成了极大的反差， 可那是他力所能及提供的唯一的娱乐，一个并不太糟糕的选择，因为除了我和我先生以外，其他都是年轻学生。第三天晚上，来了四个年轻的芬兰女孩。她们刚到，不知道一会儿要放史泰龙电影，见大家静静地坐着，就唱了起来。甜美、清澈的歌声与海水、明月遥相呼应。当我们还陶醉在美妙的歌声中时，突然，震耳的摇滚乐打破了宁静。大家不约而同地看着站在音响旁的经理，他微笑地看着大家，而在座的游客却愤愤不平， 他一下子不知所措。

经理不明白为什么。他上过旅游学校，学过职责须知，所以当他听到女孩唱歌时，以为自己没有为游客及时提供娱乐，失职了。[7] 然而游客听到刺耳的摇滚乐时，却断定，这个经理太粗鲁、太无礼了。 这时候，经理的父亲，旅游胜地的老板，觉得苗头不对，赶紧责怪儿子，因为儿子像歌星迈克尔·杰克逊（Michael Jackson）一样丢尽了脸!!! 摇滚曲子不断地重复着，"你们知道喔，我可不错！我可不错！"[8]

经理说泰语，会一点儿法语，但不会中文。他父亲说中文和泰语，但不会英语。其他游客谁也不说泰语、法语或中文，但都会说德语，大多数人知道一点儿英语。我说英语，会一点儿中文、一小点儿法语，还有大约十个德文单词——大多跟喝牛奶、吃面包有关!!! 芬兰语，一点儿也不会。我想解释这个由"鸭子-兔子"而引起的误会，可又无能为力，只好打消了念头，跟先生跳起了迪斯科。这种戏剧性的、无言的解决方法没有伤害任何人，却逗得游客开怀大笑。

---

[7] Asians try not to criticize directly but prefer hinting—especially if the complaint is from a person of lesser status. One night, soon after my younger sister arrived in the U.S. from China, she walked several times between the TV and me. This was her way of telling me that, if I were a responsible older sister, I should realize the TV volume was so loud that she couldn't study. I did nothing, thinking she was getting a soda. When she felt forced to tell me, I asked, in my Western mode, "Why didn't you just say so?"

[8] These lyrics are from the title song of Michael Jackson's 1987 album *Bad*.

VOCABULARY

offensive	adj.	of a game player who is aggressively trying to score a point/goal/basket. Together with teammates doing the same, they form the noun "offense." Also – causing displeasure, annoyance, insult, repugnance, disgust.	进攻	jìngōng
defensive	adj.	of a game player who is trying to prevent an opponent from scoring and/or protecting a teammate from attack. Together with teammates doing the same, they form the noun "defense."	防守	fángshǒu
bowling alley	n.p.	a place of leisure with long wooden lane(s) where (teams of) players roll a heavy ball from one end to knock down as many as ten wooden pins arranged at the other end.	保龄球馆	bǎolíngqiúguǎn
court	n.	a quadrangle, often standardized, where games are played. Also – a place to hold legal proceedings; a small, often open-air enclosed space; a small street; a monarch's retinue.	篮球场	lánqiúchǎng
en route	p.p.	Anglicized French phrase meaning "on the way."	在途中	zài túzhōng
backpacker	n.	people, often young and on a limited budget, who travel carrying only clothes, supplies, etc. that will fit in a soft container that is worn on the back by putting arms through straps.	背包旅行者	bēibāo lǚxíngzhě
cockroach	n.	any of several nocturnal insects characterized by a flattened body and speed, often considered a pest and associated with unclean conditions.	蟑螂	zhāngláng
divine	adj.	pertaining to god(s) and/or their celestial abode therefore "the most" wonderful, beautiful, superb.	好极了	hǎo jí le
VHS	abbr.	acronym for Video Home System, the precursor of the CD and DVD for viewing movies.	家用录像系统	jiāyòng lùxiàng xìtǒng
stark	adj.	unadorned, desolate, utter, extreme, absolute.	完全的	wánquán de
quartet	n.	a group of four, often organized to sing or play music.	四个一组	sì gè yī zǔ

生词

鸭子	鴨子	yāzi	n.	duck
兔子	兔子	tùzi	n.	rabbit
秀	秀	xiù	n.	show
红萝卜	紅蘿卜	hóngluóbo	n.	red radish
全神贯注	全神貫注	quánshén-guànzhù	f.c.w.	concentrate on sth.
幅	幅	fú	m(n)	used for paintings, cloth, silk, fabric
如此	如此	rúcǐ	adv.	in this way
反反复复	反反覆覆	fǎnfǎn-fùfù	r.f.	repeatedly
所在	所在	suǒzài	n.	location
既……又……	既……又……	jì…yòu…	conj.	both…and…
瞬间	瞬間	shùnjiān	n.	in the twinkling of an eye
当	當	dāng	v.	be
迅速	迅速	xùnsù	adj.	rapid
变换	變換	biànhuàn	v.	switch, alter
角色	角色	juésè	n.	role
转换	轉換	zhuǎnhuàn	n./v.	transformation/transform
轻松自如	輕鬆自如	qīngsōng-zìrú	f.c.w.	with ease
就像	就像	jiùxiàng	adv.	as if
防守	防守	fángshǒu	v.	defend
进攻	進攻	jìngōng	v.	attack
场地	場地	chǎngdì	n.	field, place
人种	人種	rénzhǒng	n.	ethnicity
奶奶	奶奶	nǎinai	n.	paternal grandmother
姥姥	姥姥	lǎolao	n.	maternal grandmother
保龄球馆	保齡球館	bǎolíngqiúguǎn	n.	bowling alley
信仰	信仰	xìnyǎng	n.	belief
思维	思維	sīwéi	n.	thinking
随时随地	隨時隨地	suíshí-suídì	adv.	momentarily
心态	心態	xīntài	n.	mind set
熔炉	熔爐	rónglú	n.	melting pot
描述	描述	miáoshù	v.	describe
暗示	暗示	ànshì	v.	suggest
美国化	美國化	Měiguóhuà	v.	Americanize
消除	消除	xiāochú	v.	destroy, terminate
母语	母語	mǔyǔ	n.	mother tongue
特征	特徵	tèzhēn	n.	distinctive character
仔细	仔細	zǐxì	adj.	careful

savor	v.	to unhurriedly enjoy or appreciate a flavor, usually associated with the sense of taste.	尽情享受	jìnqíng-xiǎngshòu
rock 'n roll	n.	shortened from "rock and roll" and, more recently, to just "rock," this style of music was popularized in the 1950s by Elvis Presley, Little Richard, and Chuck Berry (whose song, *Johnny B. Goode*, is "discovered" in the film, *Back to the Future*) and is characterized by a fast, very noticeable (drum) beat, (loud) electric guitar/piano accompaniment to repetitious phrasing of sound and words.	摇滚乐	yáogǔnyuè
boom box	n.	*slang* - a portable radio that also plays music tapes and CDs stereophonically so that, when the volume is very high, the effect can be deafening, i.e., like a sonic boom.	音响	yīnxiǎng
raucous	adj.	somewhat or seemingly disorderly, boisterous, harsh, strident.	刺耳的	cìěr de
refrain	n.	recurring phrase or melody in a musical or poetical composition. "To the song's refrain" is to do something like dancing, clapping or marching in time with or to the rhythm of the music. Also – v. to consciously not do something, to abstain.	重复	chóngfù

观察	觀察	guānchá	v.	observe
类似	類似	lèisì	adj.	similar
卡拉比	卡拉比	Kǎlābǐ	p.n.	Krabi
旅游胜地	旅遊勝地	lǚyóu-shèngdì	f.c.w.	resort, a place for vacationers
徒步旅行	徒步旅行	túbù lǚxíng	v.p.	backpack, hike with a backpack
棕榈树	棕櫚樹	zōnglǘshù	n.	palm
木屋	木屋	mùwū	n.	hut
拇指	拇指	mǔzhǐ	n.	thumb
蟑螂	蟑螂	zhāngláng	n.	cockroach
供	供	gōng	v.	supply
精细	精細	jīngxì	adj.	fine
沙滩	沙灘	shātān	n.	sand beach
遥望	遙望	yáowàng	v.	look into the distance
安达曼	安達曼	Āndámàn	p.n.	Andaman
景观	景觀	jǐngguān	n	scene
人间	人間	rénjiān	n.	earthly world
罕见	罕見	hǎnjiàn	v.	seldom seen
餐桌	餐桌	cānzhuō	n.	dining table
照明	照明	zhàomíng	v (c)	lighting, illumination
娱乐	娛樂	yúlè	n.	entertainment
西尔维斯特·	西爾維斯特·	Xī'ěrwéisītè		
史泰龙	史泰龙	Shǐtàilóng	p.n.	Sylvester Stallone
平和温柔	平和溫柔	pínghé-wēnróu	f.c.w.	peaceful, gentle
血腥残暴	血腥殘暴	xuèxīng-cánbào	f.c.w.	brutal
洛奇	洛奇	Luòqí		Rocky (a movie)
形成	形成	xíngchéng	v.	form
反差	反差	fǎnchā	n.	contrast
力所能及	力所能及	lìsuǒnéngjí	f.c.w.	within one's ability
甜美	甜美	tiánměi	adj.	sweet
清澈	清澈	qīngchè	adj.	crystal-clear
明月	明月	míngyuè	n.	bright moon
遥相呼应	遙相呼應	yáoxiānghūyìng	f.c.w.	harmoniously reflect each other
陶醉	陶醉	táozuì	v.	revel in, be intoxicated with
美妙	美妙	měimiào	adj.	splendid, wonderful
震耳	震耳	zhèn'ěr	v.o.	(noise) so loud that it shakes one's ears
摇滚乐	搖滾樂	yáogǔnyuè	n.	rock 'n roll music
打破	打破	dǎpò	v (c)	destroy
不约而同	不約而同	bùyuē'értóng	f.c.w.	do the same without prior consultation
愤愤不平	憤憤不平	fènfèn-bùpíng	f.c.w.	indignant
不知所措	不知所措	bùzhī-suǒcuò	f.c.w.	bewildered

第二章

在泰國的鴨子-兔子秀

 那是一只鴨子？ 一只兔子？ 一個紅蘿卜？ 一條魚？ [6]

如果你全神貫注地看這幅畫，你可能會把它看成生活中不同的東西，也可能會把它看成人們從未見過的東西。 但是不管你看到了多少東西，也不管你怎么把一只鴨子看成一只兔子，然后又把兔子看成鴨子，如此來來去去、反反復復，這幅畫在一個特定的時間里只可能表示一個東西。這就是所謂雙元文化的意思所在。我先是中國人，然后是美國人。雖然我不可能在同一瞬間既當中國人又當美國人，但是我能在兩者中間迅速變換角色，而且，我對這種角色的轉換比較輕松自如。就像一個好的籃球運動員，一會兒防守，一會兒進攻。同一場球，你在不同的場地位置，就會扮演不同的角色。從人種上說，你是個美國人，但是你在奶奶或姥姥家、在保齡球館、在公司、在學校，你的穿着、言語、思維、信仰可能會跟其他美國人不同。能夠隨時隨地從一個地方或一種心態轉換到另一個地方或另一種心態，這比用"熔爐"來描述什么是雙元文化的經驗更為準確，因為"轉換"沒有暗示如果"美國化了"就必須消除自己母語文化的特征。另外，假如你能仔細觀察，"轉換"本身也是一種學習經驗。

1993 年我們在泰國旅游的時候就遇到過類似這樣的轉換。我們在卡拉比（**Krabi**）一個比較便宜的旅游勝地住了幾天，很多徒步旅行者喜歡住在那里，他們大多是從德國來的。一間棕櫚樹的小木屋住着我和我先生，還有跟我拇指一樣大的蟑螂!!! 而且每天供電只有兩個小

---

[6] At the "On *In A Different Voice*" conference, State University of New York at Stony Brook, March 22-4, 1985, Carol Gilligan likened the background-foreground duck-rabbit drawing to the phenomenon of having different "voices" or basic outlooks.

职责	職責	zhízé	n.	duty, obligation
须知	須知	xūzhī	n.	notice, announcement
失职	失職	shīzhí	v.o.	neglect one's duty
刺耳	刺耳	cì'ěr	adj.	raucous
断定	斷定	duàndìng	v.	conclude, form a judgment
粗鲁	粗魯	cūlǔ	adj.	rough, very rude
无礼	無禮	wúlǐ	adj.	impolite
苗头	苗頭	miáotou	n.	symptom of a (new) development/trend
责怪	責怪	zéguài	v.	blame, accuse, remonstrate
歌星	歌星	gēxīng	n.	singing star
迈克尔·杰克逊	邁克爾·傑克遜	Màikèr Jiékèxùn	p.n.	Michael Jackson
丢尽	丟盡	diūjìn	v (c)	lose completely
曲子	曲子	qǔzi	n.	song
引起	引起	yǐnqǐ	v.	cause, give rise to
无能为力	無能為力	wúnéng-wéilì	f.c.w.	powerless, helpless, incapable of action
打消	打消	dǎxiāo	v (c)	give up
念头	念頭	niàntou	n.	idea
迪斯科	迪斯科	dísikē	n.	disco
戏剧性	戲劇性	xìjùxìng	adj.	dramatic
无言	無言	wúyán	adj.	non-linguistic
伤害	傷害	shānghài	v.	harm, hurt
逗	逗	dòu	v.	provoke (laughter)
开怀大笑	開懷大笑	kāihuái-dàxiào	f.c.w.	laugh heartily

時。然而，站在精細的白沙灘上遙望安達曼海（Andaman Sea）時，那景觀在人間是罕見的。第二天晚上，我們吃了晚飯，坐在外面木頭平臺上的餐桌旁，唯一一個有燈光照明的地方，我們知道旅館經理一會兒要給大家提供一點兒娛樂——放西爾維斯特·史泰龍（Sylvester Stallone）的電影錄像。平和溫柔的夜晚跟那血腥殘暴的《洛奇》(Rocky)電影形成了極大的反差，可那是他力所能及提供的唯一的娛樂，一個并不太糟糕的選擇，因為除了我和我先生以外，其他都是年輕學生。第三天晚上，來了四個年輕的芬蘭女孩。她們剛到，不知道一會兒要放史泰龍電影，見大家靜靜地坐着，就唱了起來。甜美、清澈的歌聲與海水、明月遙相呼應。當我們還陶醉在美妙的歌聲中時，突然，震耳的搖滾樂打破了寧靜。大家不約而同地看着站在音響旁的經理，他微笑地看着大家，而在座的游客卻憤憤不平，他一下子不知所措。

經理不明白為什麼。他上過旅游學校，學過職責須知，所以當他聽到女孩唱歌時，以為自己沒有為游客及時提供娛樂，失職了。[7] 然而游客聽到刺耳的搖滾樂時，卻斷定，這個經理太粗魯、太無禮了。這時候，經理的父親，旅游勝地的老板，覺得苗頭不對，趕緊責怪兒子，因為兒子像歌星邁克爾·杰克遜（Michael Jackson）一樣丟盡了臉!!! 搖滾曲子不斷地重復着，"你們知道喔，我可不錯! 我可不錯! "[8]

經理說泰語，會一點兒法語，但不會中文。他父親說中文和泰語，但不會英語。其他游客誰也不說泰語、法語或中文，但都會說德語，大多數人知道一點兒英語。我說英語，會一點兒中文、一小點兒法語，還有大約十個德文單詞——大多跟喝牛奶、吃面包有關!!! 芬蘭語，一點兒也不會。我想解釋這個由"鴨子-兔子"而引起的誤會，可又無能為力，只好打消了念頭，跟先生跳起了迪斯科。這種戲劇性的、無言的解決方法沒有傷害任何人，卻逗得游客開懷大笑。

---

[7] Asians try not to criticize directly but prefer hinting – especially if the complaint is from a person of lesser status. One night, soon after my *younger* sister arrived in the US, she walked several times between the TV and me. This was her way of telling me that, if I were a responsible older sister, I should realize the TV volume was so loud that she couldn't study. I did nothing, thinking she was getting a soda. When she felt forced to tell me, I asked, in my Western mode, "Why didn't you just say so?"

[8] These lyrics are from the title song of Michael Jackson's 1987 album *Bad*.

练习 EXERCISES

I. 思考和课堂讨论 FOOD FOR THOUGHT

A. PERSONAL 个人的

描述你生活中的一个"鸭子-兔子"经历。

Describe a "duck-rabbit" incident in your life.

B. GENERAL 普遍的

Some idiomatic words, abbreviations, or phrases are popular, useful, and thought-provoking. After reading the following explanation and sample sentence, discuss the question posed.

某些习惯用语、缩写词语或短语很流行、很有用，而且引人深思。阅读以下英语注释和例句，然后讨论问题。

> **ad lib** is derived from the Latin *ad labitum* (*ad* = "at"; *labitum* = one's pleasure).
>
> **comment:** Some politicians, even presidents, have such a poor command of their own language that they should never **ad lib** or improvise their speeches but should, if they want to avoid ridicule, always speak from a script preferably prepared by someone else **!!!**.
>
> **question:** To what extent or under what circumstances, if any, does the public have a right to witness—and the media the right to report—unrehearsed or spontaneous actions by public figures?

C. CROSS-CULTURAL 跨文化的

After reading the following, discuss <u>in English</u> whether or not you think Yo-Yo Ma's reaction was culturally motivated. Why?

阅读以下短文，并<u>用英语</u>对所提出的问题进行讨论。

> When Yo-Yo Ma, the famous Chinese-American cellist, performed in New Jersey with two non-Asian violinists and a pianist, the audience savored the music but didn't realize that they should not applaud between movements of the same composition. Then, after the last movement of the first symphony, when the quartet bowed and left the stage as is customary before proceeding to the next composition, the audience thought it was time for the intermission. About half were already out of the auditorium en route to the refreshment bar or bathroom when the musicians returned to the stage. Unlike his colleagues, Yo-Yo Ma was not offended. Understanding that the people were novices to the world of classical music and not intentionally rude, he whistled very loudly and gestured like a popular TV game host, shouting "Come on down!" As people returned to their seats, some were embarrassed but most appreciated his understanding of their ignorance and his good humor.

II. 配对 MATCHMAKER

A. VOCABULARY 词汇

找出以下两列中的对应词，并在其间划线。

Draw a connecting line between the word and its correct definition.

a.	心态	1.	concentrate on sth.
b.	熔炉	2.	the way to be addressed
c.	穿着	3.	role, part
d.	角色	4.	beach
e.	观察	5.	offensive
f.	沙滩	6.	melting pot
g.	轻松自如	7.	observe
h.	力所能及	8.	mind set
i.	全神贯注	9.	with ease
j.	进攻的	10.	within one's ability, in one's power

a.	stark	1.	尽情享受
b.	savor	2.	四个一组
c.	defensive	3.	完全的
d.	quartet	4.	重复
e.	court	5.	防守的
f.	en route	6.	好极了
g.	divine	7.	刺耳的
h.	raucous	8.	在途中
i.	backpacker	9.	篮球场
j.	refrain	10.	徒步旅行者

B. SYNONYMS & ALTERNATES 同义词和多义词

First draw a connecting line between the word or phrase in the left-hand column with the best possible <u>synonym</u> listed in the middle column, then draw a line between the synonym and an alternate meaning of the synonym listed in the right-hand column. <u>Be forewarned</u> that the part of speech may change from one column to the next and that slang terms may be used. E.g.,

"hit" ————————————— *"strike"*————————— *"stop-work action against employer"*

"warm" ——————————————— *"heat"* —————————— *"qualifying race for final contest"*

首先在第二列中找出与第一列相对应的同义词，然后在第三列中找出与第二列相关的多义词。注意：词性会有不同。

		SYNONYMS	**ALTERNATE MEANING**
a.	type	1. **suit**	i. deficient, short of
b.	speak, express vocally	2. **touched**	ii. total, complete
c.	secondhand	3. **sick**	iii. support, agree
d.	slightly crazy or "not right"	4. **angry**	iv. pre-owned
e.	matched set	5. **utter**	v. power of pleasing
f.	team up with	6. **shy**	vi. please, satisfy
g.	timid, bashful, wary	7. **charm**	vii. separate
h.	morbid, sadistic, unsound	8. **used**	viii. attack, set upon
i.	wrathful, enraged, furious	9. **sort**	ix. emotionally affected
j.	words with magical power	10. **side** with	x. inflamed, red

III. 解字/词、构字/词 DECONSTRUCTION & CONSTRUCTION

A. 将以下汉字分解成最小的构字部件，然后用每个部件构成三个汉字。例如"鸭"可以分解成 "甲"和"鸟"两个部件。"甲"能构成"押"，"岬"，"钾"；"鸟"可以构成以"鸡"，"鸦"，"鸣"。请借助字典完成练习。

Deconstruct the following characters into the smallest components, then form 3 new characters using each component.

语＿＿＿＿＿＿＿＿＿ 观＿＿＿＿＿ ＿＿＿＿＿ 苗＿＿＿＿＿＿＿＿

曼＿＿＿＿＿＿＿＿＿ 逊＿＿＿＿＿＿＿＿＿ 误＿＿＿＿＿＿＿＿

B. Using only the letters of the word "**BACKPACKER,**" form English words that are not proper nouns, abbreviations, or acronyms and that consist of 4 or more letters. A letter can only be used again if it appears in the given word more than once. E.g., "black" is not acceptable because there is no "l" and "beer" is not because there is only one "e." Like many Olympic sports, weight categories to mark performance. We filled in a few cells to get you started. Fill in the rest to achieve the highest category. If you think up more than 42, you beat the authors!

用"**BACKPACKER**"中的字母构词。新构建的词不能是专有名词、缩写词、或首字母缩略词。每个单词必须至少含有四个字母，但不能重复使用同一字母，除非该字母在"**BACKPACKER**"中出现两次。

49

CHAMPION STATUS						
FLY 6	BANTAM 12	FEATHER 18	LIGHT 24	WELTER 30	MIDDLE 36	HEAVY 42
back	care	pack				
bark	carp	peck				

C. 用"双元文化"中的每个汉字组成不同的词。看看最多能组多少个词。

Use each of the characters in "双元文化" to form as many words (of 2-4 characters) as you can.

D. Pair any two of the following 13 words to form at least 14 different, unhyphenated words.

在下列十三个词中配对、组词，新组的词只能含有两个单词，中间没有连字号。
请至少组出十三个词。

room ground fall turn above ball walk foot be breaker about board wind

IV. 阅读理解 READING QUIZ

根据课文，选择准确答案。Based on the text, choose the best answer.

1. 什么是双元文化"？

   a. "双元文化"指"熔炉"和"转换"。

   b. "双元文化"指"鸭子"和"兔子"。

   c. "双元文化"指两种不同的文化。

   d. "双元文化"指"美国化"或"中国化"。

2. 什么是"转换"？

   a. "转换"就是从中国人变成美国人。

   b. "转换"就是从美国人变成中国人。

   c. "转换"就是完全消除自己的母语文化特征。

   d. "转换"就是像运动员那样根据需要变换角色。

3. 本文用鸭子-兔子的背景-前景图来说明什么问题？

    a.   同样一幅画，不同的人从不同的角度会把它看作不同的东西。

    b.   作者借这幅画来说明一只鸭子有时候能变成一只兔子。

    c.   作者借这幅画来说明一只鸭子有时候会变成一个萝卜。

    d.   作者借这幅画来说明一只鸭子有时候还会变成一条鱼。

4. 为什么旅馆经理要放西尔维斯特·史泰龙的电影录像？

    a.   因为旅馆经理无法提供其它比这更好的娱乐。

    b.   因为旅馆经理喜欢看西尔维斯特·史泰龙的电影录像。

    c.   因为德国游客喜欢看西尔维斯特·史泰龙的电影录像。

    d.   因为芬兰女孩喜欢看西尔维斯特·史泰龙的电影录像。

5. 为什么旅游胜地的老板要责怪旅馆经理？

    a.   因为歌星丢尽了脸。

    b.   因为经理丢尽了脸。

    c.   因为老板丢尽了脸。

    d.   因为游客丢尽了脸。

6. 为什么当作者和她先生最后跳起迪斯科时，大家都笑了？

    a.   因为他们的迪斯科有戏剧性。

    b.   因为他们的迪斯科没有语言。

    c.   因为他们给大家带来了娱乐。

    d.   因为没有其他人在跳迪斯科。

V. 填空 FILL IN THE BLANK

A. 选择正确答案。Choose the correct answer.

1. 如果你＿＿＿＿＿地看这幅画，你可能会把它看成生活中不同的东西。

    a. 全力以赴   b. 全心全意   c. 全神贯注

2. 我不能在同一＿＿＿＿＿既当中国人又当美国人，但我能迅速变换这两个角色。

    a. 时间   b. 中间   c. 期间

3. 站在精细的白沙滩上遥望安达曼海时，那景观在人间是很＿＿＿＿＿的。

    a. 常见   b. 少见   c. 多见

4. 旅游胜地的老板，觉得_____不对，赶紧责怪儿子。

   a. 风头   b. 苗头   c. 念头

5. 我想解释这个由"鸭子-兔子"而引起的误会，可又_____。

   a. 无能为力   b. 无所不能   c. 无所事事

B. 在以下段落中找出与斜体词意义相近的反义词。如果你所学的外语是中文，找出相应的中文词或短语。如果你所学的外语是英语，找出相应的英语词或短语。注意：词性或时态会有变化。

Using your target language, write a word or phrase from the vocabulary lists and/or dictionary that means the <u>opposite</u> or is an <u>antonym</u> for the italicized word or phrase. Keep in mind that the part of speech and/or tense may have been adjusted to achieve grammatically correct results.

The young man thought he was being *well-mannered* _____ when he visited his girlfriend's mother and brought her a very expensive, *fancy, and brightly colored* _____ blouse. Unfortunately, a gift of clothing is very personal and not appropriate for a young man to give to an older woman on a first meeting. His mistake was followed by another—calling the politician she most admired "an idiot" and saying his opponent's ideas were innovative and not the old *same words over and over* _____. Upon hearing this, she looked at him as if he were some *hellish* _____ insect.

VI. 翻译 TRANSLATION

A. 将以下句子翻译成英文。Translate the following sentences into English.

1. 能够随时随地从一个地方或一种心态转换到另一个地方或另一种心态，这比用"熔炉"来描述什么是双元文化的经验更为准确，因为"转换"没有暗示如果"美国化了"就必须消除自己母语文化的特征。

2. 一间棕榈树的小木屋住着我和我先生，还有跟我拇指一样大的蟑螂!!! 而且每天供电只有两个小时。

3. 经理不明白为什么。他上过旅游学校，学过职责须知，所以当他听到女孩唱歌时，以为自己没有为游客及时提供娱乐，失职了。

B. Translate the following sentences into Chinese. 将以下句子翻译成中文。

1. But no matter how many you perceive, no matter how quickly you can switch from the "duck" to the "rabbit" and back again, the drawing can only be one thing at a time.

2. When we were all still savoring the last note, the quiet magic was suddenly destroyed by loud rock 'n' roll music.

3. This dramatic, non-linguistic solution made everybody laugh at no one's expense.

VII. 完型填充 CLOZE TEST

A. 在以下短文的每一空格处填入一个汉字，如有可能，给出相应的英语单词。

Fill in a Chinese character that retains the original meaning or intent of the text, then write an English equivalent, if any.

如果你全神贯注地看这幅画，你可能会把它＿＿＿＿＿成生活中不同＿＿＿＿＿东西，也可能会＿＿＿＿＿它看成人们从＿＿＿＿＿见过的东西。但＿＿＿＿＿不管你看到了＿＿＿＿＿少东西，也不管＿＿＿＿＿怎么把一只鸭＿＿＿＿＿看成一只兔子，＿＿＿＿＿后又把兔子看＿＿＿＿＿鸭子，如此来来＿＿＿＿＿去、反反复复，这＿＿＿＿＿画在一个特定＿＿＿＿＿时间里只可能＿＿＿＿＿示一个东西。这＿＿＿＿＿是所谓双元文化的意思所在。

B. Fill in an English word or phrase that retains the original meaning or intent of the text, then write a Chinese equivalent, if any.

在以下短文的每一空格处填入一个英语单词，如有可能，给出相应的汉字或词。

If you concentrate, one or the other ＿＿＿＿＿ into view. Or something no one else ＿＿＿＿＿ seen. But no matter how many you ＿＿＿＿＿, no matter how quickly you can switch ＿＿＿＿＿ the "duck" to the "rabbit" and back ＿＿＿＿＿, the drawing can only be one thing ＿＿＿＿＿ a time. This is what it's like ＿＿＿＿＿ be *at least* bicultural—I am Chinese, ＿＿＿＿＿ I am North American. I can't be ＿＿＿＿＿ simultaneously but I can get faster at ＿＿＿＿＿ from one to the other. I can ＿＿＿＿＿ be more comfortable with the changing. Like ＿＿＿＿＿ good basketball player—one second you play ＿＿＿＿＿, the next you switch to a defensive ＿＿＿＿＿. The game or circumstance is the same ＿＿＿＿＿ you see the court and your options ＿＿＿＿＿.

VIII. 身体部位 BODY PARTS

A. There are many useful idioms which contain "body parts." Choose the most appropriate to fill in the blank based on your best guess of what the idiom means.

英语中的许多习惯用语含有表示"身体部位"的单词。在下面三个习惯用语中选择最恰当的填空。

1. shake a leg 2. pulling sb.'s leg 3. give sb. a leg up

The teacher told the student, "I'm not ＿＿＿＿＿. You better ＿＿＿＿＿ and start studying. If you don't try harder, no one will think you deserve a good job or want to ＿＿＿＿＿ into a decent-paying position.

B. 将以下短文翻译成中文。注意：划线的词或短语与以上含有"身体部位"的习惯用语相对应。

Translate the following into Chinese taking note that the underlined words or phrases correspond to the meaning of the above "body parts."

After the man agreed to <u>help raise his thieving partner</u> over the window sill, the latter opened the front door from the inside without realizing there was a burglar alarm. The two had to <u>hurry</u> and steal the paintings before the police arrived. However, when they tried to sell the paintings, everyone thought the two robbers were <u>playing a joke on them</u> when they said they were by Picasso so no one believed the art was real and refused to pay more than $50 each **!!!**

C. Using your target language, create sentence(s) containing the following three English idioms or their Chinese equivalents.

用以下短语分别造句。如果你所学的外语是中文，请用中文来做这个练习。如果你所学的外语是英语，请用英语来做这个练习。

1. on one's last legs = 精疲力竭，黔驴技穷，临近结束

2. not have a leg to stand on = 站不住脚，理屈词穷

3. stretch one's legs =（做久以后）走一走，散散步

IX. 写作 PRÉCIS

用所学的外语总结课文。如果你用中文来写，请至少使用 450 个汉字，并用电脑打出摘要。如果你用英文来写，请不超过 240 个词。

Write a summary of this chapter in your target language. If writing in Chinese, use <u>more</u> than 450 characters; if writing in English, use <u>no more</u> than 240 words.

CHAPTER THREE

THUMBING YOUR *KNOWS*[7] IN VIETNAM

In 2003, we went kayaking in Vietnam. Driving from the airport, we saw wet rice paddies. This was not a surprise. What was unexpected was finding out from our guide, Nam, that the structures randomly scattered amongst them were grave markers, sometimes no more than a bump, others looking like a rectangular box of white concrete. Remembering my mother's instructions to only consider burying her in a "high, dry place with the warmth of an afternoon sun," I had jumped to the stereotypical conclusion that no Asian, lowland farmer or not, would be buried where flooding occurred. I don't think my mother would have been mollified by the fact that some Vietnamese practice an economy of space by periodically opening these familial graves and tidying the bones of the more recently interred to make room for the next "resident" !!! And she certainly would have looked at her Asian rice differently !!! Further, we were surprised to learn that the average age at death was fifty-eight. Although everyone on the street looked so healthy—lean and muscular—their internal organs were afflicted with disease and poor sanitation. Telling Nam that I was already sixty-one, he nervously complimented me on my youthful appearance. I mentioned having the advantage of a middle-class life and moisturizers fortified with aloe. I also mentioned teaching aerobics six days per week. He said, "Teaching Arabic?" I dropped the subject !!!

In Ha Long, we boarded a funky wooden boat too aptly named a "junk."[8] Thirty minutes into the bay, Nam and the crew of four brought out two kayaks—a one and a two-seater. With no discussion, Bennett clambered overboard into the one-seater. As my husband got the hang of going straight and away from the junk, I laughed and told Nam that, whenever we have a new challenge, I operate on the principle: If Bennett survives !!!, I'll try. When Nam didn't smile, I figured it was his limited English. Without further comment, Nam and I got into the two-seater. At first I tried to

---

[7]正如中文里有很多与词的发音有关的笑话，"thumb your knows" 是我创造的双关语。在这里"knows" 的发音听起来跟"nose"一样。当小孩子想作弄人或者对某些规则、法律、传统等表示不满的时候，他们会用大拇指顶着鼻子并伸出其余四个手指做出蔑视的手势，那就是"thumb their nose"。

[8]数个世纪以前马来西亚人首先将中文的"boat"读作"chuan"，后来荷兰人将其读成"junk"。在英语里，"junk"指质量很糟糕的东西。

第三章

在越南的学以致用

2003 年我们去越南作漂流旅行。在从机场去旅馆的路上，我们看到了公路两旁的水稻田。这种风景对我们来说并不陌生，新鲜的是导游纳木（Nam）告诉我们，那些三三两两散落在水稻田内的建筑都是坟墓。有的只有小土墩那么大，有的看起来像一个白色、长方形的水泥盒子。记得母亲生前曾经关照我们，等她死后要把她埋在"高高的、干干的、并且有午后阳光的温暖的地方"。我马上就得出了一个老套的结论：没有哪个亚洲人，无论是农民还是别的什么人，愿意死后埋在水里。纳木还告诉我们，为了节省空间，有些越南人会定时地打开坟墓，整理新埋进的尸骨，这样可以为后来的"居民"腾出地方。对于他们这种做法，我想母亲不会因此而感到任何安慰，但她一定会对亚洲产的大米另眼相看!!! 我们后来非常惊讶地发现，越南人的平均寿命是五十八岁。虽然大街上的每个人看起来都很健康：精瘦干练、肌肉发达，但是，由于落后的卫生条件，很多人都患有不同的疾病。当我告诉纳木我已六十一岁时，他紧张地恭维着我。我说，我的年轻归功于富裕的小康生活和滋润的护肤品，我还跟他说我每星期教六次健身课。"教阿拉伯语？"[9] 他问。我没再接他的话茬儿。

我们在哈浪（Ha Long）登上了一只很一般的木船，船名叫"junk"，这真是再确切不过了。在海湾上漂了三十分钟以后，纳木和其他四位船员为我们拿出了两条橡皮艇：一条是单人座的，一条是双人座的。我先生班尼特二话没说就爬进了那单人座的橡皮艇。当他驾着橡皮艇离开我们的大船时，我笑着对纳木说，每当遇到新的挑战时，我会按以下原则办事：如果班尼特能胜任的话，我也要尝试一下。纳木没有笑，我猜想可能是他的英文有限，没听懂吧。我俩谁也没有说什么就爬进了双人座的橡皮艇。开始我还努力地划着，可是很难协调桨的顺序。我怕因为我的失误而把纳木划进水里!!!，就停下让他一个人划。这下纳木笑了!!!

---

[9] His misunderstanding of the English was based on the similar sound of "aerobics" and "Arabic."

paddle but it was hard coordinating strokes. So, rather than knock him out by mistake **!!!**, I gave up and let him do all the work. This time he smiled **!!!**

The next day, everyone tried to hurry Bennett into the one-seater. Bennett knew better **!!!** He told Nam that it was my turn to go it alone. Nam was horrified, pointing at me and shaking his head. Indignant that I seemed to have a male chauvinist for a guide, I picked up a paddle and held it like I just stepped out of the *Crouching Tiger, Hidden Dragon* movie, ready to twirl it for battle. Wide-eyed, Nam backed away. Wearing my black bathing suit covered by a huge flowered shirt and bright orange jogging shorts (for modesty), turquoise rubber Birkenstocks (for traction), and a very tired but still electric blue skirt to fit around the rim of the kayak hole (for waterproofing) **!!!**, Nam could *see* I was crazy enough to do something drastic. Raising an eyebrow, I gave him my most stern look—the kind that left no doubt that this feminist would lift him bodily over the gender gap if he tried to prevent my getting into the one-seater. Then I grimly reminded him that I was the *paying* tourist.

Nam turned to the crew and told them the sad news of my determination. Upset, they all talked at once. I picked up a word or two. The truth hit me—I had already lived longer than their grandmothers! They weren't concerned about my being female, they were in mortal fear that I would drop dead and end up cemented in a rice paddy instead of New Jersey **!!!**

I may have invented the phrase **"Thumbing Your Knows"** to point out that not only should we dare to use what we have learned but also we should mind what Tina Turner sang in 1987, "What you *get* is what you *see*," that is, what you get or *know* depends on how well you put together all that you have seen, heard, felt, smelled, or tasted. For example, open your eyes. Then cover the left eye with your left hand. Then line up your right thumb with a straight edge like the corner of the room. Then uncover the left eye and notice the thumb seem to move. After doing the same thing but with your right eye covered, notice which eye produced a less perceptible shift in the alignment of thumb to straight edge. This is your dominant eye.

Similar "normal" variations occur in the other senses depending on age, environment, even expectation. A typical winery tour ends in the tasting room for free samples. If you care about tasting what you're drinking **!!!**, you start with the light white wines and end with robust reds because, the other way around, your tongue will have been overwhelmed. A toddler likes beer while the fourth-grader doesn't. This is because the younger taste buds don't yet register "bitter." Meanwhile, older folks often eat more candy because their sweet receptors are the last to deteriorate. The related olfactory experience depends on prior smells or a stuffed nose. Amputees **"feel"** with fingers they no

由于班尼特的技术不错，第二天，大家催着他上单人座的橡皮艇。班尼特知道我的情形，这时他对纳木说现在该轮到我划单人座的橡皮艇了。纳木指着我，直摇头，简直吓死了。碰到这么一个大男子主义的导游，我很气愤。于是我拿起桨，快速地挥舞着，准备开战，那架势好像刚从《卧虎藏龙》的电影中跑出来。纳木两眼直瞪瞪地看着我，往后退了退。那天我穿了一件黑色的泳装，外面套了一件大大的花衬衫和一条橘红色的运动短裤（为的是不要太暴露），一双青绿色的勃肯牌（Birkenstocks）橡胶鞋（为的是增加摩擦力），一件磨损了但仍然非常显眼的蓝"裙子"，用来罩在橡皮艇洞口的边沿上（为的是防止水进到船里面）。看到我这身武装，纳木知道我真的要发疯了。我严厉地瞪了他一眼。那一眼足以告诉他，如果他还试图不让我进单人橡皮艇，我这个女权主义者一定会把他从性别峡谷的那一端拽过来。然后我又提醒他，我可是付钱到这儿来旅游的呵。

当纳木转向其他船员，告诉他们我要划单人艇这一"不幸"消息时，大家顿时议论纷纷，个个诚惶诚恐。我正琢磨着说词，忽然茅塞顿开。我比他们的祖母还大，他们不是因为我是女性不让我上单人艇，而是担心我会突然死掉，再也回不去美国的新泽西州，只能永久地躺在越南的水稻田里**!!!**

"Thumbing Your Knows"[10] 是我创造的短语，表示我们不仅要使用许多已知的知识，而且要像蒂娜·特纳（Tina Turner）在 1987 年的一个演唱会上唱的那样，"你所得到的是你所看到的"。这就是说，你所得到的取决于你在多大程度上能把所看到的、听到的、摸到的、闻到的、尝到的综合起来加以运用。比如说，睁大你的眼睛，用左手挡住你的左眼，用右手的大拇指对着房角的直边，然后拿掉挡在左眼的左手，你会发现大拇指"移动"了。用同样方法再做一次，这次用右手挡住右眼，用左手的大拇指对着房角的直边，看看是哪只眼睛让你觉得大拇指离开房角直边的变动比较小。产生较小"移动"的那只眼睛是起着主要作用的眼睛。

由于不同的年龄、环境、期望，这种正常的差异同样也会体现在其他感官上。你若参观酿酒厂，最后一定会去品尝室尝酒。要是你真的很喜欢品酒，你最好先尝度数低的白

---

[10] This is a pun that I made up in English but it is like many Chinese jokes that "play on words" which sound alike but are written differently. In this case, "knows" sounds like "nose." Children "thumb their nose" at people when they want to make fun of someone or show their lack of respect for rules, laws, people, institutions, traditions, etc.

longer have, and people insist you said something when you didn't. In other words, we can make better sense if we don't "thumb our nose" by disregarding other factors and facts that we know but don't use.

VOCABULARY

kayak	n.	originally a lightweight boat used by Eskimos, now for recreation.	橡皮艇	xiàngpítǐng
paddy	n.	a field for growing rice.	水稻田	shuǐdàotián
rectangular	adj.	like a 4-sided geometric figure with 4 right angles.	矩形的	jǔxíng de
stereotypical	adj.	like a standardized and (over) simplified image of one group often held by another based on limited experience.	陈腔滥调的，老套的	chénqiāng làndiào de, lǎotào de
mollify	v.	to soften another's attitude or feeling; to placate, appease.	使……安慰	shǐ…ānwèi
economy of space	n.p.	efficient and sparing use of available area (or movement or effort, etc.)	节省空间	jiéshěng kōng-jiān
tidy	v.	to make more neat, trim, orderly.	收拾	shōushi
inter	v.	to bury a (dead) body in a grave or tomb.	埋葬	máizàng
internal organ	n.p.	a part of the body occurring beneath the surface such as the heart or liver. Also – "internals" or "innards" usually referring specifically to the bowels or entrails.	内脏器官	nèizàng qìguān
afflict	v.	to greatly distress or harm.	使……折磨	shǐ…zhémó
fortify	v.	to enhance with additional ingredients; to strengthen.	加强的	jiāqiáng de
aloe	n.	a succulent plant of which leaves yield	芦荟	lúhuì

葡萄酒，然后再尝烈性的红葡萄酒。要是你倒过来的话，你的舌头会吃不消的。一个初学走路的孩子喜欢啤酒的苦味，而一个四年级的孩子会觉得其味难忍。这是因为刚学走路的孩了还没有完全形成味觉，无法体会什么叫"苦"的滋味。而老年人比较喜欢吃糖果，是因为人对甜味感觉的功能是最后一个才衰退的。嗅觉经验取决于先前的味道或鼻子的灵敏度。被截了肢的人没有手指，但仍然能够"抚摸"；别人以为你说了什么，但事实上你什么也没说。换句话说，如果我们对其它已有的知识不嗤之以鼻，反而能够恰当地对它们加以保留、联想和运用，这样我们的为人处世才能行之有效。

生词

学以致用	學以致用	xuéyǐzhìyòng	f.c.w.	thumb your "knows" (put your knowledge into practice)
漂流	漂流	piāoliú	v.	go kayaking
水稻田	水稻田	shuǐdàotián	n.	rice paddies
导游	導游	dǎoyóu	n.	tour guide
三三两两	三三兩兩	sānsān-liǎngliǎng	f.c.w.	desolate and scattered
散落	散落	sànluò	v.	disperse
坟墓	墳墓	fénmù	n.	grave, tomb
土墩	土墩	tǔdūn	n.	bump
水泥	水泥	shuǐní	n.	concrete
盒子	盒子	hézi	n.	box
生前	生前	shēngqián	n.	before one's death, during one's lifetime
老套	老套	lǎotào	adj.	stereotypical
水里	水裡	shuǐlǐ	n.	in the water
定时地	定時地	dìngshíde	adv.	at regular intervals
埋进	埋進	máijìn	v.	inter, bury
尸骨	屍骨	shīgǔ	n.	bones of the dead (after all else has decomposed)
腾	騰	téng	v.	make room for
另眼相看	另眼相看	lìngyǎn-xiāngkàn	f.c.w.	look at sb./sth. with new eyes
精瘦干练	精瘦干練	jīngshòu-gànliàn	f.c.w.	lean but strong
肌肉发达	肌肉發達	jīròu-fādá	f.c.w.	muscular
患有	患有	huànyǒu	v.	be afflicted with
恭维	恭維	gōngwéi	v.	compliment
归功于	歸功於	guīgōngyú	v.p.	owe… to
小康	小康	xiǎokāng	n.	comparatively well off

		a liquid used on the skin to promote healing.		
Ha Long	p.n.	a bay in northwestern Vietnam known for its calm water and lime-stone mountains or karsts that are similar to those in the Lí River near Guìlín, China.	哈浪湾	Hālàng Wān
one-seater		a vehicle—bicycle, boat, carriage, etc.—with room for one person.	单人座的橡皮艇	dānrén zuò de xiàngpítǐng
funky	adj.	*slang* - having an unsophisticated, odd, quaint, unrefined or earthy character or style though sometimes "hip" or "in" style or "camp" as a result.	简单的	jiǎndān de
clamber	v.	to climb awkwardly, often leading with one's knees.	攀登	pāndēng
get the hang of	v.p.	*informal* - acquire competence or skill.	得知……窍门	dézhī…qiàomén
operate on the principle (of)	v.p.	to work, perform or proceed accord-ing to a rule.	根据……原理工作	gēnjù …yuánlǐ gōngzuò
paddle	v.	using a piece of wood, approximately 5-7 feet long, rounded at one end for holding, flat-sided at the other in the water to propel a small water craft. Shorter versions are used to play ping-pong. Also – n.	划桨	huájiǎng
knock sb. out	v.p.	to hit a person so hard that s/he loses consciousness. Also – n. a "knockout punch" is the blow in boxing that renders the opponent incapable of continuing to fight the match.	打昏	dǎhūn
know better	v.p.	to be sufficiently informed so as to make a (more) reasonable decision.	明白	míngbái

滋润	滋潤	zīrùn	adj.	moisturizing
护肤品	護膚品	hùfūpǐn	n.	lotion
阿拉伯语	阿拉伯語	Ālābóyǔ	p.n.	Arabic language
话茬儿	話茬兒	huàchár	n.	thread of conversation
确切不过	確切不过	quèqiè-búguò	f.c.w.	precisely
海湾	海灣	hǎiwān	n.	bay
船员	船員	chuányuán	n.	crew of a ship
橡皮艇	橡皮艇	xiàngpítǐng	n.	kayak
二话没说	二話沒說	èrhuà-méishuō	f.c.w.	say nothing
爬进	爬進	pájìn	v (c)	clamber into
胜任	勝任	shèngrèn	v.	be competent in
划进	划进	huájìn	v (c)	paddle into
桨	桨	jiāng	n.	paddle
失误	失誤	shīwù	n.	mistake, fault
停	停	tíng	v.	stop
这下	這下	zhèxià	n.	this time
轮到	輪到	lúndào	v.	be one's turn
吓死	嚇死	xiàsǐ	v (c)	be horrified
大男子主义	大男子主義	dànánzǐzhǔyì	n.	male chauvinist
挥舞	揮舞	huīwǔ	v.	twirl
开战	開戰	kāizhàn	v.o.	battle, fight
架势	架勢	jiàshi	n.	posture, appearance
卧虎藏龙	臥虎藏龍	Wòhǔcánglóng		Crouching Tiger, Hidden Dragon (a movie)
直瞪瞪	直瞪瞪	zhídèngdèng	adj.	wide-eyed
退	退	tuì	v.	move back
泳装	泳裝	yǒngzhuāng	n.	bathing suit
短裤	短褲	duǎnkù	n.	shorts
为的是	为的是	wèideshì	p.p.	for the purpose of
橡胶鞋	橡膠鞋	xiàngjiāoxié	n.	rubber shoes
摩擦力	摩擦力	mócāli	n.	traction
磨损	磨損	mósǔn	v (c)	wear and tear
显眼	顯眼	xiǎnyǎn	adj.	eye-catching
用来	用來	yònglái	p.p.	for the purpose of doing sth
洞口	洞口	dòngkǒu	n.	hole
边沿	邊沿	biānyán	n.	rim
发疯	發瘋	fāfēng	v.o.	go crazy
拽过来	拽过来	zhuàiguòlái	v (c)	lift sb. over
性别	性別	xìngbié	n.	gender
峡谷	峽谷	xiágǔ	n.	valley
议论纷纷	議論紛紛	yìlùn-fēnfēn	f.c.w.	discuss

chauvinist	n.	someone with an excessive, blind or overly devoted commitment to a cause or viewpoint. E.g., a "male chauvinist" is someone who believes that men are, by nature, superior to women in strength, intelligence, and capabilities.	沙文主义者	shāwén zhǔyìzhě
twirl	v.	to rotate, spin, revolve or whirl rapidly.	快速转动	kuàisù zhuǎndòng
turquoise	adj.	a blue-green color like that found in the mineral; a semi-precious stone of the same name.	青绿色	qīnglǜsè
traction	n.	adhering or gripping a surface as a good tire does on a road.	摩擦力	mócālì
be in mortal fear (of)	v.p.	be afraid for one's life.	对……极度害怕	duì…jídù hàipà
drop dead	v.p.	to suddenly die. Also – adj. so wonderful that one could "die" as in "to die for" or want very much.	猝死	cùsǐ
thumb your nose (at)	v.p.	a gesture or sign of disrespect when the thumb is placed on the tip of the nose and the fingers are waved up and down.	对……作蔑视手势	duì…zuò mièshì shǒushì
winery	n.	a place where wine is made.	酿酒厂	niàngjiǔ chǎng
reds	n.	the category of wine made from red or dark-skinned grapes.	红酒	hóngjiǔ
taste buds	n.	small fleshy bumps on the tongue which receive sensory stimuli.	味蕾	wèilěi
register	v.	to have some effect. Also – to record, take note, apply. Also n. - a book or device to store data.	生效	shēngxiào

诚惶诚恐	誠惶誠恐	chénghuáng-chéngkǒng	f.c.w.	upset, with fear and trepidation
琢磨	琢磨	zuómo	v.	think over, ponder
说词	說詞	shuōcí	n.	wording
茅塞顿开	茅塞頓開	máosè dùnkāi	f.c.w.	suddenly see the light
永久	永久	yǒngjiǔ	adj.	permanent
短语	短語	duǎnyǔ	n.	phrase
演唱会	演唱會	yǎnchànghuì	n.	recital
取决于	取決於	qǔjuéyú	v.p.	be determined by
比如说	比如說	bǐrúshuō	v.p.	take sth. for example
睁大	睜大	zhēngdà	v (c)	open one's eyes wide
房角	房角	fángjiǎo	n.	the corner of the room
感官	感官	gǎnguān	n.	sensory organ
酿酒厂	釀酒廠	niàngjiǔchǎng	n.	winery
品尝	品嘗	pǐncháng	v.	taste sample
品酒	品酒	pǐnjiǔ	v.	taste wine
度数	度數	dùshu	n.	degree
葡萄酒	葡萄酒	pútáojiǔ	n.	wine made from grapes
烈性	烈性	lièxìng	adj.	robust
吃不消	吃不消	chībùxiāo	v (c)	overwhelm, be unable to withstand
初学	初學	chūxué	v.	just begin to learn sth.
苦味	苦味	kǔwèi	n.	bitterness
难忍	難忍	nánrěn	v.	hard to bear
味觉	味覺	wèijué	n.	taste
滋味	滋味	zīwèi	n.	taste, flavor
糖果	糖果	tángguǒ	n.	candy, sweets
甜味	甜味	tiánwèi	n.	sweetness
衰退	衰退	shuāituì	v.	deteriorate
嗅觉	嗅覺	xiùjué	n.	sense of smell, olfactory
灵敏度	靈敏度	língmǐndù	n.	sensitivity
手指	手指	shǒuzhǐ	n.	finger
抚摸	撫摸	fǔmō	v.	touch
嗤之以鼻	嗤之以鼻	chīzhīyǐbí	f.c.w.	give a snort of contempt
处世	處世	chǔshì	v.o.	conduct oneself in society
行之有效	行之有效	xíngzhī-yǒuxiào	f.c.w.	act effectively

receptor	n.	that part of an organ that is sensitive to sensory stimuli.	感觉器官	gǎnjué qìguān
deteriorate	v.	to wear away; to become less in quality; to degenerate or worsen.	衰退	shuāituì
olfactory	adj	pertaining to the sense of smell.	嗅觉的	xiùjué de
amputee	n.	someone who has had a limb surgically removed.	截肢者	jiézhīzhě

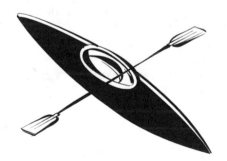

第三章

在越南的學以致用

2003 年我們去越南作漂流旅行。在從機場去旅館的路上，我們看到了公路兩旁的水稻田。這種風景對我們來說并不陌生，新鮮的是導游納木（Nam）告訴我們，那些三三兩兩散落在水稻田內的建築都是墳墓。有的只有小土墩那么大，有的看起來像一個白色、長方形的水泥盒子。記得母親生前曾經關照我們，等她死后要把她埋在"高高的、干干的、并且有午后陽光的溫暖的地方"。我馬上就得出了一個老套的結論：沒有哪個亞洲人，無論是農民還是別的什么人，願意死后埋在水里。納木還告訴我們，為了節省空間，有些越南人會定時地打開墳墓，整理新埋進的尸骨，這樣可以為后來的"居民"騰出地方。對于他們這種做法，我想母親不會因此而感到任何安慰，但她一定會對亞洲產的大米另眼相看!!! 我們后來非常驚訝地發現，越南人的平均壽命是五十八歲。雖然大街上的每個人看起來都很健康：精瘦干練、肌肉發達，但是，由于落后的衛生條件，很多人都患有不同的疾病。當我告訴納木我已六十一歲時，他緊張地恭維着我。我說，我的年輕歸功于富裕的小康生活和滋潤的護膚品，我還跟他說我每星期教六次健身課。"教阿拉伯語？"[9] 他問。我沒再接他的話茬兒。

我們在哈浪（Ha Long）登上了一只很一般的木船，船名叫"junk"，這真是再確切不過了。在海灣上漂了三十分鐘以后，納木和其他四位船員為我們拿出了兩條橡皮艇：一條是單人座的，一條是雙人座的。我先生班尼特二話沒說就爬進了那單人座的橡皮艇。當他駕着橡皮艇離開我們的大船時，我笑着對納木說，每當遇到新的挑戰時，我會按以下原則辦事：如果班尼特能勝任的話，我也要嘗試一下。納木沒有笑，我猜想可能是他的英文有限，沒聽懂吧。我倆誰也沒有說什么就爬進了雙人座的橡皮艇。開始我還努力地劃着，可是很難協調槳的順序。我怕因為我的失誤而把納木劃進水里!!!，就停下讓他一個人劃。這下納木笑了!!!

---

[9] His misunderstanding of the English was based on the similar sound of "aerobics" and "Arabic."

由于班尼特的技術不錯，第二天，大家催着他上單人座的橡皮艇。班尼特知道我的情形，這時他對納木説現在該輪到我劃單人座的橡皮艇了。納木指着我，直搖頭，簡直嚇死了。碰到這么一個大男子主義的導游，我很氣憤。于是我拿起槳，快速地揮舞着，準備開戰，那架勢好像剛從《卧虎藏龍》的電影中跑出來。納木兩眼直瞪瞪地看着我，往后退了退。那天我穿了一件黑色的泳裝，外面套了一件大大的花襯衫和一條橘紅色的運動短褲（為的是不要太暴露），一雙青綠色的勃肯牌（Birkenstocks）橡膠鞋（為的是增加摩擦力），一件磨損了但仍然非常顯眼的藍“裙子”，用來罩在橡皮艇洞口的邊沿上（為的是防止水進到船里面）。看到我這身武裝，納木知道我真的要發瘋了。我嚴厲地瞪了他一眼。那一眼足以告訴他，如果他還試圖不讓我進單人橡皮艇，我這個女權主義者一定會把他從性別峽谷的那一端拽過來。然后我又提醒他，我可是付錢到這兒來旅游的呵。

當納木轉向其他船員，告訴他們我要劃單人艇這一“不幸”消息時，大家頓時議論紛紛，個個誠惶誠恐。我正琢磨着説詞，忽然茅塞頓開。我比他們的祖母還大，他們不是因為我是女性不讓我上單人艇，而是擔心我會突然死掉，再也回不去美國的新澤西州，只能永久地躺在越南的水稻田里!!!

“Thumbing Your Knows”[10] 是我創造的短語, 表示我們不僅要使用許多已知的知識, 而且要像蒂娜 · 特納（Tina Turner）在 1987 年的一個演唱會上唱的那樣，“你所得到的是你所看到的”。這就是説，你所得到的取決于你在多大程度上能把所看到的、聽到的、摸到的、聞到的、嘗到的綜合起來加以運用。比如説，睜大你的眼睛，用左手擋住你的左眼，用右手的大拇指對着房角的直邊，然后拿掉擋在左眼的左手，你會發現大拇指“移動”了。用同樣方法再做一次，這次用右手擋住右眼，用左手的大拇指對着房角的直邊，看看是哪只眼睛讓你覺得大拇指離開房角直邊的變動比較小。產生較小“移動”的那只眼睛是起着主要作用的眼睛。

由于不同的年齡、環境、期望，這種正常的差异同樣也會體現在其他感官上。你若參觀釀酒廠，最后一定會去品嘗室嘗酒。要是你真的很喜歡品酒，你最好先嘗度數低的白葡萄

---

[10] This is a pun that I made up in English but it is like many Chinese jokes that "play on words" which sound alike but are written differently. In this case, "knows" sounds like "nose." Children "thumb their nose" at people when they want to make fun of someone or show their lack of respect for rules, laws, people, institutions, traditions, etc.

酒，然后再嘗烈性的紅葡萄酒。要是你倒過來的話，你的舌頭會吃不消的。一個初學走路的孩子喜歡啤酒的苦味，而一個四年級的孩子會覺得其味難忍。這是因為剛學走路的孩子還沒有完全形成味覺，無法體會什么叫"苦"的滋味。而老年人比較喜歡吃糖果，是因為人對甜味感覺的功能是最后一個才衰退的。嗅覺經驗取決于先前的味道或鼻子的靈敏度。被截了肢的人沒有手指，但仍然能夠"撫摸"；別人以為你說了什么，但事實上你什么也沒說。換句話說，如果我們對其它已有的知識不嗤之以鼻，反而能夠恰當地對它們加以保留、聯想和運用，這樣我們的為人處世才能行之有效。

练习　EXERCISES

I. 思考和课堂讨论　FOOD FOR THOUGHT

A. PERSONAL　个人的

描述你生活中的一个"学以致用"的经历。

Describe an instance when you "thumbed your knows" by putting two ideas together for the first time.

C. GENERAL　普遍的

Some idiomatic words, abbreviations, or phrases are popular, useful, and thought-provoking. After reading the following explanation and sample sentence, discuss the question posed.

某些习惯用语、缩写词语或短语很流行、很有用，而且引人深思。阅读以下英语注释和例句，然后讨论问题。

"m.o." is derived from the Latin *modus operandi* (*modus* = "mode"; *operandi* = operation).

example: The police detective concluded there was a serial killer because the similarity of the murders indicated the same unusual **m.o.** of writing the date on the victim's forehead.

question: What, if anything, is the difference between police drawing conclusions based on an m.o. and one based on "racial profiling" when, e.g., airport personnel are suspicious of any male who appears to be from the Middle East?

C. CROSS-CULTURAL　跨文化的

阅读以下短文，并用<u>用中文</u>对所提出的问题进行讨论。

After reading the following, discuss <u>in Chinese</u> why North Americans seem to value youthfulness more than longevity.

More likely than not, our ancestors had very definite ideas about their own culture and, just as likely, they passed their views on to their children and their children's children. In this way, our ideas about language, family, religion, food, gender roles, government, etc. were as stereotypical as theirs. Hopefully, though, as we travel, work, fall in love, and learn about things they could not have imagined, we will know better so that the views we pass on to our children will be less chauvinistic. On the other hand, operating on the principle that cultural diversity is valuable does not necessarily mean our respect for ancestral ways must deteriorate.

II. 配对　MATCHMAKER

A. VOCABULARY　词汇

找出以下两列中的对应词，并在其间划线。

Draw a connecting line between the word and its correct definition.

a.	另眼相看	1.	mistake, fault
b.	直瞪瞪	2.	overwhelm, be unable to withstand
c.	埋葬	3.	say nothing
d.	健身	4.	look at sb./sth. with new eyes
e.	茅塞顿开	5.	comparatively well off
f.	衰退	6.	sensitivity
g.	灵敏度	7.	wide-eyed
h.	失误	8.	aerobics
i.	二话没说	9.	suddenly see the light
j.	吃不消	10.	deteriorate
k.	小康	11.	inter

a.	fortify	1.	大男子主义
b.	olfactory	2.	对……作蔑视手势
c.	mollify	3.	猝死
d.	funky	4.	老套的
e.	receptor	5.	生效
f.	thumb your nose	6.	嗅觉的
g.	afflict	7.	加强
h.	drop dead	8.	感觉器官
i.	stereotypical	9.	使……安慰
j.	register	10.	使……折磨
k.	chauvinist	11.	简单的

B. ANTONYMS & ALTERNATES 反义词和多义词

First draw a connecting line between the words or phrases in the left-hand column with the best possible <u>antonym</u> listed in the middle column, then draw a line between the antonym and an alternate meaning of the antonym listed in the right-hand column. <u>Be forewarned</u> that the part of speech may change from one column to the next and that slang terms may be used. E.g.,

"hit" ——————————— *"miss"* —— ———— *"honorific for unmarried female"*

"warm" ——————————— *"cool"* ————— *"excellent"*

首先在第二列中找出与第一列相对应的反义词，然后在第三列中找出与第二列相关的多义词。注意：词性会有变化。

			ANTONYMS		ALTERNATE MEANING
a.	curved	1.	**potted**	i.	hair that has been cut short
b.	interested	2.	**pitted**	ii.	anxious, nervous
c.	secretive	3.	**fill**	iii.	effective, revealing
d.	unplanted	4.	**edgy**	iv.	opposed or set (against) sb.
e.	was still	5.	**stay**	v.	*slang* drunk, inebriated, "high"
f.	unhealthy	6.	**well**	vi.	make idea, liquid, etc. clear
g.	empty	7.	**telling**	vii.	pierced, made a hole
h.	leave	8.	**clarify**	viii.	(reproving) interjection
i.	unscarred, smooth	9.	**bored**	ix.	occupy, able to perform
j.	cloud	10.	**bobbed**	x.	brace, prop, flat stiffener

III. 解字/词、构字/词 DECONSTRUCTION & CONSTRUCTION

A. 将以下汉字分解成最小的构字部件，然后用每个部件构成三个汉字。例如"鸭"可以分解成 "甲"和"鸟"两个部件。"甲"能构成"押"，"岬"，"钾"；"鸟"可以构成以"鸡"，"鸦"，"鸣"。请借助字典完成练习。

Deconstruct the following characters into the smallest components, then form 3 new characters using each component.

国_____轮_____霉_____

醒_____架_____漂_____

B. Using only the letters of the word "**DETERIORATE**," form English words that are not proper nouns, abbreviations, or acronyms and that consist of 4 or more letters. A letter can only be used again if it appears in the given word more than once. E.g., "torn" is not acceptable because there is no "n" and "root" is not because there is only one "o." Like many Olympic sports, weight categories mark performance. We filled in a few cells to get you started. Fill in the rest to achieve the highest category. If you think up more than 90, you beat the authors!

用 "**DETERIORATE**" 中的字母构词。新构建的词不能是专有名词、缩写词、或首字母缩略词。每个单词必须至少含有四个字母，但不能重复使用同一字母，除非该字母在"**DETERIORATE**"中出现两次。

CHAMPION STATUS						
FLY 13	BANTAM 26	FEATHER 39	LIGHT 52	WELTER 65	MIDDLE 78	HEAVY 90
deer	diet	tire	rate			
deter	dieter	tired	rated			

C. 用 "学以致用" 中的每个汉字组成不同的词。看看最多能组多少个词。

Use each of the characters in "学以致用" to form as many words (of 2-4 characters) as you can.

D. Pair any two of the following 8 words to form at least 9 different, unhyphenated words.

在下列八个词中配对、组词，新组的词只能含有两个单词，中间没有连字号。
请至少组出九个词。

eyed mill cock wall up tail stone wind

IV. 阅读理解 READING QUIZ

根据课文，选择准确答案。Based on the text, choose the best answer.

1. 散落在越南公路两旁水稻田内的建筑都是什么？

    a. 是小土墩。

    b. 是水泥盒子。

    c. 是坟墓。

    d. 什么都不是。

2. 为什么有些越南人会定时地打开坟墓，整理新埋进的尸骨？

    a. 因为这样可以纪念亲人。

    b. 因为这样可以节省地方。

    c. 因为这样坟墓就会很干净。

    d. 因为这样坟墓就不会潮湿。

3. 为什么纳木担心我会突然死掉？

    a. 因为我是美国人。

    b. 因为我是女的。

    c. 因为我的年龄很大。

    d. 因为我船划得不好。

4. 根据作者，课文中哪一个人物有大男子主义思想？

    a. 导游纳木，因为他就是不让她划单人座的橡皮艇。

    b. 歌星蒂娜，因为她认为你所得到的是你所看见的。

    c. 她的先生，因为他二话没说就爬进了单人座的橡皮艇。

    d. 她的母亲，因为她希望被埋在一个舒服、温暖的地方。

    e. 作者发现自己错怪了纳木。

5. 为什么初学走路的孩子会喜欢啤酒的特殊味道？

    a. 因为他们还很小，不知道什么是酸味。

    b. 因为他们还很小，不知道什么是甜味。

    c. 因为他们还很小，不知道什么是苦味。

    d. 因为他们还很小，不知道什么是辣味。

    e. 以上都对。

6. 什么是学以致用？

    a. 把所有学到的知识综合起来用于实际。

    b. 把学到的与看到的结合起来加以运用。

    c. 把学到的与听到的结合起来加以运用。

    d. 把学到的与闻到的结合起来加以运用。

V. 填空　FILL IN THE BLANK

A. 选择正确答案。Choose the correct answer.

1. 有些越南人会_____打开坟墓，整理新埋进的尸骨。

   a. 定时　　　　b. 及时　　　　c. 准时

2. 当我告诉纳木我已六十一岁时，他紧张地_____着我。

   a. 恭候　　　　b. 恭敬　　　　c. 恭维

3. 那只非常一般的木船船名叫"junk"，这真是太_____了。

   a. 确确实实　　b. 确切不过　　c. 不过如此

4. 于是，我拿起桨，快速地_____着，准备开战。

   a. 伴舞　　　　b. 跳舞　　　　c. 挥舞

5. 然后我又_____他，我可是付钱到这儿来旅游的呵。

   a. 吵醒　　　　b. 提醒　　　　c. 唤醒

B. Using your target language, write a word or phrase from the vocabulary lists and/or dictionary that means the <u>same</u> or is a <u>synonym</u> for the italicized word or phrase. Keep in mind that the part of speech and/or tense may have been adjusted to achieve grammatically correct results.

在以下段落中找出与斜体词意义相近的同义词。如果你所学的外语是中文，找出相应的中文词或短语。如果你所学的外语是英语，找出相应的英语词或短语。注意：词性或时态会有变化。

The tourist's fear of meeting strangers was *reinforced* _____ by her ignorance of their customs. As a result, her trip *degenerated* _____ into nothing more than two weeks in a hotel room so that she returned home as much a *culturally close-minded person* _____ as before and she continued to deal *in a way that treats people as if they were all the same and without individual differences* anyone who was ethnically different _____ _____

VI. 翻译　TRANSLATION

A. 将以下句子翻译成英文。Translate the following sentences into English.

1. 记得母亲生前曾经关照我们，等她死后要把她埋在"高高的、干干的、并且有午后阳光的温暖的地方"。

2. 对于他们这种做法，我想母亲不会因此而感到任何安慰，但她一定会对亚洲产的大米另眼相看**!!!**。

3. 我严厉地瞪了他一眼。那一眼足以告诉他，如果他还试图不让我进单人橡皮艇，我这个女权主义者一定会把他从性别峡谷的那一端拽过来。

B. Translate the following sentences into Chinese. 将以下句子翻译成中文。

1. For example, open your eyes. Then cover the left eye with your left hand. Then line up your right thumb with a straight edge like the corner of the room. Then uncover the left eye and notice the thumb "move." After doing the same thing but with your right eye

covered, notice which eye produced a less perceptible shift in the alignment of thumb to straight edge. This is your dominant eye.

2. If you care about tasting what you're drinking **!!!**, you start with the light white wines and end with robust reds because, the other way around, your tongue will have been overwhelmed.

3. Amputees "feel" with fingers they no longer have; people insist you said something when you didn't. In other words, we can make better sense if we don't "thumb our nose" by disregarding other factors and facts that we know but don't use.

VII. 完型填充　CLOZE TEST

A. 在以下短文的每一空格处填入一个汉字，如有可能，给出相应的英语单词。

Fill in a Chinese character that retains the original meaning or intent of the text, then write an English equivalent, if any.

在海湾上漂了三十分钟后，纳木和其他四_____船员为我们拿_____了两条橡皮艇：_____条是单人座的，一_____是双人座的。我_____生班尼特二话_____说就爬进了那_____人座的橡皮艇。_____他驾着橡皮艇_____开我们的大船时，_____笑着对纳木说，_____当遇到新的挑_____时，我会按以下_____则办事：如果班尼特_____胜任的话，我也_____尝试一下。

B. Fill in an English word or phrase that retains the original meaning or intent of the text, then write a Chinese equivalent, if any.

在以下短文的每一空格处填入一个英语单词，如有可能，给出相应的汉字或词。

Thirty minutes into the bay, Nam and _____ crew of four brought out two kayaks—_____ one and a two-seater. With no discussion, _____ clambered overboard into the one-seater. As my _____ got the hang of going straight and _____ from the junk, I laughed and told _____ that, whenever we have a new challenge, _____ operate on the principle: If Bennett survives, _____ try. When Nam didn't smile, I figured _____ was his limited English. Without further comment, _____ and I got into the two-seater. At _____ I tried to paddle but it was _____ coordinating strokes so, rather than knock him _____ by mistake **!!!**, I gave up and let _____ do all the work. This time he_____ **!!!**

VIII. 身体部位　BODY PARTS

A. There are many useful idioms which contain "body parts". Choose the most appropriate to fill in the blank based on your best guess of what the idiom means.

英语中的许多习惯用语含有表示"身体部位"的单词。在下面三个习惯用语中选择最恰当的填空。

    1. an eye for an eye   **2.** a sight for sore eyes   **3.** in a pig's eye

Despite the many times convicted killers were later proven innocent based on new DNA evidence, the idea of _____ is still how capital punishment is justified.

Sky dive from an airplane? _____!

Although she had aged considerably, my high school sweetheart was_____.

B. 将以下短文翻译成中文。注意：划线的词或短语与以上含有"身体部位"的习惯用语相对应。

Translate the following into Chinese taking note that the underlined words or phrases correspond to the meaning of the above "body parts."

The idea that punishment should be a matter of <u>"tit for tat" or "a life for a life"</u> might make sense until you find out that some people believe it is justice to punish ordinary thieves by chopping off their hands. <u>Under no circumstances</u> is anything in a store worth a human hand. Imagining that terrible possibility makes looking at my two hands a <u>most welcome experience</u>.

C. Using your target language, create sentence(s) containing the following three English idioms or their Chinese equivalents.

用以下短语分别造句。注意：如果你所学的外语是中文，请用中文来做这个练习。如果你所学的外语是英语，请用英语来做这个练习。

    1. have an eye for = 善于鉴赏

    2. there's more than meets the eye = 某人/某事并不象看到的那样

    3. green-eyed monster = 红眼，吃醋，嫉妒

IX. 写作　PRÉCIS

用所学的外语总结课文。如果你用中文来写，请至少使用 450 个汉字，并用电脑打出摘要。如果你用英文来写，请不超过 320 个词。

Write a summary of this chapter in your target language. If writing in Chinese, use <u>more</u> than 450 characters; if writing in English, use <u>no more</u> than 320 words.

CHAPTER FOUR

CONSIDERING THE DOUBLE TAKES IN TAIPEI

The usual double take is to quickly look again because what you first saw or heard was in some way startling, even unbelievable. My version of the double take adds the idea that looking again will help you *take in* what others *take* to be the case. Happily my mother did this when she heard what her grandson did in Taiwan.

Of the three Bao daughters, I was the least connected to my Chinese roots. My elder sister was four years older and, unlike me, retained memories of our homeland. My younger sister did not emigrate from China until she was almost eighteen.[9] And, because I was also the least able to fulfill my mother's dream of who she thought I should be for the sake of completing the family's identity—get a Ph.D. and teach at a university she and her mah-jongg friends had heard of, like Cornell **!!!**—she had no hope that my son would have much of "the Chinese" in him. So, when William left Bowdoin College to spend his Junior Year Abroad in Taiwan, my mother was pleased. Of course she never said anything out loud but I knew because she readily contacted her friends, asking them to help her grandson at the beginning of his stay when his language skills were worse than mine. In this way, she indirectly let them know that William wanted to develop "the Chinese" in him so he wasn't hopelessly "Americanized" like his father **!!!**

My advice to William involved a more sexy and "sexy" concern. The year was 1992 and Keanu Reeves had just launched his career with the movie *Point Break* as an "action star." Of Chinese-Hawaiian and Irish descent, he also launched a flurry of worldwide attention to public figures with Asian-Caucasian parents. As a result, I warned our son that there would be lots of young women in Taiwan who would be impressed by his "half-half" looks and even bold about dating him. They might seem mod but they were really quite naïve so it was up to him to make sure he didn't ruin their lives and their family's reputations. (Translation: Virgins are off limits and, DON'T GET PREGNANT **!!!**)

---

[9] 有关三三的故事，请参阅包柏漪（Bette (Bao) Lord）的《秋月》。该书首先由 Harper & Row 出版社于 1964 年出版，后来又以其他语言多次再版。

第四章

在台北的恍然大悟

所谓"愣住"是指你第一次看到或听到什么令人惊讶或难以置信的事情时会有失神的反应，当然通常你会迅速再看一下。我这里所说的愣住、恍然大悟还有另一层意思。那就是，这第二次的打量会帮你理解别人所接受的东西。当我母亲得知她外孙在台湾所做的事情时，她就有这种反应。

包家的三个女儿中我最没有中国根。我们从中国来美国时，姐姐比我大四岁，所以祖国的情景她记忆犹新；妹妹快到十八岁时才来美国，有关中国的事情她了如指掌。[11] 我母亲希望她女儿能光宗耀祖：拿一个博士学位，然后在一所她和她麻将朋友听说过的大学，比如康纳尔大学（Cornell University），教教书。由于我是最没有帮母亲实现家族梦想的一个女儿，她根本就没指望过我的儿子会保留什么中国文化传统。所以当威廉离开鲍登学院（Bowdoin College）去台湾读大三时，她非常高兴。当然，她嘴上什么也没说，但是我知道，因为她马上就跟她在台湾的朋友联系，请他们在威廉到了台湾以后的头几天关照一下，因为那时候威廉的中文比我还差。她这样做也等于是拐弯抹角地告诉他们：威廉想提高自身的中国文化修养，不再是一个像他父亲那样的地地道道的美国人了!!! [12]

威廉去台湾前，我给了他一个与性有关、且比较时尚的忠告。那是 1992 年，柯努·荷菲（Keanu Reeves）——一个夏威夷华人和爱尔兰人的混血儿——领衔的电影《惊爆点》（Point Break）使他一举成名，从此开始了"动作明星"的生涯。于是对于那些父母是亚洲人和白人的公众人物，全球掀起了前所未有的关注热潮。我提醒儿子，台湾有很多年轻女孩会被他那"一半一半"的长相所迷住，而且有的会勇敢地与他约会。她们这样做也许很新潮，但也很幼稚。我要求儿子谨慎一点，千万不要毁了女孩的一生，并坏了她们家的名声（言下之意：别碰处女，别让她们怀孕了!!!）。

---

[11] For her story, read *Eighth Moon* by SanSan as told to Bette (Bao) Lord, originally published in 1964 by Harper & Row and since republished several times in many languages.

[12] The Chinese way is not to boast or praise directly. More on this later.

As usual, William slowly shook his head with the kind of what-am-I-going-to-do-with-you look that a tolerant American parent normally gives to a mischievous child **!!!** With that rueful smile, he let me know that he appreciated my blunt advice but still looked forward to the day when, maybe, I might be less cheery about his dating life **!!!**

Saying, "Okay, Mom," I was assured that he would not ignore my fears.

A few weeks after he arrived in Taipei and signed up for Mandarin classes, he called. "Mom, some lady stopped me in the street and asked if I wanted to model jeans. What do you think? Should I do it?"

I had a sinking feeling because I never wanted our son to rely on his looks to "get ahead." On the other hand, we had always jumped up and down like excited kids to encourage adventures into new territory as long as they weren't life-threatening. So I swallowed hard and said, "Sure, William. But just get very *ve-ry* suspicious if they ask you to take off *all* your clothes **!!!**"

Happily, he got paid a month's rent and wasn't tempted by the possibility of a new career in modeling—"It was boring."

What wasn't boring was that his pictures appeared all over Taipei—on billboards, department stores, *World Screen* magazine. However, the commercial artists at *Levi's* had decided to make William's eyes look artificial—like a robot or space creature—so none of my mother's friends recognized him in the advertising. Too bad the artists lost interest in the robot look. The next picture to appear in Taipei was William standing in the foreground, face forward so there was no doubt what he really looked like. Next to him was another model whose mother was probably very relieved to see that her son's face was mostly covered by a hooded sweatshirt **!!!** because, pictured behind them, wearing *Levi's* jeans of course, was a third fellow, standing in profile, looking down at his hands. At first glance, it looked like he was contemplating his navel—until you saw that he was standing in front of a urinal. This was *not* what my mother had in mind when her grandson went to establish his Chinese roots **!!!**

When my mother found out about her grandson's "bathroom picture" reproduced where her friends shopped, I told her, "Mommy, William *is* in China. But he's doing it *his* way."

She nodded.

I loved her for that. It's not easy for anyone, let alone a seventy-seven year old who left China in 1946 to *take in* what the other *takes to be* the case. For even if she "looks twice" to consider their difference in age, she also overcame the challenges of this younger "other" being a different gender,

跟平常一样，威廉慢慢地摇了摇头，同时给了我一个美国宽容父母常给淘气孩子的那种"我该拿你怎么办"的眼光。接着，他苦笑了一下，感谢我坦率的劝告，并告诉我他期待着有一天能找个女孩谈情说爱，到时也许会令我不高兴。

"好，妈妈。"他这么说我也就放心了，心想他不会一点都不理睬我的担忧吧。

威廉一到台北就修了几门中文课。几个星期后他给我来了一个电话，"妈妈，有个女的在街上拦住我，问我愿不愿意做牛仔裤的模特儿。你觉得怎么样？我该不该做？"

我心一沉，因为我从未想过要让儿子靠长相"发家"。 另一方面，我们也总是兴奋地像个孩子一样努力鼓励他敢于冒险、尝试新的经验，只要没有什么生命危险。于是，我深深地吸了口气，然后跟他说，"当然应该，威廉，但是，如果她们要你脱掉所有的衣服时，你可得千万千万小心呵!!!"

不错，威廉后来拿到了一笔钱，够他付一个月的房租。还好，他没有因为这次经验而想从事模特儿这一新职业，因为做模特儿，用他的话说，"很枯燥"。

有趣的是威廉当模特儿的广告在台北铺天盖地：广告牌、百货公司、《环球银幕》（World Screen） 杂志到处都是。但是李维斯（Levi's）公司的广告艺术家把威廉的眼睛做成机器人或者外星人的样子，所以我母亲在台湾的朋友没有一个能认出广告上的人。不幸的是广告艺术家很快就对机器人的样子失去了兴趣，接下来他们让威廉作了另一则广告。在那则广告上，威廉站在最为显著的地方，脸朝前方。站在他旁边的是另一个模特儿。那个模特儿的母亲也许很宽慰，因为她儿子的脸很大一部分被一件带有帽子的运动衫挡住了。在他们背后的是第三个模特儿，穿着李维斯的牛仔裤，侧面地站着，看着自己的手。乍一看，他好像站在那儿打坐!!! 可是你要是再仔细地看一下，就会发现他站在一个小便池的前面。我母亲压根儿没有想到她的外孙居然是以这种形象来建立他的中国根的!!!

当我母亲发现她外孙的"厕所广告"出现在她朋友购物的商店里时，我对她说，"妈妈，现在威廉在中国，他以他的方式在做一个中国人。"

她点了头。

因为这件事，我爱我母亲。理解他人对谁都不容易，更别说让一个在 1946 年就离开了中国的七十七岁的老太太来理解一个十八岁的年轻人在中国的所作所为。她"再一

and the "case" being historically revolutionized by forty-five years of political, social and economic changes. Although Chinese roots are still planted in Confucian, Taoist, and Buddhist soil, the culture is not the same as when my grandmother tried to bind her daughter's feet into "golden lotuses."

VOCABULARY

double take	n.p.	looking again quickly because one doubts that what one first saw was true or accurate.	一种开始是愣住后来才恍然大悟的反应	yīzhǒng kāishǐ shì lèngzhù hòulái cái huǎngrán dàwù de fǎnyìng
take in	v.p.	to absorb or grasp the meaning of sth.	领会，理解	lǐnghuì, lǐjiě
take to be the case	v.p.	to affirm the truth or accuracy of one's interpretation or assessment of a situation.	接受	jiēshòu
Junior Year Abroad		a program of study that is available to some college students who want to spend all or part of their 3rd year in another country.	去国外大学读三年级的项目	qù guówài dàxué dú sānniánjí de xiàngmù
sexy	adj.	*slang* - generally or currently attractive, interesting, appealing.	性感的，有趣的	xìnggǎn de, yǒuqù de
descent	n.	from an ancestor or forbearer, lineage.	后裔	hòuyì
flurry	n.	a sudden activity, excitement or commotion like a snow flurry.	阵风	zhènfēng
mod	adj.	from *mod*ern, associated with young British style of 1960s, trendy.	现代的，时髦的	xiàndài de, shímáo de
off limits	p.p.	area or topic that is not permitted; prohibited.	禁止进入，界限外	jìnzhǐ jìnrù, jièxiànwài

次"地考虑了她和年轻人的年龄差距，并且战胜了另外两个挑战：年轻人与她有性别差异；四十五年的政治、社会、经济变化使得现在的中国与从前的有着天壤之别。虽然中国的传统仍然深受儒家学说、道家思想和佛学理论的影响，但是现在的文化已不再是我外祖母时代的文化了，不会再要求她女儿把脚裹得像"三寸金莲"那么大了。

生词

恍然大悟	恍然大悟	huǎngrán-dàwù	f.c.w.	suddenly see the light
愣住	愣住	lèngzhù	v.	stand in amazement
令人	令人	lìngrén	v.o.	cause people to…, make one…
难以置信	難以置信	nányǐ-zhìxìn	f.c.w.	unbelievable, incredible
失神	失神	shīshén	v.o.	be inattentive, be absent-minded
所说	所說	suǒshuō	n.p.	what one has said
外孙	外孫	wàisūn	n.	daughter's son, grandson
记忆犹新	記憶猶新	jìyì-yóuxīn	f.c.w.	remain fresh in one's memory
了如指掌	了如指掌	liǎorúzhǐzhǎng	f.c.w.	know sth. like the palm
光宗耀祖	光宗耀祖	guāngzōng-yàozǔ	t.c.w.	bring honor to one's ancestors
博士学位	博士學位	bóshì xuéwèi	n.p.	Ph.D. degree
康纳尔大学	康納爾大學	Kāngnàěr Dàxué	p.n.	Cornell University
麻将	麻將	májiàng	n.	mah-jongg
指望	指望	zhǐwàng	v.	bank on, look forward to, pin one's hope on
鲍登学院	鮑登學院	Bàodēng Xuéyuàn	p.n.	Bowdoin College
拐弯抹角	拐彎抹角	guǎiwān-mòjiǎo	f.c.w.	indirectly, in a roundabout way
修养	修養	xiūyǎng	n.	self-cultivation
地地道道	地地道道	dìdì-dàodào	r.f.	completely
时尚	時尚	shíshàng	adj.	in fashion, in vogue
忠告	忠告	zhōnggào	n.	advice
柯努·荷菲	柯努·荷菲	Kēnǔ Héfēi	p.n.	Keanu Reeves
领衔	領銜	lǐngxián	v.o.	star in a movie/play
惊爆点	惊爆点	Jīngbàodiǎn		Point Break (a movie)
夏威夷	夏威夷	Xiàwēiyí	p.n.	Hawaii
混血儿	混血兒	hùnxuè'ér	n.	hybrid
掀起	掀起	xiānqǐ	v.	start, begin to surge
前所未有	前所未有	qiánsuǒwèiyǒu	f.c.w.	unprecedented
热潮	熱潮	rècháo	n.	crowd-pleasing attention

rueful	adj.	feeling, expressing, or showing sorrow or regret.	悲伤的，可怜的	bēishāng de, kělián de
billboard	n.	a flat surface upon which announcements or advertisements are displayed, often in public and large enough to attract attention from passers-by.	广告牌	guǎnggàopái
hood	n.	an attachment to the back collar of a shirt or jacket that can be lifted to cover the head for warmth and/or ("hoodies") style. Also – the front of a car that covers the engine; *slang* – variously a young man ranging from "wilder" to gangster; "the hood" is short for (ethnic) "neighborhood."	兜帽	dōumào
sweatshirt	n.	shirt (of heavy cotton knit) originally for athletes to absorb perspiration, now a style of casual clothing.	运动衫	yùndòngshān
in profile	p.p.	placed or seen so as the outline or side is viewed by the onlooker.	侧面地	cèmiàn de
contemplate one's navel	v.p.	from a form of meditation, to be deep in thought, often sitting cross-legged on the floor, head tilted forward, as if the person were looking down at his/her belly button.	打坐，沉思	dǎzuò, chénsī
navel	n.	the residue or scar left on the lower abdomen after severing the umbilical cord.	肚脐	dùqí
urinal	n.	a toilet fixture designed for men's (public) bathrooms.	小便池	xiǎobiànchí

长相	長相	zhǎngxiàng	n.	looks, appearance
新潮	新潮	xīncháo	adj.	mod, trendy
名声	名聲	míngshēng	n.	reputation
言下之意	言下之意	yánxiàzhīyì	f.c.w.	hidden meaning, between the lines
处女	處女	chǔnǚ	n.	virgin
宽容	寬容	kuānróng	adj.	tolerant, lenient
淘气	淘氣	táoqì	adj.	naughty, mischievous
苦笑	苦笑	kǔxiào	n.	rueful smile
坦率	坦率	tǎnshuài	adj.	blunt, candid, unadorned, frank
不埋	不理	bùlǐ	v.	ignore
担忧	擔憂	dānyōu	n.	worry, anxiety
牛仔裤	牛仔褲	niúzǎikù	n.	jeans
模特儿	模特兒	mótèr	n.	model
发家	發家	fājiā	v.o.	succeed, get ahead
兴奋地	興奮地	xìngfèn de	adv.	excitedly
一笔钱	一筆錢	yībǐqián	n.p.	a sum of money
房租	房租	fángzū	n.	rent
枯燥	枯燥	kūzào	adj.	dry and dull, uninteresting
铺天盖地	鋪天蓋地	pūtiān-gàidì	f.c.w.	all over the place
广告牌	廣告牌	guǎnggàopái	n.	billboard
百货公司	百貨公司	bǎihuògōngsī	n.	department store
环球影幕	環球影幕	Huánqiú Yíngmù		World Screen (a magazine)
李维斯	李維斯	Lǐwéisī	p.n.	Levi's
机器人	機器人	jīqìrén	n.	robot
外星人	外星人	wàixīngrén	n.	creature from outer space
认出	認出	rènchū	v (c)	recognize
一则	一則	yīzé	m (n)	a measure word for an advertisement
站在	站在	zhànzài	v.	stand at some place
最为	最為	zuìwéi	adv.	the most, extremely
宽慰	寬慰	kuānwèi	v.	be relieved
很大一部分	很大一部分	hěndà yībùfen	n.p.	a large part of
带有	帶有	dàiyǒu	v.	have
运动衫	運動衫	yùndòngshān	n	sweatshirt
侧面	側面	cèmiàn	n.	profile, side view
乍	乍	zhà	adv.	at first
打坐	打坐	dǎzuò	v.	meditate
肚脐	肚臍	dùqí	n.	navel
小便池	小便池	xiǎobiànchí	n.	urinal
压根儿	壓根兒	yàgēnr	adv.	never, not from the start
购物	購物	gòuwù	v.	go shopping

第四章

在臺北的恍然大悟

所謂"愣住"是指你第一次看到或聽到什麼令人驚訝或難以置信的事情時會有失神的反應，當然通常你會迅速再看一下。我這里所说的愣住、恍然大悟還有另一層意思。那就是，這第二次的打量會幫你理解別人所接受的東西。當我母親得知她外孫在臺灣所做的事情時，她就有這種反應。

包家的三個女兒中我最沒有中國根。我們從中國來美國時，姐姐比我大四歲，所以祖國的情景她記憶猶新；妹妹快到十八歲時才來美國，有關中國的事情她了如指掌。[11] 我母親希望她女兒能光宗耀祖：拿一個博士學位，然后在一所她和她麻將朋友聽说過的大學，比如康納爾大學（Cornell University），教教書。由于我是最沒有幫母親實現家族夢想的一個女兒，她根本就沒指望過我的兒子會保留什麼中國文化傳统。所以當威廉離開鮑登學院（Bowdoin College）去臺灣讀大三時，她非常高興。當然，她嘴上什麼也沒说，但是我知道，因為她馬上就跟她在臺灣的朋友聯系，請他們在威廉到了臺灣以后的頭幾天關照一下，因為那時候威廉的中文比我還差。她這樣做也等于是拐彎抹角地告訴他們：威廉想提高自身的中國文化修養，不再是一個像他父親那樣的地地道道的美國人了!!! [12]

威廉去臺灣前，我給了他一個與性有關、且比較時尚的忠告。那是 1992 年，柯努 • 荷菲（Keanu Reeves）——一個夏威夷華人和愛爾蘭人的混血兒——領銜的電影《驚爆點》（Point Break）使他一舉成名，從此開始了"動作明星"的生涯。于是對于那些父母是亞洲人和白人的公眾人物，全球掀起了前所未有的關注熱潮。我提醒兒子，臺灣有很多年輕女孩會被他那"一半一半"的長相所迷住，而且有的會勇敢地與他約會。她們這樣做也許很

---

[11] For her story, read *Eighth Moon* by SanSan as told to Bette (Bao) Lord, originally published in 1964 by Harper & Row and since republished several times in many languages.

[12] The Chinese way is not to boast or praise directly. More on this later.

所作所为	所作所為	suǒzuò-suǒwéi	f.c.w.	one's behavior or conduct
天壤之别	天壤之別	tiānrǎngzhībié	f.c.w.	a world of difference
扎根	扎根	zhāgēn	v.o.	be rooted in
儒家学说	儒家學說	Rújiāxuéshuō	p.n.	Confucianism
道家思想	道家思想	Dàojiāsīxiǎng	p.n.	Taoism
佛学理论	佛學理論	Fóxuélǐlùn	p.n.	Buddhism

新潮，但也很幼稚。我要求兒子謹慎一點，千萬不要毀了女孩的一生，并壞了她們家的名聲（言下之意：別碰處女，別讓她們懷孕了!!!）。

跟平常一樣，威廉慢慢地搖了搖頭，同時給了我一個美國寬容父母常給淘氣孩子的那種"我該拿你怎么辦"的眼光。接着，他苦笑了一下，感謝我坦率的勸告，并告訴我他期待着有一天能找個女孩談情說愛，到時也許會令我不高興。

"好，媽媽。"他這么說我也就放心了，心想他不會一點都不理踩我的擔憂吧。

威廉一到臺北就修了幾門中文課。幾個星期后他給我來了一個電話，"媽媽，有個女的在街上攔住我，問我願不願意做牛仔褲的模特兒。你覺得怎么樣？我該不該做？"

我心一沉，因為我從未想過要讓兒子靠長相"發家"。 另一方面，我們也總是興奮地像個孩子一樣努力鼓勵他敢于冒險、嘗試新的經驗，只要沒有什么生命危險。于是，我深深地吸了口氣，然后跟他說，"當然應該，威廉，但是，如果她們要你脫掉所有的衣服時，你可得千萬千萬小心呵!!!"

不錯，威廉后來拿到了一筆錢，夠他付一個月的房租。還好，他沒有因為這次經驗而想從事模特兒這一新職業，因為做模特兒，用他的話說，"很枯燥"。

有趣的是威廉當模特兒的廣告在臺北鋪天蓋地：廣告牌、百貨公司、《環球銀幕》（World Screen） 雜志到處都是。但是李維斯（Levi's）公司的廣告藝術家把威廉的眼睛做成機器人或者外星人的樣子，所以我母親在臺灣的朋友沒有一個能認出廣告上的人。不幸的是廣告藝術家很快就對機器人的樣子失去了興趣，接下來他們讓威廉作了另一則廣告。在那則廣告上，威廉站在最為顯著的地方，臉朝前方。站在他旁邊的是另一個模特兒。那個模特兒的母親也許很寬慰，因為她兒子的臉很大一部分被一件帶有帽子的運動衫擋住了。在他們背后的是第三個模特兒，穿着李維斯的牛仔褲，側面地站着，看着自己的手。乍一看，他好像站在那兒打坐!!! 可是你要是再仔細地看一下，就會發現他站在一個小便池的前面。我母親壓根兒沒有想到她的外孫居然是以這種形象來建立他的中國根的!!!

當我母親發現她外孫的"廁所廣告"出現在她朋友購物的商店里時，我對她說，"媽媽，現在威廉在中國，他以他的方式在做一個中國人。"

她點了頭。

　　因為這件事，我愛我母親。理解他人對誰都不容易，更別說讓一個在 1946 年就離開了中國的七十七歲的老太太來理解一個十八歲的年輕人在中國的所作所為。她"再一次"地考慮了她和年輕人的年齡差距，并且戰勝了另外兩個挑戰：年輕人與她有性別差异；四十五年的政治、社會、經濟變化使得現在的中國與從前的有着天壤之別。雖然中國的傳統仍然深受儒家學說、道家思想和佛學理論的影響，但是現在的文化已不再是我外祖母時代的文化了，不會再要求她女兒把腳裹得像"三寸金蓮"那么大了。

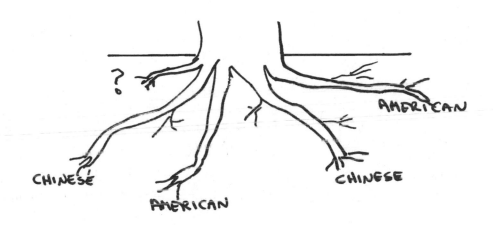

练习　EXERCISES

I. 思考和课堂讨论　FOOD FOR THOUGHT

A.　PERSONAL　个人的

描述你生活中通过再次观察然后改变己见、接受他人观点的一个经历。

When have you looked again at a situation in order to "take in what others take to be the case" and, as a result of seeing the situation from another person's viewpoint, changed your own mind?

B.　GENERAL　普遍的

An "argument" or line of reasoning is logical when a conclusion is validly deduced from premises that are assumed to be true. However, when there is an error in reasoning, then a fallacy occurs. In order to think clearly and effectively, it helps to know about these errors. After reading the following, discuss the question posed.

当某一结论是从一个正确的前提演绎出来的，那么该结论的论据符合逻辑。但是，如果推理出现错误，就会产生谬论。为了清楚、有效地思考，有必要了解这些推理错误。请阅读下面的错误，然后讨论所提出的问题。

> **ad hominem** (by being abusive) is from the Latin *argumentum ad hominem (argumentum =* "argument"; *ad* = "to"; *hominem* = "the person").

> **pattern:** Mr. X argues for the truth of his conclusion; Ms. Y refers to Mr. X's bad reputation instead of disproving what Mr. X claimed to be true. (In the U.S. courts, Ms. Y's approach is considered "prejudicial" and usually not allowed because the accused is considered innocent until proven guilty.)

> **example:** Instead of presenting physical or eye-witness evidence to the jury proving beyond a reasonable doubt that Mr. X had in fact murdered the victim, Ms. Y argues ***ad hominem*** by saying to the jury, "How can you believe Mr. X? Last year he was convicted of robbing a bank!"

> **question:** Why is Ms. Y's fallacious approach often effective but still logically irrelevant?

C.　CROSS-CULTURAL　跨文化的

After reading the following, discuss <u>in English</u> the idea of "privilege" received through personal or family connection versus "right" received by virtue of law.

阅读以下短文，并<u>用英文</u>对所提出的问题进行讨论。

> In retrospect, I now do double takes on my mother's emigrations, immigrations and *inter*grations into and out of countries and cultures. Proud of being descended from a distinguished, socially elite family, she was equally pleased with being an American citizen who had the "right" to wait on a long line, sometimes in the rain, in order to vote for the next president of the United States. Never rueful about the difference between her traditional past and her modern present, she, nevertheless, must have felt the switching was sometimes like trying to see the same snowflake twice while standing in the middle of a flurry. After she died,

Bennett and I made a T-shirt that represents her cultural journeys. On the front of the T-shirt is "Empress Dowager." On the back is "Just Another Immigrant" **!!!**

II. 配对 MATCHMAKER

A. VOCABULARY 词汇

找出以下两列中的对应词，并在其间划线。

Draw a connecting line between the word and its correct definition.

a.	地地道道	1.	unprecedented
b.	兴奋地	2.	sexy
c.	认出	3.	stand in amazement
d.	一笔钱	4.	all over the place
e.	前所未有	5.	department store
f.	百货公司	6.	a sum of money
g.	淘气	7.	recognize
h.	铺天盖地	8.	flurry
i.	愣住	9.	completely
j.	性感的，有趣的	10.	naughty, mischievous
k.	阵风	11.	excitedly

a.	rueful	1.	禁止进入
b.	in profile	2.	后裔
c.	double take	3.	接受
d.	contemplate one's navel	4.	现代的，时髦的
e.	navel	5.	可怜的
f.	off limits	6.	广告牌
g.	mod	7.	肚脐
h.	billboard	8.	运动衫
i.	take to be the case	9.	一种开始是愣住后来才恍然大悟的反应
j.	descent	10.	打坐
k.	sweatshirt	11.	侧面地

B. SYNONYMS & ALTERNATES 同义词和多义词

First draw a connecting line between the word or phrase in the left-hand column with the best possible <u>synonym</u> listed in the middle column, then draw a line between the synonym and an alternate meaning of the synonym listed in the right-hand column. <u>Be forewarned</u> that the part of speech may change from one column to the next and that slang terms may be used. E.g.,

"hit" ————————————— *"strike"* —————— *"stop-work action against employer"*

"warm" ————————————— *"heat"* ——————— *"qualifying race for final contest"*

首先在第二列中找出与第一列相对应的同义词，然后在第三列中找出与第二列相关的多义词。注意：词性会有不同。

		SYNONYMS		ALTERNATE MEANING
a.	stays, abides, stops	1. **links**	i.	corpse, dead body
b.	cold, icy	2. **formal**	ii.	*informal* thrash, beat, drub
c.	host, have guests	3. **draw**	iii.	*informal* homosexual
d.	be confident in	4. **tan**	iv.	(monopolistic) corporation
e.	joins, connects	5. **remains**	v.	"black tie" evening dress
f.	strange, odd	6. **trust**	vi.	consider possibility of plan, idea, action
g.	cure (into leather)	7. **drag**	vii.	sexually unresponsive
h.	pull hard (on cigarette)	8. **queer**	viii.	*slang* sb. who deters enjoyment
i.	inhale (air, smoke)	9. **entertain**	ix.	bring in or attract a salary, an audience
j.	not casual, official	10. **frigid**	x.	sausages strung together

III. 解字/词、构字/词 DECONSTRUCTION & CONSTRUCTION

A. 将以下汉字分解成最小的构字部件，然后用每个部件构成三个汉字。例如"鸭"可以分解成 "甲"和"鸟"两个部件。"甲"能构成"押"，"岬"，"钾"；"鸟"可以构成以"鸡"，"鸦"，"鸣"。请借助字典完成练习。

Deconstruct the following characters into the smallest components, then form 3 new characters using each component.

地_____ 迷_____ 笔_____

另_____ 掀_____ 意_____

B. Using only the letters of the word "**CONTEMPLATE**," form English words that are not proper nouns, abbreviations, or acronyms and that consist of 4 or more letters. A letter can only be used again if it appears in the given word more than once. E.g., "corn" is not acceptable because there is no "r" and "pool" is not because there is only one "o." Like many Olympic

sports, weight categories mark performance. We filled in a few cells to get you started. Fill in the rest to achieve the highest category. If you think up more than 120, you beat the authors!

用 "CONTEMPLATE" 中的字母构词。新构建的词不能是专有名词、缩写词、或首字母缩略词。每个单词必须至少含有四个字母，但不能重复使用同一字母，除非该字母在"CONTEMPLATE"中出现两次。

CHAMPION STATUS							
FLY 15	BANTAM 30	FEATHER 45	LIGHT 60	WELTER 75	MIDDLE 90	HEAVY 105	SUPER 120
cone	plea	late	mane				
cote	pleat	lace	mate				
come	plate	lame	mote				
			motel				

C. 用 "恍然大悟" 中的每个汉字组成不同的词。看看最多能组多少个词。

Use each of the characters in "恍然大悟" to form as many words (of 2-4 characters) as you can.

D. Pair any two of the following 11 words to form at least 12 different, unhyphenated words.

在下列十一个词中配对、组词，新组的词只能含有两个单词，中间没有连字号。请至少组出十二对。

heart fly brand board worm head fire ring black way wood

IV. 阅读理解　READING QUIZ

根据课文，选择准确答案。Based on the text, choose the best answer.

1. 什么是恍然大悟？

    a.　先愣住，然后再看一看。

    b.　先失神，然后再听一听。

    c.　开始稀里糊涂，后来突然一切都明白了。

    d.　开始难以置信，后来完全相信并接受了。

2. 为什么人们对公众人物中的混血儿会特别关注？

    a.　因为他们有着"一半一半" 的迷人长相。

    b.　因为他们的父母是夏威夷华人和爱尔兰人。

    c.　因为他们既很新潮，又很幼稚。

    d.　因为他们敢于冒险，尝试新的经验。

3. 威廉有没有帮李维斯公司做牛仔裤的模特儿？

    a.　他做了，还拿到了一笔钱。

    b.　他做了，还找到了一个女朋友。

    c.　他没做，因为当模特儿有生命危险。

    d.　他没做，因为当模特儿很枯燥无味。

4. 为什么我母亲在台湾的朋友没有一个能认出广告上的人就是威廉？

    a.　因为广告上的威廉长得像机器人。

    b.　因为广告上的威廉长得像美国人。

    c.　因为广告上的威廉长得像模特儿。

    d.　因为广告上的威廉长得像夏威夷人。

5. 第二则广告中的一个模特儿侧面地站在那儿做什么？

    a.　在小便。

    b.　在演戏。

    c.　在打坐。

    d.　什么也没做 。

6. 什么是中国文化的主要组成部分？

    a.　中国文化的传统包括儒家学说。

    b.　中国文化的传统包括道家思想。

c. 中国文化的传统包括佛学理论。

d. 以上都对。

V. 填空　FILL IN THE BLANK

A. 选择正确答案。Choose the correct answer.

1. 我妹妹快到十八岁时才来美国，有关中国的事情她_____。

    a. 了如指掌　　　b. 易如反掌　　c. 摩拳擦掌

2. 我给了威廉一个与性有关、且比较时尚的_____。

    a. 广告　　　　　b. 劝告　　　　c. 布告

3. 对于那些父母是亚洲人和白人的共众人物，全球一时_____了关注热潮。

    a. 举起　　　　　b. 拿起　　　　c. 掀起

4. 千万不要毁了女孩的一生，并坏了她们家的_____。

    a. 名声　　　　　b. 风声　　　　c. 笑声

5. 我心一沉，因为我从未想过要让儿子靠长相_____。

    a. 出家　　　　　b. 起家　　　　c. 成家

B. 在以下段落中找出与斜体词意义相近的反义词。如果你所学的外语是中文，找出相应的中文词或短语，如果你所学的外语是英语，找出相应的英语词或短语。注意，词性或时态会有变化。

Using your target language, write a word or phrase from the vocabulary lists and/or dictionary that means the <u>opposite</u> or is an <u>antonym</u> for the italicized word or phrase. Keep in mind that the part of speech and/or tense may have been adjusted to achieve grammatically correct results.

She would have preferred her grandmother to be more *old-fashioned* _____ and *less attractive* _____ so that people would refrain from *looking twice* at her _____ but, instead, the older woman was *not abashed* _____ about wearing short skirts. Ironically, her grandmother said the same thing about her granddaughter when the girl was a teenager and thought all styles of clothing are *permissable* _____.

VI. 翻译　TRANSLATION

A. 将以下句子翻译成英文。Translate the following sentences into English.

1. 所谓"愣住"是指你第一次看到或听到什么令人惊讶或难以置信的事情时会有失神的反应；当然通常你会迅速再看一下。我这里所说的愣住、恍然人悟还有另一层意思。那就是，这第二次的打量会帮你理解别人所接受的东西。当我母亲得知她外孙在台湾所做的事情时，她就有这种反应。

2. 跟平常一样，威廉慢慢地摇了一下头，同时给了我一个美国宽容父母常给淘气孩子的那种"我该拿你怎么办"的眼光。

3. 当我母亲发现她外孙的"厕所广告"出现在她朋友购物的商店里时，我对她说，"妈妈，现在威廉在中国，他以他的方式在做一个中国人"。

B. Translate the following sentences into Chinese. 将以下句子翻译成中文。

1. In this way, she indirectly let them know that William wanted to develop "the Chinese" in him so he wasn't hopelessly "Americanized" like his father.

2. As usual, William slowly shook his head with the kind of what-am-I-going-to-do-with-you look that a tolerant American parent normally gave to a mischievous child **!!!**

3. I loved her for that. It's not easy for anyone, let alone a seventy-seven year old who left China in 1946 to *take in* what the other *takes to be* the case.

VII. 完型填充 CLOZE TEST

A. 在以下短文的每一空格处填入一个汉字，如有可能，给出相应的英语单词。

Fill in a Chinese character that retains the original meaning or intent of the text, then write an English equivalent, if any.

我母亲希望她的 女儿能光宗耀祖：拿一个博士学_____，然后在一所她_____她麻将朋友听_____过的大学，比如_____纳尔大学，教教_____。由于我是最没 _____帮母亲实现家_____梦想的一个女_____，她根本就没指_____过我的儿子会_____留什么中国文_____传统。所以当威廉_____开鲍登学院去_____湾读大三时，她_____常高兴。

B. Fill in an English word or phrase that retains the original meaning or intent of the text, then write a Chinese equivalent, if any.

在以下短文的每一空格处填入一个英语单词，如有可能，给出相应的汉字或词。

And, because I was also the least _____ to fulfill my mother's dream of who _____ thought I should be for the sake _____ completing the family's identity—get a Ph.D _____ teach at a university she and her _____ friends had heard of, like Cornell **!!!**—she _____ no hope that my son would have _____ of "the Chinese" in him. So, when _____ left Bowdoin College to spend his Junior _____ in Taiwan, my mother was pleased. Of _____ she never said anything out loud. But _____ knew because she readily contacted her friends, _____ them to help her grandson at the _____ of his stay when his language skills _____ worse than mine.

VIII. 身体部位 BODY PARTS

A. There are many useful idioms which contain "body parts." Choose the most appropriate to fill in the blank based on your best guess of what the idiom means.

英语中的许多习惯用语含有表示"身体部位"的单词。在下面三个习惯用语中选择最恰当的填空。

1. foot-in-mouth   **2.** an arm and a leg   **3.** tongue in cheek

Critics may have their _____ when describing foreign relations as a _____ symptom when leaders who have never traveled to the Middle East, Asia, Africa, Latin America, or Europe, say the wrong thing at the wrong time. However, this can be a serious matter if you remember that, when news gets out about a country's cattle, hogs, etc., becoming infected with foot-*and*-mouth disease, other nations will isolate that country by not buying its products.

It is believed that something is very expensive if it costs "_____" because portrait artists used to charge more to paint more parts of the body.

B. 将以下短文翻译成中文。注意：划线的词或短语与以上含有"身体部位"的习惯用语相对应。

Translate the following into Chinese taking note that the underlined words or phrases correspond to the meaning of the above "body parts."

It cost her <u>dearly</u> to attend the office party because she <u>said all the wrong things</u> when toasting the boss so that, afterward, her co-workers <u>mockingly</u> referred to her by raising a hand as if holding a glass for a toast.

C. Using your target language, create sentence(s) containing the following three English idioms or their Chinese equivalents.

用以下短语分别造句。如果你所学的外语是中文，请用中文来做这个练习。如果你所学的外语是英语，请用英语来做这个练习。

1. eyes bigger than one's stomach = 嘴馋

2. by the skin of one's teeth = 好不容易才，千钧一发，幸免于难

3. head over heels in love = 颠倒，完全地，深深地

IX. 写作 PRÉCIS

用所学的外语总结课文。如果你用中文来写，请至少使用 450 个汉字，并用电脑打出摘要。如果你用中文来写，请不超过 310 个词。

Write a summary of this chapter in your target language. If writing in Chinese, use <u>more</u> than 450 characters; if writing in English, use <u>no more</u> than 310 words.

CHAPTER FIVE

CALCULATING THE CUSTOMS RATE OF EXCHANGE IN NEPAL

The Good News is that people have become increasingly aware of cultures other than their own.

*The Bad News is that people have become increasingly aware of cultures other than their own **!!!***

One result is that the rate at which this awareness happens differs from country to country, group to group, person to person, and one's self to one's other self. The confusion can happen in both directions when, for example, two corporations from different countries, without consultation, simultaneously adopt the other's etiquette. However, the consequences of not anticipating the varying rates of a customs exchange can be an opportunity to look for interesting stories. For my family, the stories are a diary which chronicles the different ways we are affected by our linguistic competence.

When I was a teenager, more interested in boyfriends than being bilingual, I spoke English at home despite my mother speaking Chinese. When I went to college, more interested in grades than living on the hyphen, I did speak Chinese but sounded like a "Banana" the day I had unexpected callers. Introducing myself to the five young Chinese men slouched in my dormitory lounge, I was immediately turned off when they made no move except with their eyes. Trying to imitate "cool" and casual, they struck me as simply rude. Even more so when one said, "Let's go."

I queried, "Go? Where?"

"Out."

"Out?"

"With us."

"Do I know you?!"

"No, but we know you," another grinned, waving a Face Book picturing all the Chinese coeds in the Boston area.

Taken aback, I said that being ethnically similar was not a good reason to cut classes. They slid off the couches, to pass the word that I was one of "those" Chinese who were no longer Chinese.

第五章

尼泊尔的风土人情

人们现在对他人文化比对自身文化给予越来越多的关注，这是一件好事。

人们现在对他人文化比对自身文化给予越来越多的关注，这是一件坏事。

这种对他人文化的逐渐关注所带来的一个结果是，文化习俗的交换率会因不同国家、不同群体、不同个人、不同自我而有所不同。文化习俗交换率指的是人们在不同场合对他人文化习俗关注、协调的程度。要是两个不同国家的公司事先未作任何咨询却同时采纳对方的文化习俗，那么双方会因此而不知所措。跟海关外汇兑换率一样，文化习俗交换率也是瞬息万变的。假如我们对文化习俗交换率的千变万化缺乏心理准备，那么就有可能碰到许多有趣的故事。以我家为例，所遇到的经历按时间顺序可编成一部叙事日记，其中的故事都跟我们的语言能力有关。

我在十几岁的时候，对男朋友比对双元文化更感兴趣，我在家说英语尽管母亲跟我说中文。到了大学以后，我对如何取得好成绩比对如何适应双元文化生活更感兴趣。虽然我开始说中文了，但是有一天当我在学校宿舍的客厅里遇到了几位不速之客并用中文跟他们交流的时候，我的中文听起来洋腔洋调。我向那五个中国男生自我介绍以后，他们毫无坐相地躺在沙发里，除了眼睛眨了几下，身子动都没动，我对他们顿失兴趣。他们试图装出一幅很酷、很潇洒的样子，但是却给我留下了粗鲁的印象。其中一个对我说，"我们出去玩玩。"

"出去，去哪儿？"我问。

"外面。"

"外面？"

"是啊，跟我们出去玩。"

Had we been less quick to judge, less set in our ways, we might have pooled our different perspectives and become better prepared for our futures, or those of our children. But our lack of mutual admiration was how I began to learn about myself, them, and how much I had oversimplified the matter of identity.[10]

When I went to graduate school, more interested in living on the hyphen than turkeys, I tried to speak Chinese while eating a huge Thanksgiving dinner. I couldn't. I was too embarrassed. The hosts—all White, all ex-China Missionaries—spoke Mandarin better than I did. Kicking myself for not having learned from my mother when I had the chance, I made a resolution: I would learn how to write in Chinese. This was one of my less brilliant decisions !!! With the vocabulary of a seven-year-old, I should have learned how to *talk* like an adult.

Meeting with the Chinese calligraphy professor, I stumbled over words. After explaining how I got to be so ignorant of my own language, I asked, in my most pardon-this-worthless-self voice, "Would you please teach me?"

He scrutinized me. I got smaller. He rose. I was an insect. He shook an accusatory finger at me. "You are a disgrace."

I looked disgraced.

"You are shameful."

I looked ashamed.

"You are a dishonor to *all* Chinese."

That was too much! Mentally I drawled like a rough cowboy, "Now, hold it right there, Buster." Aloud, I quietly reminded him that I had come to him, a Teacher, as a supplicating Student. That, obviously, he declined this Confucian relationship. That, respectfully, I withdrew my request. Before closing the door, I saw him slump back into his chair, flushed with rage and, as it turned out, pain. Weeks later, I met a local Chinese woman who was about my age. I asked in my bilingual polyglot if there was a bus to Chinatown. She replied, in English, that she had never been interested in such matters. I discovered she was the professor's daughter—the real cause of his anger at me.

When I had passed my doctoral exams, more interested in finding a dissertation topic than exploring life on Staten Island, a friend pointed out two street signs, "This used to be the intersection of Occident and Orient Avenues. After the Japanese bombed Pearl Harbor, the Borough council

---

[10]请注意，当英语的"identity"用来表示人的自我本质时，中文里找不到一个确切的对应词。第八章和第九章将对这个问题展开进一步的讨论。

"我认识你们吗？"

"你不认识我们，可是我们认识你呀！"另外一个露着牙齿笑嘻嘻地说着，一边儿说还一边晃动着一本他们制作的波斯顿地区男女同校的中国女生花名册。

我好吃惊。我说，虽然我跟你们都是中国人，但这不是我逃课的理由。他们从沙发里站了起来，然后扔给我一句话，说我是那些不再属于中国人的"中国人"。假如我们在作判断之前能够多花点时间思考问题，我们也许可以把各自不同的观点集中起来，为我们的将来或者我们孩子的将来作更好的准备。我跟这些中国男生缺乏相互了解所以双方无法沟通下去。但是，这件事情使我从此开始了解我自己，了解别人，并意识到自己以前对我（们）是谁这个问题的理解是多么地简单。[13]

我读研究生的时候，对如何驾驭双元文化生活比对吃火鸡更感兴趣。在一个大型的感恩节晚餐会上，我试着想用中文跟人们交流，可是却不成功。为此，我很尴尬。晚餐会的主人是清一色的白人，他们去过中国，在那当过传教士，说的中文比我要好得多。对于自己小时候错过了跟母亲学说中文这么一个大好机会，我真是追悔莫及。我当即发誓，要学怎么写中文。这是我所做的不太明智的决定之一，因为我当时只有七岁孩子的中文词汇量，我本应该首先学会怎样像大人那样说话，然后才开始学写中文。

在我请教中文书法教授的时候，我语无伦次，找不到确切的词汇。我向他解释自己小时候没有好好学中文，所以现在对自己的母语很无知。然后我用一种恳切的语气问他，"您能教我吗？"

他仔细地打量着我。那一刻，我变得很渺小，就像一个小虫子，而他却很高大。"你真丢脸"，他挥着手训斥我。

我真的很丢脸。

"你真可耻。"

我真的很可耻。

---

[13] Indicative of how complex this matter is, please note that there is no Chinese equivalent for the word "identity" when it refers to the nature of the Self as an Individual. This is further explained in Chapters Eight and Nine.

decided "Orient" wasn't patriotic. They renamed the street *Sunrise* Terrace" **!!!** Despite my friend's warning about the parochial atmosphere of this part of New York, I still was not prepared for the Faculty Wives Tea at the college where Bennett taught.

Leaving, I thanked the wife of the college president. She exclaimed, "We are *delighted* you *finally* joined us. You *must* come in December. You could give a talk about Christmas in China."

I didn't miss a beat, "We don't celebrate Christmas in China."

She didn't either, "Well, make something up—it'll be *so* nice."

When we moved to New Jersey and I was more interested in saving money than going to Kathmandu, Bennett went to Asia alone for the first time. Although I don't speak any of the Nepalese languages, or Thai or Japanese or Vietnamese, he previously relied on me because most Asians knew a few words of Chinese.

Checking into Happy Valley Guest House—clean, safe, cheap, and situated next to a Buddhist monastery—Bennett went straight to bed. The next day, he realized he was not suffering from jet lag but was sick. That night, he developed a high fever. Just before dawn, he heard voices. Afraid he was hallucinating, Bennett slowly realized that the fever had broken and that he was hearing chants through the open window from the gompa. Assured, he continued to drift into and out of sleep. Gradually more wakeful, a part of his groggy brain recognized the mantra. Impossible! He must be delirious! Listening more closely, he got the rhythm…then the words…then comprehension—the monks weren't preparing their minds for a day of meditation; they were teaching children how to speak English by using a popular nursery gamesong.

> *You put your right foot in,*
> *You put your right foot out,*
> *You put your right foot in*
> *And shake it all about.*
> *You do the hokey pokey*
> *And turn yourself about.*
> *That's what it's all about.*

Awake, Bennett thought, "Playing to learn and learning to play—that *is* what it's all about **!!!**"

"你把所有中国人的脸都丢尽了。"

这太过分了！"别说了，伙计！"我像个粗俗的牛仔用拉长的语调在脑子里自言自语。接着我心平气和地、人声地提醒他：我是一个诚恳的学生，特地向他这个老师来求学；他这么做跟孔夫子的教育思想是背道而驰的；我恭敬地收回了我的请求。在我离开办公室、关门的时候，我看到教授跌坐在椅子上，先是怒气冲冲，然后痛苦不堪。几个星期以后，我碰到一个跟我年龄相仿的当地中国女孩。当我用夹杂着英文的中文向她询问附近有没有去中国城的公共汽车时，她用英文说，她对跟中国有关的事从来就不感兴趣。我后来发现她原来就是那位教授的女儿，正是因为她，教授才迁怒于我。

当我通过博士资格考试以后，我对寻找博士论文课题比探索斯坦顿岛（Staten Island）上的生活更感兴趣。有个朋友指着街上的两个路牌对我说，这里以前是西方大街（Occident）与 东方大街（Orient）交汇的路口。日本人轰炸珍珠港以后，市议会觉得继续沿用"东方大街"显得不爱国，所以就改为"日出大街"！！！斯坦顿岛是纽约市的一部分，但具有狭小的地方意识。尽管朋友向我提醒了斯坦顿岛这一特点，但是我对班尼特所在大学教授太太的茶话会还是一点心理准备也没有。

当我离开茶话会跟校长太太辞行时，她人声地说，"真高兴你终于来了，你十二月份一定再来，到时可以给大家说说中国的圣诞节。"

我立即回答她，"我们中国人不过圣诞节。"

她也很快回了我一句，"那你可以编个故事说一说啊，那肯定会很有意思的。"

当我们搬到新泽西州以后，我对如何省钱比去加德满都（Kathmandu）旅游更感兴趣，班尼特只好第一次独自去亚洲旅行。虽然我不会尼泊尔语、泰语、日语或越南语，但是在这以前，班尼特一直很依赖我，因为大多数亚洲人都会说一点儿中文。

班尼特到了尼泊尔以后住进了寺庙旁一家名叫快乐峡谷的客栈 —— 一个干净、安全、便宜的小旅馆，并马上上床睡觉了。第二天，他觉得很不舒服，一种不是由时差所引起的不适，他发现原来自己病了。那个晚上，他发了高烧。凌晨的时候，听到一些声音，他以为自己在幻想什么。后来他慢慢意识到高烧退了，并觉察出他所听到的阵阵颂歌是从寺庙的窗口传来的。等弄清是怎么一回事以后，他迷迷糊糊地、时睡时醒地又睡了一会

VOCABULARY

customs rate	n.p.	"customs" refers to the idea that each country has laws about what is or is not permitted to cross the border; it also refers to the idea of what is "customary" in terms of behavior associated with that country. "Rate" refers to the relative value of currency as well as "rate" to decide relative rank or status.	海关/习俗 兑换率	hǎiguān /xísú duìhuànlǜ
etiquette	n.	rules or norms for proper behavior under various circumstances or places.	礼仪，礼节	lǐyí, lǐjié
turn off	v.p.	be no longer interested or attracted.	不感兴趣	bùgǎnxìngqù
Face Book	n.	previously a book containing pictures of incoming first-year students to facilitate identification, now a web site of the same name or myspace.com where people can register personal information and network.	花名册	huāmíngcè
coed	n.	a female college student as in a "coeducational" institution.	男女同校的 女学生	nánnǚ tóngxiào de nǚ xuésheng
slide off	v.p.	to go from one place to another in one smooth motion as a snake would slither off a rock to the ground.	滑动	huádòng
pool	v.	collect or put together (perspectives, viewpoints, opinions, money, etc.)	把观点集中 起来	bǎ guāndiǎn jízhōng qǐlái
mutual admiration	n.p.	originally a 1956 song, "mutual admiration society," the phrase now refers to people who express great esteem for each other though sometimes used sarcastically as if there were really no good reason why they should be admired.	相互赞赏， 互相了解	xiānghù- zànshǎng, hùxiāng- liǎojiě
indicative (of)	adj.	suggestive of, pointing out/to.	指示的, 象 征的, 表示 ……的	zhǐshì de, xiàngzhēng de, biǎoshì …de
kick myself/sb.	v.p.	to express regret, be rueful	严厉自责	yánlì-zìzé

儿。当他终于清醒以后，懵懵懂懂的大脑听到了歌声。这不太可能呵！他觉得自己一定是神志混乱了。他又好好地听了一下，这时他听出了旋律，接着听出了歌词，最后他听懂了那首歌。那些和尚没有潜心准备一天的打坐，却用英文儿歌教小孩子们学英语。

你把右脚跨进去，

你把右脚拿出来，

你把右脚跨进去，

你把右脚拿出来，

你做 Hokey Pokey，

摇着晃着身子，

原来就是如此!!!

班尼特这下完全醒了。他想，"玩中学，学中玩，原来就是如此!!!"

生词

尼泊尔	尼泊爾	Níbó'ěr	p.n.	Nepal
风土人情	風土人情	fēngtǔ-rénqíng	f.c.w.	local conditions and customs
习俗	習俗	xísú	n.	customs, what is customary
给予	給与	jǐyǔ	v.	give, provide
群体	群體	qúntǐ	n.	group, community
咨询	諮詢	zīxún	n.	consultation
采纳	採納	cǎinà	v.	accept, adopt
外汇兑换率	外匯兌換率	wàihuì duìhuànlǜ	n.p.	foreign currency exchange rate
瞬息万变	瞬息萬變	shùnxī-wànbiàn	f.c.w.	take place in a very short period of time
千变万化	千變萬化	qiānbiàn-wànhuà	f.c.w.	ever-changing
以......为例	以......為例	yǐ ...wéilì	p.p.	for example
叙事	叙事	xùshì	v.	narrate
对......感兴趣	對......感興趣	duì ...gǎnxìngqù	p.p.	be interested in sth./sb.
不速之客	不速之客	bùsùzhīkè	f.c.w.	uninvited or unexpected caller
洋腔洋调	洋腔洋調	yángqiāng-yángdiào	f.c.w.	foreign accent
自我介绍	自我介紹	zìwǒ jièshào	f.c.w.	introducing oneself
眨	眨	zhǎ	v.	move (i.e., eyes)
顿失兴趣	頓失興趣	dùnshī xìngqù	f.c.w.	turn off, lose interest

stumble over one's words	v.p.	to speak hesitantly, awkwardly or nervously as if trying to walk on uneven ground when the words are like rocks preventing smooth speech.	结结巴巴地说话	jiējiē-bābā de shuō huà
scrutinize	v.	to look at or examine very closely or critically.	仔细检查	zǐxì jiǎnchá
drawl	v.	to say words slowly, especially drawing out vowel sounds.	慢吞吞地说，懒洋洋地说	màntūntūn de shuō, lǎnyāngyāng de shuō
Buster		a generic name for a male, previously associated with cowboys or riders who break or "bust" untamed horses; Mister.	伙计	huǒji
supplicating	adj.	in a manner of humble prayer, entreaty, petition.	恳求的	kěnqiú de
slump into	v.p.	to drop, fall, bend, or slouch heavily as if weighted down.	陷入，掉入	xiànrù, diàorù
polyglot	n.	a mix or confusion of several languages.	数种语言的混合	shùzhǒng yǔyán de hùnhé
(the) Occident	p.n.	the countries of Europe, Britain, and America.	西方，西方人	Xīfāng, Xīfāngrén
terrace	n.	a raised level or platform area which, when adjoining a building, is usually surfaced with stone, brick, tile, etc.	大街	dàjiē
parochial	adj.	of a limited or narrow scope or outlook; of a parish or church as, e.g., a parochial school.	地方性的，狭小的	dìfāngxìng de, xiáxiǎo de
miss a beat	v.p.	to respond with hesitation and thus disrupt the established rhythm of a conversation, music, etc., usually expressed in the negative form.	错过一个节拍	cuòguò yīgè jiépāi
Kathmandu	p.n.	the capital city of Nepal.	加德满都	Jiādémǎndū
monastery	n.	a communal residence for persons, e.g., monks, who have taken religious vows and/or are committed to living a secluded life.	修道院	xiūdàoyuàn

酷	酷	kù	adj.	cool
潇洒	瀟灑	xiāosǎ	adj	casual, natural, informal
晃动	晃動	huàngdòng	v.	wave
波斯顿	波斯頓	Bōsīdùn	p.n.	Boston
花名册	花名冊	huāmíngcè	n.	Face Book
逃课	逃課	táokè	v.o.	cut class
花	花	hua	v.	spend time (money)
驾驭	駕馭	jiàyù	v.	control, master; drive (a cart, horse, etc.)
火鸡	火雞	huǒjī	n.	turkey
感恩节	感恩節	Gǎn'ēn Jié	p.n.	Thanksgiving
尴尬	尷尬	gāngà	adj.	awkward, embarrassed
晚餐会	晚餐會	wǎncānhuì	n.	dinner party
清一色	清一色	qīngyīsè	adj.	homogeneous, similar
传教士	傳教士	chuánjiàoshì	n.	missionary
机会	機會	jīhuì	n.	opportunity
追悔莫及	追悔莫及	zhuīhuǐ-mòjí	f.c.w.	be overcome with regret
当即	當即	dāngjí	adv.	at once, right away, immediately
发誓	發誓	fāshì	v.o.	vow, pledge, swear
明智	明智	míngzhì	adj.	brilliant, sagacious, sensible
词汇	詞彙	cíhuì	n.	vocabulary
量	量	liàng	n.	quantity, amount
书法	書法	shūfǎ	n.	calligraphy
语无伦次	語無倫次	yǔwúlúncì	f.c.w.	speak incoherently
确切	確切	quèqiè	adj.	precise, appropriate
无知	無知	wúzhī	adj.	ignorant, stupid
恳切	懇切	kěnqiè	adj.	sincere, genuine
渺小	渺小	miǎoxiǎo	adj.	insignificant, negligible, paltry
丢脸	丟臉	diūliǎn	v.o.	lose face, be disgraced
训斥	訓斥	xùnchì	v.	reproach, accuse
可耻	可恥	kěchǐ	adj.	shameful, disgraceful, ignominious
伙计	伙計	huǒji	n.	Buster, Mister
粗俗	粗俗	cūsú	adj.	vulgar, coarse, earthy
心平气和	心平氣和	xīnpíng-qìhé	f.c.w.	calm, even-tempered and good tempered
诚恳	誠懇	chéngkěn	adj.	supplicating
特地	特地	tèdì	adv.	for a special purpose
求学	求學	qiúxué	v.o.	pursue one's studies; seek knowledge
背道而驰	背道而馳	bèidào'érchí	f.c.w.	run in the opposite direction, run counter to
恭敬	恭敬	gōngjìng	adj.	respectful
跌坐	跌坐	diēzuò	v (c)	slump back into

hallucinate	v.	to have sensory experiences unrelated to actual or real objects, e.g., dreams are "normal" hallucinations associated with sleep whereas drug or fever-induced ones are pathological.	使……产生幻觉	shǐ… chǎnshēng huànjué
(the or sb's) fever has broken		high body temperature caused by disease or infection that ceases to climb so that the decrease indicates the patient is recovering.	退烧	tuìshāo
chant	n.	a short, simple melody often used to pray, meditate, or practice scriptures.	赞美诗，圣歌	zànměishī, shènggē
gompa	n.	a Buddhist monastery or temple generally containing a central prayer hall, a Buddha statue, benches for monks or nuns to engage in prayer or meditation as well as attached living accommodation.	寺院	sìyuàn
groggy	adj.	not clear-headed as when coming out of unconsciousness or sleep.	头昏眼花的	tóuhūn- yǎnhuā de
mantra	n.	a word or sound that is recited or sung as an aid to meditation or prayer, now any idea or statement that a person repeats.	颂歌，咒语	sònggē, zhòuyǔ
delirious	adj.	mentally and/or physically excited, disturbed, or emotional, usually temporary.	神志昏迷的	shénzhì- hūnmí de

怒气冲冲	怒氣沖沖	nùqì-chōngchōng	f.c.w.	as if flushed with rage, as if in a great rage
痛苦不堪	痛苦不堪	tòngkǔ bùkān	f.c.w.	cannot bear the suffering
夹杂	夾雜	jiāzá	v.	be mixed up with, be mingled with
中国城	中國城	Zhōngguóchéng	p.n.	Chinatown
迁怒	遷怒	qiānnù	v.o.	to take one's anger out on sb
斯坦顿岛	斯坦頓島	Sītǎndùndǎo	p.n.	Staten Island
路牌	路牌	lùpái	n.	street sign
交汇	交匯	jiāohuì	v.	intersect
轰炸	轟炸	hōngzhà	v.	bomb
珍珠港	珍珠港	Zhēnzhūgǎng	p.n.	Pearl Harbor
市议会	市議會	shìyìhuì	n.p.	city council
沿用	沿用	yányòng	v.	continue to use (an old method, system, etc.)
日出大街	日出大街	Rìchū Dàjiē	p.n.	Sunrlse Terrace
纽约市	紐約市	Niǔyuē Shì	p.n.	New York City
狭小	狹小	xiáxiǎo	adj.	narrow
地方	地方	dìfāng	n.	local area
意识	意識	yìshí	n.	sense, awareness
辞行	辭行	cíxíng	v.o.	say good-bye to the host/hostess
省钱	省錢	shěngqián	v.o.	save money, be thrifty
加德满都	加德滿都	Jiādémǎndū	p.n.	Kathmandu
尼泊尔语	尼泊爾語	Níbó'ěryǔ	p.n.	Nepali
住进	住進	zhùjìn	v (c)	check in a hotel
客栈	客棧	kèzhàn	n.	inn
时差	時差	shíchā	n.	jct lag
高烧	高燒	gāoshāo	n.	high fever
觉察	覺察	juéchá	v.	realize, sense, perceive
阵阵颂歌	陣陣頌歌	zhènzhèn sònggē	n.p.	chants
寺庙	寺廟	sìmiào	n.	Buddhist temple, monastery of other religions
弄清	弄清	nòngqīng	v (c)	understand fully, make clear
迷迷糊糊	迷迷糊糊	mími-hūhu	r.f.	dazed
懵懵懂懂	懵懵懂懂	měngměngdǒngdǒng	r.f.	groggy
神志	神志	shénzhì	n.	consciousness, senses, state of mind
旋律	旋律	xuánlǜ	n.	rhythm
歌词	歌詞	gēcí	n.	words of a song, lyrics
和尚	和尚	héshang	n.	Buddhist monk
潜心	潛心	qiánxīn	adj.	devotional
儿歌	兒歌	érgē	n.	nursery gamesong

第五章

尼泊爾的風土人情

人們現在對他人文化比對自身文化給予越來越多的關注，這是一件好事。

人們現在對他人文化比對自身文化給予越來越多的關注，這是一件壞事。

這種對他人文化的逐漸關注所帶來的一個結果是，文化習俗的交換率會因不同國家、不同群體、不同個人、不同自我而有所不同。文化習俗交換率指的是人們在不同場合對他人文化習俗關注、協調的程度。要是兩個不同國家的公司事先未作任何咨詢卻同時采納對方的文化習俗，那麼雙方會因此而不知所措。跟海關外匯兌換率一樣，文化習俗交換率也是瞬息萬變的。假如我們對文化習俗交換率的千變萬化缺乏心理準備，那麼就有可能碰到許多有趣的故事。以我家為例，所遇到的經歷按時間順序可編成一部叙事日記，其中的故事都跟我們的語言能力有關。

我在十幾歲的時候，對男朋友比對雙元文化更感興趣，我在家說英語盡管母親跟我說中文。到了大學以后，我對如何取得好成績比對如何適應雙元文化生活更感興趣。雖然我開始說中文了，但是有一天當我在學校宿舍的客廳里遇到了幾位不速之客并用中文跟他們交流的時候，我的中文聽起來洋腔洋調。我向那五個中國男生自我介紹以後，他們毫無坐相地躺在沙發里，除了眼睛眨了幾下，身子動都沒動，我對他們頓失興趣。他們試圖裝出一幅很酷、很瀟灑的樣子，但是卻給我留下了粗魯的印象。其中一個對我說，"我們出去玩玩。"

"出去，去哪兒？"我問。

"外面。"

"外面？"

"是啊，跟我們出去玩。"

"我認識你們嗎？"

"你不認識我們，可是我們認識你呀！"另外一個露着牙齒笑嘻嘻地説着，一邊兒説還一邊晃動着一本他們制作的波斯頓地區男女同校的中國女生花名冊。

我好吃驚。我説，雖然我跟你們都是中國人，但這不是我逃課的理由。他們從沙發里站了起來，然后扔給我一句話，説我是那些不再屬于中國人的"中國人"。假如我們在作判斷之前能夠多花點時間思考問題，我們也許可以把各自不同的觀點集中起來，為我們的將來或者我們孩子的將來作更好的準備。我跟這些中國男生缺乏相互了解所以雙方無法溝通下去。但是，這件事情使我從此開始了解我自己，了解別人，并意識到自己以前對我（們）是誰這個問題的理解是多么地簡單。[13]

我讀研究生的時候，對如何駕馭雙元文化生活比對吃火鷄更感興趣。在一個大型的感恩節晚餐會上，我試着想用中文跟人們交流，可是卻不成功。為此，找很尷尬。晚餐會的主人是清一色的白人，他們去過中國，在那當過傳教士，説的中文比我要好得多。對于自己小時候錯過了跟母親學説中文這么一個大好機會，我真是追悔莫及。我當即發誓，要學怎么寫中文。這是我所做的不太明智的決定之一，因為我當時只有七歲孩子的中文詞匯量，我本應該首先學會怎樣像大人那樣説話，然后才開始學寫中文。

在我請教中文書法教授的時候，我語無倫次，找不到確切的詞匯。我向他解釋自己小時候沒有好好學中文，所以現在對自己的母語很無知。然后我用一種懇切的語氣問他，"您能教我嗎？"

他仔細地打量着我。那一刻，我變得很渺小，就像一個小蟲子，而他卻很高人。"你真丟臉"，他揮着手訓斥我。

我真的很丟臉。

"你真可耻。"

我真的很可耻。

---

[13] Indicative of how complex this matter is, please note that there is no Chinese equivalent for the word "identity" when it refers to the nature of the Self as an Individual. This is further explained in Chapters Eight and Nine.

"你把所有中國人的臉都丟盡了。"

這太過分了！"別説了，伙計！"我像個粗俗的牛仔用拉長的語調在腦子里自言自語。接着我心平氣和地、大聲地提醒他：我是一個誠懇的學生，特地向他這個老師來求學；他這么做跟孔夫子的教育思想是背道而馳的；我恭敬地收回了我的請求。在我離開辦公室、關門的時候，我看到教授跌坐在椅子上，先是怒氣冲冲，然后痛苦不堪。幾個星期以後，我碰到一個跟我年齡相仿的當地中國女孩。當我用夾雜着英文的中文向她詢問附近有沒有去中國城的公共汽車時，她用英文説，她對跟中國有關的事從來就不感興趣。我后來發現她原來就是那位教授的女兒，正是因為她，教授才遷怒于我。

當我通過博士資格考試以後，我對尋找博士論文課題比探索斯坦頓島（Staten Island）上的生活更感興趣。有個朋友指着街上的兩個路牌對我説，這里以前是西方大街（Occident）與 東方大街（Orient）交匯的路口。日本人轟炸珍珠港以后，市議會覺得繼續沿用"東方大街"顯得不愛國，所以就改為"日出大街"!!! 斯坦頓島是紐約市的一部分，但具有狹小的地方意識。盡管朋友向我提醒了斯坦頓島這一特點，但是我對班尼特所在大學教授太太的茶話會還是一點心理準備也沒有。

當我離開茶話會跟校長太太辭行時，她大聲地説，"真高興你終于來了，你十二月份一定再來，到時可以給大家説説中國的聖誕節。"

我立即回答她，"我們中國人不過聖誕節。"

她也很快回了我一句，"那你可以編個故事説一説啊，那肯定會很有意思的。"

當我們搬到新澤西州以後，我對如何省錢比去加德滿都（Kathmandu）旅游更感興趣，班尼特只好第一次獨自去亞洲旅行。雖然我不會尼泊爾語、泰語、日語或越南語，但是在這以前，班尼特一直很依賴我，因為大多數亞洲人都會説一點兒中文。

班尼特到了尼泊爾以后住進了寺廟旁一家名叫快樂峽谷的客棧 —— 一個干淨、安全、便宜的小旅館，并馬上上床睡覺了。第二天，他覺得很不舒服，一種不是由時差所引起的不適，他發現原來自己病了。那個晚上，他發了高燒。凌晨的時候，聽到一些聲音，他以為自己在幻想什么。后來他慢慢意識到高燒退了，并覺察出他所聽到的陣陣頌歌是從寺廟的窗口傳來的。等弄清是怎么一回事以後，他迷迷糊糊地、時睡時醒地又睡了一會兒。當他終于清醒以后，懵懵懂懂的大腦聽到了歌聲。這不太可能呵！他覺得自己一定是神志混亂了。他又好好地聽了一下，這時他聽出了旋律，接着聽出了歌詞，最后他聽懂了那首歌。那些和尚沒有潛心準備一天的打坐，卻用英文兒歌教小孩子們學英語。

你把右腳跨進去，

你把右腳拿出來，

你把右腳跨進去，

你把右腳拿出來，

你做 Hokey Pokey，

搖着晃着身子，

原來就是如此!!!

班尼特這下完全醒了。他想，"玩中學，學中玩，原來就是如此!!!"

练习 EXERCISES

I. 思考和课堂讨论 FOOD FOR THOUGHT

A. PERSONAL 个人的

描述你曾期望父母能拥有某一观点、想法或某种习俗，然而他们却使你失望的经历。

Describe one "perspective," opinion, idea, or custom that you would have liked your own parents to have had when you were young but which they didn't.

B. GENERAL 普遍的

An "argument" or line of reasoning is logical when a conclusion is validly deduced from premises that are assumed to be true. However, when there is an error in reasoning, then a fallacy occurs. In order to think clearly and effectively, it helps to know about these errors. After reading the following, discuss the question posed.

当某一结论是从一个正确的前提演绎出来的，那么该结论的论据符合逻辑。但是，如果推理出现错误，就会产生谬论。为了清楚、有效地思考，有必要了解这些推理错误。请阅读下面的错误，然后讨论所提出的问题。

ad hominem (by citing the person's circumstance) is from the Latin *argumentum ad hominem* (*argumentum* = "argument"; *ad* = "to"; *hominem* = "the person").

pattern: Ms. Y argues for the truth of her conclusion; Mr. X refers to Ms. Y's personal circumstance or position instead of disproving what Ms. Y claimed to be true.

example: Instead of presenting physical or eye-witness evidence to the jury proving that the person accused of the murder was at the scene of the murder when it was committed and not with his grandmother robbing a bank **!!!**, Mr. X argues ***ad hominem*** by saying, "How can we believe Ms. Y? She's the grandmother of the accused so, of course, she'll say anything—even lie—to help her grandson."

question: Why is Mr. X's fallacious approach often effective but still logically irrelevant? Is the mother more believable because her testimony is <u>against her own interest</u> in that she can now be arrested for robbing the bank?

C. CROSS-CULTURAL 跨文化的

After reading the following, discuss <u>in Chinese</u> the difference between teaching to <u>understand</u> religious ideas or doctrines and proselytizing, that is, teaching to <u>believe</u> in them.

阅读以下短文，并<u>用中文</u>对所提出的问题进行讨论。

Education for believers varies from one religion to another, from one culture to another, and from one century to another. The variations also occur within each religion as to what to teach and learn as well as to answers for the "who," "where," "how," and "when" questions. Some immigrants to the United States become more committed to being part of a religious community while others become less involved. There are many reasons why but almost all soon experience what citizens do—the difficulty of providing a free public education to all children when parents think that their religious beliefs are being weakened by what is taught in history, science, math, etc. The Founding Fathers were men with different religious beliefs, including those who had none at all. However, they were all "spiritual" and valued an education that would convey the principles which produced the Constitution they wrote.

II. 配对 **MATCHMAKER**

A. VOCABULARY 词汇

找出以下两列中的对应词，并在其间划线。

Draw a connecting line between the word and its correct definition.

a.	花名册	1.	parochial
b.	地方性的，狭小的	2.	save money
c.	神志昏谜的	3.	homogenous, similar, identical
d.	省钱	4.	chant
e.	千变万化	5.	ever changing
f.	清一色	6.	calm, even-tempered, good-tempered
g.	恳求的	7.	delirious
h.	心平气和	8.	self-introduction, introduce oneself
i.	自我介绍	9.	Face Book
j.	赞美诗，圣歌	10.	supplicating

a.	slump into	1.	习俗
b.	stumble over one's words	2.	不感兴趣
c.	hallucinate	3.	陷入、掉入
d.	scrutinize	4.	洋腔洋调
e.	mutual admiration	5.	使……产生幻觉
f.	foreign accent	6.	仔细检查
g.	turn off	7.	相互赞赏
h.	custom, customs and habit	8.	男女同校的女学生
i.	etiquette	9.	结结巴巴地说话
j.	coed	10.	礼仪，礼节

115

B. ANTONYMS & ALTERNATES 反义词和多义词

First draw a connecting line between the words or phrases in the left-hand column with the best possible <u>antonym</u> listed in the middle column, then draw a line between the antonym and an alternate meaning of the antonym listed in the right-hand column. <u>Be forewarned</u> that the part of speech may change from one column to the next and that slang terms may be used. E.g.,

"hit" —————————————— *"miss"* ———————— *"honorific for unmarried female"*

"warm" —————————————— *"cool"* ————————— *"excellent"*

首先在第二列中找出与第一列相对应的反义词，然后在第三列中找出与第二列相关的多义词。注意：词性会有变化。

		ANTONYMS		ALTERNATE MEANING
a.	easy-going, smooth	1. **still**	i.	obsessive behavior or idea of self
b.	back of the hand	2. **stand**	ii.	device to distill "hard liquor"
c.	novel, new	3. **rocky**	iii.	involuntary startled response
d.	conclude, end	4. **plotted**	iv.	conceal in the hand
e.	active	5. **stale**	v.	*slang* complaining criticism
f.	noisy, raucous	6. **complex**	vi.	schemed to act illegally
g.	free, not busy	7. **start**	vii.	unsteady, unsure, hazardous
h.	simple	8. **static**	viii.	affianced to marry
i.	uncharted, unexplored	9. **engaged**	ix.	overworked, trite, hackneyed
j.	recline, sit	10. **palm**	x.	*informal* treat, pay for drinks, etc.

III. 解字/词、构字/词 DECONSTRUCTION & CONSTRUCTION

A. 将以下汉字分解成最小的构字部件，然后用每个部件构成三个汉字。例如"鸭"可以分解成 "甲"和"鸟"两个部件。"甲"能构成"押"，"岬"，"钾"；"鸟"可以构成以"鸡"，"鸦"，"鸣"。请借助字典完成练习。

Deconstruct the following characters into the smallest components, then form 3 new characters using each component.

好_____ 传 _____ 病 _____

椅_____ 潜 _____ 趣 _____

B. Using only the letters of the word "**ADMIRATION**," form English words that are not proper nouns, abbreviations, or acronyms and that consist of 4 or more letters. A letter can only be used again if it appears in the given word more than once. E.g., "mourn" is not acceptable because there is no "u" and "doom" is not because there is only one "o." Like many Olympic

sports, weight categories mark performance. We filled in a few cells to get you started. Fill in the rest to achieve the highest category. If you think up more than 44, you beat the authors!

用 "ADMIRATION" 中的字母构词。新构建的词不能是专有名词、缩写词、或首字母缩略词。每个单词必须至少含有四个字母，但不能重复使用同一字母，除非该字母在 "ADMIRATION"中出现两次。

CHAMPION STATUS			
LIGHT **11**	**WELTER** **22**	**MIDDLE** **33**	**HEAVY** **44**
main	arid	rain	train

C. 用 "千变万化" 中的每个汉字组成不同的词。看看最多能组多少个词

Use each of the characters in "千变万化" to form as many words (of 2-4 characters) as you can.

D. Pair any two of the following 9 words to form at least 10 different, unhyphenated words

在下列九个词中配对、组词，新组的词只能含有两个单词，中间没有连字号。
请至少组出十个词。

proof box water sound car fire back read sund

IV. 阅读理解 READING QUIZ

根据课文，选择准确答案。Based on the text, choose the best answer.

1. 为什么对他人文化比对自身文化给予更多的注意既是一件好事又是一件坏事？

    a. 因为不同国家有着不同的文化习俗。

b. 因为不同群体有着不同的文化习俗。

c. 因为不同个人有着不同的文化习俗。

d. 如果大家同时按他人文化习俗办事，这样有可能会使别人和自己都不知所措。

2. 作者在十几岁的时候，对交男朋友很感兴趣。可是为什么她对那几个中国男生没有兴趣？

a. 因为他们都说中文，而她的中文说得不好。

b. 因为他们的举止言行给她留下了坏的印象。

c. 因为他们要她逃课，而她不想这么做。

d. 因为他们太酷、太潇洒了。

3. 为什么那位中文书法教授训斥我（作者）？

a. 因为我让他，"别说了，伙计"！

b. 因为他很高大，而我很渺小。

c. 因为他怒气冲冲、痛苦不堪。

d. 因为我跟他女儿一样没有学好中文。

4. 班尼特去尼泊尔旅行时住在下面哪一个地方？

a. 寺庙。

b. 峡谷。

c. 旅馆。

d. 饭店。

5. 什么是尴尬？

a. 中文不好，无能为力。

b. 错过机会，追悔莫及。

c. 不好处理，不好意思。

d. 语无伦次，找不到词汇。

6. 以下哪一个答案是这篇课文想要说明的问题？

a. 文化习俗的交换因时间的不同而变化。

b. 文化习俗的交换因地点的不同而变化。

c. 文化习俗的交换因人物的不同而变化。

d. 以上都是，另外，文化习俗的交换需要大家的共同努力和协作。

V. 填空　FILL IN THE BLANK

A. 选择正确答案。Choose the correct answer.

1. 人们现在越来越多地_____他人文化。

   a. 贯注　　　b. 灌注　　　c. 关注

2. 但是，这件事情_____我从此开始了解我自己。

   a. 让　　　b. 把　　　c. 叫

3. 虽然我很不高兴，但我还是_____地跟他说话。

   a. 心平气和　b. 心狠手辣　c. 心宽体胖

4. 你把所有中国人的脸都_____了。

   a. 丢光　　　b. 丢失　　　c. 丢人

5. 那家_____很不错，里面住着很多来自世界各地的游客。

   a. 客店　　　b. 客厅　　　c. 客房

6. 他发高烧了，一个晚上都_____，时睡时醒。

   a. 清清楚楚　b. 明明白白　c. 迷迷糊糊

B. Using your target language, write a word or phrase from the vocabulary lists and/or dictionary that means the <u>same</u> or is a <u>synonym</u> for the italicized word or phrase. Keep in mind that the part of speech and/or tense may have been adjusted to achieve grammatically correct results.

在以下段落中找出与斜体词意义相近的同义词。如果你所学的外语是中文，找出相应的中文词或短语。如果你所学的外语是英语，找出相应的英语词或短语。注意：词性或时态会有变化。

www.myspace.com is a like a *journal* _____. Once only used as a *catalog of student pictures* _____ at big universities, it now contains personal information about politicians running for office, children at small *Catholic* _____ schools, and university graduates. Some of the latter are now facing a problem because, when they apply for jobs, people will *carefully check* _____ everything, including the internet, and may find pictures of the applicants in situations that are silly if not also completely not *socially acceptable* _____.

VI. 翻译　TRANSLATION

A. 将以下句子翻译成英文。Translate the following sentences into English.

1. 这是我所做的不太明智的决定之一，因为我当时只有七岁孩子的中文词汇量，我本应该首先学会怎样像大人那样说话，然后才开始学写中文。

119

2. 在我请教中文书法教授的时候，我语无伦次，找不到确切的词汇。我向他解释自己小时候没有好好学中文，所以现在对自己的母语很无知。

3. 当我用夹杂着英文的中文向她询问附近有没有去中国城的公共汽车时，她用英文说，她对这种事情不感兴趣。

B. Translate the following sentences into Chinese. 将以下句子翻译成中文。

1. The confusion can happen in both directions when, for example, two corporations, without consultation, simultaneously adopt the other's etiquette.

2. For my family, the stories are a diary which chronicles the different ways we are affected by our linguistic competence.

3. Introducing myself to the five young Chinese men slouched in my dormitory lounge, I was immediately turned off when they made no move except with their eyes.

VII. 完型填充　CLOZE TEST

A. 在以下短文的每一空格处填入一个汉字，如有可能，给出相应的英语单词。

Fill in a Chinese character that retains the original meaning or intent of the text, then write an English equivalent, if any.

我读研究生的时候，对如何驾驭＿＿＿＿＿＿元文化生活比＿＿＿＿＿＿吃火鸡更感兴＿＿＿＿＿＿。在一个大型的＿＿＿＿＿＿恩节晚餐会上，＿＿＿＿＿＿试着想用中文＿＿＿＿＿＿人们交流，可是＿＿＿＿＿＿不成功。为此，我＿＿＿＿＿＿尴尬。晚餐会的＿＿＿＿＿＿人是清一色的白＿＿＿＿＿＿，他们去过中国，＿＿＿＿＿＿那当过传教士，＿＿＿＿＿＿的中文比我要＿＿＿＿＿＿得多。对于自己＿＿＿＿＿＿时候错过了跟＿＿＿＿＿＿亲学说中文这＿＿＿＿＿＿一个大好机会，我真追悔莫及。

B. Fill in an English word or phrase that retains the original meaning or intent of the text, then write a Chinese equivalent, if any.

在以下短文的每一空格处填入一个英语单词，如有可能，给出相应的汉字或词。

Our lack of mutual admiration was how ＿＿＿＿＿＿ began to learn about myself, them, and ＿＿＿＿＿＿ much I had oversimplified the matter of ＿＿＿＿＿＿. When I went to graduate school, more ＿＿＿＿＿＿ in living on the hyphen than turkeys, ＿＿＿＿＿＿ tried to speak Chinese while eating ＿＿＿＿＿＿ huge Thanksgiving Day dinner. I couldn't. I ＿＿＿＿＿＿ too embarrassed. The hosts—all White, all ＿＿＿＿＿＿ Missionaries—spoke Mandarin better than I did. ＿＿＿＿＿＿ myself for not having learned from my ＿＿＿＿＿＿ when I had the chance, I made ＿＿＿＿＿＿ resolution: I would learn how to write ＿＿＿＿＿＿ Chinese. This was one of my less ＿＿＿＿＿＿ decisions !!! With the vocabulary of a seven-year ＿＿＿＿＿＿, I should have learned how to *talk* ＿＿＿＿＿＿ an adult.

VIII. 身体部位 BODY PARTS

A. There are many useful idioms which contain "body parts." Choose the most appropriate to fill in the blank based on your best guess of what the idiom means.

英语中的许多习惯用语含有表示"身体部位"的单词。在下面三个习惯用语中选择最恰当的填空。

1. high-handed **2.** hand in glove **3.** eating out of sb.'s hand

When the boss found out his new employee worked _____ with the newspaper reporters because her family was in the media business, he put aside his usually arrogant and _____ manner. By the end of her first week on the job, he was _____, not because her family was important but because she was both competent and pleasant.

B. 将以下短文翻译成中文。注意：划线的词或短语与以上含有"身体部位"的习惯用语相对应。

Translate the following into Chinese taking note that the underlined words or phrases correspond to the meaning of the above "body parts."

When parents realized nothing was accomplished by being <u>overbearing and bossy</u> with their children's teachers, they ended up <u>totally willing to do anything the teachers wanted</u> in order to help the children learn more. After working <u>closely</u> for a few months, everyone developed a mutual admiration for each other's efforts.

C. Using your target language, create sentence(s) containing the following three English idioms or their Chinese equivalents.

用以下短语分别造句。注意：如果你所学的外语是中文，请用中文来做这个练习。如果你所学的外语是英语，请用英语来做这个练习。

1. hand over fist = 不费力地，节节往上地，稳而快地

2. sit on one's hands = 不予鼓掌，坐守不前，按兵不动，袖手旁观

3. with a heavy hand = 粗手粗脚地，粗枝大叶地，严厉地，高压地

IX. 写作 PRÉCIS

用所学的外语总结课文。如果你用中文来写，请至少使用 450 个汉字，并用电脑打出摘要。如果你用英文来写，请不超过 360 个词。

Write a summary of this chapter in your target language. If writing in Chinese, use <u>more</u> than 450 characters; if writing in English, use <u>no more</u> than 360 words.

CHAPTER SIX

CHOOSING TIME ZONES IN THE UNITED STATES

To live in and with different cultures, keep in mind that traditions may require more time than modern life can afford. This is especially problematic in the United States where the phrase "instant gratification" was probably invented. When one culture thinks "long ago" means two millennia and the other two months, being at least bicultural may require living in several time zones simultaneously.

Our son, William, found this out in 1979 when his friend, Eric, turned five and had something called a Birthday Party. We had always marked William's birthdays with presents and, sometimes, a special dinner but certainly, I hadn't been so foolish as to invite pre-adults en masse into the house. We hadn't spent all those years renovating the place only to have it destroyed in two hours. So William knew about celebrating his birthday. He just didn't know that most of the American population regarded having the celebrant's friends—as in children—to be a necessary component of such occasions.

Walking into Eric's house, careening with hyperglycemic little people, festooned with balloons and presents and streamers, I could tell right away that William thought this was a Good Thing. One look at Frankie, Eric's mother, and I knew otherwise. I found her in the bedroom, trying to become one with the corner wall. Had she been a cartoon, her eyes would have been drawn as spirals and there would have been lots of "parentheses" around her head.

She moaned, "Oh Cath, I should've followed The Rule of Thumb."

"Frankie, what are you talking about?"

"Eric's five. I should've had six. You're supposed to invite one more than the kid is old. But no, I invited dozens! Whaddami gonna do? Have you seen the chaos out there?!"

"It is impressive," I understated and calmly assured her. "It's okay. We'll do this together. You do food. I'll do children."

We did it. It happened in some kind of time warp when a minute equaled a day but we did it. I formed a circle and we played games. William alternated between galloping joy and immobilizing

第六章

美国的文化时区

生活在多元文化环境中的人和具有不同文化背景的人得记住，保持传统需要时间，而时间是现代生活所无法提供的。在美国，要给出时间尤其困难，难怪美国人有"即刻满足"这么一个短语。"很久以前"在一种文化里表示两千年的时间，而在另一文化中有可能是两个月的时间。从这个角度来说，一个双元文化的人必须学会如何在同一瞬间跨越不同的时区。

我儿子威廉在 1979 年发现了这个秘密，当时他的朋友埃里克（Eric）刚过完五岁生日。每当威廉过生日时，我们总会给他很多礼物，有时也会给他做一顿很特殊的晚餐。但是，我还从来没有傻到请一帮小孩子到家中来庆祝一番，这样好不容易刷新的房子两个小时内就被弄得一塌糊涂。所以威廉知道什么叫庆祝生日，但是他不知道大多数美国人会把小寿星的朋友也请过来一起庆祝，而且还把这当作生日聚会一个必不可少的部分。

当我和威廉走进有着气球、礼物和装饰品的埃里克家时，一群兴奋的孩子正玩得开心着呢，那房子似乎也跟着一起在蹦蹦跳跳，变得歪歪扭扭。我能马上感觉到威廉肯定觉得这个生日聚会不错。可是当我看到埃里克的妈妈弗兰克丽 （Frankie）时，我才知道其实并非如此。弗兰克丽吓得躲在卧室的一边，脸上一副不知所措的神情。如果把她画进漫画，那她的眼睛一定会是螺旋形状，大脑两边是一道道的括号。

弗兰克丽带着呜咽的声音说："凯斯（Cath），我真应该按常规做事的。"

"怎么啦？"

"埃里克五岁，我本应该只请六个孩子来过生日的。邀请多少孩子参加聚会，只需要把小寿星的年龄加一就可以了。但是，现在我请了二十几个。怎么办呢？你没有看到家里乱七八糟的?!"

"你真行啊!"我又安慰她说："没事，我们一起来做，你管饭，我管孩子。"

fascination at seeing his mother putting her right foot in, then putting her right foot out, then putting her right foot in again, then shaking it all about **!!!**

After the last one left, Frankie and I would have smiled to each other had we had the strength. Standing by the door to see us out, Eric politely thanked us for attending his party. I wished him a wonderful year.

"Thank you, Mrs. Bean. Isn't it great? Now that I'm five, I don't have to take a nap anymore."

I didn't know William could do a double take. He did. "What did you say, Eric?"

Covering up his ears, I pulled his head out the door just as Eric repeated himself. I was too late. In the car, William asked, "Māma? What did Eric mean about five-year olds not having to take naps?"

"William, some people think that, as children grow older, they don't need naps."

"Māma, I'm five. Can I stop taking naps? Like Eric?"

"No, William. We're Chinese. Because you're five, you can stop taking *two* naps **!!!**

A sigh. And then a deep breath, "Māma? When I'm six…"

I knew what was coming. "Yes, William?"

"When I'm six, can I have a Birthday Party—with children?"

"William, we're Chinese **!!!** We don't start getting personal Birthday Parties until we're sixty—when we begin a whole new cycle. Until then, we all grow one year older together at the Chinese New Year."

"When will I be sixty?"

"In the year 2034."

"Oh."

"All right, William. Since we're also Americans, how about a compromise?"

"What kind? How?"

"Do you know why Pópo calls you Xiǎohǔ—Little Tiger?"

"Yes. Because I was born in the Year of the Tiger. Like her."

"That's right. You and Pópo are both Wood Tigers. This means you are exactly sixty years apart in age. Chinese like to refer to the Animal Year they're born in. It's special because it only happens every twelve years. Not as special as the sixtieth but pretty special. So maybe we can do something

我们最后居然做成了。那一天，我们度日如年，但是我们做成了。我把孩子们围成一个圈，一起做游戏。我先把右脚放进去，然后再把右脚拿出来，接着又把右脚放进去，最后把右脚晃来晃去。看到我这样跟小朋友们一起玩，威廉一会儿欢呼雀跃，一会儿目瞪口呆。

当最后一个孩子走了以后，我和弗兰克丽连笑的力气都没有了。等到我们要回家的时候，埃里克站在门口，很有礼貌地感谢我们参加他的生日晚会。我祝福他拥有美好的一年。

"谢谢你，比恩太太，现在我五岁了，再也不需要午睡了，这真好！"

威廉开始一愣，然后恍然大悟。在这之前，我不知道威廉会有这种反应。"你说什么，埃里克？"

我正捂着威廉的耳朵，拉着他的头往外走时，埃里克又重复了他刚才说的那句话。我慢了一拍。回到车里，威廉问我："妈妈，埃里克说五岁的孩子不需要午睡了，那是什么意思？"

"威廉，有人认为小孩长大了就不需要午睡了！"

"妈妈，我已经五岁了，我也可以不用午睡了吧？就像埃里克那样？"

"不行，威廉，我们是中国人。因为你已经五岁，所以你不用睡两个午睡了!!!"

威廉叹了一口气，接着又做了一个深呼吸。"妈妈，等我六岁时……"
我知道他要说什么了。"威廉，怎么呢？"

"等我六岁时，我也要开一个生日聚会，和小朋友们一起过的聚会，好吗？"

"威廉，我们是中国人!!! 我们中国人一直要等到六十岁，开始新一轮时，才过生日。到那个时候的中国新年，我们大家都长大一岁。"

"那我什么时候才能六十岁呢？"

"2034年。"

"唉！"

special in 1986, when you're twelve. It'll be a Fire Tiger year but I'm willing to compromise if you are."

Trying to figure how long that would take, William got lost between the right thumb and the left index finger. Holding up seven of my own, I said, "*Then* you can have a Birthday Party at home. With children. Okay?"

Although there still seemed to be entirely too many, it was still less than two full hands' worth. And a lot less than sixty. He agreed to wait, "Okay, Māma."

And so we each redefined "instant gratification" in terms of different cultural time zones. William accepted seven years to be an "instant" relative to Chinese millennia while I made the "long" wait relative to the American clock worth waiting for. By making his 12th and 24th birthday parties the hottest ticket in town, he was gratified by the uniqueness of the occasion. Indeed, the fun had by all has continued to be gratifying in that his friends still party at our house even when William is in Hong Kong.

VOCABULARY

instant gratifi-cation	n.p.	associated with "Generation X" (born 1968-78 or so) whose parents were the "Baby Boomers," their attitude of living for the moment and getting what they want quickly arises from being accustomed to the speed of technology, and the uncertainty of life.	即刻满足	jíkè mǎnzú
millennia	n.	plural of "millennium," a period of 1,000 years.	千年	qiānnián
en masse	p.p.	(French) in a group, altogether, as a mass.	全体地	quántǐ de
renovate	v.	to make new again, restore to good condition.	装修	zhuāngxiū
careen	v.	to lean or sway as if blown by a strong wind.	使……倾斜	shǐ…qīngxié
hyperglycemic	adj.	having too much glucose or sugar in the bloodstream ("hyper" is the slang for "hyperactive" which is to be excessively active).	高糖的, 好动的	gāotáng de, hàodòng de

"好吧，威廉，既然我们也是美国人，我们来个折中吧！"

"什么样的折中？"

"你知道为什么婆婆叫你小虎吗？"

"当然知道，因为我跟她一样生在虎年。"

"对，你和婆婆都属虎，是木虎。这就是说，你们两个人正好相差六十岁。中国人喜欢用动物来指自己出生的那一年，这很特别，因为每过十二年才轮换一次。虽然第十二年不像第六十年那么特别，但还是不同一般。所以到一九八六年，等你十二岁时，我们开一个特别的生日聚会。那一年是火虎年，如果你愿意折中，我也愿意到那时候把你的朋友们都请来一起庆祝生日。"

威廉用两只手数着，想要算出还要等多久，可是卡在右手的大拇指和左手的食指中间。我伸出七个手指对他说，"好，到那时你可以在家里开生日聚会，请小朋友们过来跟你一起庆祝。"

虽然七年要等很长时间，但是，比起十年还是要少得多，而且比六十年更是要少很多。"好吧，妈妈"，威廉同意等了。

我和威廉用不同文化时区的标准各自重新定义了"即刻满足"。与千年相比七年实在是个"瞬间"，威廉接受了这一事实，而我也将"长时间"的等待变得更适合美国人的时间观念。后来威廉真的等了七年，这一等还真值。他十二岁、二十四岁的生日聚会成了我们镇上最为抢手的聚会，这种独一无二的聚会令他心满意足。事实上，参加聚会的每个人都玩得很开心，以至于虽然现在威廉已去了香港工作，可他的朋友仍然还常来我们家参加聚会。

streamer	n.	a long strip of colored crepe paper hung from two high points, entwined around poles, etc. to decorate for a festive occasion.	装饰品	zhuāng-shìpǐn
spiral	n.	a coil or shape formed by connecting circles around a single point but on different planes.	螺旋	luóxuán
rule of thumb	n.p.	a general principle based on practical experience (rather than science).	原则	yuánzé
whaddami gonna do?		slurred, slangy, spoken version of "What am I going to do?" as portrayed in comic books.	我该怎么办呢？	Wǒ gāi zěnme bàn ne?
time warp	n.p.	in science fiction or "sci fi," the possibility of worm holes, parallel universes, etc. allows for nonlinear space travel because time is bent or warped so one can go from one place/time to another in seconds rather than (light) years.	时间隧道	shíjiān suìdào
gallop	v.	to run like a horse at full speed.	飞奔	fēibēn
immobilize	v.	to stop movement.	使……不动	shǐ…bùdòng
index finger	n.p.	the first or pointing finger, next to the thumb. When counting with fingers in America, the index finger would be "1," the middle finger "2," etc. so the thumb is "5." If continuing, "6" is the index finger on the other. In China, the thumb is "1," the index finger "2," etc.	食指	shízhǐ

生词

时区	時區	shíqū	n.	time zone
即刻	即刻	jíkè	adv.	at once, immediately
跨越	跨越	kuàyuè	v.	cross over
好不容易	好不容易	hǎobùróngyì	f.c.w.	after all the trouble
刷新	刷新	shuāxīn	v (c)	renovate
一塌糊涂	一塌糊塗	yītā-hútú	f.c.w.	in an awful or terrible state
寿星	壽星	shòuxīng	n.	sb. who celebrates his/her birthday
聚会	聚會	jùhuì	n.	party
必不可少	必不可少	bìbùkěshǎo	f.c.w.	indispensable, necessary
走进	走進	zǒujìn	v (c)	walk into
气球	氣球	qìqiú	n.	balloon
装饰品	裝飾品	zhuāngshìpǐn	n.	streamer
群	群	qún	m (n)	group (of people)
兴奋	興奮	xìngfèn	adj.	hyperglycemic
蹦蹦跳跳	蹦蹦跳跳	bèngbèng-tiàotiào	f.c.w.	jumping
歪歪扭扭	歪歪扭扭	wāiwāi-niǔniǔ	f.c.w.	careening
并非如此	並非如此	bìngfēirúcǐ	f.c.w.	not so
卧室	臥室	wòshì	n.	bedroom
脸上	臉上	liǎnshàng	n.	on the face
螺旋	螺旋	luóxuán	n.	spiral
括号	括號	kuòhào	n.	parentheses
呜咽	嗚咽	wūyè	v.	moan
凯斯	凱斯	Kǎisī	p.n.	shortened form for "Cathy"
乱七八糟	亂七八糟	luànqībāzāo	f.c.w.	be in a mess
常规	常規	chángguī	n.	rule of thumb, conventional measure
管	管	guǎn	v.	take care of
度日如年	度日如年	dùrì-rúnián	f.c.w.	spending a day like a year
晃来晃去	晃來晃去	huàngláihuàngqù	f.c.w.	move around
欢呼雀跃	歡呼雀躍	huānhū-quèyuè	f.c.w.	galloping joy
目瞪口呆	目瞪口呆	mùdèng-kǒudāi	f.c.w.	mouth agape with immobilizing fascination
祝福	祝福	zhùfú	v.	wish sb. happiness
午睡	午睡	wǔshuì	n.	nap
捂	捂	wǔ	v.	cover up
深呼吸	深呼吸	shēnhūxī	n.	deep breath
折中	折中	zhézhōng	n./v.	compromise
小虎	小虎	Xiǎohǔ	p.n.	nickname "Little Tiger"
相差	相差	xiāngchà	v.	differ

第六章

美國的文化時區

生活在多元文化環境中的人和具有不同文化背景的人得記住，保持傳統需要時間，而時間是現代生活所無法提供的。在美國，要給出時間尤其困難，難怪美國人有＂即刻滿足＂這么一個短語。＂很久以前＂在一種文化裏表示兩千年的時間，而在另一文化中有可能是兩個月的時間。從這個角度來說，一個雙元文化的人必須學會如何在同一瞬間跨越不同的時區。

我兒子威廉在 1979 年發現了這個秘密，當時他的朋友埃里克（Eric）剛過完五歲生日。每當威廉過生日時，我們總會給他很多禮物，有時也會給他做一頓很特殊的晚餐。但是，我還從來沒有傻到請一幫小孩子到家中來慶祝一番，這樣好不容易刷新的房子兩個小時內就被弄得一塌糊涂。所以威廉知道什麼叫慶祝生日，但是他不知道大多數美國人會把小壽星的朋友也請過來一起慶祝，而且還把這當作生日聚會一個必不可少的部分。

當我和威廉走進有着氣球、禮物和裝飾品的埃里克家時，一群興奮的孩子正玩得開心着呢，那房子似乎也跟着一起在蹦蹦跳跳，變得歪歪扭扭。我能馬上感覺到威廉肯定覺得這個生日聚會不錯。可是當我看到埃里克的媽媽弗蘭克麗 （Frankie）時，我才知道其實并非如此。弗蘭克麗嚇得躲在卧室的一邊，臉上一副不知所措的神情。如果把她畫進漫畫，那她的眼睛一定會是螺旋形狀，大腦兩邊是一道道的括號。

弗蘭克麗帶着嗚咽的聲音說：＂凱斯（Cath），我真應該按常規做事的。＂

＂怎么啦？＂

＂埃里克五歲，我本應該只請六個孩子來過生日的。邀請多少孩子參加聚會，只需要把小壽星的年齡加一就可以了。但是，現在我請了二十幾個。怎么辦呢？你沒有看到家裏亂七八糟的?!＂

轮换	輪換	lúnhuàn	v.	take turns, rotate
数	數	shǔ	v.	count
卡	卡	kǎ	v.	get lost, get stuck
食指	食指	shízhǐ	n.	index finger, forefinger
算出	算出	suànchū	v (c)	calculate
值	值	zhí	v.	be worth
镇上	鎮上	zhènshàng	n.	in the town
抢手	搶手	qiǎngshǒu	adj.	hottest
独一无二	獨一無二	dúyī-wú'èr	f.c.w.	unique
心满意足	心滿意足	xīnmǎn-yìzú	f.c.w.	be perfectly content or satisfied
以至于	以至於	yǐzhìyú	conj.	so…that…

"你真行啊！"我又安慰她说："沒事，我們一起來做，你管飯，我管孩子。"

我們最后居然做成了。那一天，我們度日如年，但是我們做成了。我把孩子們圍成一個圈，一起做游戲。我先把右腳放進去，然后再把右腳拿出來，接着又把右腳放進去，最后把右腳晃來晃去。看到我這樣跟小朋友們一起玩，威廉一會兒歡呼雀躍，一會兒目瞪口呆。

當最后一個孩子走了以后，我和弗蘭克麗連笑的力氣都沒有了。等到我們要回家的時候，埃里克站在門口，很有禮貌地感謝我們參加他的生日晚會。我祝福他擁有美好的一年。

"謝謝你，比恩太太，現在我五歲了，再也不需要午睡了，這真好！"

威廉開始一愣，然后恍然大悟。在這之前，我不知道威廉會有這種反應。"你说什么，埃里克？"

我正捂着威廉的耳朵，拉着他的頭往外走時，埃里克又重復了他剛才说的那句話。我慢了一拍。回到車里，威廉問我："媽媽，埃里克說五歲的孩子不需要午睡了，那是什么意思？"

"威廉，有人認為小孩長大了就不需要午睡了！"

"媽媽，我已經五歲了，我也可以不用午睡了吧？就像埃里克那樣？"

"不行，威廉，我們是中國人。因為你已經五歲，所以你不用睡兩個午睡了!!!"

威廉嘆了一口氣，接着又做了一個深呼吸。"媽媽，等我六歲時……"

我知道他要说什么了。"威廉，怎么呢？"

"等我六歲時，我也要開一個生日聚會，和小朋友們一起過的聚會，好嗎？"

"威廉，我們是中國人!!! 我們中國人一直要等到六十歲，開始新一輪時，才過生日。到那個時候的中國新年，我們大家都長大一歲。"

"那我什么時候才能六十歲呢？"

"2034 年。"

"唉！"

"好吧，威廉，既然我們也是美國人，我們來個折中吧！"

"什么樣的折中？"

"你知道為什麼婆婆叫你小虎嗎？"

"當然知道，因為我跟她一樣生在虎年。"

"對，你和婆婆都屬虎，是木虎。這就是說，你們兩個人正好相差六十歲。中國人喜歡用動物來指自己出生的那一年，這很特別，因為每過十二年才輪換一次。雖然第十二年不像第六十年那麼特別，但還是不同一般。所以到一九八六年，等你十二歲時，我們開一個特別的生日聚會。那一年是火虎年，如果你願意折中，我也願意到那時候把你的朋友們都請來一起慶祝生日。"

威廉用兩只手數着，想要算出還要等多久，可是卡在右手的大拇指和左手的食指中間。我伸出七個手指對他說，"好，到那時你可以在家里開生日聚會，請小朋友們過來跟你一起慶祝。"

雖然七年要等很長時間，但是，比起十年還是要少得多，而且比六十年更是要少很多。"好吧，媽媽"，威廉同意等了。

我和威廉用不同文化時區的標準各自重新定義了"即刻滿足"。與千年相比七年實在是個"瞬間"，威廉接受了這一事實，而我也將"長時間"的等待變得更適合美國人的時間觀念。后來威廉真的等了七年，這一等還真值。他十二歲、二十四歲的生日聚會成了我們鎮上最為搶手的聚會，這種獨一無二的聚會令他心滿意足。事實上，參加聚會的每個人都玩得很開心，以至于雖然現在威廉已去了香港工作，可他的朋友仍然還常來我們家參加聚會。

练习 EXERCISES

I. 思考和课堂讨论 FOOD FOR THOUGHT

A. PERSONAL 个人的

描述你生活中的一个"跨越时区"的经历。

Describe an experience of yours which made you cross different "time zones."

B. GENERAL 普遍的

An "argument" or line of reasoning is logical when a conclusion is validly deduced from premises that are assumed to be true. However, when there is an error in reasoning, then a fallacy occurs. In order to think clearly and effectively, it helps to know about these errors. After reading the following, discuss the question posed.

当某一结论是从一个正确的前提演绎出来的,那么该结论的论据符合逻辑。但是,如果推理出现错误,就会产生谬论。为了清楚、有效地思考,有必要了解这些推理错误。请阅读下面的错误,然后讨论所提出的问题。

> **ad populum** is from the Latin *argumentum ad populum (argumentum* = "argument"; *ad* = "to"; *populum* = "masses" or "a majority of people").

> **pattern:** Mr. X argues for the truth of his conclusion; Ms. Y says he's wrong because the masses or majority of people disagree with Mr. X and, therefore, agree with her.

> **example:** Instead of presenting physical or eye-witness evidence to the jury proving beyond a reasonable doubt that Mr. X had in fact murdered the victim, Ms. Y argues ***ad populum*** by saying to the jury, "How can you believe Mr. X? All your neighbors think he's guilty!"

> **question:** Why is Ms. Y's fallacious approach often effective but still logically irrelevant? How is this approach similar to TV advertisers who use celebrities to endorse their products?

C. CROSS-CULTURAL 跨文化的

After reading the following, discuss <u>in English</u> the recent effect of naming dozens of different routes traveled over many centuries and several continents as "The Silk Road" as if there was only one.

阅读以下短文,并<u>用英文</u>对所提出的问题进行讨论。

> There is a very real difference between renovating an old structure and restoring it. For example, what is now called the "Great Wall of China," originally built to prevent invasions, has been continuously repaired since the late 15th century. At first, earth and bricks were used to restore the wall but stone became preferable in terms of maintaining the structure for defensive purposes. However, since the 1980s, renovations were made—not to conserve but to provide modern facilities for the tourist trade. So now, instead of original materials to restore and repair, metal, concrete, steel, plastic, etc. have been used to construct recreational slides for sledding, chair lifts to carry people up high for a better view, fast-food restaurants, etc. Some historians

think millions of "invading" tourists from the West are more frightening and dangerous to Chinese culture than an equal number of barbarians **!!!**

II. 配对 **MATCHMAKER**

A. VOCABULARY 词汇

找出以下两列中的对应词，并在其间划线。

Draw a connecting line between the word and its correct definition.

a.	螺旋	1.	instant gratification
b.	食指	2.	spiral
c.	使……不动	3.	renovate
d.	即刻满足	4.	immobilize
e.	飞奔	5.	rule of thumb
f.	千年	6.	index finger
g.	使……倾斜	7.	*en masse*
h.	装修	8.	careen
i.	常规，凭经验来做的方法	9.	millennium
j.	全体地	10.	gallop

a.	a flash, a very short moment	1.	算出
b.	careening, swaying	2.	折中
c.	sb. who celebrates his/her birthday	3.	心满意足
d.	compromise	4.	一瞬间
e.	in a hopeless mess	5.	装饰品
f.	nap, break	6.	寿星
g.	be perfectly content	7.	独一无二
h.	calculate	8.	高糖的, 好动的
i.	unique, unparalleled	9.	午睡
j.	hyperglycemic	10.	一塌糊涂
k.	streamer	11.	歪歪扭扭

135

B. **SYNONYMS & ALTERNATES** 同义词和多义词

First draw a connecting line between the word or phrase in the left-hand column with the best possible <u>synonym</u> listed in the middle column, then draw a line between the synonym and an alternate meaning of the synonym listed in the right-hand column. <u>Be forewarned</u> that the part of speech may change from one column to the next and that slang terms may be used. E.g.,

"hit" ———————————— *"strike"*————— *"stop-work action against employer"*

"warm"———————————— *"heat"* ————— *"qualifying race for final contest"*

首先在第二列中找出与第一列相对应的同义词，然后在第三列中找出与第二列相关的多义词。注意：词性会有不同。

			SYNONYMS		**ALTERNATE MEANING**
a.	held title to	1	**hooks**	i.	surpass, complete, top
b.	medicinal tablet	2.	**cap**	ii.	*slang* disagreeable person
c.	hat of soft fabric	3.	**reel**	iii.	*slang* a pretty, attractive female
d.	boxing punches	4.	**possessed**	iv.	*slang* hands or fingers
e.	murder, slay	5.	**pill**	v.	controlled by an evil spirit
f.	emotionally affect	6.	**dish**	vi.	make a formal request/motion
g.	rumor, gossip, news	7.	**kill**	vii.	*informal* telephone call
h.	receiver of signals	8.	**move**	viii.	spend unprofitably
i.	voluntarily leaves a job	9.	**buzz**	ix.	lively folk dance
j.	sway, rock or whirl	10.	**quits**	x.	on equal terms by repayment

III. 解字/词、构字/词 DECONSTRUCTION & CONSTRUCTION

A. 将以下汉字分解成最小的构字部件，然后用每个部件构成三个汉字。例如"鸭"可以分解成"甲"和"鸟"两个部件。"甲"能构成"押"，"岬"，"钾"；"鸟"可以构成以"鸡"，"鸦"，"鸣"。请借助字典完成练习。

Deconstruct the following characters into the smallest components, then form 3 new characters using each component.

间_____ 歪_____ 饭_____

蹦_____ 摆_____ 婆_____

B. Using only the letters of the word "**STREAMER**," form English words that are not proper nouns, abbreviations, or acronyms and that consist of 4 or more letters. A letter can only be used again if it appears in the given word more than once. E.g., "starve" is not acceptable because there is no "v" and "stammer" is not because there is only one "m." Like many Olympic sports, weight categories mark performance. We filled in a few cells to get you started. Fill in the rest to achieve the highest category. If you think up more than 64, you beat the authors!

用 "STREAMER" 中的字母构词。新构建的词不能是专有名词、缩写词、或首字母缩略词。每个单词必须至少含有四个字母，但不能重复使用同一字母，除非该字母在 "STREAMER" 中出现两次。

CHAMPION STATUS					
FLY 11	BANTAM 22	FEATHER 33	WELTER 44	MIDDLE 55	HEAVY 64
stream					
seam					
team					

C. 用 "度日如年" 中的每个汉字组成不同的词。看看最多能组多少个词。

Use each of the characters in "度日如年" to form as many words (of 2-4 characters) as you can.

D. Pair any two of the following 7 words to form at least 9 different, unhyphenated words.

在下列七个词中配对、组词，新组的词只能含有两个单词，中间没有连字号。请至少找出九对。

head wall point pin stone long line

IV. 阅读理解 READING QUIZ

根据课文，选择准确答案。Based on the text, choose the best answer.

1. 为什么美国人有 "即刻满足" 这么一个短语？

a. 因为美国文化只有两个月的时间。

b. 因为美国文化有着两千年的时间。

c. 因为美国文化只有一刹那的时间。

d.　因为美国人工作忙，时间紧，没有耐心等待。

2.　大多数美国父母通常是怎样为自己的小孩庆祝生日的？

　　a.　他们会给小孩买很多好玩的礼物。

　　b.　他们会给小孩做一顿好吃的晚饭。

　　c.　他们会刷房子，把家里布置得漂亮一点儿。

　　d.　他们会给小孩开个生日聚会，并把小孩的朋友也请过来一起庆祝。

3.　埃里克过生日的那天，为什么她妈妈躲在卧室里？

　　a.　因为来了二十几个小朋友，家里乱得一团糟，她吓坏了。

　　b.　因为来了二十几个小朋友，她想给他们一个突然的惊喜。

　　c.　因为那些小朋友个个很好动、走路歪头歪脑，她怕他们。

　　d.　因为那些小朋友拿着气球、礼物和装饰品要找她一起玩。

4.　在美国为小孩开生日聚会，应该请多少小朋友参加？

　　a.　请二十几个。

　　b.　请六个。

　　c.　请两个。

　　d.　把小孩的年龄加一就得出要请的人数。

5.　中国人的一轮是多少年？

　　a.　十二年。

　　b.　二十四年。

　　c.　六十年。

　　d.　七年。

6.　在请小朋友参加生日聚会这个问题上，威廉和他母亲最后达成什么样的协议？

　　a.　家里再也不给威廉过生日。

　　b.　家里不请小朋友参加聚会。

　　c.　每过十二年才开个聚会，并请小朋友参加。

　　d.　每过十二年才开个聚会，但不邀请小朋友。

V.　填空　FILL IN THE BLANK

A.　选择正确答案。Choose the correct answer.

　　1.　一个双元文化的人要学会如何在同一瞬间不时地跨越不同_____。

       a. 地区　　　　b. 时区　　　　c. 灾区

2. 请小寿星的朋友一起来玩是美国小孩生日聚会的一个_____的部分。

       a. 必然　　　　b. 必定　　　　c. 必不可少

3. 如果把弗兰克丽画进_____，那她的眼睛一定会夸张得像个螺旋形状。

       a. 漫画　　　　b. 油画　　　　c. 中国画

4. 人们通常都喜欢按_____做事，因为这比较简单。

       a. 成规　　　　b. 常规　　　　c. 正规

5. 一共来了二十几个小孩子，他们把家里搞得_____。

       a. 乱七八糟　b. 七手八脚　c. 七嘴八舌

6. 中国人用动物来指自己出生的那一年，每过十二年_____一次。

       a. 交换　　　　b. 轮换　　　　c. 转换

B. 在以下段落中找出与斜体词意义相近的反义词。如果你所学的外语是中文，找出相应的中文词或短语，如果你所学的外语是英语，找出相应的英语词或短语。注意，词性或时态会有变化。

Using your target language, write a word or phrase from the vocabulary lists and/or dictionary that means the <u>opposite</u> or is an <u>antonym</u> for the italicized word or phrase. Keep in mind that the part of speech and/or tense may have been adjusted to achieve grammatically correct results.

If he didn't eat every four hours, he would be *lacking blood sugar* _____ and he would *slow to a snail's pace* _____ so that grass growing seemed more *alert and ready to go* _____ than he did **!!!**

VI. 翻译　TRANSLATION

A. 将以下句子翻译成英文。Translate the following sentences into English.

1. 生活在多元文化环境中的人和具有不同文化背景的人得记住，保持传统需要时间，而时间是现代生活所无法提供的。

2. 但是，我还从来没有傻到请一帮小孩子到家中来庆祝一番，这样好不容易刷新的房子两个小时内就被弄得一塌糊涂。

3. 看到我这样跟小朋友们一起玩，威廉一会儿欢呼雀跃，一会儿目瞪口呆。

B. Translate the following sentences into Chinese. 将以下句子翻译成中文。

1. "William, we're Chinese **!!!** We don't start getting personal Birthday Parties until we're sixty—when we begin a whole new cycle. Until then, we all grow one year older together at the Chinese New Year.

2. "That's right. You and *PoPo* are both Wood Tigers. This means you are exactly sixty years apart in age.

3. And so we each redefined "instant gratification" in terms of different cultural time zones. William accepted seven years to be an "instant" relative to Chinese millennia while I made the "long" wait relative to the American clock worth waiting for.

VII. 完型填充　CLOZE TEST

A. 在以下短文的每一空格处填入一个汉字，如有可能，给出相应的英语单词。

Fill in a Chinese character that retains the original meaning or intent of the text, then write an English equivalent, if any.

后来威廉真的等了七年，这一等还真值。＿＿＿＿＿十二岁、二十四＿＿＿＿＿的生日聚会成＿＿＿＿＿我们镇上最为＿＿＿＿＿手的聚会；这种＿＿＿＿＿一无二的聚会＿＿＿＿＿他心满意足。事＿＿＿＿＿上，参加聚会的＿＿＿＿＿个人都玩得很＿＿＿＿＿心，以至于直到＿＿＿＿＿在威廉已去了＿＿＿＿＿港工作，可他的＿＿＿＿＿友仍然还常来＿＿＿＿＿们家参加聚会。

B. Fill in an English word or phrase that retains the original meaning or intent of the text, then write a Chinese equivalent, if any.

在以下短文的每一空格处填入一个英语单词，如有可能，给出相应的汉字或词。

Holding up seven of my own, I ＿＿＿＿＿, "*Then* you can have a Birthday Party ＿＿＿＿＿ home. With children. Okay?" Although there still ＿＿＿＿＿ to be entirely too many, it was ＿＿＿＿＿ less than two full hands' worth. And ＿＿＿＿＿ lot less than sixty. He agreed to ＿＿＿＿＿, "Okay, *MaMa*." And so we each redefined "＿＿＿＿＿ gratification" in terms of different cultural time ＿＿＿＿＿. William accepted seven years to be an "＿＿＿＿＿" relative to Chinese millennia while I made ＿＿＿＿＿ "long" wait relative to the American clock ＿＿＿＿＿ waiting for. By making his 12th and ＿＿＿＿＿ birthday parties the hottest ticket in town, ＿＿＿＿＿ was gratified by the uniqueness of the ＿＿＿＿＿. Indeed, the fun had by all has ＿＿＿＿＿ to be gratifying in that his friends ＿＿＿＿＿ party at our house even when William ＿＿＿＿＿ in Hong Kong.

VIII. 身体部位　BODY PARTS

A. There are many useful idioms which contain "body parts." Choose the most appropriate to fill in the blank based on your best guess of what the idiom means.

英语中的许多习惯用语含有表示 "身体部位" 的单词。在下面三个习惯用语中选择最恰当的填空。

1. take a five-finger discount　　**2.** high five　　**3.** not lift a finger

When he was a student in New York, guys would greet each other with a _____ so, whenever someone held his hand up, palm toward him, he would clap the palm with his own.

Big department stores like Wal-Mart and Macy's lose millions of dollars every year because so many thieves _____.

One sister was always ready to help her brother while the other sister did _____ unless their parents were watching.

B. 将以下短文翻译成中文。注意：划线的词或短语与以上含有"身体部位"的习惯用语相对应。

Translate the following into Chinese, taking note that the underlined words or phrases correspond to the meaning of the above "body parts."

Some very rich people steal things at stores, not because they want or need the items but because they need the thrill of possibly getting caught.

When people first started to slap another's palm in the air, it wasn't always clear if they were saying "hello" or telling you to stop.

When her aunt visited, she sometimes stayed for weeks yet she did not help but expected everybody else to cook and clean.

C. Using your target language, create sentence(s) containing the following three English idioms or their Chinese equivalents.

用以下短语分别造句。注意：如果你所学的外语是中文，请用中文来做这个练习。如果你所学的外语是英语，请用英语来做这个练习。

1. slip through one's fingers = 错过机会，坐失良机

2. twist around one's little finger = 任意摆布某人，左右某人

3. put one's finger on = 正确地指出（错误）

IX. 写作 PRÉCIS

用所学的外语总结课文。如果你用中文来写，请至少使用 450 个汉字，并用电脑打出摘要。如果你用英文来写，请不超过 305 个词。

Write a summary of this chapter in your target language. If writing in Chinese, use more than 450 characters; if writing in English, use no more than 305 words.

CHAPTER SEVEN

SPECIALIZING MINORITY MINUTES[11] IN BEIJING

Before visiting China in 1987, I bought clothes in yellow, fuchsia, and orange. Bennett looked at the pile and wondered what had come over me because, generally, I wear black.

"You've never had to find me in a crowd before," I explained.

Laughing, he asked, "What about Chinatown?"

"That's nothing compared to what it'll be like in Beijing during August! At five feet, at least the *colors* will stand out."

I was right. Although velveteen skirts were replacing Mao suits, we saw none more daring than dark green. However, after getting separated in the crush of vacationing foreign and domestic tourists, Bennett said after we were reunited, "I could have found you no matter what color you wore. Even in this crowd, your body language is completely American!"

Asian students studying in the U.S. have also discovered that they can be a member of the "minority" when they return home, even after only one semester. The reasons can be obvious—like clothing, make-up, hair style, ways of moving—but there are more subtle changes like casual references to "foreign" people, places, practices, politics, pronunciations, and possibilities. Similar changes happen when a student returns to a small town after going away to a city or college and strikes up a conversation with a high school buddy who, physically and psychologically, went directly from cutting study hall to pumping gas. In the case of the Asian, the changes may be, often derisively, labeled "Americanization." Maybe, to some extent, they are but I think a more accurate and helpful way to think about them is in terms of adding a "radish" option to what used to be just the "duck" and "rabbit." That is, in terms of becoming more multicultural in ways other than by ethnicity so that, when in their home countries, they are now part of the "minority" but when debarking at the international arrival gate, they are part of the "majority."

---

[11]这里的"specializing"和"minutes"分别具有两种不同的意思。前者表示（1）成为专家；（2）使某事或某人变得独特，后者指（1）时间；（2）记载。当两者结合起来使用时，产生了更多的意义。

第七章

北京的"少数族群"

1987 年我们去中国旅游之前，我买了一些黄色、粉红色和橘红色的衣服。班尼特看着那堆衣服，纳闷着：这是怎么回事呢？因为我平时穿的可都是黑色的衣服。

"因为以前你没有必要在人群中找我呀，"我跟他解释。

"在中国城我不是也要找你吗？"他笑着说。

"可那没法跟八月份的北京比呀！五英尺高的人，至少鲜艳的色彩能更醒目一点吧。"

没错，那个时候的中国，虽然柔软的绒布裙子替代了毛式的制服，但是除了深绿色以外，我们很少看到其它鲜艳的颜色。成群结队的海内外游客把我和班尼特挤散了，当我们重新会合时，他说，"现在不管你穿什么颜色的衣服，我都可以在人群中找到你，因为你的一举一动完全是美国式的。"

在美国读过书的亚洲学生，哪怕只是读了一个学期，也会发现，当回到自己的国家以后，他们居然成了"少数族群"。这其中的理由很明显——衣服、化妆、发型、走路的姿势都跟原来的有所不同。当然，在随便的交谈中，比如，说起"外国人"，地方、习俗、政治，或在发音上以及在选择不同话题时也都显出一些比较微妙的变化。一个从小镇出去到大城市发展或去外地大学读书的学生，回到家乡后跟从前高中时期读书不那么用功、现在只能在加油站打工的朋友聊天时，也会有类似这样的变化。拿前面一个例子来说，发生在一个亚洲学生身上的变化常常会被人们可笑地贴上"美国化"的标签。也许，在某种程度上，他们是美国化了。但是，对于这种变化，仅仅用"鸭子"和"兔子"两个角度看还不够，也许还应该增加"红萝卜"这么一个角度。这就是说，除了用种族标

The experience can be frightening and exhilarating, exhausting and energizing. Many ex-GIs have stopped me at the store in our small New Jersey town and announced, apropos of nothing happening at the time, that they had been "in the East" during the war. "The war" could have been any of three from WW II to Vietnam. It didn't seem to matter that the country from which I came could have been the enemy, or the issues over which nations had fought were still being debated. They would see my face and feel nostalgia for those "Glory Days," ready to recall a "Time of Their Lives" when they were on foreign soil, drafted to do something, rightly or wrongly, of international importance. Students who voluntarily travel, seek the experience of being part of the "minority," often learning how to communicate in a language or style they weren't born into. And then there is former President Bill Clinton. He has his office in Harlem. Some say he is trying to attract more Whites into the African-American neighborhood while many local residents say, "He was *our* only Black President and is right at home here."

My first home-away-from-home was in Berkeley, California. I lived there for three months but I felt "in the majority"—not because there were many Asians there in the mid-1960s but because people *expected* each person to be truly individual as a "minority of one." Meanwhile, I could say less about what I was doing and feeling to my mother: Conversing with her became "work" and I was better able to relax when elsewhere. Yet, even then, while my parents were alive, every time I said *jiā* or "home" to them, I felt somewhat disloyal if I was referring to some place other than their house.

My younger sister, Sānsan, didn't feel similarly when she arrived in the U.S. in 1962. Instantly, *jiā* was in New Jersey even though we were strangers to her. Nevertheless, for her there was no re-laxing. By 1965, she had progressed from singing "A, B, C, D..." to taking the SATs and entering college. In between, our older sister got married and we were two of her four bridesmaids. There were eight groomsmen and a thousand guests. At the rehearsal, Sānsan kept taking the wrong arm for the recessional. They were all Caucasian. They all looked alike **!!!** Instead of taking a chance on a traffic jam in the aisle, her groomsman wore a different color boutonnière so Sānsan could target the flower rather than the face.

Whenever I get impatient or even angry with someone who is or has been a member of some "minority," I remember that flower. After all, Sānsan had been a wee bit busy that year—learning how to spell, use shampoo, ride buses, not to mention getting used to food instead of famine. There had been little time left over to study how to differentiate one Caucasian from another. Taking this lesson seriously, I facilitate fun and function whenever we host a large party when almost two hun-

准以外，还要用多元文化的标准来看问题。那些亚洲学生在自己的国家里被看作是"少数族群"，但是一旦下了飞机，踏进国际大门，却成为"多数族群"中的一员。[14]

这种经验可能令人生畏，但又令人振奋。可能让人疲乏不堪、但也使人精力旺盛。在我住的新泽西州小镇上，许多参加过二战、韩战或越战的老兵在商店里看到我常常会莫名其妙地跟我讲起他们在战争年代曾去过东方的经历。他们并不在乎我所来自的国家曾是他们的敌人，也不在乎那些他们曾为之战斗过的信仰仍是具有争议的话题。只是看到我这亚洲人的脸就对从前那段峥嵘岁月产生出一股浓浓的怀旧感，情不自禁地回忆起当年奔赴异国他乡为正义热血奋战的瑰丽人生。自愿外出旅行的学生追寻成为"少数族群"的经历，学习如何用自己毫不熟悉的语言跟外国人交流。前总统比尔·克林顿把办公室设在纽约市的哈莱姆（Harlem）。有人说他这么做是想吸引更多的白人搬到非裔-美国人的居住区，但许多当地的居民说："比尔·克林顿是我们黑人唯一的一个总统，他就在我们家。"

加利福尼亚的伯克利是我离开父母家以后第一个可以称之为家的地方。我在那里只住了三个月，但是我在那儿却感觉自己是"多数族群"中的一员。这不是因为六十年代中期的伯克利有很多亚裔人，而是因为那里的人都希望别人把自己看作是一个真正的"少数族群"中的一个独立的个体成员。那段时间，我不需要跟母亲汇报我在做什么、我有什么感受。跟母亲的那种聊天是份"工作"，所以我只有在父母家以外才能觉得轻松悠闲。父母在世的时候，每当我在他们面前把父母家以外的地方也称为"家"时，我就会有一种不孝之感。

我妹妹三三 1962 年来美国的时候就没有这种麻烦。虽然我们对她来说都是陌生人，但是新泽西州一下子就成了她的"家"。然而她在"家"里没有什么悠闲的时刻，因为到 1965 年，她已经从只会唱"A, B, C, D……"到通过美国大学入学考试（SAT），并进入大学读书。在此期间，我姐姐结婚时，我和她充当了四个伴娘中的两个。婚礼的场面极其壮观：八个伴郎，一千多来宾。记得我们彩排退场那一段，三三总是挽错伴郎的手，

---

[14] Although I realize that it is unlikely that governments or even adults — whether numerically in the majority or minority — will ever be "color-blind" when it comes to not seeing people, including themselves, in terms of visible differences, I am heartened by the fact that young children only notice them after they are taught to do so.

dred people of all ages, genders, ethnicities, and vocations attend. When they arrive, they see a box with a punning sign that I created:

> *Zhuāngzǐ says:*
>
> *Avoid Mask Confucian,[12]*
>
> *Wear a name tag and*
>
> *Help "Save a Face" !!!*

VOCABULARY

minutes	n.	at least two sixteenth of an hour; the official written record of a meeting.	分钟，纪录	fēnzhōng, jìlù
fuchsia	n.	a bright purplish red color as is the drooping flower of the same name.	粉红色	fěnhóngsè
velveteen	n.	a fabric made of various materials with a short pile that is like velvet but softer and lighter.	绒布	róngbù
daring	adj.	adventurous, bold, audacious.	鲜艳的	xiānyàn de
in the crush of …	p.p.	being within a group formed by many occupying too small a space to avoid bodily contact.	在拥挤的人群中	zài yōngjǐ de rénqún zhōng
derisively	adv.	with a mocking manner, making fun of someone in a demeaning way.	可笑地，嘲弄地	kěxiào de, cháonòng de
debark	v.	to get off a ship (or plane), to land.	使……下船，使……登陆	shǐ…xiàchuán, shǐ…dēnglù
ex-GI	abbr.	20th century slang abbrev. for a U.S. soldier possibly from "**G**eneral **I**nfantry," "**G**alvanized **I**ron, "**G**overnment **I**ssue."	战争老兵	zhànzhēng lǎobīng
apropos of nothing	p.p.	with no purpose or reference to anything in particular.	凭空地，突如其来地，没有任何联系地	píngkōng de, tūrúqílái de, méiyǒu rènhé liánxì de

---

[12]"mask Confucian"是一个双关语："mask" 是面具（一种遮住脸的东西），在这里指"mass"许多、大量，"Confucian, 孔夫子" 在这里指 "confusion" 糊涂。

因为他们都是白人，看起来一个模样。为了避免走道上可能造成的拥挤，她的伴郎特意佩戴不同颜色的胸花以帮助三三识别，这样她只需分辨花的颜色，而不是人的面孔。

每当我对某个"少数族群"中的一员感到不耐烦甚或有点气愤时，我就会想起那朵胸花。那一年三三真有点忙——她得学习怎么拼写英语字母、怎么使用洗发水、怎么乘坐公共汽车，更不用说怎么从常常吃不饱到适应如何从丰富的食物中挑选自己喜欢吃的东西。她因为那么忙，所以几乎没有时间去研究、区分白种人的不同面孔特征。通过这个教训，也为了给大家增添乐趣，每当我家举行拥有男女老少、不同肤色、各行各业近两百人的大型聚会时，来客一进家门就会在醒目的地方看到我做的一张双关语的指示牌：

庄子说：

不戴孔老夫子面具，[15]

佩戴尊姓大名标签

以此确保不丢脸面!!!

生词

纳闷	納悶	nàmèn	v.	wonder, be puzzled
回	回	huí	m (n)	a measure word for sth.
没法	沒法	méifǎ	v.	have no way to do sth.
醒目	醒目	xǐngmù	adj.	eye-catching
绒布	絨布	róngbù	n.	velveteen
替代	替代	tìdài	v.	substitute for, replace, supersede
毛式	毛式	máoshì	n	the Mao style
制服	制服	zhìfú	n.	uniform
深绿色	深綠色	shēnlǜsè	adj.	dark green
成群结队	成群結隊	chéngqún-jiéduì	f.c.w.	in crowds
海内外	海內外	hǎinèiwài	n.p.	home and abroad
会合	會合	huìhé	v.	join, meet
一举一动	一舉一動	yījǔ-yīdòng	f.c.w.	body language
化妆	化妝	huàzhuāng	v.	make up

---

[15] Here is a double pun on "mask Confucian." "mask" (something that hides the face) for "mass"; "Confucian" for "confusion."

nostalgia	n.	a desire to return in thought or in fact to a former time in one's life. It is interesting that the song Americans sing with nostalgia at the New Year "Auld Lang Syne," meaning "old long days," is/was one of the best known in China.	乡愁, 怀旧之情	xiāngchóu, huái-jiù zhī qíng
Harlem	p.n.	northwestern New York City and site of The New Negro Movement or The Harlem Renaissance when African-American music, dance, literature, and art flourished.	哈莱姆	Hāláimǔ
SAT	abbr.	**S**tandard **A**ptitude **T**ests in Mathematics or Critical Reading and Writing taken by high school students applying to a college.	美国大学的入学考试	Měiguó dàxué de rùxué kǎoshì
Caucasian	p.n.	although scholars have good reasons to debate the very concept of "race," our use of such terms reverts to their normative or popularly accepted meaning as descriptive of one's appearance, albeit vague, even erroneous, in this case to "White" people. The other racial "colors" are "Red," "Yellow," and "Black."	白种人	Báizhǒngrén
bridesmaid	n.	woman who attends the bride as her witness to the marriage.	伴娘	bànniáng
groomsman	n.	man who attends the groom as his witness to the marriage, usually a brother or friend.	伴郎	bànláng
boutonnière	n.	a flower or small bouquet worn on the lapel of a man's suit.	胸花	xiōnghuā
wee	adj.	little, small amount.	很少的	hěnshǎo de

有所不同	有所不同	yǒusuǒ-bùtóng	f.c.w.	somewhat different
微妙	微妙	wēimiào	adj.	subtle
城市	城市	chéngshì	n.	city
加油站	加油站	jiāyóu zhàn	n.p.	gas station
标签	標簽	biāoqiān	n.	label, tag
程度	程度	chéngdù	n.	degree, extent
范畴	範疇	fànchóu	n.	category, domain, range
这就是说	這就是說	zhè jiù shì shuo		that is to say…
看作	看作	kànzuò	v.	regard as, consider, look upon as
一员	一員	yīyuán	n.	one of the members
令人生畏	令人生畏	lìngrén-shēngwèi	f.c.w.	frightening
令人振奋	令人振奮	lìngrén-zhènfèn	f.c.w.	exhilarating
疲乏不堪	疲乏不堪	pífá bùkān	f.c.w.	exhausting
精力旺盛	精力旺盛	jīnglì wàngshèng	f.c.w.	energizing
二战	二戰	Èrzhàn	p.n.	World War Two
韩战	韓戰	Hánzhàn	p.n.	The Korean War
越战	越戰	Yuèzhàn	p.n.	The Vietnam War
老兵	老兵	lǎobīng	n.	veteran
在乎	在乎	zàihu	v.	(oft. used in the negative) care about, mind
峥嵘岁月	峥嵘岁月	zhēngróng-suìyuè	f.c.w.	memorable years of one's life
浓浓	濃濃	nóngnóng	adj.	(of degree or extent) great, strong
怀旧	懷舊	huáijiù	v.o.	remember past times
情不自禁	情不自禁	qíngbùzìjīn	f.c.w.	cannot help oneself (doing sth.)
奔赴	奔赴	bēnfù	v.	be drafted to go (somewhere)
异国他乡	異國他鄉	yìguó-tāxiāng	f.c.w.	foreign country
热血奋战	熱血奮戰	rèxuè-fènzhàn	f.c.w.	fight bravely and with enthusiasm
瑰丽	瑰麗	guīlì	adj.	magnificent
外出	外出	wàichū	v.	go out
追寻	追尋	zhuīxún	v.	pursue
比尔·克林顿	比爾·克林頓	Bǐ'ěr Kèlíndùn	p.n.	Bill Clinton
哈莱姆	哈萊姆	Hāláimǔ	p.n.	Harlem
居住区	居住區	jūzhùqū	n.p.	dwelling district
称之为	稱之為	chēngzhīwéi	v.p.	call it…
中期	中期	zhōngqī	n.	middle period
亚裔	亞裔	Yàyì	p.n.	Asian descendent
轻松悠闲	輕鬆悠閑	qīngsōng-yōuxián	f.c.w.	relaxed, carefree, ease
在世	在世	zàishì	v.	exist, be alive
陌生人	陌生人	mòshēngrén	n	stranger

第七章

北京的 "少數族群"

1987 年我們去中國旅游之前，我買了一些黃色、粉紅色和橘紅色的衣服。班尼特看着那堆衣服，納悶着：這是怎么回事呢？因為我平時穿的可都是黑色的衣服。

"因為以前你沒有必要在人群中找我呀，"我跟他解釋。

"在中國城我不是也要找你嗎？"他笑着説。

"可那沒法跟八月份的北京比呀！五英尺高的人，至少鮮艷的色彩能更醒目一點吧。"

沒錯，那個時候的中國，雖然柔軟的絨布裙子替代了毛式的制服，但是除了深綠色以外，我們很少看到其它鮮艷的顏色。成群結隊的海內外游客把我和班尼特擠散了，當我們重新會合時，他説，"現在不管你穿什么顏色的衣服，我都可以在人群中找到你，因為你的一舉一動完全是美國式的。"

在美國讀過書的亞洲學生，哪怕只是讀了一個學期，也會發現，當回到自己的國家以后，他們居然成了"少數族群"。這其中的理由很明顯——衣服、化妝、發型、走路的姿勢都跟原來的有所不同。當然，在隨便的交談中，比如，説起"外國人"，地方、習俗、政治，或在發音上以及在選擇不同話題時也都顯出一些比較微妙的變化。一個從小鎮出去到大城市發展或去外地大學讀書的學生，回到家鄉后跟從前高中時期讀書不那么用功、現在只能在加油站打工的朋友聊天時，也會有類似這樣的變化。拿前面一個例子來説，發生在一個亞洲學生身上的變化常常會被人們可笑地貼上"美國化"的標簽。也許，在某種程度上，他們是美國化了。但是，對于這種變化，僅僅用"鴨子"和"兔子"兩個角度看還不夠，也許還應該增加"紅蘿卜"這么一個角度。這就是説，除了用種族標準以外，還要用多元文化的標

150

充当	充當	chōngdāng	v.	serve as, act as
伴娘	伴娘	bànniáng	n.	bridesmaid
壮观	壯觀	zhuàngguān	adj.	magnificent
挽错	挽錯	wǎncuò	v (c)	take wrongly
伴郎	伴郎	bànláng	n.	groomsman
彩排	彩排	cǎipái	v.	rehearse
退场	退場	tuìchǎng	n.	recessional, formally exit
特意	特意	tèyì	adv.	for a special purpose, especially
佩戴	佩戴	pèidài	v.	wear (a boutonnière, badge, etc.)
胸花	胸花	xiōnghuā	n.	boutonnière
需	需	xū	v.	need
分辨	分辨	fēnbiàn	v.	identify, distinguish
耐烦	耐煩	nàifán	adj.	patient
甚或	甚或	shènhuò	conj.	even
拼写	拼寫	pīnxiě	v.	spell
洗发水	洗髮水	xǐfàshuǐ	n.	shampoo
乘坐	乘坐	chéngzuò	v.	embark, take a ride (in a car, ship, etc.)
不用说	不用說	bùyòngshuō	conj.	without saying
区分	區分	qūfēn	v.	distinguish, differentiate
增添	增添	zēngtiān	v.	facilitate, augment
男女老少	男女老少	nánnǚ-lǎoshào	f.c.w.	men, women, old and young
肤色	膚色	fūsè	n.	color of skin
各行各业	各行各業	gèháng-gèyè	f.c.w.	all walks of life
双关语	雙關語	shuāngguānyǔ	n.	pun, a play upon words
庄子	莊子	Zhuāngzǐ	p.n.	369-286 B.C.E., Daoist philosopher, Master Zhuāng, also known as Zhuang Zhou
面具	面具	miànjù	n.	mask
尊姓大名	尊姓大名	zūnxìng-dàmíng	f.c.w.	one's surname and given name
以此	以此	yǐcǐ	adv.	so that
确保	確保	quèbǎo	v.	ensure, assure

準來看問題。那些亞洲學生在自己的國家里被看作是"少數族群"，但是一旦下了飛機，踏進國際大門，卻成為"多數族群"中的一員。[14]

這種經驗可能令人生畏，但又令人振奮。可能讓人疲乏不堪、但也使人精力旺盛。在我住的新澤西州小鎮上，許多參加過二戰、韓戰或越戰的老兵在商店里看到我常常會莫名其妙地跟我講起他們在戰爭年代曾去過東方的經歷。他們并不在乎我所來自的國家曾是他們的敵人，也不在乎那些他們曾為之戰斗過的信仰仍是具有爭議的話題。只是看到我這亞洲人的臉就對從前那段崢嶸歲月產生出一股濃濃的懷舊感，情不自禁地回憶起當年奔赴异國他鄉為正義熱血奮戰的瑰麗人生。自願外出旅行的學生追尋成為"少數族群"的經歷，學習如何用自己毫不熟悉的語言跟外國人交流。前總統比爾‧克林頓把辦公室設在紐約市的哈萊姆（Harlem）。有人說他這么做是想吸引更多的白人搬到非裔-美國人的居住區，但許多當地的居民說："比爾‧克林頓是我們黑人唯一的一個總統，他就在我們家。"

加利福尼亞的伯克利是我離開父母家以后第一個可以稱之為家的地方。我在那里只住了三個月，但是我在那兒卻感覺自己是"多數族群"中的一員。這不是因為六十年代中期的伯克利有很多亞裔人，而是因為那里的人都希望別人把自己看作是一個真正的"少數族群"中的一個獨立的個體成員。那段時間，我不需要跟母親匯報我在做什么、我有什么感受。跟母親的那種聊天是份"工作"，所以我只有在父母家以外才能覺得輕松悠閑。父母在世的時候，每當我在他們面前把父母家以外的地方也稱為"家"時，我就會有一種不孝之感。

我妹妹三三 1962 年來美國的時候就沒有這種麻煩。雖然我們對她來說都是陌生人，但是新澤西州一下子就成了她的"家"。然而她在"家"里沒有什么悠閑的時刻，因為到 1965 年，她已經從只會唱"A, B, C, D……"到通過美國大學入學考試（SAT），并進入大學讀書。在此期間，我姐姐結婚時，我和她充當了四個伴娘中的兩個。婚禮的場面極其壯觀：八個伴郎，一千多來賓。記得我們彩排退場那一段，三三總是挽錯伴郎的手，因為他們都是白人，看起來一個模樣。為了避免走道上可能造成的擁擠，她的伴郎特意佩戴不同顏色的胸花以幫助三三識別，這樣她只需分辨花的顏色，而不是人的面孔。

---

[14] Although I realize that it is unlikely that governments or even adults—whether numerically in the majority or minority—will ever be "color-blind" when it comes to not seeing people, including themselves, in terms of visible differences, I am heartened by the fact that young children only notice them after they are taught to do so.

每當我對某個 "少數族群" 中的一員感到不耐煩甚或有點氣憤時，我就會想起那朵胸花。那一年三三真有點忙 —— 她得學習怎么拼寫英語字母、怎么使用洗髮水、怎么乘坐公共汽車，更不用說怎么從常常吃不飽到適應如何從豐富的食物中挑選自己喜歡吃的東西。她因為那么忙，所以幾乎沒有時間去研究、區分白種人的不同面孔特征。通過這個教訓，也為了給大家增添樂趣，每當我家舉行擁有男女老少、不同膚色、各行各業近兩百人的大型聚會時，來客一進家門就會在醒目的地方看到我做的一張雙關語的指示牌：

莊子說:

不戴孔老夫子面具, [15]

佩戴尊姓大名標簽

以此確保不丢臉面!!!

---

[15] Here is a double pun on "mask Confucian." "mask" (something that hides the face) for "mass"; "Confucian" for "confusion."

练习　EXERCISES

I. 思考和课堂讨论　FOOD FOR THOUGHT

A. PERSONAL　个人的

描述你充当"少数族群"的一个经历。

Describe a time you felt "in the minority." What were the circumstances? What, if anything, did you do about it? Did it make a difference in how you felt?

B. GENERAL　普遍的

An "argument" or line of reasoning is logical when a conclusion is validly deduced from premises that are assumed to be true. However, when there is an error in reasoning, then a fallacy occurs. In order to think clearly and effectively, it helps to know about these errors. After reading the following, discuss the question posed.

当某一结论是从一个正确的前提演绎出来的，那么该结论的论据符合逻辑。但是，如果推理出现错误，就会产生谬论。为了清楚、有效地思考，有必要了解这些推理错误。请阅读下面的错误，然后讨论所提出的问题。

> **appeal to fear** or threat of **force** is from the Latin *argumentum ad baculum* (*argumentum* = "argument"; *ad* = "to"; *baculum* = "stick, staff").
>
> **pattern:** Ms. Y argues for the truth of her conclusion; Mr. X threatens Ms. Y and/or her supporters with harmful results if they don't agree with him by disagreeing with her.
>
> **example:** *Instead of presenting physical or eye-witness evidence to the jury proving beyond a reasonable doubt that Ms. Y had in fact murdered the victim, Mr. X argues* **ad baculum** *by appealing to the jurors' fear of being harmed by saying, "If you want to be safe, you have to put murderers like Ms. Y in jail."*
>
> **question:** Why is Mr. X's fallacious approach often effective but still logically irrelevant? How is this approach similar to the idea that "might makes right" or "strong-arm" tactics or bullying"?

C. CROSS-CULTURAL　跨文化的

After reading the following, discuss <u>in Chinese</u> how the internet has confirmed what Pop Artist, Andy Warhol said in 1968, "In the future everyone will be famous for fifteen minutes."

阅读以下短文，并<u>用中文</u>对所提出的问题进行讨论。

> People like feeling special. Years ago, Forest Lawn MemorialParks & Mortuaries became a draw. Then and now, it is a company that charges an arm and a leg to embalm, cremate, and bury the dead. As a result, the company became associated with the socially elite (meaning wealthy) clientele of southern California. Ordinary people liked the idea of rubbing elbows with the rich, especially Hollywood movie stars—even if they were dead **!!!** However, just being buried there was not enough—after all, how much fun can it be if you're dead too **!!!** So people started holding their weddings there. Now Forest Lawn attracts the living with a museum that exhibits copies of "famous" art from Michelangelo marble statues to Walt Disney cartoons as well as

holds special events for children and educational shows. It is hard to imagine a Chinese daughter in California taking her traditional grandmother to Forest Lawn for a birthday party **!!!**

II. 配对 **MATCHMAKER**

A. VOCABULARY 词汇

找出以下两列中的对应词，并在其间划线。

Draw a connecting line between the word and its correct definition.

a.	白种人	1.	bridesmaid
b.	使……下船, 使……登陆	2.	groomsman
c.	可笑地，嘲弄地	3.	boutonnière
d.	战争老兵	4.	debark
e.	胸花	5.	Harlem
f.	伴郎	6.	derisively
g.	乡愁, 怀旧之情	7.	ex-GIs
h.	伴娘	8.	Caucasian
i.	鲜艳的	9.	nostalgia
j.	哈莱姆	10.	daring

a.	body language	1.	醒目
b.	eye-catching, attractive	2.	说起
c.	label, tag	3.	在某种程度上
d.	men, women, old and young	4.	一举一动
e.	mask	5.	标签
f.	care about	6.	双关语
g.	mention	7.	纪录，分钟
h.	to some extent	8.	凭空地，突如其来地，没有任何联系地
i.	pun, a play upon words	9.	面具
j.	minutes	10.	在乎
k.	apropos of nothing	11.	男女老少

155

B. ANTONYMS & ALTERNATES 反义词和多义词

First draw a connecting line between the words or phrases in the left-hand column with the best possible <u>antonym</u> listed in the middle column, then draw a line between the antonym and an alternate meaning of the antonym listed in the right-hand column. <u>Be forewarned</u> that the part of speech may change from one column to the next and that slang terms may be used. E.g.,

"hit" —————————— *"miss"* ————— *"honorific for unmarried female"*

"warm" —————————— *"cool"* ————— *"excellent"*

首先在第二列中找出与第一列相对应的反义词，然后在第三列中找出与第二列相关的多义词。注意：词性会有变化。

	ANTONYMS	ALTERNATE MEANING
a. experienced	1. **wax**	i. slightly cooked meat
b. secondary, ancillary	2. **salty**	ii. not dried or fired wood, clay
c. unimportant, minor	3. **green**	iii. of legal age to vote, drive, etc.
d. plentiful, ordinary	4. **major**	iv. ocean, high sea
e. wane, grow smaller	5. **rare**	v. grow, become fuller
f. front	6. **clean**	vi. bet on
g. an unbroken length of sth.	7. **joint**	vii. witty, racy, sharp
h. rough, irregular	8. **main**	viii. honorable, innocent
i. touch with a heavy hand	9. **back**	ix. unconvincing, glib, facile
j. sweet	10. **pat**	x. *slang* a marijuana cigarette

III. 解字/词、构字/词 DECONSTRUCTION & CONSTRUCTION

A. 将以下汉字分解成最小的构字部件，然后用每个部件构成三个汉字。例如"鸭"可以分解成 "甲" 和 "鸟" 两个部件。"甲" 能构成 "押"， "岬"， "钾"；"鸟" 可以构成以 "鸡"， "鸦"， "鸣"。请借助字典完成练习。

Deconstruct the following characters into the smallest components, then form 3 new characters using each component.

瑰_____ 朵_____ 宾_____

贫_____ 望_____ 随_____

B. Using only the letters of the word "**DERISIVELY**," form English words that are not proper nouns, abbreviations, or acronyms and that consist of 4 or more letters. A letter can only be used again if it appears in the given word more than once. E.g., "dime" is not acceptable because there is no "m" and "lively" is not because there is only one "l." Like many Olympic

sports, weight categories mark performance. We filled in a few cells to get you started. Fill in the rest to achieve the highest category. If you think up more than 81, you beat the authors!

用 "DERISIVELY" 中的字母构词。新构建的词不能是专有名词、缩写词、或首字母缩略词。每个单词必须至少含有四个字母，但不能重复使用同一字母，除非该字母在 "DERISIVELY" 中出现两次。

CHAMPION STATUS								
FLY 9	BANTAM 18	FEATHER 27	LIGHT 36	WELTER 45	MIDDLE 54	LGT HEAVY 63	HEAVY 72	SUPER 81
deer	sire							
dire	sired							
dive								

C. 用 "少数族群" 中的每个汉字组成不同的词。看看最多能组多少个词。

Use each of the characters in "少数族群" to form as many words (of 2-4 characters) as you can.

D. Pair any two of the following 10 words to form at least 12 different, unhyphenated words.

在下列十个词中配对、组词，新组的词只能含有两个单词，中间没有连字号。请至少组出十二个词。

horse side clothes man top hair tree long way line

IV. 阅读理解 READING QUIZ

根据课文，选择准确答案。Based on the text, choose the best answer.

1. 为什么作者去中国前买了一堆色彩鲜艳的衣服？

    a. 因为她以前穿的都是黑色的衣服，现在想换一换颜色。

    b. 因为中国人喜欢穿大红大绿的衣服，她去中国要入乡随俗。

    c. 因为中国人喜欢穿深绿色的衣服，她去中国希望有所不同。

    d. 因为中国人很多，鲜艳的衣服可以使她在人群中醒目一点。

2. 为什么许多老兵看到作者常常会跟她炫耀他们战争年代去过东方的经历？

    a. 因为作者是亚洲人，她的相貌使他们想起从前 。

    b. 因为作者说中国话，他们很想跟她练习说中文。

    c. 因为他们非常伤感，想找一个人讲讲从前的事。

    d. 因为他们没有朋友，想找一个人说说话。

3. 在美国学习过的亚洲学生，回到自己的国家后，常常被别人看作 "少数族群"。以下哪个方面可以说明他们跟原先的朋友有所不同？

    a. 他们的穿着打扮。

    b. 他们的语言用词。

    c. 他们的走路姿势。

    d. 他们的聊天话题。

    e. 以上都是。

4. 为什么前总统克林顿把办公室设在纽约市的哈莱姆非裔-美国人社区？

    a. 因为他想争取非裔-美国人。

    b. 因为他想讨好非裔-美国人。

    c. 因为他想吸引非裔-美国人。

    d. 作者没有解释。

5. 为什么作者的妹妹三三在婚礼彩排的时候总是挽错男傧相的膀子？

    a. 因为一共有八个伴郎，看起来都很帅。

    b. 因为一共有八个伴郎，看起来都很白。

    c. 因为一共有八个伴郎，看起来都一样。

    d. 因为一共有八个伴郎，看起来都像模特儿。

6. 什么是"少数族群"？

    a. "少数族群"指伴娘伴郎。

    b. "少数族群"指男女老少。

    c. "少数族群"指婚礼来宾。

    d. "少数族群"指海外游客。

    e. "少数族群"与"多数族群"相对而言,指占总人数中一小部分的一个群体。

V. 填空 FILL IN THE BLANK

A. 选择正确答案。Choose the correct answer.

1. 我们开始被成群结队的游客挤散了，后来我们才重新_____。

    a. 会面　　　　　　b. 会见　　　　　c. 会合

2. 有的人不愿意在公共场所讨论自己的信仰，因为那是一个有争议的_____。

    a. 话题　　　　　　b. 考题　　　　　c. 问题

3. 虽然你长得跟中国人一样，但是你的_____就像一个美国人。

    a. 一颦一笑　　　　b. 一唱一和　　　c. 一举一动

4. 她认不出谁是他的伴郎，因为她无法区分白种人的不同_____。

    a. 面部表情　　　　b. 庐山面目　　　c. 面孔特征

5. 大家都_____别人把自己看作是一个真正、独立的个体。

    a. 期望　　　　　　b. 展望　　　　　c. 探望

6. 那位伴郎_____佩戴不同颜色的胸花以帮助三三识别。

    a. 特别　　　　　　b. 特殊　　　　　c. 特地

B. Using your target language, write a word or phrase from the vocabulary lists and/or dictionary that means the <u>same</u> or is a <u>synonym</u> for the italicized word or phrase. Keep in mind that the part of speech and/or tense may have been adjusted to achieve grammatically correct results.

在以下段落中找出与斜体词意义相近的同义词。如果你所学的外语是中文，找出相应的中文词或短语。如果你所学的外语是英语，找出相应的英语词或短语。注意：词性或时态会有变化。

> When she smelled the *soap used to wash her hair* _____, she *suddenly and unexpectedly* _____ thought about her childhood and, *with great fondness, remembered* _____ her mother's flower garden as if only *sixty seconds* _____ had passed, not sixty years.

VI. 翻译 TRANSLATION

A. 将以下句子翻译成英文。Translate the following sentences into English.

1. 没错，那个时候的中国，虽然柔软的绒布裙子替代了毛式的制服，但是除了深绿色以外，我们很少看到其它鲜艳的颜色。

2. 这种经验可能令人生畏，但又令人振奋；可能让人疲乏不堪、但也使人精力旺盛。

3. 自愿外出旅行的学生追寻成为"少数族群"的经历，学习如何用自己毫不熟悉的语言跟外国人交流。

B. Translate the following sentences into Chinese. 将以下句子翻译成中文。

1. I could have found you no matter what you wore. Even in this crowd, your body language is completely American.

2. Asian students studying in the U.S. have also discovered they can be a member of the "minority" when they return home, even after only one semester.

3. Taking this lesson seriously, I facilitate fun and function whenever we host a large party when almost two hundred people of all ages, genders, ethnicities, and vocations arrive.

VII. 完型填充　CLOZE TEST

A. 在以下短文的每一空格处填入一个汉字，如有可能，给出相应的英语单词。

Fill in a Chinese character that retains the original meaning or intent of the text, then write an English equivalent, if any.

加利福尼亚的伯克利是我离开父母_____以后第一个可_____称之为家的地_____。我在那里只住_____三个月，但是我_____那儿却感觉自_____是"多数族群"中_____一员，这不是因_____六十年代中期_____伯克利有很多_____裔人，而是因为_____里的人都希望_____人把自己看作_____一个真正的"少_____族群"中的一个_____立的个体成员。

B. Fill in an English word or phrase that retains the original meaning or intent of the text, then write a Chinese equivalent, if any.

在以下短文的每一空格处填入一个英语单词，如有可能，给出相应的汉字或词。

My first home-away-from-home was _____ Berkeley, California. I lived there for three _____ but I felt "in the majority"—not _____ there were many Asians there in the mid- _____ but because people *expected* each person to _____ truly individual as a "minority of one." _____, I could say less about what I _____ doing and feeling to my mother: Conversing _____ her became "work" and I was better _____ to relax when elsewhere. Yet, even then, _____ my parents were alive, every time I _____ *jiā* or "home" to them, I felt _____ disloyal if I was referring to some _____ other than their house.

My younger sister, _____, didn't feel similarly when she arrived _____ the U.S. in 1962, at age seventeen. _____, *jiā* was in New Jersey even _____ we were strangers to her.

VIII. 身体部位　BODY PARTS

A. There are many useful idioms which contain "body parts." Choose the most appropriate to fill in the blank based on your best guess of what the idiom means.

英语中的许多习惯用语含有表示"身体部位"的单词。在下面三个习惯用语中选择最恰当的填空。

    1. bleeding heart liberals   **2.** heart and soul   **3.** heart of darkness

In 1902, Joseph Conrad's novel, _____, presented the idea that beneath the appearance of civilized behavior can be a capacity for horrible or brutal violence.

People who think that the government should be responsive to the needs of those in society who are least able to care for themselves are often criticized as "_____."

To give your _____ to someone or some organization is to care deeply that the person or cause does well.

B. 将以下短文翻译成中文。注意：划线的词或短语与以上含有"身体部位"的习惯用语相对应。

Translate the following into Chinese, taking note that the underlined words or phrases correspond to the meaning of the above "body parts."

Because so many individuals don't care about people they don't know and/or have <u>a capacity to do great harm</u>, it is good that there are others who are <u>sensitive and responsive to the needs of all humanity</u>. Indeed, of these latter, there are people who devote their <u>whole being</u> to relieving the distress of the poor.

C. Using your target language, create sentence(s) containing the following three English idioms or their Chinese equivalents.

用以下短语分别造句。如果你所学的外语是中文，请用中文来做这个练习。如果你所学的外语是英语，请用英语来做这个练习。

    1. have a change of heart = 改变主意

    2. wear one's heart on one's sleeve = 心直，坦率

    3. in one's heart of hearts = 在内心深处

IX. 写作 PRÉCIS

用所学的外语总结课文。如果你用中文来写，请至少使用 450 个汉字，并用电脑打出摘要。如果你用英文来写，请不超过 300 个词。

Write a summary of this chapter in your target language. If writing in Chinese, use <u>more</u> than 450 characters; if writing in English, use <u>no more</u> than 300 words.

PART THREE

SHAPING A LIFE

WITH THE POSSIBILITIES AND TECHNIQUES

第三辑

塑造多姿多彩的生活

CHAPTER EIGHT

DEFINING A LIFE WITH LANGUAGE

When our son was a toddler, I bought shoes objectively identifying the "right" and "left." When my great aunt in Hong Kong heard William was walking, she sent shoes marked *guāi* and *guāi* to encourage his subjective development. The difference was indicative of how much language mattered in defining our world and selves.[13]

William got English from his father and Chinese from me. Although I had a tin ear for tones and the vocabulary of a child, I wanted him to be bilingual. Deciding that *any* Chinese was better than none at all, I made myself speak Chinese to him even though my brain thought in English.[14] I figured that it wouldn't be important if I couldn't hear or say the difference between "bald" and "rabbit," "mother" and "horse," and "ten" and "feces" **!!!**

Soon, it became habit—put me in front of a baby and, no matter what it looked like, I would speak Chinese. No one seemed to mind, including William. So, from the moment he was born, Bennett spoke one language to him while I used another. That was the simple rule. The reality was more complex: He got Chinese from my parents and most of their friends, English from my sisters, Bennett's family, and most passers-by. He overheard his parents converse only in English while witnessing his mother speak a polyglot to her parents and Chinese to the babies of those same passers-by.

It didn't occur to me to wonder what was going on in William's brain until, one night, sitting in his highchair, he asked for *bǐnggān*. I explained in my usual Chinese that he could have a "sweet biscuit" after he ate his dinner. Dissatisfied, he again said, "*Bǐnggān*." And I again explained the procedure of first eating his meal before getting dessert. Another "*bǐnggān*" brought him yet another lesson on good nutrition.

13若想了解这一题材的详情，请参阅 Richard E. Nisbett 的著作《思维的地理：亚洲及西方人的不同思维及其原因》（*The Geography of Thought: How Asians and Westerners Think Differently...and Why*）。该书由 The Free Press 2003 年出版。

14由于人的情感和感官先于抽象思维，所以当我在英语中找不到可以确切表达某种感觉的词的时候，我常常自然而然地会使用中文。比如，用"酸"来表示肌肉的疼痛感，用"稀饭"来描述煮烂的、但米粒仍保持原状且透明的食物。

第八章

语言塑造生活

当我儿子威廉初学走路时，我给他买的鞋子都有"左"、"右"的标记。我在香港的姨婆给我从香港寄来的鞋子都有"乖"、"乖"的标记。很明显，母语对我们的生活以及自身的成长起了很大的作用。[16]

威廉跟他父亲学说英语，跟我学说中文。虽然我的听觉不太灵，要听清小孩的声调和发音有点吃力，但是，我还是希望威廉将来能够使用中、英文这两种不同的语言。我认为会说一点中文比一点都不会要好，所以尽管我常常用英文思考问题，但我还是规定自己一定得用中文跟威廉说话。[17] 我发现，即使我听不清或说不清"秃子"和"兔子"、"妈"和"马"、"十"和"屎"之间的差异，也不重要。

我们家很快就养成了这么一个习惯：在小孩子面前，不管是谁，我都说中文。家里的其他人包括威廉在内都不反对这样做。威廉从生下来的那一刻起，班尼特就跟他说一种语言，而我则跟他说另一种语言。这条规则很简单，但是现实生活远比这复杂得多。我父母以及他们的朋友跟威廉说中文，我的姐妹、班尼特家人以及其他人跟威廉说英文。威廉发现，他的父母亲之间只用英文会话，而他母亲跟她的父母亲，却是中、英文双管齐下，跟别人的小孩子则一律都用中文。

威廉对此会想些什么，我一直没有琢磨过。直到有一天晚上，他坐在高脚椅子（一种小孩吃饭时坐的、带有一个小桌面的椅子）里，喊着要"饼干"。我用中文跟他解释，让他吃了晚饭以后再吃"甜饼干"。他不高兴，就是要"饼干"，我又给他讲先吃饭再吃甜食的道理。结果他还是要"饼干"，而我还是给他讲营养学的大道理。

---

[16] For more on this subject, read *The Geography of Thought: How Asians and Westerners Think Differently…and Why* by Richard E. Nisbett, The Free Press 2003.

[17] Since our emotions and senses precede abstract thought, I naturally reverted to Chinese when an English word did not readily convey a feeling or texture—like "suān" for the "sourness" of a sore muscle or "xīfàn" to describe the delicacy of each grain of rice that would retain its shape yet be delicately translucent.

Huffing a sigh of exasperation, he leaned his elbow on the highchair tray and locked me in place with his eyes. Squaring his tiny jaw and concentrating his brow, he snorted out a quick puff of air, signaling to me that this was my last chance so I better pay close attention. Then he slowly, deliberately, sounded out, as if to some foreigner, "*Cook-ie?*" **!!!**

He didn't speak another English word to me until he was three years old. Then, for the first time, I drove him to school, dropped him off, and went back to my car. In the parking lot, I danced toward the old '71 Subaru. Clicking my heels in the air, I sang out "Free at last! free at last!" **!!!**[15]

Hours later, I returned to that marvelous invention—Day Care **!!!** Seeing him at his desk, I asked, "Wǒmen huí jiā, hǎobuhǎo?"

Looking up, he stated, rather than asked, "Yes, Māma. But I come back tomorrow…yes?"

I was startled. Up until that moment, he spoke English only to his father. He seemed to have paused before forming the last word so I couldn't tell if it was because he was hesitant about leaving. Or how to talk to me. But William had ended his sentence with a "yes?" Without the query, it would have been a political statement, an Emancipation Proclamation. No matter that he was a child who had just been toilet-trained **!!!**—this was the United States.

Driving home, reverting to Chinese, we talked. The Chinese words I (and therefore he) knew were good enough to discuss simple activities. Thus arithmetic and body parts from the neck up or thigh down were no problem **!!!** If I could keep it going until William needed to talk about algebra or sex, he would be bilingual. But that night, sitting at the table in our country kitchen, William announced, in the language of his new peers and in a peremptory tone that I would never have used on my mother, "I speak *English*."

Quietly I responded, in Chinese, "Yes, *and* you speak Chinese."

Even more emphatically, he declared, "I speak *English*."

Not content with Emancipation, he wanted Independence as well. Was this how it would start? After only one day in school? Should I continue in Chinese the way my mother did? Should I, like her, seem to ignore the linguistic line in the cultural sand? Or should I deliver some cut-down version (which was all I could manage in Chinese) of the lecture I had subjected myself to since college, the one that starts out with "I wish I'd paid better attention when I was a child, then I could speak my native language more fluently now that I realize the importance of…"? A second later, without

---

[15]这是马丁•路德金 (Martin Luther King) 于 1963 年 8 月 28 日在华盛顿特区的林肯纪念堂发表的"我有一个梦"演说中的最后一句。第二年美国国会通过了民权法案，同年马丁•路德金获得了诺贝尔和平奖。

这时威廉叹了一口气，不耐烦地把右手肘放在高脚椅子的桌面上，两眼紧紧地盯着我。接着他拉长了下巴，锁着眉头，哼了一声，暗示这可是我最后一次机会，我得听着。然后他用英文慢慢地、故意地、一个音节一个音节地说出了"Cook -ie"这个词，他那样子好像是跟外国人说话似的。

威廉第二次用英语跟我说话是三岁。那是我第一次开车送他上学，到了学校我把他放下后，就回到车里。当我在停车场踩着舞步走向我那辆1971年的Subaru车时，我兴奋地边跳边唱，"终于解放了！终于解放了！"

几个小时后，我又回到了托儿所（在当时真是一个了不起的发明**!!!**）。威廉坐在桌子边，我问他，"我们回家，好不好？"

威廉抬头看着我，用英文并以一种陈述而不是询问的语气说，"好，妈妈，我明天再来这儿，是吧？"

我很惊讶，因为在这之前，威廉只跟他父亲说英文。这是他第一次用英文跟我说话。他停了一下才把最后的一个词说了出来。开始，我没明白威廉是因为不想离开托儿所才这么吞吞吐吐地说话还是因为他还不知道怎么用英文跟我说话。但是，他的句子是以"是吧"结尾的。要是没有一点询问的口气，那就是一个政治声明，一个解放宣言。尽管威廉还是个小孩，刚学会怎样上厕所，但是他已经宣布要做什么了。这就是美国啊**!!!**

开车回家的路上，我们又用中文聊天。我知道的中文单词也是威廉知道的单词，那些词汇足以让我们讨论简单的事项。所以聊一些简单的算术和象脖子以上或大腿以下的身体部位的话题，我们的词汇都绰绰有余。要是当初我坚持让威廉说中文，让他以后知道怎么用中文谈论代数或性方面的话题的话，那么今大他就是一个不错的中、英文双语者了。可是那天晚上，坐在我家乡村厨房的饭桌旁，威廉用他刚刚结识的朋友的语言，用一种我从来敢对我母亲使用过的专横的语气宣布，"我说英语。"

我平静地用中文回答说："好啊，但你也说中文。"

他更坚定地宣布，"我说英语。"

威廉不仅要解放，而且还要独立。他这就开始独立了吗？他可是才上了第一天的学呀？我是否应该象我母亲对我们那样坚持用中国式的方法教育他？我是否应该象我母亲那

having to explain a lifetime of reasons, I told his father, "Bennett, take him to Chinatown after school tomorrow."

The next day, Bennett and William admired the pressed ducks hanging in windows. After going into one store to buy a little jar of balm, its golden lid embossed with a leaping tiger, and another to select six different kinds of steamed dumplings, after hours of being with people who looked and spoke like his mother, they returned in the evening. Showing me his treasures, William trumpeted, "I'm half Chinese."

"Yes," I said, gratified that the visual impact had done what words could not. And then, out of curiosity, inquired, "Do you know what the other half is?" No answer. He was stumped.

But not for long. Gradually but inextricably, we both lapsed into English—the language of schoolmates, of teachers, of power, of my ideas but not all my emotions, of his choice but not all his values. If I wanted to teach beyond a second grade level, it had to be in English, the language I think in. Yet I wondered, without the words or phrases of my childhood, could William understand that part of me which still feels some experiences in Chinese? Would attending Chinese School on the weekends be enough?

VOCABULARY

tin ear	n.p.	incapable of hearing some sounds.	听觉不灵的耳朵	tīngjué bùlíng de ěrduo
feces	n.	waste discharged from the bowels, excrement.	屎	shǐ
passer-by	n.	someone, usually a stranger, who (coincidentally) walks by.	过路人	guòlùrén
huff	v.	to audibly puff or breathe out.	吹	chuī
exasperation	n.	extreme irritation, annoyance.	恼怒	nǎonù
square	v.	to firmly set (the jaw, shoulders, etc.) to indicate determination and serious intent.	拉长下巴	lācháng xiàba
click one's heels in the air	v.p.	to jump high and, while in the air, to bend both legs to the side so the heels can touch to signal joy, happiness, exuberance.	兴奋地跳起来	xīngfèn de tiàoqǐlái

样对我们各自使用不同语言这个事实视而不见？我是否应该用简单的中文，也是我有限的中文给他讲讲我自从进了大学以后就不断聆听的教训："早知道中文这么重要，我小时候真应该认真学习，这样我就可以更熟练地运用我的母语"。我没有跟他讲那么多的大道理，过了一会儿，我对他父亲说，"班尼特，明天放学后带他去趟中国城。"

第二天，班尼特和威廉在中国城的大街上欣赏着一个个倒挂在餐馆橱窗里的板鸭，进了一家商店买了一小盒万金油，万金油圆盒子的金色盖子上印着一只跳跃的老虎，后来又进了一家餐馆吃了六种不同馅的包子。在中国城里，威廉看到很多长着和他母亲一样肤色、说着跟他母亲一样语言的人。他们在那逛了几个小时才回家。那天晚上威廉给我看他的宝贝东西，并自豪地宣称，"我是半个中国人"。

"是啊"，我说。 这一个下午的所见所闻就对威廉起了这么大的作用，而且这种视觉影响是语言文字无法类比的。我很高兴，然后好奇地问他，"那你知道你另外半个是什么人吗？" 威廉没有回答我，因为他不知道该说什么。

没过多久，我和威廉渐渐地、不可避免地都说起了英语——威廉的同学、老师和权力机构使用的语言，我表达自己观点的语言（虽然它不能表达我全部的感情），威廉选择的语言（虽然它不能表达他全部的价值观）。要是我想教威廉二年级以上的知识，我必须用英语，因为那是我思考所用的语言。然而我想，如果威廉没有学会我童年的中文词汇，他能理解我身上的中国烙印吗？仅仅在周末上上中文学校就能理解双元文化吗？

生词

塑造	塑造	sùzào	v.	shape, mold, portray
鞋子	鞋子	xiézi	n.	shoe
乖	乖	guāi	adj.	being well-behaved
标记	標記	biāojì	n.	label
听觉	聽覺	tīngjué	n.	sense of hearing
灵	靈	líng	adj.	quick, alert
听清	聽清	tīngqīng	v (c)	understand
秃子	秃子	tūzi	n.	a bald person
屎	屎	shǐ	n.	feces, shit

Emancipation Proclamation	p.n.	an announcement of freedom like the document issued by President Abraham Lincoln on January 1, 1863. As the U.S. approached its third year of bloody civil war, this document declared "that all persons held as slaves" within the rebellious states "are, and henceforward shall be free."	解放宣言	Jiěfàng xuānyán
in a peremptory tone	p.p.	in a commanding or unconditional way that precludes opposition or counter-argument.	以专横的语气	yǐ zhuānhèng de yǔqì
balm	n.	something that soothes, eases pain, or heals; originally an ointment from a plant.	香油，药膏	xiāngyóu, yàogāo
emboss	v.	to print or decorate so the image is raised from the surface.	作成浮雕，以浮雕装饰	zuò chéng fúdiāo, yǐ fúdiāo zhuāngshì
stump	v.	to render completely at a loss (for words or response), nonplus, fluster, cause puzzlement. Also – n. the base of a tree after the upper portion has been cut off.	被……难住	bèi … nánzhù
inextricably	adv.	in a way that is so hopelessly intricate, complicated, tangled, or involved that it cannot be undone or avoided.	分不开地，不可避免地	fēnbùkāi de, bùkě-bìmiǎn de
lapse (into)	v.p.	to fall, sink, or return to a previous (lesser) state or standard; to fail to maintain a (higher) state or standard.	陷入	xiànrù

170

家里	家裡	jiālǐ	n.	at home
对此	對此	duìcǐ	p.p.	pertaining to this
反对	反對	fǎnduì	v.	object
姐妹	姐妹	jiěmèi	n.	sisters
双管齐下	雙管齊下	shuāngguǎn-qíxià	f.c.w.	do two things simultaneously
高脚椅	高脚椅	gāojiǎoyǐ	n.	high chair
甜食	甜食	tiánshí	n.	dessert
营养学	營養學	yíngyǎngxué	n.	nutrition
肘	肘	zhǒu	n.	elbow
两眼	兩眼	liǎngyǎn	n.	(two) eyes
下巴	下巴	xiàba	n.	chin, lower jaw
音节	音節	yīnjié	n.	syllable
舞步	舞步	wǔbù	n.	dance steps
解放	解放	jiěfàng	v.	be free, emancipate
托儿所	托兒所	tuō'érsuǒ	n.	day care
陈述	陳述	chénshù	v.	state, explain
询问	詢問	xúnwèn	v.	ask, inquire
吞吞吐吐	吞吞吐吐	tūntūn-tǔtǔ	f.c.w.	speak hesitantly
结尾	結尾	jiéwěi	v.o.	end, wind up
声明	聲明	shēngmíng	n.	statement
宣言	宣言	xuānyán	n.	proclamation
宣布	宣布	xuānbù	v.	announce
聊天	聊天	liáotiān	v.o.	chat
事项	事項	shìxiàng	n.	item, matter
算术	算術	suànshù	n.	arithmetic
脖子	脖子	bózi	n.	neck
大腿	大腿	dàtuǐ	n.	thigh
绰绰有余	綽綽有餘	chuòchuò-yǒuyú	f.c.w.	more than enough
代数	代數	dàishù	n.	algebra
双语者	雙語者	shuāngyǔzhě	n.	bilingual
结识	結識	jiéshí	v.	get acquainted with sb.
专横	專橫	zhuānhèng	adj.	peremptory
独立	獨立	dúlì	v.	be independent
中国式	中國式	zhongguóshì	adj.	Chinese style
视而不见	視而不見	shì'érbùjiàn	f.c.w.	turn a blind eye to, look but (deliberately) not see
不断	不斷	bùduàn	adv.	continuously
聆听	聆聽	língtīng	v.	listen respectfully
教训	教訓	jiàoxùn	n.	lesson, lecture
小时候	小時候	xiǎoshíhou	n.	in one's childhood, when one was young
趟	趟	tàng	m (v)	a verbal measure word indicating the frequency of

第八章

語言塑造生活

當我兒子威廉初學走路時，我給他買的鞋子都有"左"、"右"的標記。我在香港的姨婆給我從香港寄來的鞋子都有"乖"、"乖"的標記。很明顯，母語對我們的生活以及自身的成長起了很大的作用。[16]

威廉跟他父親學説英語，跟我學説中文。雖然我的聽覺不太靈，要聽清小孩的聲調和發音有點吃力，但是，我還是希望威廉將來能夠使用中、英文這兩種不同的語言。我認為會説一點中文比一點都不會要好，所以盡管我常常用英文思考問題，但我還是規定自己一定得用中文跟威廉説話。[17] 我發現，即使我聽不清或説不清"秃子"和"兔子"、"媽"和"馬"、"十"和"屎"之間的差异，也不重要。

我們家很快就養成了這么一個習慣：在小孩子面前，不管是誰，我都説中文。家里的其他人包括威廉在内都不反對這樣做。威廉從生下來的那一刻起，班尼特就跟他説一種語言，而我則跟他説另一種語言。這條規則很簡單，但是現實生活遠比這復雜得多。我父母以及他們的朋友跟威廉説中文，我的姐妹、班尼特家人以及其他人跟威廉説英文。威廉發現，他的父母親之間只用英文會話，而他母親跟她的父母親，卻是中、英文雙管齊下，跟別人的小孩子則一律都用中文。

威廉對此會想些什么，我一直沒有琢磨過。直到有一天晚上，他坐在高脚椅子（一種小孩吃飯時坐的、帶有一個小桌面的椅子）里，喊着要"餅干"。我用中文跟他解釋，讓他吃了晚飯以后再吃"甜餅干"。 他不高興，就是要"餅干"，我又給他講先吃飯再吃甜食的道理。結果他還是要"餅干"，而我還是給他講營養學的大道理。

---

[16] For more on this subject, read *The Geography of Thought: How Asians and Westerners Think Differently…and Why* by Richard E. Nisbett, The Free Press 2003.

[17] Since our emotions and senses precede abstract thought, I did naturally revert to Chinese when an English word did not readily convey a feeling or texture—like "suān" for the "sourness" of a sore muscle or "xīfàn" to describe the delicacy of each grain of rice that would retain its shape yet be delicately translucent.

				going/coming
漫步	漫步	mànbù	v.o.	stroll, roam
欣赏	欣賞	xīnshǎng	v.	admire
倒挂	倒掛	dàoguà	v.	be hung upside
橱窗	櫥窗	chúchuāng	n.	show or display window
板鸭	板鴨	bǎnyā	n.	pressed duck
万金油	萬金油	wànjīnyóu	n	analgesic balm for muscle soreness, headache, etc.
金色	金色	jīnsè	n.	gold color
盖子	蓋子	gàizi	n.	lid
跳跃	跳躍	tiàoyuè	v.	leap
馅	餡	xiàn	n.	stuffing
逛	逛	guàng	v.	look around shops, stroll
自豪	自豪	zìháo	adj.	proud
宣称	宣稱	xuānchēng	v.	announce
所见所闻	所見所聞	suǒjiàn-suǒwén	f.c.w.	what one has seen and heard
视觉	視覺	shìjué	n.	vision
影响	影響	yǐngxiǎng	n.	impact
无法类比	無法類比	wúfǎ lèibǐ	f.c.w.	beyond analogy or comparison
不可避免	不可避免	bùkě-bìmiǎn	f.c.w.	inextricable
价值观	價值觀	jiàzhíguān	n.	value system
童年	童年	tóngnián	n.	childhood
烙印	烙印	làoyìn	n.	branding, lasting impression
中文学校	中文學校	zhōngwén xuéxiào	n.p.	Chinese school

這時威廉嘆了一口氣，不耐煩地把右手肘放在高腳椅子的桌面上，兩眼緊緊地盯着我。接着他拉長了下巴，鎖着眉頭，哼了一聲，暗示這可是我最后一次機會，我得聽着。 然后他用英文慢慢地、故意地、一個音節一個音節地説出了 "Cook -ie" 這個詞，他那樣子好像是跟外國人説話似的。

威廉第二次用英語跟我説話是三歲。那是我第一次開車送他上學，到了學校我把他放下后，就回到車里。當我在停車場踩着舞步走向我那輛 1971 年的 Subaru 車時，我興奮地邊跳邊唱，"終于解放了！終于解放了！"

幾個小時后，我又回到了托兒所（在當時真是一個了不起的發明!!!）。威廉坐在桌子邊，我問他，"我們回家，好不好？"

威廉抬頭看着我，用英文并以一種陳述而不是詢問的語氣説，"好，媽媽，我明天再來這兒，是吧？！"

我很驚訝，因為在這之前，威廉只跟他父親説英文。這是他第一次用英文跟我説話。他停了一下才把最后的一個詞説了出來。開始，我沒明白威廉是因為不想離開托兒所才這麼吞吞吐吐地説話還是因為他還不知道怎麼用英文跟我説話。但是，他的句子是以 "是吧" 結尾的。要是沒有一點詢問的口氣，那就是一個政治聲明，一個解放宣言。盡管威廉還是個小孩，剛學會怎樣上廁所，但是他已經宣布要做什麼了。這就是美國啊!!!

開車回家的路上，我們又用中文聊天。我知道的中文單詞也是威廉知道的單詞，那些詞匯足以讓我們討論簡單的事項。所以聊一些簡單的算術和象脖子以上或大腿以下的身體部位的話題，我們的詞匯都綽綽有余。要是當初我堅持讓威廉説中文，讓他以后知道怎麼用中文談論代數或性方面的話題的話，那麼今天他就是一個不錯的中、英文雙語者了。可是那天晚上，坐在我家鄉村廚房的飯桌旁，威廉用他剛剛結識的朋友的語言，用一種我從未敢對我母親使用過的專橫的語氣宣布，"我説英語。"

我平靜地用中文回答説："好啊，但你也説中文。"

他更堅定地宣布，"我説英語。"

威廉不僅要解放，而且還要獨立。他這就開始獨立了嗎？他可是才上了第一天的學呀？我是否應該象我母親對我們那樣堅持用中國式的方法教育他？我是否應該象我母親那樣對我們各自使用不同語言這個事實視而不見？我是否應該用簡單的中文，也是我有限的中文給他講講我自從進了大學以后就不斷聆聽的教訓：＂早知道中文這么重要，我小時候真應該認真學習，這樣我就可以更熟練地運用我的母語＂。我沒有跟他講那么多的大道理，過了一會兒，我對他父親說，＂班尼特，明天放學后帶他去趟中國城。＂

第二天，班尼特和威廉在中國城的大街上欣賞着一個個倒挂在餐館櫥窗里的板鴨，進了一家商店買了一小盒萬金油，萬金油圓盒子的金色蓋子上印着一只跳躍的老虎，后來又進了一家餐館吃了六種不同餡的包子。在中國城里，威廉看到很多長着和他母親一樣膚色、說着跟他母親一樣語言的人。他們在那逛了幾個小時才回家。那天晚上威廉給我看他的寶貝東西，并自豪地宣稱，＂我是半個中國人＂。

＂是啊＂，我說。這一個下午的所見所聞就對威廉起了這么大的作用，而且這種視覺影響是語言文字無法類比的。我很高興，然后好奇地問他，＂那你知道你另外半個是什么人嗎？＂威廉沒有回答我，因為他不知道該說什么。

沒過多久，我和威廉漸漸地、不可避免地都說起了英語——威廉的同學、老師和權力機構使用的語言，我表達自己觀點的語言（雖然它不能表達我全部的感情），威廉選擇的語言（雖然它不能表達他全部的價值觀）。要是我想教威廉二年級以上的知識，我必須用英語，因為那是我思考所用的語言。然而我想，如果威廉沒有學會我童年的中文詞匯，他能理解我身上的中國烙印嗎？僅僅在周末上上中文學校就能理解雙元文化嗎？

练习　EXERCISES

I. 思考和课堂讨论　FOOD FOR THOUGHT

A. PERSONAL　个人的

当你阅读、分析、计算、做数学题、表达感情或做梦的时候，你用什么语言思考？

What languages do you think in when reading, analyzing, calculating, doing mathematics, expressing strong emotions, dreaming, intuiting, etc.?

B. GENERAL　普遍的

An "argument" or line of reasoning is logical when a conclusion is validly deduced from premises that are assumed to be true. However, when there is an error in reasoning, then a fallacy occurs. In order to think clearly and effectively, it helps to know about these errors. After reading the following, discuss the question posed.

当某一结论是从一个正确的前提演绎出来的，那么该结论的论据符合逻辑。但是，如果推理出现错误，就会产生谬论。为了清楚、有效地思考，有必要了解这些推理错误。请阅读下面的错误，然后讨论所提出的问题。

appeal to pity is from the Latin *argumentum ad misericordiam (argumentum* = "argument"; *ad* = "to"; *misericordiam* = "mercy").

pattern: Mr. X argues for the truth of his conclusion; Ms. Y tries to evoke pity for the defendant so that the jury will feel sorry for the defendant and not wish to make his situation worse by finding him guilty.

example: Instead of presenting reasons for doubting Mr. X's case against her client, Ms. Y defends the teenager who is accused of murdering his parents by saying, "Have pity on this young orphan." **!!!**

question: Why is Ms. Y's fallacious approach often effective but still logically irrelevant? Does this approach mean we should never be merciful?

C. CROSS-CULTURAL　跨文化的

After reading the following, discuss in English the difference between an opinion that is "objective" and one that is "subjective."

阅读以下短文，并用英文对所提出的问题进行讨论。

Scientists have studied how and why people teach and learn language. Those who speak English tend to emphasize nouns. They call attention to objects by pointing and naming—"This is a fence." In doing so, categories of things with similar physical characteristics are important. E.g., "Fences made of wood can be burned." Those who speak an Asian language tend to emphasize verbs by calling attention to relationships between and among things. E.g., "The fence was built by Mr. Li to separate his property from mine." When students were shown pictures of a chicken, cow, and grass, and then asked to place two together, the English-speaking preferred to put the chicken and cow together as they both belong to the category of "animal," while the Asian-speaking preferred grouping the cow with the grass as they have a relationship of being eater and eaten. The vocabulary of those in Hong Kong who learned both English and Chinese as children were more evenly divided into nouns and verbs.

II. 配对 MATCHMAKER

A. VOCABULARY 词汇

找出以下两列中的对应词，并在其间划线。

Draw a connecting line between the word and its correct definition.

a.	分不开地, 不可避免地	1.	lapse into
b.	以专横的语气	2.	balm
c.	使……难住	3.	indicative of
d.	堕入，陷入	4.	stump
e.	指示的,象征的	5.	click one's heels in the air
f.	过路人	6.	in a peremptory tone
g.	恼怒	7.	tin ear
h.	兴奋地跳起来	8.	passer-by
i.	听觉不灵	9.	inextricably
j.	香油，药膏	10.	exasperation

a.	get acquainted with sb.	1.	暗示
b.	just begin to learn sth.	2.	初学
c.	dessert	3.	结识
d.	hesitate in speech	4.	大腿
e.	Chinese style	5.	童年
f.	thigh	6.	板鸭
g.	childhood	7.	中国式
h.	pressed duck	8.	作成浮雕, 以浮雕装饰
i.	drop a hint, suggest	9.	甜食
j.	emboss	10.	吞吞吐吐

B. SYNONYMS & ALTERNATES 同义词和多义词

First draw a connecting line between the word or phrase in the left-hand column with the best possible <u>synonym</u> listed in the middle column, then draw a line between the synonym and an alternate meaning of the synonym listed in the right-hand column. <u>Be forewarned</u> that the part of speech may change from one column to the next and that slang terms may be used. E.g.,

"hit" —————————————— "strike"————————— "stop-work action against employer"

"warm"—————————————— "heat" ——————— "qualifying race for final contest"

首先在第二列中找出与第一列相对应的同义词，然后在第三列中找出与第二列相关的多义词。注意：词性会有不同。

		SYNONYMS		ALTERNATE MEANING
a.	path, distance, space	1. **port**	i.	lessening of stress, pain, anxiety
b.	space to be filled in	2. **milk**	ii.	vassal, one who is under sb.'s authority
c.	lose blood, spread	3. **part**	iii.	feel pity, sorrow or sympathy
d.	extract liquid from	4. **relief**	iv.	without interest, emotion
e.	help for the needy	5. **subject**	v.	manner, condition, style
f.	theme, course of study	6. **must**	vi.	dividing line in hair
g.	shut with force and noise	7. **blank**	vii.	*slang* harsh criticism, verbally attack
h.	mold, moldiness	8. **bleed**	viii.	vital or necessary
i.	role in a play or movie	9. **way**	ix.	very sweet wine
j.	left-hand side of ship/vessel	10. **slam**	x.	*slang* exploit or drain other's assets

III. 解字/词、构字/词 DECONSTRUCTION & CONSTRUCTION

A. 将以下汉字分解成最小的构字部件，然后用每个部件构成三个汉字。例如"鸭"可以分解成 "甲" 和 "鸟" 两个部件。"甲" 能构成"押"，"岬"，"钾"；"鸟" 可以构成以"鸡"，"鸦"，"鸣"。请借助字典完成练习。

Deconstruct the following characters into the smallest components, then form 3 new characters using each component.

秃＿＿＿＿＿＿＿＿＿＿＿＿ 管＿＿＿＿＿＿＿＿＿＿＿＿ 陌＿＿＿＿＿＿＿＿＿＿＿＿

跟＿＿＿＿＿＿＿＿＿＿＿＿ 逛＿＿＿＿＿＿＿＿＿＿＿＿ 暗＿＿＿＿＿＿＿＿＿＿＿＿

B. Using only the letters of the word "**LAPSE**," form English words that are not proper nouns, abbreviations, or acronyms and that consist of 4 or more letters. A letter can only be used again if it appears in the given word more than once. E.g., "pole" is not acceptable because there is no "o" and "please" is not because there is only one "e." Like many Olympic sports, weight categories mark performance. We filled in a few cells to get you started. Fill in the rest to achieve the highest category. If you think up more than 16, you beat the authors!

用 "LAPSE" 中的字母构词。新构建的词不能是专有名词、缩写词、或首字母缩略词。每个单词必须至少含有四个字母，但不能重复使用同一字母，除非该字母在 "LAPSE" 中出现两次。

CHAMPION STATUS			
LIGHT 4	WELTER 8	MIDDLE 12	HEAVY 16
peal	plea	pale	leap

C. 用"中文学校"中的每个汉字组成不同的词。看看最多能组多少个词。

Use each of the characters in "中文学校" to form as many words (of 2-4 characters) as you can.

D. Pair any two of the following 10 words to form at least 13 different, unhyphenated words.

在下列十个词中配对、组词，新组的词只能含有两个单词，中间没有连字号。请至少组出十三个词。

keeper fast store stand house maker break book match hand

IV. 阅读理解 READING QUIZ

根据课文，选择准确答案。Based on the text, choose the best answer.

1. 为什么在美国买的鞋子有"左"、"右"的 标记，而在香港买的鞋子有"乖"、"乖"的标记？

    a. 这说明不同的语言决定不同的生活价值观。

    b. 这说明美国人对鞋子的标记比香港人的好。

    c. 这说明香港人对鞋子的标记比美国人的好。

    d. 这说明美国人和香港人对鞋子有不同看法。

2. 为什么作者在小孩子面前一律只说中文？

    a. 因为她要给儿子创造一个说中文的环境。

    b. 因为她要给儿子创造一个说英文的环境。

    c. 因为她希望所有的小孩子都学会说中文。

d. 因为她希望所有的小孩子都跟她学中文。

3. 作者教育儿子的方法跟她母亲教育她的方法有什么不同？

a. 作者没有坚持用中国式的方法教育儿子。

b. 作者用适合美国孩子的方法教育儿子。

c. 作者运用双语、双元文化教育儿子。

d. 以上都对。

4. 假如威廉跟一个能说中、英文的中国学生讨论数学，你认为他会用什么语言？

a. 中文。

b. 英文。

c. 香港话。

d. 中、英文。

5. 威廉第二次用英语说的话是以下哪一句？

a. "饼干"。

b. "好，妈妈，我明天再来这儿，是吧？！"

c. "我说英语"。

d. "我是半个中国人"。

6. 为什么威廉说他是半个中国人？

a. 因为他在中国城看到了挂在餐馆橱窗里的中国板鸭。

b. 因为他在中国城吃了六种不同馅的中国包子。

c. 因为他在中国城买了一盒中国生产的万金油。

d. 因为他在中国城看到了很多长得跟他母亲一样的中国人。

V. 填空 FILL IN THE BLANK

A. 选择正确答案。Choose the correct answer.

1. 这条规则很简单，但是_____生活远比这复杂得多。

    a. 现代   b. 现在   c. 现实

2. 因为我的听力不太好，所以要听懂小孩子说的话有点_____。

    a. 费力   b. 尽力   c. 用力

3. 威廉的母亲跟她的父母说话时，中文、英文_____。

    a. 一箭双雕   b. 一石二鸟   c. 双管齐下

4. 我给他讲了很多先吃饭再吃甜食的道理，＿＿＿＿＿＿他还是要"饼干"。

    a. 结果   b. 如果   c. 后果

5. 威廉哼了一声，＿＿＿＿＿＿我这可是我最后一次机会。

    a. 指示   b. 暗示   c. 表示

6. 没过多久，我们慢慢地、＿＿＿＿＿＿地都说起了英文。

    a. 不可思议   b. 不可避免   c. 不可或缺

B. 在以下段落中找出与斜体词意义相近的反义词。如果你所学的外语是中文，找出相应的中文词或短语。如果你所学的外语是英语，找出相应的英语词或短语。注意：词性或时态会有变化。

Using your target language, write a word or phrase from the vocabulary lists and/or dictionary that means the <u>opposite</u> or is an <u>antonym</u> for the italicized word or phrase. Keep in mind that the part of speech and/or tense may have been adjusted to achieve grammatically correct results.

    Not wishing to be an *irritant* ＿＿＿＿＿＿＿, the son did *persist* ＿＿＿＿＿＿＿but was still *patient and calm* ＿＿＿＿＿＿, when he said to his mother *in a pleading way* ＿＿＿＿＿, "I hope you agree that my singing demonstrates my *musical ability* ＿＿＿＿＿＿. Please, may I take lessons to develop my voice further?"

VI. 翻译 TRANSLATION

A. 将以下句子翻译成英文。Translate the following sentences into English.

1. 即使我听不清或说不清"秃子"和"兔子"、"妈"和"马"、"十"和"屎"之间的差异，也不重要。

2. 然后他用英文慢慢地、故意地、一个音节一个音节地的说出了"饼-干"这个词，他那样子好像是跟外国人说话似的。

3. 开始，我没明白威廉是因为不想离开托儿所才这么吞吞吐吐地说话还是因为他还不知道怎么用英文跟我说话。

B. Translate the following sentences into Chinese. 将以下句子翻译成中文。

1. Soon, it became habit—put me in front of a baby and, no matter what it looked like, I would speak Chinese.

2. But that night, sitting at the table in our country kitchen, William announced, in the language of his new peers and in a peremptory tone that I would never have used on my mother, "I speak *English.*"

3. Gradually but inextricably, we both lapsed into English—the language of schoolmates, of teachers, of power, of my ideas but not all my emotions, of his choice but not all his values.

VII. 完型填充　CLOZE TEST

A. 在以下短文的每一空格处填入一个汉字，如有可能，给出相应的英语单词。

Fill in a Chinese character that retains the original meaning or intent of the text, then write an English equivalent, if any.

威廉跟他父亲_____说英语，跟我学_____中文。虽然我的_____觉不太灵，要听_____小孩子的声调_____发音有点吃力，_____是，我还是希望威廉_____来能够使用中、_____文这两种不同_____语言。我认为会_____一点中文比什_____也不会要好，所_____尽管我常常用_____文思考问题，我 _____是规定自己一_____ 得用中文跟威廉说话。

B. Fill in an English word or phrase that retains the original meaning or intent of the text, then write a Chinese equivalent, if any.

在以下短文的每一空格处填入一个英语单词，如有可能，给出相应的汉字或词。

When our son was a toddler, I _____ shoes marked "right" and "left." When my _____ aunt in Hong Kong heard William was _____, she sent shoes marked "guai" and "guai." _____ difference was indicative of how much language _____ in shaping our lives and selves. William _____ English from his father and Chinese from _____. Although I had a tin ear for _____ and the vocabulary of a child, I _____ him to be bi-lingual. Deciding that *any* _____ was better than none at all, I _____ myself speak Chinese to him even though _____ brain thought in English. I figured that _____ wouldn't be important if I couldn't hear _____ say the difference between "bald" and "rabbit," "_____" and "horse," and "ten" and "feces" **!!!**

VIII. 身体部位　BODY PARTS

A. There are many useful idioms which contain "body parts." Choose the most appropriate to fill in the blank based on your best guess of what the idiom means.

英语中的许多习惯用语含有表示"身体部位"的单词。在下面三个习惯用语中选择最恰当的填空。

    1. no stomach for   **2.** cannot stomach   **3.** knot in the pit of sb.'s stomach

After only a few days of being a vegetarian, she said, "I _____ the sight of meat!"

After the men entered the dark cave, they heard the sound of a large animal growling and immediately broke out in a cold sweat and felt a _____.

After three miles of winding road, he said, "I have _____ driving in the country—the scenery is lovely but the dizzying motion makes it difficult for me to enjoy the experience."

B. 将以下短文翻译成中文。注意：划线的词或短语与以上含有"身体部位"的习惯用语相对应。

Translate the following into Chinese taking note that the underlined words or phrases correspond to the meaning of the above "body parts."

The man had <u>no desire to go</u> hunting because, having been a soldier, the sound of gun fire caused him to have a <u>case of nerves and tension</u> so he decided, "I <u>can't willingly do</u> this.

C. Using your target language, create sentence(s) containing the following three English idioms or their Chinese equivalents.

用以下短语分别造句。如果你所学的外语是中文，请用中文来做这个练习。如果你所学的外语是英语，请用英语来做这个练习。

1. spill one's guts = 把自己知道的一切原原本本地说出来，告密

2. gutless wonder = 没有勇气或不愿意面对困境

3. gutsy = 勇敢的

IX. 写作 PRÉCIS

用所学的外语总结课文。如果你用中文来写，请至少使用 450 个汉字，并用电脑打出摘要。如果你用英文来写，请不超过 350 个词。

Write a summary of this chapter in your target language. If writing in Chinese, use <u>more</u> than 450 characters; if writing in English, use <u>no more</u> than 350 words.

CHAPTER NINE

WEAVING A LIFE IN A WEB

The second time I escorted William to his classroom, I expected him to behave the same as he did the first day when he immediately went in and sat down. Like the day before, I gave him a hug and told him that I would see him later. Turning, I again walked through the phalanx of parents and children huddling and sobbing near the door, performing the "First Day at School Ritual" that is standard in North America. Feeling rather smug that we didn't need it, I was a few steps away when I heard, "Māma!" Going back through the crowd, I saw William standing by himself, arms at his side, tears rolling down his face.

"Zěnme la?"

"Nothing," he replied in his being-at-school language.

"Nà nǐ wèishénme kū ne?"

"I'm supposed to."

"Nǐ yīnggāi kū, zhè shì shénme yìsi?"

"Children cry when parents leave them at school."

As he continued crying, I asked, "Nǐ wèishénme juéde tāmen yīnggāi kū?"

"Because they're going to miss their mothers."

Happy he understood enough about their ritual to be concerned that I might need his tearful good-bye, I reassured him by stating the obvious in my Jewish accent **!!!** , "Nǐ zěnme huì xiǎng wǒ? "Wǒ bú jiù zài zhèr !"

"But I might. Later."

While his "later" gave me pause, I continued being practical, "Búhuìde, nǐ yìhuǐr jiù mángde méiyǒu shíjiān xiǎng wǒ le. Bù guǎn zěnyàng, nǐ xiān bié kū, yàobù bízi huì dǔsè de."

"Okay, Māma."

第九章

在蜘蛛网里

我第二次送威廉上学的时候，期望他跟第一天那样，马上走进教室坐下来。跟第一次一样，我拥抱了他一下，告诉他下课以后我再来接他。说完后我就转过身，从一群站在门口、抱在一起、哭哭啼啼的小孩及其父母身旁走过去，他们正重演"开学第一天的仪式"，那是北美学校的惯例。我和威廉没有那些麻烦，为此我觉得很庆幸。可是快走到门口时，我突然听到威廉喊，"妈妈"。我穿过人群走回去，看见威廉一个人站在那里，耷拉着两个膀了，眼泪从脸上滚了下来。

"怎么啦？"

"没什么，"他用学校语言回答我。

"那你为什么哭呢？"

"我应该哭啊！"

"'你应该哭'，这是什么意思？"

"当爸爸、妈妈离开的时候，小朋友都应该哭啊！"

他还在继续哭着，我问他"你为什么觉得他们应该哭？"

"因为他们会想妈妈呀！"

我很欣慰，儿子这么小就明白了学校的"仪式"，要给我一个伤感的再见。我用犹太人的幽默语气安慰他，"你怎么会想我？我不就在这儿！"

"但我会想你呀，以后。"

他停了一下才说"以后"。我接着说，"不会的，你一会儿就忙得没有时间想我了。不管怎样，先别哭，要不鼻子会堵塞的。"

Hearing less than wholehearted belief, I rummaged in my purse for a photo. "Názhe, bǎ zhè fàng jìn kǒudài. Yào shì nǐ juéde nǐ xiàng wǒ huò Bàba de huà, jiù bǎ zhèzhāng zhàobiān náchūlǎi kànkan."

Holding it, he studied it before putting it in his pocket, instinctively !!! treating it like an Asian handles a business card. Giving me a serious nod, his second "Okay" closed the subject.

Waving good-bye, I left. No more hugs or kisses. I didn't want him to think that his thoughtful decision needed reinforcement or that he was being consoled for a loss. Parents who had been watching us looked horrified. How could I leave my child with tears in his eyes (and none in mine)? I must be heartless. Unloving. Without emotions. Another "Inscrutable Oriental" raising an inscrutable child.

There wasn't time to explain how we are shaped differently by our cultures. When Chinese, we are each the hub of a web formed by relationships to immediate, extended, and ancestral family. Everyone interdependent, the spokes are strengthened when children do their duty as good students and adults provide the means. Mutually responsible, there is no "please" or "thank you." To say either implies that you might not have done your duty without request or public acknowledgement.[16]

Mutuality may require the long view—as when my uncle left his wife and young daughter to work for ten years half-way around the world. Believing this was their best alternative, there was no shame that they sacrificed their immediate home life for bettering a future one. Feeling guilty about missing out on family dinners or the "First Day at School Ritual" made no sense. My parents felt similarly about my younger sister. Left in China as a baby, she was seventeen when we were finally reunited.

Like so many immigrants before us, we lived as part of each other but apart, as present to each other but absent. We lived with physical separation but not emotional distance. We were each with many selves—mothers, fathers, sons, and daughters—who, daily, yearly, lived without spouses, siblings, and parents because we were bonded by something more urgent than tears. The Americanized understand military duty but cannot easily imagine how good and real people could otherwise be "married" without living together, or "loving" without hugging.

---

[16]同样，给餐馆服务员付小费就像是贿赂他们。

186

"好吧，妈妈。"

听他那语气还不坚定，我就从手提包里找出了一张照片。"拿着，把这放进口袋。要是你觉得你想我或爸爸的话，就把这张照片拿出来看看。"

他接过照片，端详了一会儿才放进口袋，他那本能的恭敬态度如同一个东方人接受别人的名片。他认真地向我点了一下头，说了一声"好"，我们就没有再说下去。

我跟他挥了挥手，说了再见，就走了，没有更多的拥抱和亲吻，因为我不想让他觉得他经过深思熟虑的决定还需要我的认可，或者他做错了什么需要我的安慰。其他家长惊讶地看着我们：这个人怎么能抛下流泪的孩子一走了之，居然一点也不伤心？她一定很残酷，没有爱心，没有感情。又一个不可思议的东方人养着一个不可思议的孩子！

我没有时间解释我们的文化是如何影响了我们的生活。作为中国人，我们与家人包括近亲、远亲及祖先的关系就像 张 蜘蛛网，我们处在蜘蛛网的中心。在这个蜘蛛网里，每个人都是相互依 赖的。当孩子们在学校能成为一个好学生，而家长们能为他们提供一定 的经济保障时，彼此的关系就得到了进一步的强化。我们各自对他人负责，所以我们不需要整天把"请"或"谢谢"挂在嘴上。如果你真说了"请"或"谢谢"倒意味着你没有尽到自己的责任，或者你在指望别人的感谢。[18]

每个人对他人的责任需要从长远的角度来看，就象我伯父离开他太太和女儿到世界的另一端，一工作就是十年。我伯父相信这是唯一最佳的选择，为了将来更美好的前景而暂时牺牲家庭生活，他对此问心无愧。对没有能赶上跟家人吃顿团圆饭、没有能在孩子第一天上学时陪伴而行而感到内疚实在是没有意义的。我妹妹在婴儿时就被留在中国，直到快十八岁才来美国与家人团圆，但我父母对此问心无愧。

就象许多早先的移民那样，我们每个人的生活都是他人生活中的一部分。但是，我们是可以分离的。每个人尽管不在他人身边，但都与他人同在。我们之间有时空上的距离，但我们的感情是没有距离的。我们每个人都同时扮演着不同的角色：母亲，父亲，儿子，女儿，我们常常一年到头身边没有丈夫，妻子，兄妹，父母，因为维持我们关系的

---

[18] Similarly, tipping a waiter to get good service is like bribing.

I wanted William to learn that family can't be **"missed,"**[17] that, when he is in school gathering new experiences, so are we. Those experiences are what can be missed, not family. Yet there is a downside to this web identity. *In the extreme,* it can mean that nothing is personal. *In the extreme,* it can mean that it is shameful to act singly or alone. Only by keeping this downside in mind could I not feel guilty when my mother died telling me, "I hate you and everything you stand for!"

Although she gave me a wonderful childhood, she nevertheless had **"only"** three daughters. Raising us as sons, our duties and allegiance would remain in her web, not our in-laws'. Thus:

- My older sister was to be powerful so benefits could devolve to family. She did this.

- My younger sister was to be a lady-in-waiting. Without complaint, she complied. Monthly driving 500 miles to do errands, she even promised to be buried in the same plot so they would be served in the afterlife.

- And I was to be the scholar.

Had we lived in traditional China, I would have passed the examinations and elevated the clan from the provincial to the imperial. Living in North America, I should have earned a Ph.D. and taught at an Ivy League university. I didn't. Nor did I stop talking about why it was important to *me* that I didn't fulfill her vision of my duty. In other words, I never expressed feeling guilty or regretful about my decisions. After our mother died, I said to my younger sister—"Mommy loved you Chinese style but did not respect you American style. She hated me Chinese style but respected me American style." Living on the hyphen sometimes means having to make difficult choices. Yet, then and since then, I did miss hearing the words my Caucasian friends got from their parents—"Well done," "Good job," and "I'm proud of you."

VOCABULARY

phalanx	n.	from ancient Greek warfare, now any compact formation of people, animals or things, united for a common purpose.	方阵, 密集队人群	fāngzhèn, mìjíduì rénqún

---

[17]这个双关语有"未得到"和"渴望"两层意思。所谓"思念（miss）"某人以至于"很想家（homesick）"的情形常常指被送到夏令营的孩子由于跟父母分开而无法正常地喜欢平时觉得好玩的活动，比如，游泳、游戏。

是一种比感情和眼泪更重要的东西。美国人能理解因军事责任而与家人分开的情形，但是无法想象一个有血有肉的人可以"结了婚"却不和家人生活在一起，也不能理解有"爱情"却没有拥抱。

我要威廉明白，在这个蜘蛛网式的关系中，家庭是不可能"被遗忘"的。当他在学校获取新的经历时，他的家人也与他一起分享。这些经历也许会被忘却，但是家庭不可能被忘记。不过，这种蜘蛛网式的关系有个不好的地方。用极端的话说，这里没有"个人的东西"。一个人要是"独立"地做些什么事，这种行为是羞耻的。我理解并记住了这一点，所以当母亲在弥留之际对我说"我恨你和你所代表的价值观"这句话时，我没有感到任何的内疚。

我母亲给了我一个幸福的童年。但是，她只有三个女儿，她把我们当作"儿子"来培养，要我们孝顺、尽职，永远生活在她的，而不是我们公公、婆婆家的蜘蛛网中。所以

- 她期望我姐姐名利双收，光宗耀祖。姐姐如愿以偿，成功了。

- 她期望我妹妹当个宫女。妹妹毫无怨言地顺从了，每月开车 500 英里去父母家服侍他们，她甚至允诺死后要和父母合葬一地，这样来世的日子里仍然可以继续服侍他们。

- 她期望我成为一个学者。

假如我们今天还生活在传统的中国社会，那么我肯定会通过层层考试，将我家从省级荣升到宫廷。可是我却生活在北美。我应该拥有一个博士学位，并在一所常春藤大学任教，但是我未能做到。我不明白自己未能实现母亲强加于我的梦想这跟我又有什么重要的关系，而且我还喋喋不休地说个没完。换句话说，我应该对自己所作的决定向母亲表示歉意，但是我没有。母亲去世后，我对妹妹说，"妈妈喜欢你的中式传统，但不欣赏你的美式风格。她厌恶我的中式做法，但尊重我的美式风格"。在双元文化环境中生活，这意味着必须作出困难的选择。自从母亲去世到现在，我耳畔时常萦绕着我白人朋友的父母常常对他们说的那几句话："棒极了"，"不错"，"我以你为荣"。

huddle	v.	to crowd or crouch together; to form a close group as players do in an American football game in order to plan strategy.	拥挤	yōngjǐ
sob	v.	to cry convulsively or loudly with a catching of breath.	哭诉, 哭泣	kūsù, kūqì
ritual	n.	an established or prescribed way of proceeding; a formal ceremony, often religious in nature.	仪式	yíshì
reassure	v.	to restore confidence; to support, comfort.	使……安心	shǐ…ānxīn
rummage	v.	to actively search through a place or receptacle for an object or idea.	到处翻寻,搜出,检查	dàochù fānxún, sōuchū, jiǎnchá
instinctively	adv.	natural, inborn, innate or unlearned impulse, pattern, or way of doing sth.	本能地	běnnéng de
reinforcement	n.	an additional supply of people, equipment, structural components, etc. to support or bolster a need, purpose, aim.	加强	jiāqiáng
Inscrutable Oriental		this phrase has a long history of use, mostly by non-Asians, to describe the(ir) difficulty in reading Asian facial expressions (or the lack thereof). At its worst, it was associated with the "The Insidious Dr. Fu Manchu" character created by novelist Sax Rohmer and visually immortalized in the movies as the personification of the cruel cunning and evil genius that underlies the "Yellow Peril." At its most naïve, it refers to the self-control exercised by Asians who do not "wear their heart on their sleeves" and are less likely to express their feelings in public and who are, therefore, mysterious, not easily understood or seen through.	不可思议的东方人	bùkě-sīyì de dōngfāngrén

生词

蜘蛛网	蜘蛛網	zhīzhūwǎng	n.	spider web
拥抱	擁抱	yōngbào	v./n.	hug
哭哭啼啼	哭哭啼啼	kūku-títí	f.o.w.	sob
重演	重演	chóngyǎn	v.	repeat, reenact
北美	北美	Běiměi	p.n.	North America
惯例	慣例	guànlì	n.	ritual
庆幸	慶幸	qìngxìng	v.	feel smug
耷拉	耷拉	dāla	v.	hang down
膀子	膀子	bǎngzi	n.	arms
欣慰	欣慰	xīnwèi	adj.	conforming
伤感	傷感	shānggǎn	adj.	emotional
堵塞	堵塞	dǔsè	v.	stop up, block, block up
手提包	手提包	shǒutíbāo	n.	purse, pocketbook
端详	端詳	duānxiang	v.	scrutinize carefully
本能	本能	běnnéng	n.	instinct
名片	名片	míngpiàn	n.	business card, name card
挥	揮	huī	v.	wave
亲吻	親吻	qīnwěn	n.	kiss
深思熟虑	深思熟慮	shēnsī-shúlǜ	f.c.w.	think deeply and carefully
认可	認可	rènkě	n.	approval
抛	抛	pāo	v.	leave behind
流泪	流淚	liúlèi	v.o.	shed tears
一走了之	一走了之	yīzǒu-liǎozhī	f.c.w.	leave
残酷	殘酷	cánkù	adj.	heartless
爱心	愛心	àixīn	n.	love, compassion, sympathy
不可思议	不可思議	bùkě-sīyì	f.c.w.	inscrutable
近亲	近親	jìnqīn	n.	immediate family
远亲	遠親	yuǎnqīn	n.	extended family
祖先	祖先	zǔxiān	n.	ancestors
相互	相互	xiānghù	adv.	each other
依赖	依賴	yīlài	v.	rely on, depend on
经济	經濟	jīngjì	n.	finance, economy
保障	保障	bǎozhàng	n.	means
彼此	彼此	bǐcǐ	pron.	one another, each other
强化	強化	qiánghuà	n.	reinforcement
整天	整天	zhěngtiān	n.	the whole day
挂	掛	guà	v.	put in

spoke	n.	one of several bars, rods or rungs radiating from the central hub of a wheel or cylinder.	辐，辐条	fú, fútiáo
double en-tendre	n.p.	from the French for "double meaning," i.e., to have two different meanings in the context.	双关语	shuāngguānyǔ
lady-in-waiting	n.	female attendant to a queen, princess, et al., usually a noblewoman of lower rank than the one she attends but is not a common servant.	宫女	gōngnǚ
elevate	v.	to move or raise to a higher physical, spiritual, intellectual or political place or level; to promote to greater stature by an increase in rank, status, or office.	提拔，举起	tíba, jǔqǐ

意味	意味	yìwèi	v.	imply
尽	盡	jìn	v.	do (one's duty)
指望	指望	zhǐwàng	v.	expect, pin one's hopes on, hope for
一端	一端	yīduān	n.	one end, the other side of the world
暂时	暫時	zànshí	n.	temporary
牺牲	犧牲	xīshēng	v.	sacrifice
问心无愧	問心無愧	wènxīn-wúkuì	f.c.w.	have a clear conscience
团圆饭	團圓飯	tuányuánfàn	n.	family reunion dinner
陪伴	陪伴	péibàn	v.	accompany
内疚	內疚	nèijiù	adj.	remorse, compunction, twinge of guilt
婴儿	嬰兒	yīng'ér	n.	baby
早先	早先	zǎoxiān	n.	previous time, before
时空	時空	shíkōng	n.	space-time
扮演	扮演	bànyǎn	v.	play a role
一年到头	一年到頭	yī'nián-dàotóu	f.c.w.	throughout the year
兄妹	兄妹	xiōngmèi	n.	brother and sister
有血有肉	有血有肉	yǒuxuè-yǒuròu	f.c.w.	true to life
遗忘	遺忘	yíwàng	v.	forget
忘却	忘卻	wàngquè	v.	forget, unlearn
极端	極端	jíduān	adj.	extreme
羞耻	羞恥	xiūchǐ	adj.	shameful
弥留之际	彌留之際	míliúzhījì	f.c.w.	before dying, at the time of dying
尽职	盡職	jìnzhí	v.o.	fulfill one's duty
公公	公公	gōnggong	n.	husband's father, father-in-law
名利双收	名利雙收	mínglìshuāngshōu	f.c.w.	gain both fame and wealth
如愿以偿	如願以償	rúyuànyǐcháng	f.c.w.	achieve what one wishes
宫女	宮女	gōngnǚ	n.	lady-in-waiting
毫无怨言	毫無怨言	háowú-yuànyán	f.c.w.	without complaint
顺从	順從	shùncóng	v.	comply
服侍	服侍	fúshì	v.	wait upon, attend to
允诺	允諾	yǔnnuò	v.	promise, undertake
合葬	合葬	hézàng	v.	be buried together
来世	來世	láishì	n.	afterlife
继续	繼續	jìxù	v.	continue
层层	層層	céngcéng	adv.	layer upon layer
省级	省級	shěngjí	n.	provincial level
荣升	榮升	róngshēng	v.	elevate
宫廷	宮廷	gōngtíng	n.	palace, royal court
常春藤大学	常春藤大學	chángchūnténg dàxué	n.p.	the Ivy League colleges and universities

第九章

在蜘蛛網里

我第二次送威廉上學的時候，期望他跟第一天那樣，馬上走進教室坐下來。跟第一次一樣，我擁抱了他一下，告訴他下課以后我再來接他。說完后我就轉過身，從一群站在門口、抱在一起、哭哭啼啼的小孩及其父母身旁走過去，他們正重演"開學第一天的儀式"，那是北美學校的慣例。我和威廉沒有那些麻煩，為此我覺得很慶幸。可是快走到門口時，我突然聽到威廉喊，"媽媽"。我穿過人群走回去，看見威廉一個人站在那里，耷拉着兩個膀子，眼泪從臉上滾了下來。

"怎么啦？"

"沒什么，"他用學校語言回答我。

"那你為什么哭呢？"

"我應該哭啊！"

"'你應該哭'，這是什么意思？"

"當爸爸、媽媽離開的時候，小朋友都應該哭啊！"

他還在繼續哭着，我問他"你為什么覺得他們應該哭？"

"因為他們會想媽媽呀！"

我很欣慰，兒子這么小就明白了學校的"儀式"，要給我一個傷感的再見。我用猶太人的幽默語氣安慰他，"你怎么會想我？我不就在這兒！"

"但我會想你呀，以后。"

他停了一下才說"以后"。我接着說，"不會的，你一會兒就忙得沒有時間想我了。不管怎樣，先別哭，要不鼻子會堵塞的。"

强加	強加	qiángjiā	v.	impose, force (upon), impose by force
喋喋不休	喋喋不休	diédié-bùxiū	f.c.w.	talk endlessly
歉意	歉意	qiànyì	n.	regret
去世	去世	qùshì	v.o.	die, pass away
美式	美式	měishì	n.	the American style
厌恶	厭惡	yànwù	v.	hate
尊重	尊重	zūnzhòng	v.	respect
耳畔	耳畔	ěrpàn	n.	around one's ears
萦绕	縈繞	yíngrào	v.	linger on
棒极了	棒極了	Bàng jí le		Well done!
以……为荣	以……為榮	yǐ…wéiróng	p.p.	be proud of

"好吧，媽媽。"

聽他那語氣還不堅定，我就從手提包里找出了一張照片。"拿着，把這放進口袋。要是你覺得你想我或爸爸的話，就把這張照片拿出來看看。"

他接過照片，端詳了一會兒才放進口袋，他那本能的恭敬態度如同一個東方人接受別人的名片。他認真地向我點了一下頭，説了一聲"好"，我們就沒有再説下去。

我跟他揮了揮手，説了再見，就走了，沒有更多的擁抱和親吻，因為我不想讓他覺得他經過深思熟慮的決定還需要我的認可，或者他做錯了什麼需要我的安慰。其他家長驚訝地看着我們：這個人怎麼能拋下流泪的孩子一走了之，居然一點也不傷心？她一定很殘酷，沒有愛心，沒有感情。又一個不可思議的東方人養着一個不可思議的孩子!

我沒有時間解釋我們的文化是如何影響了我們的生活。作為中國人，我們與家人包括近親、遠親及祖先的關系就像一張蜘蛛蜘蛛網里，每個人都是相互依賴的。當家長們能為他們提供一定的經濟保障網，我們處在蜘蛛網的中心。在這個孩子們在學校能成為一個好學生，而時，彼此的關系就得到了進一步的強化。我們各自對他人負責，所以我們不需要整天把"請"或"謝謝"挂在嘴上。如果你真説了"請"或"謝謝"倒意味着你沒有盡到自己的責任，或者你在指望別人的感謝。[18]

每個人對他人的責任需要從長遠的角度來看，就象我伯父離開他太太和女兒到世界的另一端，一工作就是十年。我伯父相信這是唯一最佳的選擇，為了將來更美好的前景而暫時犧牲家庭生活，他對此問心無愧。對沒有能趕上跟家人吃頓團圓飯、沒有能在孩子第一天上學時陪伴而行而感到內疚實在是沒有意義的。我妹妹在嬰兒時就被留在中國，直到快十八歲才來美國與家人團圓，但我父母對此問心無愧。

就象許多早先的移民那樣，我們每個人的生活都是他人生活中的一部分。但是，我們是可以分離的。每個人盡管不在他人身邊，但都與他人同在。我們之間有時空上的距離，但我們的感情是沒有距離的。我們每個人都同時扮演着不同的角色：母親，父親，兒子，女兒，我們常常一年到頭身邊沒有丈夫，妻子，兄妹，父母，因為維持我們關系的是一種比感

---

[18] Similarly, tipping a waiter to get good service is like bribing.

情和眼泪更重要的東西。美國人能理解因軍事責任而與家人分開的情形，但是無法想象一個有血有肉的人可以"結了婚"卻不和家人生活在一起，也不能理解有"愛情"卻沒有擁抱。

我要威廉明白，在這個蜘蛛網式的關系中，家庭是不可能"被遺忘"的。當他在學校獲取新的經歷時，他的家人也與他一起分享。這些經歷也許會被忘卻，但是家庭不可能被忘記。不過，這種蜘蛛網式的關系有個不好的地方。用極端的話說，這里沒有"個人的東西"。一個人要是"獨立"地做些什么事，這種行為是羞恥的。我理解并記住了這一點，所以當母親在彌留之際對我說"我恨你和你所代表的價值觀"這句話時，我沒有感到任何的内疚。

我母親給了我一個幸福的童年。但是，她只有三個女兒，她把我們當作"兒子"來培養，要我們孝順、盡職，永遠生活在她的，而不是我們公公、婆婆家的蜘蛛網中。所以

- 她期望我姐姐名利雙收，光宗耀祖。姐姐如願以償，成功了。

- 她期望我妹妹當個宮女。妹妹毫無怨言地順從了，每月開車 500 英里去父母家服侍他們，她甚至允諾死后要和父母合葬一地，這樣來世的日子里仍然可以繼續服侍他們。

- 她期望我成為一個學者。

假如我們今天還生活在傳統的中國社會，那么我肯定曾通過層層考試，將包家從省級榮升到宮廷。可是我卻生活在北美。我應該擁有一個博士學位，并在一所常春藤大學任教，但是我未能做到。我不明白自己未能實現母親強加于我的夢想這跟我又有什么重要的關系，而且我還喋喋不休地說個沒完。換句話說，我應該對自己所作的決定向母親表示歉意，但是我沒有。母親去世后，我對妹妹說，"媽媽喜歡你的中式傳統，但不欣賞你的美式風格。她厭惡我的中式做法，但尊重我的美式風格"。在雙元文化環境中生活，這意味着必須作出困難的選擇。自從母親去世到現在，我耳畔時常縈繞着我白人朋友的父母常常對他們說的那幾句話："棒極了"，"不錯"，"我以你為榮"。

练习　EXERCISES

I. 思考和课堂讨论　FOOD FOR THOUGHT

A. PERSONAL　个人的

描述你在家中的责任。你的责任跟你兄弟姐妹的责任是非不同？为什么？

Did you have a certain sociological role or set of duties which you were expected to perform for the family? Was yours very different from what was expected of your siblings or friends by their relatives? Why or why not?

B. GENERAL　普遍的

An "argument" or line of reasoning is logical when a conclusion is validly deduced from premises that are assumed to be true. However, when there is an error in reasoning, then a fallacy occurs. In order to think clearly and effectively, it helps to know about these errors. After reading the following, discuss the question posed.

当某一结论是从一个正确的前提演绎出来的，那么该结论的论据符合逻辑。但是，如果推理出现错误，就会产生谬论。为了清楚、有效地思考，有必要了解这些推理错误。请阅读下面的错误，然后讨论所提出的问题。

> **appeal to authority** is from the Latin *argumentum ad verecundiam (argumentum* = "argument"; *ad* = "to"; *verecundiam* = "reverence" or "respect" for authority/expertise.

> **pattern:** Ms. Y argues for the truth of her conclusion; Mr. X calls Dr. Z as an expert witness to counter some of Ms. Y's conclusions, hoping that the jurors' respect for Dr. Z will persuade them to disagree totally with Ms. Y.

> **example:** Instead of proving beyond a reasonable doubt that Ms. Y's plea of "Not Guilty by reason of mental defect," was not true because she in fact knew "right" from "wrong" and was, therefore, sane at the time she committed murder, Mr. X **appeals to the authority** of Dr. Z's well-known reputation for exposing people who fake mental illness (but Dr. Z never gives any reason to believe that Ms. Y was faking).

> **question:** Is Mr. X's approach less fallacious if we <u>assume</u> that people who achieve an expert status are probably more intelligent and well-informed so it makes sense to pay more attention to their opinions than to those who are less smart or educated?

C. CROSS-CULTURAL　跨文化的

After reading the following, discuss <u>in Chinese</u> why the "ritual" of traditional classroom behavior—students standing up when the teacher enters—is no longer practiced in the U.S.

阅读以下短文，并<u>用中文</u>对所提出的问题进行讨论。

> We each perform personal rituals that are repeated so many times that they seem instinctive rather than habitual like the order in which we dry ourselves after a shower—first the face, then the back, then the arms, etc. We also reinforce our cultural habits by elevating them to the

category of "common sense" as when we wait our turn and refrain from raising our voices when trying to be persuasive. The ritual and reinforcement combine to put us at ease by reassuring us with comfortable and reasonable expectations. If you doubt this, try drying yourself in reverse order and then asking a stranger for a favor by yelling your request. Nevertheless, keep in mind that standing naked in the open air to get dry makes sense in some cultures while others consider a person to be uncommitted, uninvolved, or insincere if the person does not interrupt others in a high-pitched voice. In other words, we would all benefit if we carefully observe our own and others' behavior before judging them to be too stubborn or too rude to learn new ways.

II. 配对 MATCHMAKER

A. VOCABULARY 词汇

找出以下两列中的对应词，并在其间划线。

Draw a connecting line between the word and its correct definition.

a.	荣升, 提拔	1.	inscrutable
b.	方阵, 密集队, 密集的人群	2.	phalanx
c.	本能地	3.	reinforcement
d.	辐，辐条	4.	stop up, block
e.	使……安心	5.	expect, pin one's hopes on, hope for
f.	堵塞	6.	instinctively
g.	指望	7.	ritual
h.	欣慰	8.	elevate
i.	强化	9.	comforting
j.	不可思议的	10.	reassure
k.	仪式	11.	spoke

a.	shed tears	1.	北美
b.	North America	2.	一年到头
c.	repeat	3.	团圆
d.	love, compassion	4.	哭诉, 哭泣
e.	throughout the year	5.	价值观
f.	reunion	6.	双关语
g.	value system	7.	以……为荣

199

h.   think deeply and carefully   8.   爱心

i.   be proud of sth.   9.   流泪

j.   sob   10.   重演

k.   double entendre   11.   深思熟虑

B. ANTONYMS & ALTERNATES 反义词和多义词

First draw a connecting line between the words or phrases in the left-hand column with the best possible <u>antonym</u> listed in the middle column, then draw a line between the antonym and an alternate meaning of the antonym listed in the right-hand column. <u>Be forewarned</u> that the part of speech may change from one column to the next and that slang terms may be used. E.g.,

"hit" ———————————— *"miss"* ———————— *"honorific for unmarried female"*

"warm" ———————————— *"cool"* ———————— *"excellent"*

首先在第二列中找出与第一列相对应的反义词，然后在第三列中找出与第二列相关的多义词。注意：词性会有变化。

		ANTONYMS		ALTERNATE MEANING
a.	cheerful or good times	1.	**bull**	i.	African-American jazz song
b.	save, conserve	2.	**bomb**	ii.	*slang* failure, flop, fiasco
c.	spiritually save, bless	3.	**the blues**	iii.	group of animals, cards, etc.
d.	not fancy, shabby	4.	**run**	iv.	*informal* a thousand dollars
e.	lengthen	5.	**damn**	v.	*slang* cocaine drugs
f.	of little extent, narrow	6.	**pack**	vi.	curse; extremely, very
g.	bear, seller of stocks	7.	**cut**	vii.	*slang* a (promiscuous) woman
h.	succeed, be popular	8.	**blow**	viii.	*slang* nonsense, big lies
i.	walk	9.	**grand**	ix.	*informal* share, payment
j.	take out, unpack	10.	**broad**	x.	*slang* smuggle

III. 解字/词、构字/词 DECONSTRUCTION & CONSTRUCTION

A. 将以下汉字分解成最小的构字部件，然后用每个部件构成三个汉字。例如"鸭"可以分解成 "甲"和"鸟"两个部件。"甲"能构成"押"，"岬"，"钾"；"鸟"可以构成以"鸡"，"鸦"，"鸣"。请借助字典完成练习。

Deconstruct the following characters into the smallest components, then form 3 new characters using each component.

提	_____	情	_____	袋	_____
室	_____	谢	_____	然	_____

B. Using only the letters of the word **"ENTENDRE,"** form English words that are not proper nouns, abbreviations, or acronyms and that consist of 4 or more letters. A letter can only be used again if it appears in the given word more than once. E.g., "tone" is not acceptable because there is no "o" and "dented" is not because there is only one "d" Like many Olympic sports, weight categories mark performance. We filled in a few cells to get you started. Fill in the rest to achieve the highest category. If you think up more than 20, you beat the authors!

用 **"ENTENDRE"** 中的字母构词。新构建的词不能是专有名词、缩写词、或首字母缩略词。每个单词必须至少含有四个字母，但不能重复使用同一字母，除非该字母在**"ENTENDRE"**中出现两次。

CHAMPION STATUS			
FEATHER 5	**WELTER** 10	**MIDDLE** 15	**HEAVY** 20
rend			
dent			
enter			

C. 用 "深思熟虑" 中的每个汉字组成不同的词。看看最多能组多少个词。

Use each of the characters in "深思熟虑" to form as many words (of 2-4 characters) as you can.

D. Pair any two of the following 11 words to form at least 13 different, unhyphenated words.

在下列十一个词中配对、组词，新组的词只能含有两个单词，中间没有连字号。
请至少组出十三个词。

light over side run turn come weight state stop out paper

IV. 阅读理解 READING QUIZ

根据课文，选择准确答案。Based on the text, choose the best answer.

1. 为什么威廉第二次上学的时候哭了？

   a. 因为他看到别的小朋友都在哭。

   b. 因为他看到别的父母亲都在哭。

   c. 因为他觉得学校要求学生哭。

d. 因为他觉得学校希望学生哭。

2. 为什么威廉哭了以后作者没有拥抱他一下就走了？

a. 因为她没有看见。

b. 因为她没有感情。

c. 因为她没有爱心。

d. 因为她没有时间。

e. 以上都不对。

3. 以下哪一个答案准确描述了"蜘蛛网式的"人际关系？

a. 在"蜘蛛网"里，人与人之间相互依赖。

b. 在"蜘蛛网"里，人与人之间不能分开。

c. 在"蜘蛛网"里，人人都有自己的隐私。

d. 在"蜘蛛网"里，人人都很独立。

4. 作者的母亲生前曾对女儿说过以下哪句话？

a. "棒极了"。

b. "不错"。

c. "我以你为荣"。

d. "我恨你及你所代表的价值观"。

5. 为什么作者的妹妹直到快十八岁才来美国与家人团圆？

a. 因为她不喜欢来美国。

b. 因为她无法离开中国。

c. 因为她父母问心无愧。

d. 作者没有解释。

6. 作者的母亲对她女儿的期望是什么？

a. 光宗耀祖。

b. 名利双收。

c. 孝顺尽职。

d. 以上都是。

V. 填空　FILL IN THE BLANK

A. 选择正确答案。Choose the correct answer.

1. 我送威廉上学的时候，我们都没有哭哭啼啼的麻烦，为此我觉得很_____。

    a. 不幸　　　　b. 荣幸　　　　c. 庆幸

2. 我不想让威廉觉得他的深思熟虑的决定还需要我的_____。

    a. 认识　　　　b. 认同　　　　c. 认知

3. 作者认为，在"蜘蛛网"里的每个人都同时_____着不同的角色。

    a. 扮演　　　　b. 重演　　　　c. 表演

4. 我们全家人都_____着儿子在学校所获得的成功。

    a. 分担　　　　b. 分忧　　　　c. 分享

5. 我母亲厌恶我的中式_____，但尊重我的美式风格。

    a. 办法　　　　b. 做法　　　　c. 说法

6. 拿个博士学位，然后在大学教教书，这是我母亲的_____。

    a. 梦话　　　　b. 梦乡　　　　c. 梦想

B. Using your target language, write a word or phrase from the vocabulary lists and/or dictionary that means the <u>same</u> or is a <u>synonym</u> for the italicized word or phrase. Keep in mind that the part of speech and/or tense may have been adjusted to achieve grammatically correct results.

在以下段落中找出与斜体词意义相近的同义词。如果你所学的外语是中文，找出相应的中文词或短语。如果你所学的外语是英语，找出相应的英语词或短语。注意：词性或时态会有变化。

To *boost* _____ their spirits before facing a *tight formation* _____ of opponents, the team repeated their pre-game *ceremony* _____ which was to *gather in a tight circle* _____ so that each player got *additional strength* _____ from their mutual proximity.

VI. 翻译　TRANSLATION

A. 将以下句子翻译成英文。Translate the following sentences into English.

1. 我很欣慰，儿子这么小就明白了学校的"仪式"，要给我一个伤感的再见。

2. 他拿着照片，端详了一会儿才放进口袋，他那本能的恭敬态度如同一个东方人接受别人的名片。

3. 作为中国人，我们与家人包括近亲、远亲及祖先的关系就像一张蜘蛛网，我们处在蜘蛛网的中心。

B. Translate the following sentences into Chinese. 将以下句子翻译成中文。

1. The second time I escorted William to his classroom, I expected him to behave the same as he did the first day when he immediately went in and sat down.

2. Like so many immigrants before us, we lived as part of each other but apart, as present to each other but absent.

3. Parents who had been watching us looked horrified. How could I leave my child with tears in his eyes and none in mine?

VII. 完型填充　CLOZE TEST

A. 在以下短文的每一空格处填入一个汉字，如有可能，给出相应的英语单词。

Fill in a Chinese character that retains the original meaning or intent of the text, then write an English equivalent, if any.

我第二次送威廉上学的时候，期望他跟第一_____那样，马上走进_____室坐下来。跟第_____次一样，我拥抱_____他一下，告诉他_____课以后我再来_____他。说完后我就_____过身，从一群站_____门口、抱在一起、_____哭啼啼的小孩_____其父母身旁走_____去，他们正重演"_____学第一天的仪_____"，那是北美学校_____惯例。我和威廉_____有那些麻烦, 为_____我觉得很庆幸。

B. Fill in an English word or phrase that retains the original meaning or intent of the text, then write a Chinese equivalent, if any.

在以下短文的每一空格处填入一个英语单词，如有可能，给出相应的汉字或词。

The second time I escorted William _____ his classroom, I expected him to behave _____ same as he did the first day _____ he immediately went in and sat down. _____ the day before, I gave him a _____ and told him that I would see _____ later. Turning, I again walked through the _____ of parents and children huddling and sobbing _____ the door, performing the "First Day At _____ Ritual" that is standard in North America. _____ rather smug that we didn't need it, _____ was a few steps away when I _____, "Māma!" Going back through the crowd, I _____ William standing by himself, arms at his _____, tears rolling down his face.

VIII. 身体部位　BODY PARTS

A. There are many useful idioms which contain "body parts." Choose the most appropriate to fill in the blank based on your best guess of what the idiom means.

英语中的许多习惯用语含有表示"身体部位"的单词。在下面三个习惯用语中选择最恰当的填空。

    1. by the skin of sb's teeth   **2.** thick skin   **3.** get under sb's skin

He has a _____ so didn't care that his opponent continued to criticize his narrow victory. The attacks, however, did _____ of his supporters. He told them that whether he won _____ or by a large margin wasn't important as long as he won.

B. 将以下短文翻译成中文。注意：划线的词或短语与以上含有"身体部位"的习惯用语相对应。

Translate the following into Chinese taking note that the underlined words or phrases correspond to the meaning of the above "body parts."

The runner finished the race seconds before the last person so she escaped <u>by a hair's breadth</u> being the worst athlete of the day.

The writer was used to being corrected by his editor so had developed an <u>immunity to criticism</u>.

His mother's habit of talking loud could <u>annoy him very much</u>.

C. Using your target language, create sentence(s) containing the following three English idioms or their Chinese equivalents.

用以下短语分别造句。如果你所学的外语是中文，请用中文来做这个练习。如果你所学的外语是英语，请用英语来做这个练习。

1. no skin off sb's back or nose = 毫无兴趣；没有风险

2. skin alive = 严厉申斥，决定性地击败

3. all skin and bones = 骨瘦如柴，瘦得皮包骨

IX. 写作 PRÉCIS

用所学的外语总结课文。如果你用中文来写，请至少使用 450 个汉字，并用电脑打出摘要。如果你用英文来写，请不超过 390 个词。

Write a summary of this chapter in your target language. If writing in Chinese, use <u>more</u> than 450 characters; if writing in English, use <u>no more</u> than 390 words.

CHAPTER TEN

CONSTRUCTING A LIFE IN A PYRAMID

When William insisted on responding in English to his mother's Chinese, or crowed with pride "I'm half Chinese!" he was not being more loyal to one culture over the other. Rather, he was, at three, already switching between a "duck" and "rabbit" way of being—one moment self-identifying more vividly with one, the next moment, the other. When he cried on his second day at school, his tears took shape within the pyramidal universe of being a modern American. In this universe, the Constitution, corporate by-laws, religious belief, and educational system form the major institutions which always have a pinnacle. Here the president, CEO, pope, and principal hold the highest office and have the most power while the "baser"[18] voters, workers, parishioners, and students "below" continue to compete for the leftover resources.

This universe is populated with separate individuals. Each is independently free to choose relationships *and* free to sever them by divorce, adoption, lawsuit, and refusal to sign on the dotted line. Relationships are continually reinforced by proximity, hugs, and words like "I love you," "I miss you," "I do," as well as by the force of law. In this kind of culture, homesick children reassure parents that "home is where the heart is." Here a person can get what (s)he deserves regardless how the punishment or reward may affect family members so that no one but the perpetrator *legally* serves time in jail or only the actual lottery ticket-holder can claim the prize. Sharing the ignominy or money is a matter of choice and conscience. In a society of individuals, any experience—whether good or bad, triumphant or debasing, at the "top" with the elite, or at the "bottom" with the common people—can be a lonely one. Achieving success, status, and salvation is a matter of "going *up* the ladder," "breaking through the glass *ceiling*," and "sitting *on top* of the world." *In the extreme*, life is a zero-sum game so winning only happens because there are losers. *In the extreme*, all matters are "personal."

However, not all matters are important even if personal. Yet those shaped by the pyramid ask, "Which is your *favorite* color?" "Who is your *best* friend?" "What is your *worst* subject?" so children

---

[18]"baser"是一个双关语，指金字塔的塔底和平民百姓。

206

第十章

在金字塔里

当威廉坚持要用英语来回答他母亲的中文问题，或自豪地称自己为"半个中国人"时，他并不是热衷于某一文化而疏于另一文化。他三岁的时候就已经能熟练地穿梭在"鸭子"和"兔子"之间，知道什么时候该认同这一类，而什么时候认同另一类。在他第二天上学哭的时候，他的眼泪标志着当代美国式的金字塔文化。国家宪法、公司章程、宗教信仰和教育系统是这个金字塔的主要结构，各自都有一个顶点。在这里，总统、执行长官、教皇、校长拥有至高无上的行政权力，而处在金字塔"底部"的老百姓、选民、工人、教民和学生只能在下面角逐、竞争余下的资源。

这个金字塔世界是由不同的个体所组成的。在这里，人人独立，每个人都可以自由自在地用不同的方式选择和终止某种关系，比如离婚、领养、诉讼、拒绝签字。处在金字塔世界中的人际关系必须靠亲近、拥抱和诸如"我爱你"、"我想你"、"我会"等文字来维持，当然也得借助于法律的力量。在这里，一人做事一人当，尽管他/她所遭到的惩罚或所获取的荣誉会影响家人，但是，最后只是他/她一个人或锒铛入狱，或中奖享福。是否与他人同甘共苦、荣辱与共完全由选择和良心而定。在这个由独立个体所组成的社会里，任何经验，不管是好是坏、是成是败、是在"塔顶"的精英还是在"塔底"的平民，都是独自的。获得成功、取得地位、得到拯救无非都是一个"爬楼梯"、"打破天花板"、"坐在世界之巅"的过程。用极端的话说，在这个文化世界中，生活就是一场零和游戏，之所以有人成功是因为有人失败了。也就是说，这一切的一切都是"个人的"。

然而，即使一切都是个人的，但这并不表明所有一切都很重要。由金字塔文化熏陶、培养出来的人常常会问以下问题，"你最喜欢什么颜色？""谁是你最好的朋友？""你最不喜欢的科目是什么？"孩子们从小就学会怎样在万事中间决定优先次序。当民意

naturally prioritize everything. When pollsters ask, "What is *the most important* issue facing voters?" adults habitually simplify world conditions into a list of separate problems. Being unable to choose *one* smacks of being wishy-washy and indecisive.

Characterizing cultures as "web" or "pyramid" may be dangerously close to stereotyping yet our (grand)parents did this when we were still tied to their apron strings. For them it was no big deal to say, "Chinese do this, not that" or "Irish like that, not this." They handed down their heritage and gave us our starting point with the noodles we slurped or twirled, the dances we skipped or stomped, the sounds we hushed or shouted. Most thought their way was "normal," maybe even "best." Few gave a hoot about being politically correct. However, just because it was our (grand)parents who handed it to us doesn't mean we have a clue what we got. So we need to understand what the slurping, twisting, skipping, stomping, hushing and shouting was about, and then move on from these generalizations to acquire the "ifs, ands, and buts" of specific cases. In this way, we can change those first impressions into globally functional ones.

When William was born, I had to figure out how to do this. Putting him into a "melting pot" where all cultural differentiation would be destroyed was unacceptable. "Tossed salad" and "smorgasbord" were somewhat better but still lacked descriptions of how individual ingredients are to be grown and prepared. For me, part of this "figuring" was to avoid shaping either the web or pyramid *in the extreme.*

Imagining William's future growth, I remembered my past. As the only Chinese attending my suburban high school in 1959, I was also a candidate for the Student Council. Winning the Vice Presidency would accomplish two goals:

- I would establish myself as a leader and, thereby, beef up my college application.

- I would give my mother the opportunity to "complain" (and, thereby, brag) that Daughter No. 2 was not much good as a "Little Ambassador" of 650,000,000 Chinese since she, as Vice President, would only have access to 650 high school students **!!!**

The problem was campaigning. Besides posters, each candidate would have two minutes before the school-wide assembly. The trouble is that:

- My American Self needed to persuade the voters that I was "the best."

测验专家问，"什么是选民面临的最重要的问题？"成年人也习惯于将复杂的社会现实逐一简化为不同问题，因为在这个文化世界里，不会选择就等于软弱无力、优柔寡断。

把文化归为"蜘蛛网式的"或"金字塔式的"几乎是一种带有偏见的分类，这很危险，然而我们的（祖）父母在我们还未成年的时候就这么做了。他们常说，"中国人这么做，不那么做"，或者"爱尔兰人喜欢那，不喜欢这"。对于他们，说这些话不是什么大不了的事。他们把自己的文化习俗传了下来，使得我们在吃面条的时候要么发出稀溜稀溜的声音，要么用叉子转来转去；使得我们在跳舞的时候要么轻盈飞舞，要么用力顿足；使得我们在说话的时候要么细声细语，要么粗声粗气。大多数人认为自己的做法很正常，也许是最好的。没有人在乎"政治上正确"的东西。然而，并非因为祖父母传给了我们某些传统就表明我们真的理解了所继承的东西。我们首先得弄明白为什么我们吃面时会发出稀溜稀溜的声音或用叉子转来转去，为什么在跳舞时会轻盈飞舞或用力顿足，为什么在说话时会细声细语或粗声粗气。然后从这些笼统的概括中学会对不同情况作不同处理，这样我们才能将"第一印象"转换成通用、实际的知识。

我生下威廉以后就想着应该怎样把以上这些付诸实施。如果把他放进"大熔炉"，各种文化的特点都被毁得面目全非，这显然不能接受。"拌色拉"和"大杂烩"似乎比"大熔炉"好得多，但是对其中的每个成分是如何生长的、我们该如何准备仍缺乏解释。对于我来说，怎样付诸实施的一个重要方面就是避免打造极端的蜘蛛网或极端的金字塔。

当我在设想威廉将来的发展时，我想起了我的过去。1959 年我是我们郊区高中唯一的一个中国人，也是学生会的候选人之一。我竞选学生会副主席有两个目的：

- 我想锻炼自己的领导才能，以此加重我大学申请材料的分量。

- 我想给母亲一个可以抱怨的机会（也是吹牛的机会）：我们二女儿当不了六亿五千万中国人的"小大使"，作为学生会副主席，她只能指挥六百五十个中学生!!!

我的挑战是竞选。每个候选人除了准备海报以外，还得在全校集会上发表两分钟的演讲，而麻烦的是：

- 我那美国的一面需要劝说选民让他们知道我是最好的。

- My Chinese Self needed to keep a low profile so the gods wouldn't notice that I was tooting my own horn.[19]

- My Teenage Self needed to avoid hurting the feelings of friends who also happened to be my opponents.

By the time it was my turn to speak at the assembly, the audience was bored to tears. Since students in office had very little power to actually do anything, everybody had said the same thing about being conscientious, hard-working, responsive, etc. My speech was no different...except that I delivered it in Chinese. At first people thought the problem was caused by their dozing off. Then, awake, it took another second to figure out why I still wasn't making any sense to them. Then everyone laughed. We all knew that, whatever language I used, I couldn't say much more or less than the dozen previous speakers but I could empathize with their need for a diversion. I won the election.

At the time, the victory felt right but for reasons I didn't know how to talk about. Since that time, I have learned how from many sources. By "charting" the way, I am clearer about the strategies valued by my dual heritage and more hopeful about creating multiple realities.

PYRAMID	WEB
"Nature"	"Nurture"[20]
Independence	Mutuality
Overcoming	Balancing
Integrity and Honor	Moral rectitude and "Face"
Introspection	Contemplation
(Objective) Knowledge	(Practical) Wisdom
Humility	Modesty
Power	Authority
Sympathy	Compassion
Potentialities of Future/ Youth	Actualities of Experience/Age

---

[19]中国大约有一百五十种神，但是没有一个是全能的。其中大多数神不喜欢人们吹牛，而且很多并不聪敏。像许多亚洲人一样，我的家人都不相信神，但是我们的行为，比如某些庄重的礼仪，却让人觉得那些神真的存在似的。

[20]当培养"nurture"的分量大于自然"nature"时，人的行为就变成为一种克己的意志力，而不是生物遗传或物质环境的结果。

- 我那中国的一面需要保持低调，这样众神不会注意到我在炫耀。[19]

- 我那少年的一面需要避免伤害既是我朋友又是我竞选对手的感情。

轮到我演讲时，同学们早已被枯燥的发言听得坐不住了。因为学生会没有权力做具体实事，所以每个竞选者都讲自己有多诚实、多努力、多负责等等。我说的也是这些话，但是与他们唯一不同的是我用中文发表了演讲。刚开始大家还在打瞌睡，没有在意，接着清醒了，等过了一秒钟弄清为什么还没有听懂我在说什么的时候大家哄堂大笑。谁都知道，不管我用什么语言演讲，我无非还是重复前面十几位学生所说的陈词滥调，但是因为我能顺应大家对多元文化的需求，所以我的竞选成功了。

赢了竞选我很高兴，但那时候我不知道如何谈论这种胜利。打那以后，我从不同的渠道逐渐学会了应该怎样做。在这里，我将"金字塔"和"蜘蛛网"这两个不同文化世界的特点列表如下，以供参考。通过比较两者，我对自己双元文化的价值观越来越清楚，同时也越来越希望建立多元化的现实世界。

金字塔式的文化	蜘蛛网式的文化
自然	培养[20]
独立自主	相互依赖
战胜	制衡
正直和诚实	道德和面子
内省	沉思
客观的知识	实际的智慧
谦卑	谦虚
权力	权威
同情	怜悯
将来的潜力/年轻	实际的经验/年长

---

[19] Of the 150 or so Chinese gods, none are all-powerful, most don't like people who brag, and many aren't all that bright !!! Like many Asians, our family didn't "believe in" the gods but we *behaved* as if they exist—like *serious* etiquette.

[20] When Nurture outweighs Nature, behavior is primarily a matter of self-control and will-power, not biological inheritance or physical environment.

VOCABULARY

crow	v.	to boast, exult, or proclaim loudly like the sound made by the bird of the same name.	自豪地吹嘘	zìháo de chuīxū
take shape	v.p.	to become like a certain form; to attain or obtain the character of sth.	以……形式出现	yǐ… xíngshì chūxiàn
by-laws	n.	rule by which an organization governs itself and conducts its business.	章程	zhāngchéng
pinnacle	n.	the highest peak; the pointed or towering top of a formation.	尖峰，高峰，顶点	jiānfēng, gāofēng, dǐngdiǎn
parishioner	n.	the people or residents of a religious or civil parish or district.	教区居民	jiàoqū jūmín
sever	v.	to separate (from), to divide, break off, disunite, dissolve (ties) often in a forcible or drastic way.	终止	zhōngzhǐ
sign on the dotted line	v.p.	to signify legal agreement in that the place on a contract where one's signature is written is usually indicated by a line, possibly appearing as a series of dots which is how early typewriters made a line on the paper.	签字，在虚线上签名	qiānzì, zài xūxiàn shàng qiānmíng
ignominy	n.	disgrace, dishonor, shame, public contempt.	羞耻，屈辱	xiūchǐ, qūrǔ
debase	v.	to reduce in value or quality; to lower in rank, significance or dignity; adulterate.	衰落，失败	shuāiluò, shībài
zero-sum game	n.p.	a game where the losses and gains are exactly balanced by the gains and losses so that the total of gain and loss is zero and there is a winner only when there is also a loser.	零和游戏	línghé yóuxì
prioritize	v.	to list or rate in order of preference or precedence.	区分优先次序	qūfēn yōuxiān cìxù
smack of	v.p.	to have a (slight) taste, flavor, touch, or trace of.	带有……味道,有点象	dàiyǒu… wèidao, yǒudiǎn xiàng

生词

金字塔	金字塔	jīnzìtǎ	n.	pyramid
热衷	熱衷	rèzhōng	v.	be loyal to
疏于	疏於	shūyú	v.	neglect
穿梭	穿梭	chuānsuō	v.	switch back and forth
一类	一類	yīlèi	n.	one category
标志	標誌	biāozhì	v.	indicate
宪法	憲法	xiànfǎ	n.	constitution
章程	章程	zhāngchéng	n.	bylaws, regulations
宗教	宗教	zōngjiào	n.	religion
执行长官	執行長官	zhíxíng zhǎng-guān	n.p.	chief executive officer (CEO)
教皇	教皇	jiàohuáng	n.	pope
至高无上	至高無上	zhìgāo-wúshàng	f.c.w.	highest
底部	底部	dǐbù	n.	base, low level
教民	教民	jiàomín	n.	parishioner
角逐	角逐	juézhú	v.	compete, enter into rivalry with
自由自在	自由自在	zìyóu-zìzài	f.c.w.	free
终止	終止	zhōngzhǐ	v.	sever, terminate
领养	領養	lǐngyǎng	v.	adopt (a child)
诉讼	訴訟	sùsòng	v.	file a lawsuit, litigate
拒绝	拒絕	jùjué	v.	refuse
签字	簽字	qiānzì	v.o.	sign on the dotted line, affix one's signature
诸如	諸如	zhūrú	v.	such as
借助于	借助於	jièzhùyú	v.p.	by the force of, obtain support from
一人做事一人当	一人做事一人當	yīrénzuòshì yīréndāng		one is responsible for what one has done
惩罚	懲罰	chéngfá	n.	punishment, penalty
荣誉	榮譽	róngyù	n.	reward, honor, credit
锒铛入狱	銀鐺入獄	lángdāng-rùyù	f.c.w.	serve time in jail, be imprisoned
中奖	中獎	zhòngjiǎng	v.o.	win the lottery
享福	享福	xiǎngfú	v.o.	live in ease and comfort
同甘共苦	同甘共苦	tónggān-gòngkǔ	f.c.w.	share well-being and woe
荣辱与共	榮辱與共	róngrǔ-yǔgòng	f.c.w.	share honor and disgrace
良心	良心	liángxīn	n.	conscience
由......而定	由......而定	yóu...érdìng	p.p.	depending on
顶	頂	dǐng	n.	the top of a structure

wishy-washy	adj.	watery, that is, lacking substance, charac-ter, strength; indecisive; thin and weak.	软弱无力	ruǎnruò-wúlì
be tied to mother's apron strings	v.p.	be overly influenced by one's mother es-pecially if an adult and still (too) strongly motivated by the desire to please a parent as if one is still a child. Defining "too much" or "adult" varies with cultures.	受母亲的控制	shòu mǔqīn de kòngzhì
slurp	v.	to noisily suck in food or drink.	吃/喝东西时发出稀溜溜的声音	chī /hē dōngxi shí fāchū xīliūliū de shēngyīn
stomp	v.	to stamp the foot heavily; to dance by stamping the feet to (fast) music.	跺（脚）,重踩	duò (jiǎo), zhòngcǎi,
give a hoot about sth.	v.p.	to care, be concerned or have interest (usually phrased in the negative).	在乎	zàihu
politically cor-rect	adj.p.	initially, being careful not to offend, espe-cially in speech or writing, those people who are ethnically, religiously, linguisti-cally, economically, or physically different; later, shortened to "p.c." with increasing sarcasm, disapproval and/or criticism of the resultant limitations on one's freedom to speak one's mind regardless of other's (hurt) feelings and/or inhibitions lest one inadvertently offends another.	政治上正确的	zhèngzhì shàng zhèngquè de
tossed salad	n.p.	a food item of loose, raw, green, leafy vegetables, sometimes combined with cooked meat, cheese, etc. which are placed in a large bowl and mixed with a dressing or cold sauce by "tossing" the ingredients u-sing a large spoon or fork in each hand.	拌色拉	bànsèlā
smorgasbord	n.	originally Swedish, now a style of serving a meal buffet style when a variety of differ-ent dishes are placed on a long table and diners serve themselves; a miscellany, mé-lange, assortment.	大杂烩	dàzáhuì
beef up	v.p.	to make more powerful, strengthen.	加重	jiāzhòng

214

精英	精英	jīngyīng	n.	elite
平民	平民	píngmín	n.	common or ordinary people
拯救	拯救	zhěngjiù	n.	salvation
无非	無非	wúfēi	adv.	simply, only
天花板	天花板	tiānhuābǎn	n.	ceiling
世界之颠	世界之巔	shìjièzhīdiān	n.p.	the top of the world
零和	零和	línghé	n.	zero sum
游戏	游戏	yóuxì	n.	game
熏陶	熏陶	xūntáo	v.	shape, be influenced by
科目	科目	kēmù	n.	school subject
万事	萬事	wànshì	n.	everything
决定	決定	juédìng	v.	determine
优先次序	優先次序	yōuxiān-cìxù	f.c.w.	priority
民意测验	民意測驗	mínyì-cèyàn	f.c.w.	poll or survey of public opinion
成年人	成年人	chéngniánrén	n.	adult
逐一	逐一	zhúyī	adv.	one by one
软弱无力	軟弱無力	ruǎnruò-wúlì	f.c.w.	weak
优柔寡断	優柔寡斷	yōuróu-guǎduàn	f.c.w.	indecisive, irresolute, hesitant
偏见	偏見	piānjiàn	n.	stereotype, preconception
大不了	大不了	dàbuliǎo	adj.	no big deal, not problematic
面条	麵條	miàntiáo	n.	noodles
要么	要麼	yàome	conj.	or, either...or…
稀溜稀溜	稀溜稀溜	xīliūxīliū	r.f.	slurping
转来转去	轉來轉去	zhuànlái-zhuànqù	f.c.w.	twirl
轻盈飞舞	輕盈飛舞	qīngyíng-fēiwǔ	f.c.w.	skip
用力顿足	用力頓足	yònglì-dùnzú	f.c.w.	stomp
细声细语	細聲細語	xìshēng-xìyǔ	f.c.w.	hushed voice
粗声粗气	粗聲粗氣	cūshēng-cūqì	f.c.w.	shout
笼统	籠統	lǒngtǒng	adj.	general
付诸实施	付諸實施	fùzhū-shíshī	f.c.w.	put into effect
放进	放進	fàngjìn	v.o.	place in
面目全非	面目全非	miànmù-quánfēi	f.c.w.	beyond recognition, completely changed
拌	拌	bàn	v.	mix in, toss (a salad)
色拉	色拉	sèlā	n.	salad
大杂烩	大雜燴	dàzáhuì	n.	smorgasbord
竞选	竞選	jìngxuǎn	v.	campaign
副主席	副主席	fùzhǔxí	n.p.	vice chairman
加重	加重	jiāzhòng	v.	beef up, make or become more weighty

assembly	n.	a (large) gathering of people for a specific political, religious, social, etc. purpose; in schools, bringing all or portions of the student body together to witness or be part of a program.	集会	jíhuì
toot one's horn	v.p.	to tell people how good one is in general or in particular; brag, boast.	炫耀	xuànyào
doze off	v.p.	to sleep lightly or "nod off" when sitting or standing, that is, when not intending to sleep as in a bed.	打瞌睡	dǎ kēshuì
chart the way	v.p.	to pilot, guide, lead, map.	指引（航向）	zhǐyǐn (hángxiàng)
nurture	n.	upbringing, training, breeding, education. Also – v.	培养	péiyǎng
rectitude	n.	moral virtue; rightness of practice, correctness.	诚实，正直	chéngshí, zhèngzhí
introspection	n.	observation or examination of one's mental and emotional state; looking within for better understanding of self.	内省	nèixǐng
contemplation	n.	full, deep, or thoughtful observation or consideration of general conditions, God, humanity, nature, etc.	沉思	chénsī

亿	億	yì	num.	a hundred million
海报	海報	hǎibào	n.	poster
全校	全校	quánxiào	n.	the whole school
集会	集會	jíhuì	n.	assembly, gathering
劝说	勸說	quànshuō	v.	persuade
低调	低調	dīdiào	n.	low profile
神	神	shén	n.	god
炫耀	炫耀	xuànyào	v.	toot one's horn, show off, flaunt
实事	實事	shíshì	n.	work
打瞌睡	打瞌睡	dǎkēshuì	v.p.	doze off
在意	在意	zàiyì	v.	take notice of
秒钟	秒鐘	miǎozhōng	m(n)	second (of time)
哄堂大笑	哄堂大笑	hōngtáng-dàxiào	f.c.w.	the whole room burst into laughter
陈词滥调	陳詞濫調	chéncí-làndiào	f.c.w.	redundant, hackneyed
渠道	渠道	qúdào	n.	channels, sources
将……列表	將……列表	jiāng…lièbiǎo	p.p.	put sth. on the list
参考	參考	cānkǎo	v.	guide
独立自主	獨立自主	dúlì-zìzhǔ	f.c.w.	independence and self-reliance
制衡	制衡	zhìhéng	v.	balance
正直	正直	zhèngzhí	adj.	honest, upright, fair-minded
内省	內省	nèixǐng	v.	introspect
沉思	沉思	chénsī	v.	contemplate
谦卑	謙卑	qiānbēi	adj.	humble, modest
怜悯	憐憫	liánmǐn	v.	express sympathy for, have passion for
潜力	潛力	qiánlì	n.	potentiality
年长	年長	niánzhǎng	adj.	senior

第十章

在金字塔里

當威廉堅持要用英語來回答他母親的中文問題，或自豪地稱自己為"半個中國人"時，他并不是熱衷于某一文化而疏于另一文化。他三歲的時候就已經能熟練地穿梭在"鴨子"和"兔子"之間，知道什麼時候該認同這一類，而什麼時候認同另一類。在他第二天上學哭的時候，他的眼淚標志着當代美國式的金字塔文化。國家憲法、公司章程、宗教信仰和教育系統是這個金字塔的主要結構，各自都有一個頂點。在這里，總統、執行長官、教皇、校長擁有至高無上的行政權力，而處在金字塔"底部"的老百姓、選民、工人、教民和學生只能在下面角逐、竞爭余下的資源。

這個金字塔世界是由不同的個體所組成的。在這里，人人獨立，每個人都可以自由自在地用不同的方式選擇和終止某種關系，比如離婚、領養、訴訟、拒絕簽字。處在金字塔世界中的人際關系必須靠親近、擁抱和諸如"我愛你"、"我想你"、"我會"等文字來維持，當然也得借助于法律的力量。在這里，一人做事一人當，盡管他/她所遭到的懲罰或所獲取的榮譽會影響家人，但是，最后只是他/她一個人或銀鐺入獄，或中獎享福。是否與他人同甘共苦、榮辱與共完全由選擇和良心而定。在這個由獨立個體所組成的社會里，任何經驗，不管是好是壞、是成是敗、是在"塔頂"的精英還是在"塔底"的平民，都是獨自的。獲得成功、取得地位、得到拯救無非都是一個"爬樓梯"、"打破天花板"、"坐在世界之巔"的過程。用極端的話說，在這個文化世界中，生活就是一場零和游戲，之所以有人成功是因為有人失敗了。也就是說，這一切的一切都是"個人的"。

然而，即使一切都是個人的，但這并不表明所有一切都很重要。由金字塔文化熏陶、培養出來的人常常會問以下問題，"你最喜歡什麼顏色？""誰是你最好的朋友？""你最不喜歡的科目是什麼？"孩子們從小就學會怎樣在萬事中間決定優先次序。當民意測驗專家問，"什么是選民面臨的最重要的問題？"成年人也習慣于將復雜的社會現實逐一簡化為不同問題，因為在這個文化世界里，不會選擇就等于軟弱無力、優柔寡斷。

把文化歸為"蜘蛛網式的"或"金字塔式的"幾乎是一種帶有偏見的分類，這很危險，然而我們的（祖）父母在我們還未成年的時候就這么做了。他們常說，"中國人這么做，不那么做"，或者"愛爾蘭人喜歡那，不喜歡這"。對于他們，說這些話不是什么大不了的事。他們把自己的文化習俗傳了下來，使得我們在吃面條的時候要么發出稀溜稀溜的聲音，要么用叉子轉來轉去；使得我們在跳舞的時候要么輕盈飛舞，要么用力頓足；使得我們在說話的時候要么細聲細語，要么粗聲粗氣。大多數人認為自己的做法很正常，也許是最好的。沒有人在乎"政治上正確"的東西。然而，并非因為祖父母傳給了我們某些傳統就表明我們真的理解了所繼承的東西。我們首先得弄明白為什么我們吃面時會發出稀溜稀溜的聲音或用叉子轉來轉去，為什么在跳舞時會輕盈飛舞或用力頓足，為什么在說話時會細聲細語或粗聲粗氣。然后從這些籠統的概括中學會對不同情況作不同處理，這樣我們才能將"第一印象"轉換成通用、實際的知識。

我生下威廉以后就想着應該怎樣把以上這些付諸實施。如果把他放進"大熔爐"，各種文化的特點都被毀得面目全非，這顯然不能接受。"拌色拉"和"大雜燴"似乎比"大熔爐"好得多，但是對其中的每個成分是如何生長的、我們該如何準備仍缺乏解釋。對于我來說，怎樣付諸實施的一個重要方面就是避免打造極端的蜘蛛網或極端的金字塔。

當我在設想威廉將來的發展時，我想起了我的過去。1959 年我是我們郊區高中唯一的一個中國人，也是學生會的候選人之一。我竟選學生會副主席有兩個目的：

- 我想鍛煉自己的領導才能，以此加重我大學申請材料的分量。

- 我想給母親一個可以抱怨的機會（也是吹牛的機會）：我們二女兒當不了六億五千萬中國人的"小大使"，作為學生會副主席，她只能指揮六百五十個中學生!!!

我的挑戰是竟選。每個候選人除了準備海報以外，還得在全校集會上發表兩分鐘的演講，而麻煩的是：

- 我那美國的一面需要勸說選民讓他們知道我是最好的。

- 我那中國的一面需要保持低調，這樣眾神不會注意到我在炫耀。[19]

- 我那少年的一面需要避免傷害既是我朋友又是我竞選對手的感情。

輪到我演講時，同學們早已被枯燥的發言聽得坐不住了。因為學生會沒有權力做具體實事，所以每個竞選者都講自己有多誠實、多努力、多負責等等。我説的也是這些話，但是與他們唯一不同的是我用中文發表了演講。剛開始大家還在打瞌睡，沒有在意，接着清醒了，等過了一秒鐘弄清為什麼還沒有聽懂我在説什麼的時候大家哄堂大笑。誰都知道，不管我用什麼語言演講，我無非還是重復前面十幾位學生所説的陳詞濫調，但是因為我能順應大家對多元文化的需求，所以我的竞選成功了。

贏了竞選我很高興，但那時候我不知道如何談論這種勝利。打那以后，我從不同的渠道逐漸學會了應該怎樣做。在這里，我將"金字塔"和"蜘蛛網"這兩個不同文化世界的特點列表如下，以供參考。通過比較兩者，我對自己雙元文化的價值觀越來越清楚，同時也越來越希望建立多元文化的現實世界。

金字塔式的文化	蜘蛛網式的文化
自然	培養[20]
獨立自主	相互依賴
戰勝	制衡
正直和誠實	道德和面子
內省	沉思
客觀的知識	實際的智慧
謙卑	謙虛
權力	權威
同情	憐憫
將來的潛力/年輕	實際的經驗/年長

---

[19] Of the 150 or so Chinese gods, none are all-powerful, most don't like people who brag, and many aren't all that bright !!! Like many Asians, our family didn't "believe in" the gods but we *behaved* as if they exist – like *serious* etiquette.

[20] When Nurture outweighs Nature, behavior is primarily a matter of self-control and will-power, not biological inheritance or physical environment.

练习 EXERCISES

I. 思考和课堂讨论 FOOD FOR THOUGHT

A. PERSONAL 个人的

在你生活中哪些方面是"蜘蛛网"式的，哪些是"金字塔"式的？区分两种不同的文化世界有没有困难？为什么？

Which aspects of your life, if any, are more pyramidal? Which more web-like? Is the difference problematic? If so, how? If not, why not?

B. GENERAL 普遍的

An "argument" or line of reasoning is logical when a conclusion is validly deduced from premises that are assumed to be true. However, when there is an error in reasoning, then a fallacy occurs. In order to think clearly and effectively, it helps to know about these errors. After reading the following, discuss the question posed.

当某一结论是从一个正确的前提演绎出来的，那么该结论的论据符合逻辑。但是，如果推理出现错误，就会产生谬论。为了清楚、有效地思考，有必要了解这些推理错误。请阅读下面的错误，然后讨论所提出的问题。

begging the question is from the Latin *petitio principii* = request for the beginning.

pattern: Mr. X argues for the truth of a conclusion or "the matter in question" by assuming that very same conclusion (usually worded differently) as a premise, that is, is true by assumption, not true by proof or argument.

example: Someone is **begging the question** if they say "Ms. Y is a great writer. How do I know? Because all the good readers agree Ms. Y is a great writer. And what makes them good readers? Because they all read Ms. Y's books."

question: Why is Mr. X's fallacious approach described as **"going in circles"** or **"circular reasoning"**? What if Ms. Y really is a great writer? Does Mr. X's circular reasoning change that opinion?

C. CROSS-CULTURAL 跨文化的

After reading the following, discuss <u>in English</u> why members of a family should complement rather than compete with each other. Relate this to the idea that every kind of animal year is necessary because, if the explosive and dramatic Tiger year is not followed by the placid and calm Rabbit Year, we'd be exhausted **!!!**

阅读以下短文，并<u>用英文</u>对所提出的问题进行讨论。

The "Model Minority" myth in America rests on the fact that many Chinese and Japanese students earned a reputation for being good students, especially during the mid-twentieth century. Obviously, a long history of valuing education accounted for their performance. However, in recent decades, the criteria for being a "good student" has been mixed with

American standards so that doing well academically is no longer sufficient. So, in addition to the academic requirements, a high school student is pushed to attain a wide range of "bests" as an athlete, musician, worker, and volunteer. Among these "bests," are also socially "popular" as well as inventor, business owner, published writer, bird-watcher, and/or gourmet cook !!! At the same time, changes in immigration laws have resulted in many more Asians from many other countries with many different backgrounds and disadvantages. Thus the former simple reality is now a complex myth that is used to measure "an" Asian minority that is actually very multicultural. The pressure for every child in a family to be a "good student" by this revised standard in a pyramidal world is tremendous, often overwhelming.

II. 配对 MATCHMAKER

A. VOCABULARY 词汇

找出以下两列中的对应词，并在其间划线。

Draw a connecting line between the word and its correct definition.

a.	章程	1.	smack of
b.	尖峰，高峰，顶点	2.	give a hoot about sth.
c.	打瞌睡	3.	ignominy
d.	受母亲的控制	4.	by-laws
e.	软弱无力	5.	nurture
f.	内省	6.	doze off
g.	在乎	7.	tossed salad
h.	培养	8.	be tied to mother's apron strings
i.	拌色拉	9.	wishy-washy
j.	带有……味道，有点象	10.	pinnacle
k.	羞耻，屈辱	11.	introspection

a.	human relation	1.	金字塔
b.	noodles	2.	领养孩子
c.	beyond recognition	3.	由……而定
d.	adopt a child	4.	良心
e.	pyramid	5.	衰落，失败
f.	depending on	6.	正直

222

g. conscience   7. 面目全非

h. poster   8. 面条

i. upright   9. 人际关系

j. zero-sum game   10. 零和游戏

k. debase   11. 海报

B. SYNONYMS & ALTERNATES 同义词和多义词

First draw a connecting line between the word or phrase in the left-hand column with the best possible <u>synonym</u> listed in the middle column, then draw a line between the synonym and an alternate meaning of the synonym listed in the right-hand column. <u>Be forewarned</u> that the part of speech may change from one column to the next and that slang terms may be used. E.g.,

"hit" ——————————— *"strike"* ————— *"stop-work action against employer"*

"warm" ——————————— *"heat"* ————— *"qualifying race for final contest"*

首先在第二列中找出与第一列相对应的同义词，然后在第三列中找出与第二列相关的多义词。注意：词性会有不同。

			SYNONYMS	ALTERNATE MEANING
a.	suddenly run, escape, flee	1.	**noodle**	i. to install secret listening device
b.	a loud sudden sound	2.	**bug**	ii. joking trick or harmless deception
c.	flash as lightning	3.	**blast**	iii. run naked in a public place
d.	edge of mouth, canyon, etc.	4.	**con**	iv. a short period of self-indulgence
e..	pasta, food item	5.	**plant**	v. *slang* impudent talk, sass
f.	put in soil or mind for growth	6.	**bolt**	vi. *slang* the head, brain
g.	annoy, bother, pester	7.	**gag**	vii. wild party
h.	violently throw or hurl	8.	**lip**	viii hurriedly eat or drink
i.	retch, choke	9.	**streak**	ix. company building, land, etc.
j.	memorize, study	10.	**fling**	x. swindle, deceive

III. 解字/词、构字/词 DECONSTRUCTION & CONSTRUCTION

A. 将以下汉字分解成最小的构字部件，然后用每个部件构成三个汉字。例如"鸭"可以分解成 "甲"和"鸟"两个部件。"甲"能构成"押"，"岬"，"钾"；"鸟"可以构成以"鸡"，"鸦"，"鸣"。请借助字典完成练习。

Deconstruct the following characters into the smallest components, then form 3 new characters using each component.

进_____   跳_____   实_____

懂_____ 赢_____ 瞓_____

B. Using only the letters of the word **"PINNACLE,"** form English words that are not proper nouns, abbreviations, or acronyms and that consist of 4 or more letters. A letter can only be used again if it appears in the given word more than once. E.g., "pack" is not acceptable because there is no "k" and "peel" is not because there is only one "e." Like many Olympic sports, weight categories mark performance. We filled in a few cells to get you started. Fill in the rest to achieve the highest category. If you think up more than 40, you beat the authors!

用 **"PINNACLE"** 中的字母构词。新构建的词不能是专有名词、缩写词、或首字母缩略词。每个单词必须至少含有四个字母，但不能重复使用同一字母，除非该字母在 **"PINNACLE"**中出现两次。

CHAMPION STATUS			
FEATHER **10**	**WELTER** **20**	**MIDDLE** **30**	**HEAVY** **40**
pain	clean	lean	acne

C. 用 "金字塔" 中的每个汉字组成不同的词。看看最多能组多少个词。

Use each of the characters in "金字塔" to form as many words (of 2-4 characters) as you can.

D. Pair any two of the following 12 words to form at least 13 different, unhyphenated words.

在下列十二个词中配对、组词，新组的词只能含有两个单词，中间没有连字号。请至少组出十三个词。

wink sister bat step spread hood stop bed back door boy wing

IV. 阅读理解 READING QUIZ

根据课文，选择准确答案。Based on the text, choose the best answer.

1. 对于不同的文化我们应该持有什么态度？

   a. 应该热衷一种文化。

   b. 应该冷淡一种文化。

   c. 应该认同一种文化。

   d. 学习、了解不同文化。

2. 以下哪些人是站在"金字塔世界"的顶点的？

   a. 工人， 工头。

   b. 学生，教师。

   c. 总统，教皇。

   d. 选民，竞选者。

3. 以下哪一个答案准确描述了"金字塔式的"人际关系？

   a. 在"金字塔"里，人们可以自山选择某种关系。

   b. 在"金字塔"里，人们可以自由终止某种关系。

   c. 在"金字塔"里，人们喜欢说，"我爱你"，并喜欢亲吻、拥抱 。

   d. 以上都对。

4. 为什么在"金字塔的文化世界"中，生活是一场零和游戏？

   a. 因为在这里，只有成功者才能登上高峰。

   b. 因为在这里，人人都想打破天花板。

   c. 因为在这里，人人都想坐在世界之巅。

   d. 因为在这里，人人天天都在爬楼梯。

5. 人们应该怎样看待祖父母传给下一代的文化习俗？

   a. 一切都是正确的，应该毫无保留地继承下去。

   b. 要理解这些习俗，通过分析，得出不同结论。

   c. 他们从小就这么做，所以是"政治上正确的"。

   d. 大多数做法都很正常，也许是有道理的。

6. 在全校的集会上，作者为什么用中文发表演讲？

   a. 因为她只会说中文。

   b. 因为同学喜欢中文。

   c. 因为她想练习中文。

   d. 因为她想显示多元化。

V. 填空　FILL IN THE BLANK

A.　选择正确答案。Choose the correct answer.

1.　威廉＿＿＿＿地称自己为"半个中国人"。

　　a.　自豪　　　　b.　自信　　　　c.　自私

2.　威廉的眼泪＿＿＿＿着当代美国式的金字塔文化。

　　a.　标明　　　　b.　标志　　　　c.　标示

3.　处在金字塔世界中的人际关系必须靠文字来＿＿＿＿。

　　a.　维持　　　　b.　保持　　　　c.　坚持

4.　我们应该避免打造＿＿＿＿的"蜘蛛网"或"金字塔"文化。

　　a.　极点　　　　b.　极顶　　　　c.　极端

5.　我想竞选学生议员以＿＿＿＿我的大学申请材料的分量。

　　a.　加快　　　　b.　加重　　　　c.　加强

6.　我的竞选演讲强调了同学对多元文化的＿＿＿＿。

　　a.　请求　　　　b.　寻求　　　　c.　需求

B.　在以下段落中找出与斜体词意义相近的反义词。如果你所学的外语是中文，找出相应的中文词或短语。如果你所学的外语是英语，找出相应的英语词或短语。注意：词性或时态会有变化。

Using your target language, write a word or phrase from the vocabulary lists and/or dictionary that means the <u>opposite</u> or is an <u>antonym</u> for the italicized word or phrase. Keep in mind that the part of speech and/or tense may have been adjusted to achieve grammatically correct results.

When the movie star got sick and *lost his muscle tone* ＿＿＿＿＿＿, he was relieved to find out that his *"tough guy"* ＿＿＿＿＿＿ reputation depended more on his acting ability than on his good physical condition. This discovery so *purified* ＿＿＿＿＿＿ his spirits of doubt that he felt *reconnected with* ＿＿＿＿＿＿ the confident self he was before becoming famous.

VI. 翻译　TRANSLATION

A.　将以下句子翻译成英文。Translate the following sentences into English.

1.　他三岁的时候就已经能熟练地穿梭在"鸭子"和"兔子"之间，知道什么时候该认同这一类，而什么时候认同另一类。

2.　在这个由独立个体所组成的社会里，任何经验，不管是好是坏、是成是败、是在"塔顶"的精英还是在"塔底"的平民，都是独自的。

3.　把文化归为"蜘蛛网式的"或"金字塔式的"几乎是一种带有偏见的分类，这很危险，然而我们的（祖）父母在我们还未成年的时候就这么做了。

B. Translate the following sentences into Chinese. 将以下句子翻译成中文。

1. The second time I escorted William to his classroom, I expected him to behave the same as he did the first day when he immediately went in and sat down.

2. This universe is populated with separate individuals. Each is independently free to choose relationships *and* free to sever them by divorce, adoption, lawsuit, and refusal to sign on the dotted line.

3. By charting the way, I am more clear about the strategies valued by my dual heritage and more hopeful about creating multiple realities.

VII. 完型填充　CLOZE TEST

A. 在以下短文的每一空格处填入一个汉字，如有可能，给出相应的英语单词。

Fill in a Chinese character that retains the original meaning or intent of the text, then write an English equivalent, if any.

> 当威廉坚持要用英文来回答他母亲的中文问题，或白豪地称白_____为"半个中国人"_____，他并不是热衷_____一文化而疏于_____一文化。他三岁_____时候就已经能 _____练地穿梭在"鸭_____"和"兔子"之间，知_____什么时候该认_____这一类，而什么_____候认同另一类。_____他第二天上学_____的时候，他的眼_____标志着当代美_____式的金字塔文_____。

B. Fill in an English word or phrase that retains the original meaning or intent of the text, then write a Chinese equivalent, if any.

在以下短文的每一空格处填入一个英语单词，如有可能，给出相应的汉字或词。

> When William insisted on responding in English _____ his mother's Chinese, or crowed with pride "_____ half Chinese!" he was not being more _____ to one culture over the other. Rather, _____ was, at three, already switching between a "_____" and "rabbit" way of being—one moment _____ more vividly with one, the next _____, the other. When he cried on his _____ day at school, his tears took shape _____ the pyramidal universe of (a modern American). _____ this universe, the Constitution, corporate by-laws, religious _____, and educational system form the major institutions _____ always have a pinnacle. Here the president, _____, pope, and principal hold the highest office _____ have the most power.

VIII. 身体部位　BODY PARTS

A. There are many useful idioms which contain "body parts." Choose the most appropriate to fill in the blank based on your best guess of what the idiom means.

227

英语中的许多习惯用语含有表示"身体部位"的单词。在下面三个习惯用语中选择最恰当的填空。

1. look down one's nose   2. cut off one's nose to spite one's face   3. pay through the nose

To _____ for a gift that was totally overpriced to make his wife feel better about how much money they owed the bank proved that his brain was several "noodles" shy of a full bowl **!!!**

When she first brought her new boyfriend home for a family dinner, her father was very cordial but, when she saw her snobbish mother _____ at his unsophisticated ways and lack of "good" breeding, the daughter knew things would not be easy for them as a couple.

To punish his neighbors for having a dog that barked all night, he let the garbage accumulate for weeks. The foul smell permeated the air so he really _____ since he also had to breathe the same air.

B. 将以下短文翻译成中文。注意：划线的词或短语与以上含有"身体部位"的习惯用语相对应。

Translate the following into Chinese taking note that the underlined words or phrases correspond to the meaning of the above "body parts."

She <u>looked condescendingly</u> at the battered old car and declined his offer to drive her to the gas station, preferring to walk rather than be seen in such a vehicle. As it turned out, she only <u>hurt herself</u> because the nearest station was closed and the next one was not only miles away but priced higher so she also had to <u>pay through the nose for a tankful</u>.

C. Using your target language, create sentence(s) containing the following three English idioms or their Chinese equivalents.

用以下短语分别造句。如果你所学的外语是中文，请用中文来做这个练习。如果你所学的外语是英语，请用英语来做这个练习。

1. keep or hold one's nose to the grindstone = 努力工作，埋头苦干

2. count noses = 清点人数

3. on the nose = 正是，正好，恰到好处

IX. 写作 PRÉCIS

用所学的外语总结课文。如果你用中文来写，请至少使用 450 个汉字，并用电脑打出摘要。如果你用英文来写，请不超过 350 个词。

Write a summary of this chapter in your target language. If writing in Chinese, use <u>more</u> than 450 characters; if writing in English, use <u>no more</u> than 350 words.

CHAPTER ELEVEN

ABIDING WITH MULTIPLE REALITIES

British author, Rudyard Kipling, captured the Pyramid spirit in his poem "*If you can keep your head when all about you are losing theirs…you'll be a Man, my son!*" Had Kipling been from a Web culture, his poem might have been, "*If you can keep your head when all about you are losing theirs…then there is probably something *very* wrong with you, your family, your village, your ruler, *and* your ancestors* **!!!**"

 This is what I visualize when I think about the multiple realities that shape my life. By truncating the pyramid, I prioritize people, places and things but make room for more than one at the top. By participating in many webs, I diversify who I am. By linking the webs, I am challenged to connect them with compassion, intelligence, loyalty, and humor. The result looks messy but it isn't boring, especially when the webs involve dating and mating **!!!**

For many reasons—social conditioning, biological determination, religious teaching, and so on—gender happens **!!!**[21] If we then take into account generational, economic, political, psychological, "racial" and/or astrological factors,[22] all premarital and marital matters are cross-cultural.

For example, after giving a talk at a university, a man of about forty years asked, "Can you help me?"

I answered, "I'll try."

He continued, "I'm like your son—half-half. My mother is Chinese, my father Caucasian. Last week I brought my date home where I have a basement apartment. My mother went ballistic because the date had blond hair and blue eyes! It's crazy for her to get mad at me for going out with a non-Chinese. My father is one!"

---

[21]关于性别这一题材有两本畅销书：一本是 Deborah Tannen 的 *You Just Don't Understand: Women and Men in Conversation*；一本是 John Gray 的 *Men Are from Mars, Women Are from Venus: A Practical Guide for Improving Communication and Getting What You Want in Your Relationships*。

[22]虽然人们不相信占星术可以预测未来，但是大家仍然喜欢阅读有关自己的星座。男人也总爱用"你是什么星座"这样的问题与单身女子搭讪。美国人在吹牛时常常会"摸摸木头"，希望能走好运。同样，中国人深知神的威力也常在神的面前说好话，并表现得规规矩矩以讨好他们**!!!**

第十一章

多元化的现实

英国作家鲁迪·杰卜林（Rudyard Kipling）有一首诗曾这样描写金字塔文化世界的精髓：“当你周围的人都已惊慌失措，而你还能保持镇静…… 那你是一个勇敢者，我的儿子！” 如果杰卜林来自蜘蛛网文化世界，那么这首诗可能会这样说：“当你周围的人都已惊慌失措，而你还能保持镇静……那么很有可能你本人、你全家、你的村庄、你的领导人乃至你的祖先都很有问题。”

我的生活是一个多元化的现实世界，可以用以下这个图形来表示：这是一个包含多个蜘蛛网但又没有顶的金字塔。我之所以切掉了金字塔的塔顶，是因为我要强调人物、地点和事情的重要性，并使金字塔的顶部可容得下一个以上的人物、地点和事情。参与多个不同的蜘蛛网使我变得更具多元化，能够接受挑战，并学会如何用爱心、智慧、忠诚和幽默将不同的蜘蛛网结合在一起。虽然其结果看起来乱七八糟，但其实一点也不枯躁，尤其是涉及到约会和成家这两件事。

很多不同因素，如社会条件、生物基因、宗教宣道等，导致男女有别。[21] 如果我们考虑代沟、经济、政治、心理学、人种学或占星学等因素，[22] 那么所有婚前、婚后的事情都是“跨文化的”。

举个例子来说，有一次，我在大学作完报告以后，一个大约四十左右的男听众问我，“你能帮个忙吗？”

---

[21] Two popular authors who write about this are Deborah Tannen in *You Just Don't Understand: Women and Men in Conversation* and John Gray in *Men Are from Mars, Women Are from Venus: A Practical Guide for Improving Communication and Getting What You Want in Your Relationships* respectively.

[22] Although people do not “believe in” predicting the future by astrology, they still like to read their horoscope. A hackneyed “pick-up line” is to ask someone at a singles bar what their sign is. Similarly, Americans often “knock on wood” when they say something boastful or wishful to prevent Fate from hearing. Meanwhile Chinese try to fool the gods with optimistic talk and behavior because these spirits are powerful but not all that bright.

I asked, "Was she an important date? Is she someone you might marry?"

"No."

I laughed, "Then *why* would you bring her home? !!!" You have limited credit in the "blood bank."[23] Don't spend it for no good reason !!! She's obliged to give good advice (even when she doesn't have any !!!) so the gods and ancestors know she's a dutiful mother who honors their line-age."

"That's crazy—she's not religious."

"This isn't about belief. It's about good behavior."

"But my father is White so it's not like the gods don't already know about us being "mixed up"[24] down here."

"Well, then consider the psychological impact of seeing you with someone who looks her complete opposite."

"Yeah, I guess so. But what if I do end up marrying a Caucasian?"

"Time is on your side. The longer you wait to give her grandchildren, the less she's going to care that they don't look like her !!!"

I told him not to forget his frustration because, one day, his daughter may feel the same way about him. This kind of remembering is even harder when dating leads to mating. I know—I've been at both ends. First, I married Bennett and ignored how seriously my parents believed in one of the few Universal Truths, that is, *no* father, *regardless* of culture, *ever* says to his daughter, "*Please, marry an artist.*" !!! Happily, Bennett stuck it out—for years he faithfully visited my parents, being a filial son while they talked about him in uncomplimentary Chinese.

And then it was my turn. I can imagine a variety of women hoping for a "good marriage." I can also imagine the variety in what is considered "good" based on race, sex, national origin, age, height, and so on. What I would find very hard to imagine is many women falling to their knees, fervently praying for a Chinese mother-in-law !!! And, when I became one, there were too many times when I saw the reason why there are so many jokes about this complex relationship.

After William and Lisa got married, they continued to live in San Francisco where they crafted a very nice life indeed. However, when he left abruptly to take a job in Taipei, Lisa stayed in California

---

[23]"blood bank" 是一个双关语，指血库和家庭关系价值观。
[24]这是另一个双关语，指把不同的成分混合在一起，也指糊涂。

我回答说，"试试看吧。"

他接着说，"我跟你儿子一样，一半一半。我母亲是中国人，父亲是白人。上星期我把一个女朋友带回家，我的房间在地下室。当我母亲发现女友是金发碧眼后一下子就爆发了。我找了一个白人女朋友，她就这样，这不是太过分了吗？我父亲就是个白人!"

我问他，"你们的关系定下来了吗？你是不是要娶她？"

"不。"

我笑了。"那么你为什么要把她带回家呢？你的'血库'里没有多少本钱、信誉，不要随便乱花在不值钱的东西上。你母亲有责任劝告你（就算她什么忠告也没有，她也得说点儿什么!!!），这样众神和祖先才知道她是一个尊重血统、尽责任的母亲。"

"这很荒谬，她可不信神。"

"这跟信仰没关，这跟行为有关。"

"但是，我父亲是个白人。难道众神不知道我们家的血源早已有问题了吗!"

"看你找了一个跟她长得完全不同的女人，你母亲一定有很多心理压力，你也得为她想一想呀？"

"也许吧。但是，如果我最后真的要娶个白人太太，那怎么办？"

"时间操纵在你手里呀！你让她等得越久才能抱上孙子和孙女，她就越不计较他们长得是不是跟她一样!!!"

我提醒他记住这些烦恼，因为总有一天他的女儿会对他有同样的看法。当约会最后走到成家这条路，要记住这些烦恼尤其艰难。对此，我深有体会，因为这两个方面我都经历过。第一，我嫁给了班尼特，完全忽略了父母深信不疑的人世间的真理，那就是，没有哪个父亲，不管哪种文化，会对他女儿说，"你嫁个艺术家吧！"幸运的是，班尼特总算熬了过来。过去的几十年里他一直忠实地探访我父母，不管他们怎么用中文对他评头论足，他都一如既往地孝敬他们。

接下来就轮到我了。我可以想象为什么很多妇女希望有个好的婚姻，我也能想象为什么由于种族、性别、性生活、国家、年龄、身高等不同因素，有的婚姻被看作是很幸福

to sell the car and pack up their apartment. That was June. Come September, Lisa still owned the car and nothing was packed. She loved San Francisco. One day she telephoned. When I detected in her voice less of the dutiful cheerfulness that I and countless others have forced during those "have to" calls, I asked, "Lisa, what's wrong? You sound really down."

"I am. My mother just called, my father just called. Even my grandmother called. They're telling me I'm a terrible wife because I'm not over there helping William."

Suppressing an urge to crow my joy at the opportunity of having a mother-daughter relationship that only incidentally came about by legal contract, I said, "Don't worry. William is my son. He can cook, iron, clean and sew. He's found a great furnished apartment near his office. He's fine. You go when *you're* ready."

To which Lisa wailed, "But they keep calling me," followed by a sober, quiet, "And I feel so guilty."

In my Empress Dowager voice, I responded, "Call your mother. Call your father. *And* call your grandmother. You tell them that *I'm* your Chinese mother-in-law—I *own* you !!!

Stunned silence from California.

I continued in my smiling voice, "Tell them you cannot possibly leave San Francisco until *I* say you can !!!"

Then I heard Lisa chuckle and felt that her "double take" on the "duck-rabbit" I had just pulled out of a hat was priceless at a modern "customs rate of exchange" because "thumbing our knows" allowed us to cross "time zones" and enjoy "minority minutes" as in-laws who had not outlawed each other.

VOCABULARY

visualize	v.	to form a mental image or picture; imagine.	将事物放在心里想像	jiāng shìwù fàngzài xīn lǐ xiǎngxiàng
truncate	v.	to cut off a part, apex or end.	切去头端, 缩短, 截成平面	qiēqù tóuduān, suōduǎn, jié-chéng píngmiàn

的，而有的则不是。但是我想，没有人会跪下来虔诚地祈祷，希望有个中国婆婆吧**!!!** 当我成了别人的婆婆以后，我多次思考这个问题，终于明白了为什么在复杂的婆媳关系上会有那么多的笑话。

威廉和丽莎结婚后，继续住在旧金山，在那儿他们生活得很安逸。可是，不久威廉突然获得一份工作去了台北，而丽莎仍然留在加州。她得把车子卖了、把家收拾好后才能走。那时是六月份，但一直到了九月份，丽莎的车子还是没有卖掉，东西也还没有整好，因为她喜欢旧金山，不想动。一天，她打来了一个电话。我听不出她以往那种带有"责任"性的、快活的声音，那种我们常常会在"不得不要打"的电话中流露出来的语调。我问，"丽莎，你怎么啦？听起来不开心吗。"

"是啊。我妈刚给我打电话。我爸也给我打电话，连我姥姥也打过。他们都说我是一个不负责的太太，因为我没有去台湾帮助威廉。"

一张结婚纸居然能给我带来这样的婆媳关系，我真是欣喜若狂。但我还是按捺住内心的喜悦，对她说："不要急，威廉是我的儿子，他会做饭，烫衣，打扫，缝补。他在台北的办公室附近找了一个设施具备的公寓，他在那儿没问题。你什么时候想走，再走。"

听了我的话，丽莎呜咽着，"可是他们不停地给我打电话呀"，接着她又认真、平静地说，"我自己也觉得很内疚。"

接着我以慈禧太后的口气命令她，"给你妈打电话。给你爸打电话。给你姥姥打电话。告诉他们，我是你的中国婆婆，我拥有你**!!!**"

电话那头——加利福尼亚——鸦雀无声。

我继续兴奋地说："告诉他们，我说你什么时候能离开旧金山，你就什么时候走!"

这时我听到丽莎在电话那头吃吃地轻笑。我就"鸭子-兔子"这个问题神奇般地向她大显了身手，她"先是一愣，然后恍然大悟"。她的这种反应用当代"文化习俗兑换率"是有钱都买不到的，因为"学以致用"让我们跨越了多元文化的"不同时区"，使我们能消除婆媳间的隔阂走到一起，共同欣赏"少数族群的光辉记载"。

premarital	adj.	preceding marriage.	婚前	hūnqián
go ballistic	v.p.	to (re)act explosively and forcefully like the projectile motion of a bullet or missile.	爆发	bàofā
blood bank	n.p.	a place, usually a hospital facility, to preserve blood for transfusions.	血库	xuèkù
be obliged to do sth.	v.p.	be required to do by law, conscience, sense of duty, contract, etc.	被迫做事	bèipò zuòshì
honor one's lineage	v.p.	to respect or carry on one's family (blood) line or name.	尊重家庭传统,光宗耀祖	zūnzhòng jiātíng chuántǒng, guāngzōng-yàozǔ
end up (doing sth.)	v.p.	to conclude or finalize a process with a particular action.	以做某事而结束	yǐ zuò mǒushì ér jiéshù
fall to one's knees	v.p.	to drop down to the ground landing on both knees as an act of prayer or gratitude.	跪下	guìxià
fervently	adv.	with much warmth or great intensity of spirit, enthusiasm, feeling.	热诚地, 热心地	rèchéng de, rèxīn de
craft	v.	to make or fashion using acquired techniques or skills.	编织	biānzhī
pack up	v.p.	to arrange (into boxes, vehicles, etc.) things to be carried or moved from one place to another.	收拾	shōushi
wail	v.	to grieve with prolonged cries or high-pitched sounds.	哭泣	kūqì
pull out of the hat	v.p.	to suddenly or surprisingly produce a result, idea, or plan without prior warning like the stage trick when a performer "magically" lifts a live rabbit out of what seemed to be an empty top hat.	神奇般地给出结果、观点、计划	shénqíbān de gěichū jiéguǒ、guāndiǎn、jìhuà

生词

鲁迪·杰卜林	魯迪·傑卜林	Lǔdí Jiébǔlín	p.n.	Rudyard Kipling
精髓	精髓	jīngsuǐ	n.	spirit, essence
惊慌失措	驚慌失措	jīnghuāng-shīcuò	t.c.w.	losing one's head, seized with panic
保持	保持	bǎochí	v.	keep, maintain
镇静	鎮靜	zhènjìng	adj.	calm
乃至	乃至	nǎizhì	conj.	even
图形	圖形	túxíng	n.	sketch, drawing
之所以	之所以	zhīsuǒyǐ	conj.	the reason why
强调	強調	qiángdiào	v.	emphasize
重要性	重要性	zhòngyàoxìng	n.	importance, significance
顶部	頂部	dǐngbù	n.	the top part
容得下	容得下	róngdexià	v.	hold, contain, make room for
参与	參與	cānyù	v.	participate in
接受	接受	jiēshòu	v.	take, accept
挑战	挑戰	tiǎozhàn	n	challenge
幽默	幽默	yōumò	n.	humor
结合	結合	jiéhé	v.	connect
涉及	涉及	shèjí	v.	involve, concern
成家	成家	chéngjiā	v.o.	marry, mate
基因	基因	jīyīn	n.	gene
男女有别	男女有別	nánnǚ-yǒubié	f.o.w.	difference between men and women
占星学	占星學	zhānxīngxué	n.	astrology
婚前	婚前	hūnqián	n.	premarital, before marriage
婚后	婚後	hūnhòu	n.	postnuptial, after marriage
跨文化的	跨文化的	kuàwénhuàde	adj.	cross-cultural
听众	聽眾	tīngzhòng	n.	audience, listener
地下室	地下室	dìxiàshì	n.	basement
金发碧眼	金髮碧眼	jīnfà-bìyǎn	f.c.w.	blonde
娶	娶	qǔ	v.	marry (a woman), take a wife
对象	對象	duìxiàng	n.	girlfriend/boyfriend, also spouse
血库	血庫	xuèkù	n.	blood bank
本钱	本錢	běnqián	n.	principal (used to gain or pursue profit)
信誉	信譽	xìnyù	n.	credit
值钱	值錢	zhíqián	adj.	valuable, worthwhile
血统	血統	xuètǒng	n.	blood lineage
荒谬	荒謬	huāngmiù	adj.	crazy, ridiculous, absurd, preposterous
操纵	操縱	cāozòng	v.	operate, handle

第十一章

多元化的現實

英國作家魯迪・杰卜林（Rudyard Kipling）有一首詩曾這樣描寫金字塔文化世界的精髓：" 當你周圍的人都已驚慌失措，而你還能保持鎮靜…… 那你是一個勇敢者，我的兒子！ " 如果杰卜林來自蜘蛛網文化世界，那么這首詩可能會這樣說：" 當你周圍的人都已驚慌失措，而你還能保持鎮靜……那么很有可能你本人、你全家、你的村莊、你的領導人乃至你的祖先都很有問題。 "

我的生活是一個多元化的現實世界，可以用以下這個圖形來表示：這是一個包含多個蜘蛛網但又沒有頂的金字塔。我之所以切掉了金字塔的塔頂，是因為我要強調人物、地點和事情的重要性，并使金字塔的頂部可容得下一個以上的人物、地點和事情。參與多個不同的蜘蛛網使我變得更具多元化，能夠接受挑戰，并學會如何用愛心、智慧、忠誠和幽默將不同的蜘蛛網結合在一起。雖然其結果看起來亂七八糟，但其實一點也不枯燥，尤其是涉及到約會和成家這兩件事。

很多不同因素，如社會條件、生物基因、宗教宣道等，導致男女有別。[21] 如果我們考慮代溝、經濟、政治、心理學、人種學或占星學等因素，[22] 那么所有婚前、婚后的事情都是 " 跨文化的 "。

舉個例子來說，有一次，我在大學作完報告以后，一個大約四十左右的男聽眾問我，" 你能幫個忙嗎？ "

---

[21] Two popular authors who write about this are Deborah Tannen in *You Just Don't Understand: Women and Men in Conversation* and John Gray in *Men Are from Mars, Women Are from Venus: A Practical Guide for Improving Communication and Getting What You Want in Your Relationships* respectively.

[22] Although people do not "believe in" predicting the future by astrology, they still like to read their horoscope. A hackneyed "pick-up line" is to ask someone at a singles bar what their sign is. Similarly, Americans often "knock on wood" when they say something boastful or wishful to prevent Fate from hearing. Meanwhile Chinese try to fool the gods with optimistic talk and behavior because these spirits are powerful but not all that bright.

手里	手裡	shǒulǐ	n.	in one's hand
计较	計較	jìjiào	v.	care about
忽略	忽略	hūlüè	v	ignore
深信无疑	深信無疑	shēnxìn-wúyí	f.c.w.	firmly convinced
人世间	人世間	rénshìjiān	n.	human world
嫁	嫁	jià	v.	(of a woman) marry
熬	熬	áo	v.	stick out
探访	探訪	tànfǎng	v.	visit
评头论足	評頭論足	píngtóu-lùnzú	f.c.w.	be critical, nit-pick
一如既往	一如既往	yīrú-jìwǎng	f.c.w.	all the time, for years, just as in the past
孝敬	孝敬	xiàojìng	v.	be filial and respectful to one's elders
身高	身高	shēngāo	n.	(a person's) height
跪	跪	guì	v.	kneel
虔诚	虔誠	qiánchéng	adj.	fervent, sincere
祈祷	祈禱	qídǎo	v.	pray
旧金山	舊金山	Jiùjīnshān	p.n.	San Francisco, CA
安逸	安逸	ānyì	adj.	nice and comfortable
收拾	收拾	shōushi	v.	pack up
打来	打來	dǎlái	v (c)	make (a telephone call)
流露	流露	liúlù	v.	reveal, show
婆媳	婆媳	póxí	n.	mother-in-law and daughter-in-law
欣喜若狂	欣喜若狂	xīnxǐ-ruòkuáng	f.c.w.	be joyful
按捺	按捺	ànnà	v.	suppress, restrain
喜悦	喜悦	xǐyuè	n.	joy
烫	燙	tàng	v.	iron
缝补	縫補	fénghǔ	v.	sow
设施	設施	shèshī	n.	facility
具备	具備	jùbèi	v.	furnish, be equipped with
慈禧太后	慈禧太后	Cíxǐ Tàihòu	p.n.	Empress Dowager (1835-1908), ruling over Manchu Qing dynasty in China for 47 years
鸦雀无声	鴉雀無聲	yāquè-wúshēng	f.c.w.	stunned silence
神奇	神奇	shénqí	adj.	magical
大显身手	大显身手	dàxiǎn-shēnshǒu	f.c.w.	pull out of the hat, accomplish
隔阂	隔閡	géhé	n.	misunderstanding, gap
光辉	光輝	guānghuī	adj.	momentous
记载	記載	jìzǎi	n.	minutes

我回答説，"試試看吧。"

他接着説，"我跟你兒子一樣，一半一半。我母親是中國人，父親是白人。上星期我把一個女朋友帶回家，我的房間在地下室。當我母親發現女友是金發碧眼后一下子就爆發了。我找了一個白人女朋友，她就這樣，這不是太過分了嗎？我父親就是個白人！"

我問他，"你們的關系定下來了嗎？你是不是要娶她？"

"不。"

我笑了。"那么你為什么要把她帶回家呢？你的'血庫'里沒有多少本錢、信譽，不要隨便亂花在不值錢的東西上。你母親有責任勸告你（就算她什么忠告也沒有，她也得説點兒什么!!!），這樣眾神和祖先才知道她是一個尊重血統、盡責任的母親。"

"這很荒謬，她可不信神。"

"這跟信仰沒關，這跟行為有關。"

"但是，我父親是個白人。難道眾神不知道我們家的血源早已有問題了嗎！"

"看你找了一個跟她長得完全不同的女人，你母親一定有很多心理壓力，你也得為她想一想呀？"

"也許吧。但是，如果我最后真的要娶個白人太太，那怎么辦？"

"時間操縱在你手里呀！你讓她等得越久才能抱上孫子和孫女，她就越不計較他們長得是不是跟她一樣!!!"

我提醒他記住這些煩惱，因為總有一天他的女兒會對他有同樣的看法。當約會最后走到成家這條路，要記住這些煩惱尤其艱難。對此，我深有體會，因為這兩個方面我都經歷過。第一，我嫁給了班尼特，完全忽略了父母深信不疑的人世間的真理，那就是，沒有哪個父親，不管哪種文化，會對他女兒説，"你嫁個藝術家吧！"幸運的是，班尼特總算熬了過來。過去的幾十年里他一直忠實地探訪我父母，不管他們怎么用中文對他評頭論足，他都一如既往地孝敬他們。

接下來就輪到我了。我可以想象為什么很多婦女希望有個好的婚姻，我也能想象為什么由于種族、性別、性生活、國家、年齡、身高等不同因素，有的婚姻被看作是很幸福的，而有的則不是。但是我想，沒有人會跪下來虔誠地祈禱，希望有個中國婆婆吧!!! 當我成了別人的婆婆以后，我多次思考這個問題，終于明白了為什么在復雜的婆媳關系上會有那么多的笑話。

威廉和麗莎結婚后，繼續住在舊金山，在那兒他們生活得很安逸。可是，不久威廉突然獲得一份工作去了臺北，而麗莎仍然留在加州。她得把車了賣了、把家收拾好后才能走。那時是六月份，但一直到了九月份，麗莎的車子還是沒有賣掉，東西也還沒有整好，因為她喜歡舊金山，不想動。一天，她打來了一個電話。我聽不出她以往那種帶有"責任"性的、快活的聲音，那種我們常常會在"不得不要打"的電話中流露出來的語調。我問，"麗莎，你怎么啦? 聽起來不開心嗎。"

"是啊。我媽剛給我打電話。我爸也給我打電話，連我姥姥也打過。他們都说我是一個不負責的太太，因為我沒有么臺灣幫助威廉。"

一張結婚紙居然能給我帶來這樣的婆媳關系，我真是欣喜若狂。但我還是按捺住内心的喜悅，對她說："不要急，威廉是我的兒子，他會做飯，燙衣，打掃，縫補。他在臺北的辦公室附近找了一個什么設施都具備的公寓，他在那兒沒問題。你什么時候想走，再走。"

聽了我的話，麗莎嗚咽着，"可是他們不停地給我打電話呀"，接着她又認真、平靜地说，"我自己也覺得很内疚。"

接着我以慈禧太后的口氣命令她，"給你媽打電話。給你爸打電話。給你姥姥打電話。告訴他們，我是你的中國婆婆，我擁有你!!!"

電話那頭—— 加利福尼亞 —— 鴉雀無聲。

我繼續興奮地說："告訴他們，我说你什么時候能離開舊金山，你就什么時候走!"

這時我聽到麗莎在電話那頭吃吃地輕笑。我就"鴨子-兔子"這個問題神奇般地向她大顯了身手，她"先是一愣，然后恍然大悟"。她的這種反應用當代"义化習俗兌換率"是有錢都買不到的，因為"學以致用"讓我們跨越了多元文化的"不同時區"，使我們能消除婆媳間的隔閡走到一起，共同欣賞"少數族群的光輝記載"。

练习 EXERCISES

I. 思考和课堂讨论 FOOD FOR THOUGHT

A. PERSONAL 个人的

你心目中的"家人"包括哪些人？包括你的近亲？包括所有与你家人有关系的亲属？包括已经过世的亲人或尚未出生的婴儿或整个人类？

When you think of "family," who do you include? How far do you "extend" it—only to the immediate? To all the living? Ancestral? To the yet-to-be-born? To all humankind?

B. GENERAL 普遍的

An "argument" or line of reasoning is logical when a conclusion is validly deduced from premises that are assumed to be true. However, when there is an error in reasoning, then a fallacy occurs. In order to think clearly and effectively, it helps to know about these errors. After reading the following, discuss the question posed.

当某一结论是从一个正确的前提演绎出来的，那么该结论的论据符合逻辑。但是，如果推理出现错误，就会产生谬论。为了清楚、有效地思考，有必要了解这些推理错误。请阅读下面的错误，然后讨论所提出的问题。

complex or "loaded" question is to ask one question grammatically but more than one in fact.

pattern: Ms. Y asks what is grammatically a single question but which is actually two or more questions so that any one answer Mr. X gives— "yes," "no," "maybe" —functions as a simultaneous response to more than one question.

example: Ms. Y asks Mr. X, "Have you stopped cheating on tests?" or "When did you stop beating your wife?" or "Are you going to be a good father and take your son to the baseball game?" So, even if there has been no prior discussion on these matters, Ms. Y takes any one answer to her **loaded question** and also concludes that Mr X did, in fact, cheat or beat his wife or agree that going to the baseball game is what a good father must do.

question: If Mr. X doesn't want to be forced to answer more than one question at a time, he should "divide the question" before responding. How?

C. CROSS-CULTURAL 跨文化的

阅读以下短文，并用<u>中文</u>对所提出的问题进行讨论。

After reading the following, discuss <u>in Chinese</u> ways, if any, to prioritize loyalties to self, family, community, province, country, humankind, and/or the planet earth.

Although being multicultural and having many different webs of relationships is probably healthier than focusing on only one kind of living with one group of people, there can arise one big problem—the Green-eyed Monster! For example, it is not uncommon that traditional cultures, including the Chinese, regarded a married daughter as belonging to the husband's clan and, therefore, no longer a member of her birth family. However, complications arise for "immigrants" into a modern setting for, after nurturing a daughter through college, parents may be both emotionally and financially invested in her. So, even if they raised her to be a good daughter-in-law, they can get very jealous and hurt when they think she has changed her allegiance upon marrying. This is not unlike the feeling of betrayal that a gang may feel when someone leaves for another kind of life after being protected on the street by its members or when a political refugee is granted asylum and then criticizes that country's policies. Although both are grateful for the benefits bestowed, neither thinks this entitles their benefactor to dictate the course of their lives. On the other hand, both would probably like to know what they can do to alleviate the sense of betrayal. The unfortunate outcome is when the benefactors won't consider ways to do this or, worse, decide that nothing will be good enough.

II. 配对 MATCHMAKER

A. VOCABULARY 词汇

找出以下两列中的对应词，并在其间划线。

Draw a connecting line between the word and its correct definition.

a.	切去头端，缩短	1.	prioritize
b.	精心编织美好的生活	2.	blood bank
c.	尊重家庭传统	3.	stunned silence
d.	鸦雀无声	4.	premarital
e.	区分优先次序	5.	honor one's lineage
f.	血库	6.	craft a nice life
g.	虔诚地	7	fervently
h.	跪下	8.	wail
i.	哭泣	9.	fall to one's knees
j.	婚前	10.	truncate

a.	blonde	1.	成家
b.	easy and comfortable	2.	孝敬
c.	generation gap	3.	公婆，婆婆
d.	psychology	4.	心理学
e.	be filial & respectful to one's elders	5.	评头论足
f.	be overcritical	6.	使……看得见,将事物在心里想像
g.	get married	7.	爆发

243

h. husband's mother   8. 代沟

i. visualize   9. 金发碧眼

j. go ballistic   10. 安逸

B. ANTONYMS & ALTERNATES 反义词和多义词

First draw a connecting line between the words or phrases in the left-hand column with the best possible <u>antonym</u> listed in the middle column, then draw a line between the antonym and an alternate meaning of the antonym listed in the right-hand column. <u>Be forewarned</u> that the part of speech may change from one column to the next and that slang terms may be used. E.g.,

"hit" ——————————— "miss" ——————— "honorific for unmarried female"

"warm" ——————————— "cool" ——————— "excellent"

首先在第二列中找出与第一列相对应的反义词，然后在第三列中找出与第二列相关的多义词。注意：词性会有变化。

		ANTONYMS		ALTERNATE MEANING
a.	uncoated (wall)	1. **landed**	i.	*slang* murder, kill
b.	deplete, reduce supply	2. **off**	ii.	shockingly, conspicuously
c.	let loose, unblock	3. **flat**	iii.	line of racial/ethnic/biological descent
d.	fragrant	4. **plastered**	iv.	soak, wet thoroughly
e.	on	5. **stock**	v.	apartment
f.	not bubbly, dull	6. **steep**	vi.	gird, ready, be determined
g.	plump, robust	7. **steel**	vii.	remove the stem
h.	cheap	8. **stem**	viii.	*slang* drunk, "looped," inebriated
i.	took off, departed	9. **rank**	ix.	*slang* insider information, "the dope"
j.	make vulnerable	10. **skinny**	x.	obtained, got

III. 解字/词、构字/词 DECONSTRUCTION & CONSTRUCTION

A. 将以下汉字分解成最小的构字部件，然后用每个部件构成三个汉字。例如"鸭"可以分解成 "甲"和"鸟"两个部件。"甲"能构成"押"，"岬"，"钾"；"鸟"可以构成以"鸡"，"鸦"，"鸣"。请借助字典完成练习。

Deconstruct the following characters into the smallest components, then form 3 new characters using each component.

神_____   信_____   若_____

围_____   碧_____   部_____

B. Using only the letters of the word "**PREMARITAL**," form English words that are not proper nouns, abbreviations, or acronyms and that consist of 4 or more letters. A letter can only be used again if it appears in the given word more than once. E.g., "port" is not acceptable because there is no "o" and "mete" is not because there is only one "e." Like many Olympic sports, weight categories mark performance. We filled in a few cells to get you started. Fill in the rest to achieve the highest category. If you think up more than 95, you beat the authors!

用 "**PREMARITAL**" 中的字母构词。新构建的词不能是专有名词、缩写词、或首字母缩略词。每个单词必须至少含有四个字母，但不能重复使用同一字母，除非该字母在 "**PREMARITAL**" 中出现两次。

CHAMPION STATUS							
FLY 12	BANTAM 24	FEATHER 36	LIGHT 48	WELTER 60	MIDDLE 72	HEAVY 84	SUPER 95
trial							
pirate							
leap							
mate							

C. 用 "大显身手" 中的每个汉字组成不同的词。看看最多能组多少个词。

Use each of the characters in "大显身手" to form as many words (of 2-4 characters) as you can.

D. Pair any two of the following 10 words to form at least 16 different, unhyphenated words.

在下列十个词中配对、组词，新组的词只能含有两个单词，中间没有连字号。请至少组出十六个词。

hold cuff hand back heavy out over link set off

IV. 阅读理解　READING QUIZ

根据课文，选择准确答案。Based on the text, choose the best answer.

1.　多元化的现实世界是一幅什么样的结构图？

　　a.　是蜘蛛网里的金字塔。

　　b.　是金字塔里的蜘蛛网。

　　c.　是含有多个蜘蛛网、但又没有顶的金字塔。

　　d.　是容不下很多人物、地点、事情的金字塔。

2.　那位男听众有什么难题需要请教作者？

　　a.　他父亲是个白人。

　　b.　他母亲是个中国人。

　　c.　他住在地下室里。

　　d.　他母亲不同意他跟白人女孩谈对象。

3.　以下哪一个答案比较有可能决定婚姻是否幸福？

　　a.　有个中国婆婆。

　　b.　有个美国婆婆。

　　c.　种族、性生活、国家、年龄等等。

　　d.　以上都对。

4.　为什么丽莎到九月份的时候还在旧金山，没有去台湾？

　　a.　因为她的车子还没有卖掉。

　　b.　因为她的家还没有收拾好。

　　c.　因为她爸爸、妈妈不让她走。

　　d.　因为她喜欢旧金山，不想走。

5.　为什么丽莎给作者打电话？

　　a.　因为作者是丽莎的婆婆。

　　b.　因为丽莎需要请教婆婆。

　　c.　因为丽莎整天没事可做。

　　d.　因为丽莎很想念作者。

6.　你认为作者与丽莎之间的婆媳关系怎样？

　　a.　不错。

　　b.　作者很凶。

   c.   婆婆拥有丽莎的房子和汽车。

   d.   丽莎不敢说话。

V. 填空　FILL IN THE BLANK

A.　选择正确答案。Choose the correct answer.

1.　英国有个作家曾作诗描写金字塔文化世界的_____。

   a.　精品　　　　b.　精华　　　　c.　精神

2.　那位问问题的男听众_____四十左右。

   a.　大概　　　　b.　大多　　　　c.　大体

3.　当母亲发现我找的女朋友是个白人以后一下子就_____了。

   a.　爆炸　　　　b.　爆发　　　　c.　爆笑

4.　她_____孙子或孙女长得跟她是不是一样。

   a.　计算　　　　b.　计较　　　　c.　计划

5.　他们住在旧金山，在那儿生活得很_____。

   a.　安全　　　　b.　安静　　　　c.　安逸

6.　过去的几十年里他一直_____地探访我父母。

   a.　忠诚　　　　b. 忠实　　　　c. 忠厚

B.　Using your target language, write a word or phrase from the vocabulary lists and/or dictionary that means the <u>same</u> or is a <u>synonym</u> for the italicized word or phrase. Keep in mind that the part of speech and/or tense may have been adjusted to achieve grammatically correct results.

在以下段落中找出与斜体词意义相近的同义词。如果你所学的外语是中文，找出相应的中文词或短语。如果你所学的外语是英语，找出相应的英语词或短语。注意：词性或时态会有变化。

> When people marry after launching their career and earning a good salary, they sometimes consider doing what many of the very wealthy do—sign *prenuptial* _____ or "prenup" contracts. This is when the soon-to-be-married couple agree how their money will be divided if their marriage is *cut shorter* _____ than originally hoped. The prenup may be a practical way to protect one's savings but it is hard to imagine a couple discussing terms for a divorce while *going out* _____ to a romantic dinner or before performing the "I do" *ceremony* _____ pledging to remain married "until death do us part"

VI. 翻译　TRANSLATION

A.　将以下句子翻译成英文。Translate the following sentences into English.

247

1. 参与多个不同的蜘蛛网使我变得更具多元化，能够接受挑战，并学会如何用爱心、智慧、忠诚和幽默将不同的蜘蛛网融合在一起。

2. 如果我们考虑代沟、经济、政治、心理学、人种学或占星学等因素，那么所有婚前、婚后的事情都是"跨文化的"。

3. 没有哪个父亲，不管哪种文化，会对他女儿说，"你嫁个艺术家吧"！

B. Translate the following sentences into Chinese. 将以下句子翻译成中文。

1. "*If* you can keep your head when all about you are losing theirs…you'll be a Man, my son!"

2. By truncating the pyramid, I prioritize people, places and things but make room for more than one at the top. By participating in many webs, I diversify who I am. By linking the webs, I am challenged to connect them with compassion, intelligence, loyalty, and humor.

3. For many reasons—social conditioning, biological determination, religious teaching, and so on—gender happens **!!!**

VII. 完型填充　CLOZE TEST

A. 在以下短文的每一空格处填入一个汉字，如有可能，给出相应的英语单词。

Fill in a Chinese character that retains the original meaning or intent of the text, then write an English equivalent, if any.

威廉和丽莎结＿＿＿＿＿后，继续住在旧＿＿＿＿＿山，在那儿他们＿＿＿＿＿活得很安逸。可＿＿＿＿＿，不久威廉突然＿＿＿＿＿到一份工作去＿＿＿＿＿台北，而丽莎仍＿＿＿＿＿留在加州，她得＿＿＿＿＿车子卖了、把家＿＿＿＿＿拾好才能走，那＿＿＿＿＿是六月份。等到＿＿＿＿＿九月份，丽莎的＿＿＿＿＿子还没有卖掉，＿＿＿＿＿西也没有整好，＿＿＿＿＿为她喜欢旧金山，＿＿＿＿＿想动。

B. Fill in an English word or phrase that retains the original meaning or intent of the text, then write a Chinese equivalent, if any.

在以下短文的每一空格处填入一个英语单词，如有可能，给出相应的汉字或词。

What I would find very hard to ＿＿＿＿＿ is many women falling to their knees, ＿＿＿＿＿ praying for a Chinese mother-in-law **!!!** And, when ＿＿＿＿＿ became one, there were too many times ＿＿＿＿＿ I saw the reason why there are ＿＿＿＿＿ many jokes about this complex relationship. After ＿＿＿＿＿ and Lisa got married, they continued to ＿＿＿＿＿ in San Francisco where they crafted a ＿＿＿＿＿ nice life indeed. However, when he left ＿＿＿＿＿ to take a job in Taipei, Lisa ＿＿＿＿＿ in California to sell the car and ＿＿＿＿＿ up their apartment. That was June. Come September, ＿＿＿＿＿ still owned the car and nothing was ＿＿＿＿＿. She loved San Francisco. One day she ＿＿＿＿＿.

VIII. 身体部位 BODY PARTS

A. There are many useful idioms which contain "body parts." Choose the most appropriate to fill in the blank based on your best guess of what the idiom means.

英语中的许多习惯用语含有表示"身体部位"的单词。在下面三个习惯用语中选择最恰当的填空。

1. hair-raising **2.** let one's hair down **3.** split hairs

He said that there is so little difference between one route and the other that arguing about which way home is better is to _____ and to waste time.

When she first rode a bicycle down a steep hill, it was a _____ experience in two ways—first because of the great speed, second because the wind blew her long hair around and she couldn't see.

After four years of working nonstop studying and earning tuition for college, she _____ and vacationed in the mountains for two weeks.

B. 将以下短文翻译成中文。注意：划线的词或短语与以上含有"身体部位"的习惯用语相对应。

Translate the following into Chinese taking note that the underlined words or phrases correspond to the meaning of the above "body parts."

When the pilot announced that one of the engines had gone dead and he would make an emergency landing, the passengers braced themselves for a <u>terrifying</u> experience. When they arrived at the airport safely, half celebrated by <u>abandoning inhibitions</u> while half could not stop talking about what they did during the descent, even <u>arguing over unimportant factors</u> like whether crossing fingers for good luck was more effective than praying.

C. Using your target language, create sentence(s) containing the following three English idioms or their Chinese equivalents.

用以下短语分别造句。如果你所学的外语是中文，请用中文来做这个练习。如果你所学的外语是英语，请用英语来做这个练习。

1. without turning a hair = 不动声色

2. tear one's hair out = 撕扯自己的头发（表示愤怒、焦急等情绪）

3. get in sb's hair = 使某人不高兴，惹恼某人

IX. 写作 PRÉCIS

用所学的外语总结课文。如果你用中文来写，请至少使用 450 个汉字，并用电脑打出摘要。如果你用英文来写，请不超过 320 个词。

Write a summary of this chapter in your target language. If writing in Chinese, use <u>more</u> than 450 characters; if writing in English, use <u>no more</u> than 320 words.

CHAPTER TWELVE

PLAYING WITH MULTIPLE FANTASIES

My mother's fantasy emerged when I returned to teaching philosophy soon after William started school.

- She lamented that I only got a part-time position.

- She was sorry that I would have to commute so far from home.

- She thought it was a shame that the twice-a-month housekeeper couldn't work full-time and take care of William so I could concentrate on my career.

- She claimed never to have heard of Montclair State. What kind of a school was it?

- She worried about my teaching night classes.

- She considered it a good idea if I immediately applied for a full-time position at Princeton or Rutgers instead—some place with a recognizable name.

- She was concerned that William wouldn't get as much necessary attention from me now that I was going to spend so much time away from home.

- She wondered if I couldn't get a job at that place in Teaneck—what's it called?—so that I'd be even closer to her house and could have dinner there before class, maybe stay overnight.

- She suggested I get a later schedule—then I wouldn't have to leave home until after William was in bed.

We both laughed when I said, "Mommy, you want me to get a full-time *and* part-time job at a college you have *and* haven't heard of but which is nearer your house *and* mine, with a schedule that meets earlier *and* later so that the twice-a-month housekeeper *and* I can both take care of William all the time *and* part of the time **!!!** "

My mother's laughter was short-lived but her disapproval grew into an abiding hatred while my laughter grew longer and stronger. The smiles sustained my optimism that life on the hyphen could be fun. With conscious, sometimes constant, effort, a sense of humor can help achieve a balance

第十二章

多元化的幻想

威廉上学后不久我就回到学校教哲学，这时我母亲的一大堆幻想也就应运而生了：

- 我只有一份半日制的教书工作，她为我叹惜。

- 我得开很长时间的车去上班，她深表同情。

- 女管家一个月只来家两次，无法全日制地照看威廉使我可以集中精力干我自己的事，她觉得是一大遗憾。

- 蒙特克莱尔（Montclair）州立大学是个什么样的学校，她声称从未听说过。

- 我得晚上教书，她为此很担忧。

- 她认为我应该立即在普林斯顿（Princeton）或若哥（Rutgers）那样有名望的大学申请一份全日制的工作。

- 由于我大部分时间在外工作，她担心我没有时间在家照顾威廉。

- 她想不通为什么我不能在提纳克（Teaneck）镇随便哪所学校找一份工作，这样我可以离她家更近一点，并且可以吃了晚饭再去上课，也许晚上还可以睡在她家里。

- 她建议我应该把上班的时间安排晚一点，这样我可以等威廉上床睡觉后再出家门。

等她开完那一长条一厢情愿的单子，我说，"妈，你要我在一个离你家和我家都很近、在你听说过和没听说过的大学里找一份既是全日制又是半日制的工作，有一个又早

between different, seemingly opposing, cultural forces. With it, we can better explain "right" and "wrong" clearly enough so the immature can grasp the concepts yet not too categorically so that the mature won't consider degrees of difference. With it, maybe we could create fantasies but prepare for realities. With it, maybe I could figure out what to do about the jolly man in the red suit and the woman with a dental fixation **!!!**

Before William attended school, I controlled his environment, both the realities and the fantasies. Once he entered the classroom, the values, rituals, and beliefs could come from Cinderella wimps, Pinocchio liars, and Sleeping Beauty do-nothings. I could counter the effect of these stories but for weeks after Thanksgiving—an eternity for a child—St. Nicholas actually showed up in stores and street corners asking, "What do you want for Christmas?" buttressed by musical warnings, "You better watch out, you better not cry, you better be good, I'm telling you why. Santa Claus is coming to town!"[25] And, throughout the year, young and old would talk about finding shiny quarters under pillows in exchange for a toothless grin.

Did I want to go along with these cultural icons? Did I want to take a chance that, one day, my son might say "Yes," when I asked, "Have I ever lied to you?" Part of me said, "Get real! We're talking about 'HoHoHo' not philosophy." The upshot was that I told our son about the "*Imaginary* Tooth Fairy" and the "*Make-Believe* Santa Claus." By dubbing the two with qualifiers, I hoped to give our son fantasy and reality simultaneously.

When William was five, the dubbing hit the fan **!!!** It happened one night when I had to teach so I took William to school with me. Driving home after class, he was tugging at a loose tooth while I, too tired to face cooking, kept an eye out for a restaurant. We both succeeded.

Spotting the bloody incisor on the table, the Chinese waiter asked, "Nǐ yéye nǎinai shìbushì yào mǎi nǐ de yáchǐ?"

Alert to financial transactions of any kind **!!!**, William was interested but perplexed. He could still understand some of the waiter's words but had become accustomed to conversing in English. William looked up at the man, then down at the tooth. I could guess what he was thinking. He knew about The Imaginary Tooth Fairy who gave him real money for actual teeth. He knew my parents gave him Red Envelopes of money on special occasions. Quickly, I told the waiter, "Wǒmen ān Měiguórén de zuòfǎ chúlǐ diàoxiàlái de yáchǐ."

---

[25]当威廉第一次听到这首歌时，他哭了虽然这首歌没有说他做错什么，甚至都没有一点暗示说他不乖。

又晚的工作时间表，这样，一个月来两次的女管家和我就可以全日制和半日制地照看威廉了。" 我们俩都笑了。

没过多久母亲的笑就变成了不满，最后发展成了永久的怨恨。而我的笑，随着时间的推移变得越加根深蒂固。微笑使我对双元文化的生活保持乐观。如果我们能自觉努力，坚持不懈，幽默感能使我们在不同、有时甚至是对立的文化势力中保持平衡。有了这种幽默感，我们可以更加清楚地解释什么是"对"，什么是"错"，这样涉世不深的人可以理解 "对""错"之间的灰白地带，而过于世故的人不再考虑"对""错"之间的差异程度。这种幽默感也能使我们建立幻想，但同时又能面对现实。有了这种幽默感，我明白该怎样在孩子面前处理穿红衣服的圣诞老人和对牙齿情有独钟的牙仙女!!!

威廉上学以前，他的周围环境，包括现实和幻想的东西都是由我一手控制的。进了学校后，他的价值观、行为和信仰就被灰姑娘（Cinderella）的唯唯诺诺、皮诺丘（Pinocchio）的撒谎成性、和睡美人（Sleeping Beauty）的无所事事所影响。虽然我可以抵挡这些故事对孩子的影响，但是我无法与永远吸引孩子的另一种诱惑力所抗衡。感恩节以后的那几个星期里，圣诞老人站在商店或街头问孩子："圣诞节你要什么礼物？"另外，你到处都能听到这样的歌声："你得注意呵，最好不要哭，最好乖一点，我告诉你为什么，因为圣诞老人就要来了！" [23] 除此以外，一年四季，不论大人小孩，大家都会兴致勃勃地谈论怎么因为在枕头下发现闪闪发亮的硬币而乐得露齿而笑（露出掉了牙的牙床!!!）。

我是否应该随大溜认同这些文化观念？如果有朝一日我问儿子，"我对你撒过谎吗？"而儿子的回答是，"撒过"！我是否愿意冒这个险？有时我会说，"现实一点吧，我们谈论的是圣诞老人的笑声'哈-哈-哈'，而不是哲学"。所以我最后决定给儿子讲一讲"想象中的牙仙女"和"虚构中的圣诞老人"的故事。我希望诸如"想象"和"虚构"这样的限制词可以培养儿子的想象力，同时又能提高他接受现实的能力。

威廉五岁的时候，我那自以为管用的限制词惹出了麻烦。事情发生在一个晚上，我接了威廉去我学校。下课后开车回家的路上，威廉正用力拔着他那颗松动的牙齿，而我

---

[23] When William, in his Chinese mode, first heard this song, he cried. Although the song didn't accuse him of wrong-doing, even the implication that he could fail to be "guāi guāi" was an indictment.

The waiter left to get our tea and milk, having picked up on my desire to avoid discussing the ontological status of fairies or the limited market value of baby teeth !!! William did not.

"I don't understand. What did he mean? What did *you* mean?"

Overly casual, I quickly explained, "In China, children get money from their grandparents. In America, they get it from the Imaginary Tooth Fairy."

His neck extended like a turtle so his eyes could see my face clearly. His words were slow and deliberate, "*Who* is the Imaginary Tooth Fairy?"

Meeting him halfway so he could watch me even more closely, I said, "Who do you think it is?" Then added, "Remember: It's the *Imaginary* Tooth Fairy." And flashed him a wink and my This-Is-A-Good-Joke-If-You're-Smart-Enough-To-Get-It smile.

Sitting back, he thought. No conclusion came forth. Figuring he needed another clue, I added, "You know, William, 'imaginary' means '*not* real'."

No reaction.

Slightly exasperated, I continued, "You know, William, Māma is real. Māma always called it the Imaginary Tooth Fairy. Māma tucks you in bed. Māma has access to your pillow. Now, *THINK!*' !!!

As I started to wonder how, at this rate, the kid would finish kindergarten !!!, he stretched toward me again, furrowed what little brow he had, and slowly intoned, as if to the dimwitted, "Maybe the Tooth Fairy is Real, and You're *NOT* !!!" A split second later, he gave me a blink and his This-Is-A-Good-Joke-If-You're-Smart-Enough-To-Get-It smile.

Later, he held the tooth toward me. Uncertain of his own wish, he asked, "Do you want it…now?"

Gently I suggested, "Why don't you put it under your pillow tonight?"

Pleased with my answer, he again focused on the tooth. Turning it with his little fingers, he said to it, in a voice I could hear, "Santa Claus may not 'exist,' but he's real to me."

Even more gently, I said, "Yes, William, that'll be fine."

In the morning, the heft and sheen of the quarter helped resolve his mixed feelings and give reality to his new perspective. That evening, he completed the transition. During the lull between dinner and bedtime, William climbed into Bennett's lap and began, "Bàba, let *me* tell *you* about the *Imaginary* Tooth Fairy. Did you know…?!"

呢，因为太累不想做饭，正边开车边寻找餐馆。最后威廉把牙齿搞下来了，我也找到了一家中餐馆。

看到威廉把血淋淋的门牙放在桌上，服务员就问他，"你爷爷、奶奶是不是要把它买去呀？"

威廉对任何种类的金融交易都比较敏感，听服务员这么一说顿时饶有兴致，可是又有点困惑。虽然他能听懂服务员的一些中文词，但是他已习惯用英语会话。威廉抬起头看了一下服务员，然后又看了一下桌上的牙齿。我能猜出威廉在想什么，他知道想象中的牙仙女曾经用钱跟他交换过他的牙齿，他也知道我父母亲在某些场合给过他红包。我很快对服务员说，"我们按美国人的做法处理掉下来的牙齿。"

服务员看出我不想继续讨论牙仙女是否存在，或小孩的牙齿是否有经济价值的问题，就离开餐桌去取茶和牛奶了，可是威廉好像对此还兴趣盎然。

"我不明白。他说的是什么意思？你说的又是什么意思？"

我漫不经心地解释说，"在中国，小孩子从爷爷、奶奶、姥姥、姥爷那儿拿到钱。但在美国，小孩从想象中的牙仙女那儿得到钱。"

这时威廉的脖子伸得长长的像个乌龟，两眼大大地盯着我的脸，慢慢地、小心翼翼地问："谁是想象中的牙仙女？"

我看着他，然后问，"你觉得她应该是谁呢？"接着我又加了一句："记住呵，是想象中的牙仙女。"我对他挤了一眼，又笑了笑。我的笑意味着：假如你聪明绝顶的话，这可是一个有趣的笑话呵！

威廉往后靠了靠，想着问题，什么也没说。我想他可能需要一点儿提示，就加了一句，"威廉，你知道，'想象中的'就是'不真实的'。"

威廉还是没有反应。

对于威廉这种没有反应的表情，我有点失望。但我还是继续对他说，"你知道，威廉，妈妈是真实的，妈妈总是把她称为想象中的牙仙女。妈妈为你盖被子、妈妈可以拿你的枕头。好，你再想想。"

255

Tears welled up as I gratefully witnessed our son test his learning by teaching, by having a father whom he trusted to listen carefully, by my knowing that William felt comfortable with multiple realities and fantasies.

VOCABULARY

lament	v.	to feel or express sorrow, regret, rue.	叹惜	tànxī
sustain	v.	to support, bear, hold up.	支撑	zhīchēng
jolly	adj.	cheerful, gay, merry, jovial.	愉快的，高兴的	yúkuài de, gāoxìng de
dental fixation	n.p.	a complex or unnatural interest in teeth !!! More psychologically common are fixations on a celebrity, parent, or, in the case of foot-binding, female feet.	对牙齿的眷恋	duì yáchǐ de juànliàn
wimp	n.	someone who is ineffectual or does not stand firm but easily gives way to others.	懦弱的人，无用的人	nuòruò de rén, wúyòng de rén
buttress	v.	to support, hold up, reinforce.	伴随着……	bànsuí zhe…
toothless grin	n.p.	smiling broadly so that the lack of teeth is visible.	露齿而笑（露出掉了牙齿的牙床）	lòuchǐ-érxiào (lùchū diàole yáchǐ de yáchuáng)
ho ho ho		the sound of laughter associated with Santa Claus as in the poem, "He had a broad face and a little round belly that shook, when he laughed, like a bowl full of jelly."	ho ho ho !!!	ho ho ho !!!
make-believe	adj.	pretended, fantasized, unreal.	虚构的	xūgòu de
upshot	n.	result, outcome, conclusion.	结果，结局	jiéguǒ, jiéjú
qualifier	n.	sth. that describes, limits or modifies.	限制词	xiànzhìcí
(when the shit) hits the fan	v.p.	taken literally, it is easy to imagine why the phrase is a metaphor for what happens when those who were previously "kept in the dark"	真相大白所导致的后果	zhēnxiàng-dàbái suǒ dǎozhì de

按这种智力水平，这小孩什么时候才能上完幼儿园呢！我正琢磨着这个问题，威廉又把头朝我伸过来，紧锁着眉头，然后郑重其事地说，"也许想象中的牙仙女是真实的，但你不是真实的。"他那神情和语气好像在跟傻瓜说话。刹那间，他用双眼对我眨了一眨、笑了一笑，意思是假如你聪明绝顶的话，这可是一个有趣的笑话呵！

威廉后来拿起牙，不知道究竟想要什么，就问，"你要不要这颗牙……现在？"

我温柔地建议他，"你为什么今晚不把它放在你枕头下呢？"

听我这么一说威廉很高兴，接着他又继续拨弄那颗牙，几个小手指把牙齿拨来拨去，一边玩一边小声地说，"圣诞老人可能并不存在，可是他对于我来说是真实的。"

我更加温柔地说，"对，威廉，你可以这么说。"

威廉的复杂情感在第二天早晨得到了安抚，而且他还学会了用新的、现实的眼光看问题，这应归功于两毛五分硬币那实实在在的重量和光泽。那天晚上，他完成了从幻想到现实的转变。吃过晚饭后，威廉爬到班尼特的大腿上说，"爸爸，我来给你讲讲想象中的牙仙女的故事。你知道吗……?"

看到儿子能运用刚学来的知识，看到他有个值得信赖、并细心聆听他的父亲，看到他能从容不迫地应付多元现实和多元幻想，我情不自禁地热泪盈眶。

生词

幻想	幻想	huànxiǎng	n.	fantasy
一大堆	一大堆	yīdàduī	n.p.	a large pile of
应运而生	應運而生	yìngyùn'érshēng	f.c.w.	emerge
半日制	半日制	bànrìzhì	n.	part-time
叹惜	嘆惜	tànxī	v.	lament
深表同情	深表同情	shēnbiǎotóngqíng	f.c.w.	sympathize
管家	管家	guǎnjiā	n.	housekeeper
全日制	全日制	quánrìzhì	n.	full-time
照看	照看	zhàokàn	v.	take care of
集中精力	集中精力	jízhōng-jīnglì	f.c.w.	concentrate on
遗憾	遺憾	yíhàn	n.	shame, pity, regret

		about sth. suddenly discover the truth and are, to say the very least, not happy about the situation.		hòuguǒ
tug	v.	to pull, drag, or move.	拔（牙齿）	bá (yáchǐ)
incisor	n.	one of the two upper or lower front or anterior teeth used primarily for biting or cutting into. See "incisive".	门牙	ményá
perplexed	adj.	to be confused, bewildered, puzzled. Also – v. to perplex, confuse, puzzle, etc.	困惑的	kùnhuò de
ontological	adj.	pertaining to metaphysics or the study of being, existence or reality (independent of the physical).	方法论的	fāngfǎlùn de
wink	v.	to quickly close and open one eye indicating good humor or joke, sometimes as a way to be flirtatious.	眨一眼使眼神	zhǎ yī yǎn shǐ yǎnshén
furrow	v.	to make a fold or, in this case, wrinkle the area between the eyebrows and/or forehead.	弄绉	nòngzhòu
intone	v.	to speak or vocalize, in this case in a monotone.	郑重其事地说	zhèngzhòngqíshì de shuō
blink	v.	to quickly close and open the eyes, in this case intentionally and because he didn't yet know how to wink.	眨两只眼睛使眼神	zhǎ liǎng zhī yǎnjing shǐ yǎnshén
heft	n.	heaviness often measured by placing or balancing sth. in the hand then moving the hand up and down to gauge weight.	重量	zhòngliàng
sheen	n.	surface shine, luster, reflective brightness.	光泽	guāngzé
lull	n.	a temporary period of inactivity or quiet. Also – v. to soothe or induce sleep or rest.	间歇	jiànxiē
well up	v.p.	to rise, pool or gather. In this case the tears form and moisten the eyes but not so much as to fall down the face.	（泪如）泉涌	(lèi rú) quányǒng

蒙特克莱尔	蒙特克萊爾	Méngtèkèlái'ěr	p.n.	Montclair
声称	聲稱	shēngchēng	v.	claim
普林斯顿	普林斯頓	Pǔlínsīdùn	p.n.	Princeton
若哥	若哥	Ruògē	p.n.	Rutgers
名望	名望	míngwàng	n.	renown
提纳克	提納克	Tínàkè	p.n.	Teaneck
在外	在外	zàiwài	p.p.	outside
照顾	照顧	zhàogù	v.	take care of (a child, a senior, et al.)
一长条	一長條	yīchángtiáo	n.p.	a long list
一厢情愿	一廂情願	yīxiāng-qíngyuàn	f.c.w.	one's wishful thinking
单子	單子	dānzi	n.	list (of items)
时间表	時間表	shíjiānbiǎo	n.	schedule, time-table
怨恨	怨恨	yuànhèn	n.	hatred, intense dislike
推移	推移	tuīyí	n.	elapse (of time)
越加	越加	yuèjiā	adv.	more and more
根深蒂固	根深蒂固	gēnshēn-dìgù	f.c.w.	deep-rooted
乐观	樂觀	lèguān	n.	optimism
坚持不懈	堅持不懈	jiānchí-bùxiè	f.c.w.	persistent, unremitting, persevering
幽默感	幽默感	yōumògǎn	n.	sense of humor
涉世不深	涉世不深	shèshìbùshēn	f.c.w.	the immature who have scanty experience of life
灰白地带	灰白地帶	huībáidìdài	f.c.w.	degrees of difference between "right" and "wrong"
圣诞老人	聖誕老人	Shèngdàn Lǎorén	p.n.	Santa Claus
牙齿	牙齒	yáchǐ	n.	tooth
情有独钟	情有獨鍾	qíngyǒudúzhōng	f.c.w.	fixation, focus on sb./sth. with great passion
仙女	仙女	xiānnǚ	n.	fairy
掌控	掌控	zhǎngkòng	v.	control
灰姑娘	灰姑娘	Huīgūniang	p.n.	Cinderella
唯唯诺诺	唯唯諾諾	wěiwěi-nuònuò	r.f.	wimp
皮诺丘	皮諾丘	Pínuòqiū	p.n.	Pinocchio
撒谎成性	撒謊成性	sāhuǎngchéngxìng	f.c.w.	chronic liar
睡美人	睡美人	Shuìměirén	p.n.	Sleeping Beauty
无所事事	無所事事	wúsuǒshìshì	f.c.w.	do nothing, idle away one's time
抵挡	抵擋	dǐdǎng	v.	counter the effect of
诱惑力	誘惑力	yòuhuòlì	n.	attraction
抗衡	抗衡	kànghéng	v.	counter the effect of
街头	街頭	jiētóu	n.	street corner
除此以外	除此以外	chúcǐ yǐwài	p.p.	beyond this, in addition to this
一年四季	一年四季	yī'nián-sìjì	f.c.w.	all the year round
兴致勃勃	興致勃勃	xìngzhì-bóbó	f.c.w.	take delight in doing a sth.

第十二章

多元化的幻想

威廉上學后不久我就回到學校教哲學，這時我母親的一大堆幻想也就應運而生了：

- 我只有一份半日制的教書工作，她為我嘆惜。

- 我得開很長時間的車去上班，她深表同情。

- 女管家一個月只來家兩次，無法全日制地照看威廉使我可以集中精力干我自己的事，她覺得是一大遺憾。

- 蒙特克萊爾（Montclair）州立大學是個什麼樣的學校，她聲稱從未聽説過。

- 我得晚上教書，她為此很擔憂。

- 她認為我應該立即在普林斯頓（Princeton）或若哥（Rutgers）那樣有名望的大學申請一份全日制的工作。

- 由于我大部分時間在外工作，她擔心我沒有時間在家照顧威廉。

- 她想不通為什麼我不能在提納克（Teaneck）鎮隨便哪所學校找一份工作，這樣我可以離她家更近一點，并且可以吃了晚飯再去上課，也許晚上還可以睡在她家里。

- 她建議我應該把上班的時間安排晚一點，這樣我可以等威廉上床睡覺后再出家門。

等她開完那一長條一廂情願的單子，我説，"媽，你要我在一個離你家和我家都很近、在你聽説過和沒聽説過的大學里找一份既是全日制又是半日制的工作，有一個又早又晚

闪闪发亮	閃閃發亮	shǎnshǎnfāliàng	f.c.w.	shiny
硬币	硬幣	yìngbì	n.	coin
露齿而笑	露齒而笑	lòuchǐ'érxiào	f.c.w.	grin
牙床	牙床	yáchuáng	n.	gum
随大溜	隨大溜	suídàliù	v.o.	follow the general trend
观念	觀念	guānniàn	n.	icons, concept
冒险	冒險	màoxiǎn	v.o.	take a chance
笑声	笑聲	xiàoshēng	n.	sound of laughter
哲学	哲學	zhéxué	n.	philosophy
虚构	虛構	xūgòu	v.	make-believe
想象	想象	xiǎngxiàng	v.	imagine
限制词	限制詞	xiànzhìcí	n.	qualifier
管用	管用	guǎnyòng	v.	be of use, be effective
惹	惹	rě	v.	provoke
拔	拔	bá	v.	tug (a tooth)
松动	鬆動	sōngdòng	adj.	loose
中餐馆	中餐館	zhōngcānguǎn	n.	Chinese restaurant
血淋淋	血淋淋	xiělínlín	adj.	bloody
门牙	門牙	ményá	n.	incisor
金融	金融	jīnróng	n.	finance
交易	交易	jiāoyì	n.	transaction
饶有兴致	饒有興致	ráoyǒu-xingzhi	f.c.w.	be interested in
困惑	困惑	kùnhuò	adj.	perplexed, puzzled
抬起	抬起	táiqǐ	v (c)	look up at
曾经	曾經	céngjīng	adv.	once
用钱	用錢	yòngqián	p.p.	by means of money, using money
交换	交換	jiāohuàn	v.	exchange
红包	紅包	hóngbāo	n.	red paper envelope to hold money as a gift
兴趣盎然	興趣盎然	xìngqù'àngrán	f.c.w.	have great interest in sth.
漫不经心	漫不經心	mànbùjīngxīn	f.c.w.	casually
伸	伸	shēn	v.	extend
乌龟	烏龜	wūguī	n.	turtle
聪明绝顶	聰明絕頂	cōngming-juédǐng	f.c.w.	extremely smart, bright
提示	提示	tíshì	n.	clue
智力	智力	zhìlì	n.	intelligence, intellect, brains, wit
紧锁	緊鎖	jǐnsuǒ	v.	furrow
郑重其事	郑重其事	zhèngzhòng-qíshì	f.c.w.	intone
傻瓜	傻瓜	shǎguā	n.	the dimwitted
刹那间	剎那間	chànàjiān	n.	split second
拿起	拿起	náqǐ	v (c)	pick up

的工作時間表，這樣，一個月來兩次的女管家和我就可以全日制和半日制地照看威廉了。"
我們倆都笑了。

沒過多久母親的笑就變成了不滿，最后發展成了永久的怨恨。而我的笑，隨着時間的
推移變得越加根深蒂固。微笑使我對雙元文化的生活保持樂觀。如果我們能自覺努力，堅持
不懈，幽默感能使我們在不同、有時甚至是對立的文化勢力中保持平衡。有了這種幽默感，
我們可以更加清楚地解釋什么是"對"，什么是"錯"，這樣涉世不深的人可以理解"對"
"錯"之間的灰白地帶，而過于世故的人不再考慮"對""錯"之間的差异程度。這種幽默
感也能使我們建立幻想，但同時又能面對現實。有了這種幽默感，我明白該怎樣在孩子面前
處理穿紅衣服的聖誕老人和對牙齒情有獨鐘的牙仙女!!!

威廉上學以前，他的周圍環境，包括現實和幻想的東西都是由我一手控制的。進了學校
后，他的價值觀、行為和信仰就被灰姑娘（Cinderella）的唯唯諾諾、皮諾丘（Pinocchio）的
撒謊成性、和睡美人（Sleeping Beauty）的無所事事所影響。雖然我可以抵擋這些故事對孩子
的影響，但是我無法與永遠吸引孩子的另一種誘惑力所抗衡。感恩節以后的那幾個星期里，
聖誕老人站在商店或街頭問孩子："聖誕節你要什么禮物？"另外，你到處都能聽到這樣的
歌聲："你得注意呵，最好不要哭，最好乖一點，我告訴你為什么，因為聖誕老人就要來
了！"[23] 除此以外，一年四季，不論大人小孩，大家都會興致勃勃地談論怎么因為在枕頭下
發現閃閃發亮的硬幣而樂得露齒而笑（露出掉了牙的牙床!!!）。

我是否應該隨大流認同這些文化觀念？如果有朝一日我問兒子，"我對你撒過謊
嗎？"而兒子的回答是，"撒過"！我是否願意冒這個險？有時我會説，"現實一點吧，我們
談論的是聖誕老人的笑聲'哈-哈-哈'，而不是哲學"。所以我最后決定給兒子講一講"想象
中的牙仙女"和"虛構中的聖誕老人"的故事。我希望諸如"想象"和"虛構"這樣的限制
詞可以培養兒子的想象力，同時又能提高他接受現實的能力。

威廉五歲的時候，我那自以為管用的限制詞惹出了麻煩。事情發生在一個晚上，我接
了威廉去我學校。下課后開車回家的路上，威廉正用力拔着他那顆松動的牙齒，而我呢，因

---

[23] When William, in his Chinese mode, first heard this song, he cried. Although the song didn't accuse him of
wrong-doing, even the implication that he could fail to be "guāi guāi" was an indictment.

拨弄	撥弄	bōnong	v.	play with sth.
小声	小聲	xiǎoshēng	adj.	in a soft, low voice
安抚	安撫	ānfǔ	v.	settle one's mixed feelings
实实在在	實實在在	shíshí-zàizài	r.f.	concretely existing
重量	重量	zhòngliàng	n.	heft
光泽	光澤	guāngzé	n.	sheen
信赖	信賴	xìnlài	v.	trust
细心	细心	xìxīn	adj.	careful
从容不迫	從容不迫	cóngróng-bùpò	f.c.w.	confidently and without haste
应付	應付	yìngfu	v.	cope with, handle
热泪盈眶	熱淚盈眶	rèlèi-yíngkuàng	f.c.w.	tears well up, tearful

為太累不想做飯，正邊開車邊尋找餐館。最后威廉把牙齒搞下來了，我也找到了一家中餐館。

看到威廉把血淋淋的門牙放在桌上，服務員就問他，"你爺爺、奶奶是不是要把它買去呀？"

威廉對任何種類的金融交易都比較敏感，聽服務員這麼一説頓時饒有興致，可是又有點困惑。雖然他能聽懂服務員的一些中文詞，但是他已習慣用英語會話。威廉抬起頭看了一下服務員，然后又看了一下桌上的牙齒。我能猜出威廉在想什麼，他知道想象中的牙仙女曾經用錢跟他交換過他的牙齒，他也知道我父母親在某些場合給過他紅包。我很快對服務員説，"我們按美國人的做法處理掉下來的牙齒。"

服務員看出我不想繼續討論牙仙女是否存在，或小孩的牙齒是否有經濟價值的問題，就離開餐桌去取茶和牛奶了，可是威廉好像對此還興趣盎然。

"我不明白。他説的是什麼意思？你説的又是什麼意思？"

我漫不經心地解釋説，"在中國，小孩子從爺爺、奶奶、姥姥、姥爺那兒拿到錢。但在美國，小孩從牙仙女那兒得到錢。"

這時威廉的脖子伸得長長的像個烏龜，兩眼大大地盯着我的臉，慢慢地、小心翼翼地問："誰是想象中的牙仙女？"

我看着他，然后問，"你覺得她應該是誰呢？"接着我又加了一句："記住呵，是想象中的牙仙女。"我對他擠了一眼，又笑了笑。我的笑意味着：假如你聰明絕頂的話，這可是一個有趣的笑話呵！

威廉往后靠了靠，想着問題，什麼也沒説。我想他可能需要一點兒提示，就加了一句，"威廉，你知道，'想象中的'就是'不真實的'。"

威廉還是沒有反應。

對于威廉這種沒有反應的表情，我有點失望。但我還是繼續對他説，"你知道，威廉，媽媽是真實的，媽媽總是把她稱為想象中的牙仙女。媽媽為你蓋被子、媽媽可以拿你的枕頭。好，你再想想。"

按這種智力水平，這小孩什么时候才能上完幼兒園呢！我正琢磨着這個問題，威廉义把頭朝我伸過來，緊鎖着眉頭，然后鄭重其事地説，"也許想象中的牙仙女是真實的，但你不是真實的。"他那神情和語氣好像在跟傻瓜説話。刹那間，他用雙眼對我眨了一眨、笑了一笑，意思是假如你聰明絕頂的話，這可是一個有趣的笑話呵！

威廉后來拿起牙，不知道究竟想要什么，就問，"你要不要這顆牙……現在？"

我溫柔地建議他，"你為什么今晚不把它放在你枕頭下呢？"

聽我這么説威廉很高興，接着他又繼續撥弄那顆牙，幾個小手指把牙齒撥來撥去，一邊玩一邊小聲地説，"聖誕老人可能并不存在，可是他對于我來説是真實的。"

我更加溫柔地説，"對，威廉，你可以這么説。"

威廉的復雜情感在第二天早晨得到了安撫，而且他還學會了用新的、現實的眼光看問題，這應歸功于兩毛五分硬幣那實實在在的重量和光澤。那天晚上，他完成了從幻想到現實的轉變。吃過晚飯后，威廉爬到班尼特的大腿上説，"爸爸，我來給你講講想象中的牙仙女的故事。你知道嗎……？"

看到兒子能運用剛學來的知識，看到他有個值得信賴、并細心聆聽他的父親，看到他能從容不迫地應付多元現實和多元幻想，我情不自禁地熱淚盈眶。

练习 EXERCISES

I. 思考和课堂讨论 FOOD FOR THOUGHT

A. PERSONAL 个人的

在你生活中你是否有过基于不现实的梦幻、希望和计划？你是如何面对的？

Have you experienced a time when people told you that your dreams/hopes/plans were based on an "impossible" combination of cultural, professional, religious, political, financial/economic, educational, social, geographic, sexual, etc. factors and that you were being "unrealistic"? If not, why not? If so, did you resolve the supposed discrepancies? How?

B. GENERAL 普遍的

An "argument" or line of reasoning is logical when a conclusion is validly deduced from premises that are assumed to be true. However, when there is an error in reasoning, then a fallacy occurs. In order to think clearly and effectively, it helps to know about these errors. After reading the following, discuss the question posed.

当某一结论是从一个正确的前提演绎出来的，那么该结论的论据符合逻辑。但是，如果推理出现错误，就会产生谬论。为了清楚、有效地思考，有必要了解这些推理错误。请阅读下面的错误，然后讨论所提出的问题。

> **non sequitor** is from the Latin *non* = does not; *sequitor* = follow.

> **pattern:** Mr. X argues for the truth of his conclusion by arguing for the truth of another, different conclusion. In other words, the premises he assumes to be true do not lead to the conclusion he actually wants to make. Also known as a "red herring" which "smell" leads listeners away from the real issue.

> **example:** Instead of showing why a particular plan for building low-cost housing is a good idea, Mr. X presents a **non sequitor** by citing reasons why low-cost housing is, in general, a good idea, and then talking about how much the bad economy has affected low-income families, and then discussing how we should all do our part in helping the less fortunate, and then, finally, concluding that his particular plan is a good one.

> **question:** Why is Mr. X's fallacious approach often effective but still logically irrelevant?

C. CROSS-CULTURAL 跨文化的

阅读以下短文，并用英文讨论三个习惯用语是如何看待过去的。

After reading the following, discuss in English the following idioms that deal with how to perceive the past:

1. **should've, could've, would've** (in any order) = what might have been done instead of the past event that did happen.

2. **water under the bridge** = a past event that is no longer judged to be important.

3. **crying over spilt** (or spilled) **milk** = a past event that cannot be undone or restored.

There is no easy way to know when your fantasies will probably never be realities. For example, artists should make art and writers should write—not just *talk* about doing it. This often requires, at the very least, a commitment to living without getting a regular paycheck. While unappreciated artists may have been driven by the romance of fame after death—like the posthumous recognition of Van Gogh and Kafka—this is not nearly as much fun as eating on a regular basis !!! So if, after ten years, only your mother likes what you make !!!, you should seriously consider spending your time doing something else with your life. Similarly, there is no easy way to know when your realities will probably never fulfill your fantasies. So if, after ten years of living in a new country, you still talk as if you wished you'd never emigrated, you should seriously consider inventing new fantasies. The result of never trying to make your fantasies and realities merge is that you could end up with a mantra of regretting. Yet, even so, you can make good stories out of any experience!

II. 配对 **MATCHMAKER**

A. VOCABULARY 词汇

找出以下两列中的对应词，并在其间划线。

Draw a connecting line between the word and its correct definition.

a.	叹惜	1.	incisor
b.	光泽	2.	tears well up, tearful
c.	门牙	3.	sheen
d.	间歇	4.	a dental fixation
e.	热泪盈眶	5.	intone
f.	结果，结局	6.	lull
g.	郑重其事地说	7.	lament
h.	对牙齿的眷恋	8.	upshot
i.	伴随着……	9.	sustain
j.	支撑	10.	buttress

a.	Thanksgiving	1.	一大堆
b.	concentrate on	2.	想象力
c.	take care of	3.	无所事事
d.	a pile of	4.	重量

e.	have nothing to do	5.	懦弱的人，无用的人
f.	sense of humor	6.	照顾
g.	imagination, vision	7.	感恩节
h.	tell a lie	8.	集中精力
i.	wimp	9.	撒谎
j.	heft	10.	幽默感

B. SYNONYMS & ALTERNATES 同义词和多义词

First draw a connecting line between the word or phrase in the left-hand column with the best possible <u>synonym</u> listed in the middle column, then draw a line between the synonym and an alternate meaning of the synonym listed in the right-hand column. <u>Be forewarned</u> that the part of speech may change from one column to the next and that slang terms may be used. E.g.,

"hit" ——————————————— *"strike"* ———————— *"stop-work action against employer"*

"warm" ——————————————— *"heat"* ———————— *"qualifying race for final contest"*

首先在第二列中找出与第一列相对应的同义词，然后在第三列中找出与第二列相关的多义词。注意：词性会有不同。

		SYNONYMS		**ALTERNATIVE MEANING**
a.	plaza, open public area	1. **hoot**	i.	obviously stylish in dress
b.	even, horizontal	2. **level**	ii.	*slang* run-down, dirty place to live
c.	urge, insist, plead	3. **spread**	iii.	force into military service
d.	extend out, overlay	4. **dump**	iv.	the least bit of care or concern
e.	empty out, overturn	5. **press**	v.	large body of water, ocean
f.	express displeasure	6. **lower**	vi.	*informal* threat/pressure to obtain favor
g.	debase	7. **sharp**	vii.	*slang* many dishes of food served
h.	compress, extract juice	8. **drink**	viii	disgrace, degrade
i.	acute, keen-minded	9. **square**	ix.	well-balanced, even-tempered
j.	water, liquor, juice, etc.	10. **squeeze**	x.	honest, just, fair

III. 解字/词、构字/词 DECONSTRUCTION & CONSTRUCTION

A. 将以下汉字分解成最小的构字部件，然后用每个部件构成三个汉字。例如"鸭"可以分解成"甲"和"鸟"两个部件。"甲"能构成"押"，"岬"，"钾"；"鸟"可以构成以"鸡"，"鸦"，"鸣"。请借助字典完成练习。

Deconstruct the following characters into the smallest components, then form 3 new characters using each component.

制 _____ 称 _____ 钟 _____

茶 _____ 照 _____ 露 _____

B. Using only the letters of the word "**MAKE-BELIEVE**," form English words that are not proper nouns, abbreviations, or acronyms and that consist of 4 or more letters. A letter can only be used again if it appears in the given word more than once. E.g., "bask" is not acceptable because there is no "k" and "alibi" is not because there is only one "i." Like many Olympic sports, weight categories mark performance. We filled in a few cells to get you started. Fill in the rest to achieve the highest category. If you think up more than 45, you beat the authors!

用 "**MAKE-BELIEVE**" 中的字母构词。新构建的词不能是专有名词、缩写词、或首字母缩略词。每个单词必须至少含有四个字母，但不能重复使用同一字母，除非该字母在 "**MAKE-BELIEVE**" 中出现两次。

CHAMPION STATUS				
FLY 9	**FEATHER** 18	**WELTER** 27	**MIDDLE** 36	**HEAVY** 45
make	bake	bale	kale	

C. 用 "一年四季" 中的每个汉字组成不同的词。看看最多能组多少个词。

Use each of the characters in "一年四季" to form as many words (of 2-4 characters) as you can.

D. Pair any two of the following 9 words to form at least 10 different, unhyphenated words.

在下列九个词中配对、组词，新组的词只能含有两个单词，中间没有连字号。请至少组出十个词。

mind meal piece master script time war writer post

IV. 阅读理解 READING QUIZ

根据课文，选择准确答案。Based on the text, choose the best answer.

1. 微笑和幽默感在日常生活中有什么功能？

   a. 可以使人们在对立的文化势力中保持平衡。

   b. 可以帮助人们建立幻想，同时又能面对现实。

   c. 可以帮助人们识别"对"与"错"。

   d. 以上都对。

2. 以下哪些故事对美国孩子有着永久的吸引力？

   a. 灰姑娘的故事。

   b. 睡美人的故事。

   c. 皮诺丘的故事。

   d. 圣诞老人的故事。

3. 牙仙女特别喜欢什么？

   a. 牙齿。

   b. 硬币。

   c. 红包。

   d. 小朋友。

4. 对孩子掉下来的牙齿美国人是怎样处理的？

   a. 放在孩子的枕头下。

   b. 卖给爸爸、妈妈。

   c. 卖给姥姥、姥爷。

   d. 卖给爷爷、奶奶。

5. 在威廉的眼中，世界上有没有圣诞老人？

   a. 他觉得圣诞老人是存在的。

   b. 他觉得圣诞老人是真实的。

   c. 他觉得圣诞老人是虚构的。

   d. 他觉得圣诞老人是想象中的。

6. 这个故事发生的时候威廉在上几年级？

   a. 小学。

   b. 中学。

   c. 幼儿园。

   d. 还没上学。

V. 填空　FILL IN THE BLANK

A. 选择正确答案。Choose the correct answer.

1. 普林斯顿是一所很有_____的大学。

    a.　名气　　　　b.　名声　　　　c.　名字

2. 微笑能使人对双元文化的生活保持_____的态度。

    a.　宏观　　　　b.　乐观　　　　c.　主观

3. 他能从容不迫地_____多元现实和多元幻想。

    a.　支付　　　　b.　交付　　　　c.　对付

4. 我们应该学会用现实的_____看问题。

    a.　眼睛　　　　b.　眼光　　　　c.　眼神

5. 我希望_____"想象"和"虚拟"这样的词可以培养他的想象力。

    a.　比如　　　　b.　诸如　　　　c.　假如

6. 我对他这种没有反应的_____有点失望。

    a.　感情　　　　b.　心情　　　　c.　表情

B. 在以下段落中找出与斜体词意义相近的反义词。如果你所学的外语是中文，找出相应的中文词或短语。如果你所学的外语是英语，找出相应的英语词或短语。注意：词性或时态会有变化。

Using your target language, write a word or phrase from the vocabulary lists and/or dictionary that means the opposite or is an antonym for the italicized word or phrase. Keep in mind that the part of speech and/or tense may have been adjusted to achieve grammatically correct results.

When a solution to the problem became suddenly *clear in her mind* _____, she *rejoiced* _____. It would mean she would have to lay low and not attract attention while working *nonstop with no rest* _____ for months to get her discovery on paper but her lifelong dream was soon to be a *reality* _____.

VI. 翻译　TRANSLATION

A. 将以下句子翻译成英文。Translate the following sentences into English.

1. 除此以外，一年四季，不管是小孩还是老人，大家都兴致勃勃地谈论怎么因为在枕头下发现闪闪发亮的硬币而乐得露齿而笑（露出掉了牙的牙床!!!）。

2. 威廉对任何种类的金融交易都比较敏感，听服务员这么一说顿时饶有兴致，可是又有点困惑。

3. 我给他挤了一眼，又笑了一笑，我的笑意味着：假如你聪明绝顶的话，这可是一个有趣的笑话呵！

271

B. Translate the following sentences into Chinese. 将以下句子翻译成中文。

1. My mother's laughter was short-lived but her disapproval grew into an abiding hatred while my laughter grew longer and stronger.

2. Overly casual, I quickly explained, "In China, children get money from their grandparents. In America, they get it from the Imaginary Tooth Fairy."

3. Tears welled as I gratefully witnessed our son test his learning by teaching, by having a father whom he trusted to listen carefully, by my knowing that William felt comfortable with multiple realities and fantasies.

VII. 完型填充　CLOZE TEST

A. 在以下短文的每一空格处填入一个汉字，如有可能，给出相应的英语单词。

Fill in a Chinese character that retains the original meaning or intent of the text, then write an English equivalent, if any.

威廉五岁的时＿＿＿＿＿＿，我那自以为管＿＿＿＿＿＿的限制词惹出＿＿＿＿＿＿麻烦。事情发生＿＿＿＿＿＿一个晚上，我接＿＿＿＿＿＿威廉去我学校。＿＿＿＿＿＿课后开车回家＿＿＿＿＿＿路上，威廉正用＿＿＿＿＿＿拔着他那颗松＿＿＿＿＿＿的牙齿，而我呢，＿＿＿＿＿＿为太累不想做＿＿＿＿＿＿，正边开车边寻＿＿＿＿＿＿餐馆，最后威廉＿＿＿＿＿＿牙齿搞下来了，＿＿＿＿＿＿也找到了一家＿＿＿＿＿＿餐馆。

B. Fill in an English word or phrase that retains the original meaning or intent of the text, then write a Chinese equivalent, if any.

在以下短文的每一空格处填入一个英语单词，如有可能，给出相应的汉字或词。

Did I want to take a chance ＿＿＿＿＿＿, one day, my son might say "Yes," ＿＿＿＿＿＿ I asked, "Have I ever lied to ＿＿＿＿＿＿?" Part of me said, "Get real! We're ＿＿＿＿＿＿ about 'HoHoHo' not philosophy." The upshot was ＿＿＿＿＿＿ I told our son about the "*Imaginary* ＿＿＿＿＿＿ Fairy" and the "*Make-Believe* Santa Claus." By ＿＿＿＿＿＿ the two with qualifiers, I hoped to ＿＿＿＿＿＿ our son fantasy and reality simultaneously. When ＿＿＿＿＿＿ was five, the dubbing hit the fan **!!!** ＿＿＿＿＿＿ happened one night when I had to ＿＿＿＿＿＿ so I took William to school with ＿＿＿＿＿＿. Driving home after class, he was tugging ＿＿＿＿＿＿ a loose tooth while I, too tired ＿＿＿＿＿＿ face cooking, kept an eye out for ＿＿＿＿＿＿ restaurant. We both succeeded.

VIII. 身体部位　BODY PARTS

A. There are many useful idioms which contain "body parts." Choose the most appropriate to fill in the blank based on your best guess of what the idiom means.

英语中的许多习惯用语含有表示"身体部位"的单词。在下面三个习惯用语中选择最恰当的填空。

1. get off one's back   **2.** with one's back to the wall   **3.** stab in the back

He yelled, "_____, I'm sick and tired of your complaining day in and day out about how little time I spend with you."

He thought she was his friend and would help him get the job but, instead, he got a double _____ when she misled him about what he should wear as well as told the interviewer that he was not always reliable.

_____, I have no other choice but to work on weekends in order to pay back the bank loan so it won't foreclose on our house."

B. 将以下短文翻译成中文。注意：划线的词或短语与以上含有"身体部位"的习惯用语相对应。

Translate the following into Chinese taking note that the underlined words or phrases correspond to the meaning of the above "body parts."

She finally realized that she must <u>stop annoying him</u> with her suggestions because her son interpreted them as criticisms.

She still feels <u>the betrayal</u> by her teacher who used her research in his article but did not credit her with the discovery. On the other hand, <u>with her hands tied</u>, she could do nothing other than to keep quiet or risk not graduating.

C. Using your target language, create sentence(s) containing the following three English idioms or their Chinese equivalents.

用以下短语分别造句。如果你所学的外语是中文，请用中文来做这个练习。如果你所学的外语是英语，请用英语来做这个练习。

1. put one's back into it = 发奋努力做事

2. back out = 违背诺言，违约，收回（承担的责任）

3. back up = 支持

IX. 写作 PRÉCIS

用所学的外语总结课文。如果你用中文来写，请至少使用 450 个汉字，并用电脑打出摘要。如果你用英文来写，请不超过 420 个词。

Write a summary of this chapter in your target language. If writing in Chinese, use <u>more</u> than 450 characters; if writing in English, use <u>no more</u> than 420 words.

ENGLISH VOCABULARY

ABC	abbr.	American Born Chinese.	生在美国的华人	shēng zài Měiguó de Huárén	1
afflict	v.	to greatly distress or harm.	使……折磨	shǐ…zhémó	3
aloe	n.	a succulent plant of which leaves yield a liquid used on the skin to promote healing.	芦荟	lúhuì	3
amputee	n.	someone who has had a limb surgically removed.	截肢者	jiézhīzhě	3
apropos of nothing	p.p.	with no purpose or reference to anything in particular.	凭空地，突如其来地，没有任何联系地	píngkōng de, tūrúqílái de, méiyǒu rènhé liánxì de	7
assembly	n.	a (large) gathering of people for a specific political, religious, social, etc. purpose; in schools, bringing all or portions of the student body together to witness or be part of a program.	集会	jíhuì	10
backpacker	n.	people, often young and on a limited budget, who travel carrying only clothes, supplies, etc. that will fit in a soft container that is worn on the back by putting arms through straps.	背包旅行者	bēibāo lǚxíngzhě	2
balm	n.	something that soothes, eases pain, or heals; originally an ointment from a plant.	香油，药膏	xiāngyóu, yàogāo	8
"Banana"	p.n.	during the 1950s, even though 38% of Teaneck, New Jersey was Jewish, the dominant culture was "WASP" or White Anglo-Saxon Protestant. New terms like "Banana" to describe Asians (yellow on the outside, white on the inside) and "Oreo" (a cookie that is black on the outside, white on the inside) to describe African-Americans came into use as People of Color became conscious of how much they were influenced by the	指具有英国后裔白人价值观的黄种人 指具有英国后裔白人价值观	zhǐ jùyǒu Yīngguó hòuyì báirén jiàzhíguān de huángzhǒngrén zhǐ jùyǒu Yīngguó hòuyì báirén jiàzhíguān de hēirén	1

275

		WASP values and attitudes—even to the extent they were prejudiced about their own cultures.	的黑人		
be in mortal fear (of)	v.p.	be afraid for one's life.	对……极度害怕	duì…jídù hàipà	3
be obliged to do sth.	v.p.	be required to do by law, conscience, sense of duty, contract, etc.	被迫做事	bèipò zuòshì	11
be tied to mother's apron strings	v.p.	be overly influenced by one's mother especially if an adult and still (too) strongly motivated by the desire to please a parent as if one is still a child. Defining "too much" or "adult" varies with cultures.	受母亲的控制	shòu mǔqīn de kòngzhì	10
beef up	v.p.	to make more powerful, strengthen.	加重	jiāzhòng	10
Berkeley	p.n.	the University of California in Berkeley was, like San Francisco, the birthplace of the "Hippie," "Flower Children," anti-Vietnam and anti-establishment movements—those who felt that no (government) agency could be trusted to honor individual freedom to be different from those in the mainstream or (WASP) norm.	伯克利，加利福尼亚大学伯克利分校 反-权力	Bókèlì, Jiālìfúníyà Dàxué Bókèlì Fēnxiào fǎn-quánlì	1
billboard	n.	a flat surface upon which announcements or advertisements are displayed, often in public and large enough to attract attention from passers-by.	广告牌	guǎnggàopái	4
Birkenstock	n.p.	a German-made shoe popularized in the 1960s by the "hippies" and "flower children" that is characterized by a solid, not delicate, thick sole.	勃肯牌	Bókěnpái	1
blink	v.	to quickly close and open the eyes, in this case intentionally and because he didn't yet know how to wink.	眨两只眼睛使眼神	zhǎ liǎng zhī yǎnjing shǐ yǎnshén	12
blood bank	n.p.	a place, usually a hospital facility, to preserve blood for transfusions.	血库	xuèkù	11
boom box	n.	slang - a portable radio that also plays music tapes and CDs stereophonically so that, when the volume is very high, the effect can be deafening, i.e., like a sonic boom.	音响	yīnxiǎng	2

boutonnière	n.	a flower or small bouquet worn on the lapel of a man's suit.	胸花	xiōnghuā	7
bowling alley	n.p.	a place of leisure with long wooden lane(s) where (teams of) players roll a heavy ball from one end to knock down as many as ten wooden pins arranged at the other end.	保龄球馆	Bǎolíngqiú-guǎn	2
bridesmaid	n.	woman who attends the bride as her witness to the marriage.	伴娘	bànniáng	7
Buster		a generic name for a male, previously associated with cowboys or riders who break or "bust" untamed horses; Mister.	伙计	huǒji	5
buttress	v.	to support, hold up, reinforce.	伴随着……	bànsuí zhe...	12
by-laws	n.	rule by which an organization governs itself and conducts its business.	章程	zhāngchéng	10
careen	v.	to lean or sway as if blown by a strong wind.	使……倾斜	shǐ...qīngxié	6
Caucasian	p.n.	although scholars have good reasons to debate the very concept of "race," our use of such terms reverts to their normative or popularly accepted meaning as descriptive of one's appearance, albeit vague, even erroneous, in this case to "White" people. The other racial "colors" are "Red," "Yellow," and "Black."	白种人	Báizhǒngrén	
chant	n.	a short, simple melody often used to pray, meditate, or practice scriptures.	赞美诗，圣歌	zànměishī, shènggē	5
chart the way	v.p.	to pilot, guide, lead, map.	指引（航向）	zhǐyǐn (hángxiàng)	10
chauvinist	n.	someone with an excessive, blind or overly devoted commitment to a cause or viewpoint. E.g., a "male chauvinist" is someone who believes that men are, by nature, superior to women in strength, intelligence, and capabilities.	沙文主义者	shāwén zhǔyìzhě	3
chill	v.	*Slang* - like "be cool," the idea is to calm down, not get upset.	冷静	lěngjìng	1
chronicle	v.	to write a chronological record of events, history, annals.	把……载入编年史，记述	bǎ...zǎirù biānniánshǐ, jìshù	1

clamber	v.	to climb awkwardly, often leading with one's knees.	攀登	pāndēng	3
click one's heels in the air	v.p.	to jump high and, while in the air, to bend both legs to the side so the heels can touch to signal joy, happiness, exuberance.	兴奋地跳起来	xīngfèn de tiàoqǐlái	8
clunky	adj.	not refined or delicate, awkward-looking.	笨拙	bènzhuō	1
cockroach	n.	any of several nocturnal insects characterized by a flattened body and speed, often considered a pest and associated with unclean conditions.	蟑螂	zhāngláng	2
coed	n.	a female college student as in a "coeducational" institution.	男女同校的女学生	nánnǚ tóngxiào de nǚ xuésheng	5
concierge	n.	French term for a hotel employee in charge of welcoming guests and providing special services.	大堂经理	dàtáng jīnglǐ	1
contemplate one's navel	v.p.	from a form of meditation, to be deep in thought, often sitting cross-legged on the floor, head tilted forward, as if the person were looking down at his/her belly button.	打坐，沉思	dǎzuò, chénsī	4
contemplation	n.	full, deep, or thoughtful observation or consideration of general conditions, God, humanity, nature, etc.	沉思	chénsī	10
court	n.	a quadrangle, often standardized, where games are played. Also – a place to hold legal proceedings; a small, often open-air enclosed space; a small street; a monarch's retinue.	篮球场	lánqiúchǎng	2
craft	v.	to make or fashion using acquired techniques or skills.	编织	biānzhī	11
crow	v.	to boast, exult, or proclaim loudly like the sound made by the bird of the same name.	自豪地吹嘘	zìháo de chuīxū	10
customs rate	n.p.	"customs" refers to the idea that each country has laws about what is or is not permitted to cross the border; it also refers to the idea of what is "customary" in terms of behavior associated with that	海关/习俗兑换率	hǎiguān /xísú duìhuànlǜ	5

country. "Rate" refers to the relative value of currency as well as "rate" to decide relative rank or status.

daring	adj.	adventurous, bold, audacious.	鲜艳的	xiānyàn de	7
debark	v.	to get off a ship (or plane), to land.	使……下船，使……登陆	shǐ…xiàchuán, shǐ…dēnglù	7
debase	v.	to reduce in value or quality; to lower in rank, significance or dignity; adulterate.	衰落，失败	shuāiluò, shībài	10
debutante	n.	a young woman who "comes out" or is formally introduced to society as was the custom among daughters of those in the *Social Register* [see below].	初进社交界的女子	chū jìn shèjiāojiè de nǚzǐ	1
defensive	adj.	of a game player who is trying to prevent an opponent from scoring and/or protecting a teammate from attack. Together with teammates doing the same, they form the noun "defense."	防守	fángshǒu	2
delirious	adj.	mentally and/or physically excited, disturbed, or emotional, usually temporary.	神志昏迷的	shénzhì-hūnmí de	5
dental fixation	n.p.	a complex or unnatural interest in teeth !!! More psychologically common are fixations on a celebrity, parent, or, in the case of foot-binding, female feet.	对牙齿的眷恋	duì yáchǐ de juànliàn	12
derisively	adv.	with a mocking manner, making fun of someone in a demeaning way.	可笑地，嘲弄地	kěxiào de, cháonòng de	7
descent	n.	from an ancestor or forbearer, lineage.	后裔	hòuyì	4
deteriorate	v.	to wear away; to become less in quality; to degenerate or worsen.	衰退	shuāituì	3
Diary of Anne Frank		this very important play, translated into 67 languages, was based on the personal record written by a 13-year old Jewish girl who hid from the Nazis for 25 months. The climax occurs when she screams at seeing the police.	《安妮少女日记》	《Ānnī Shàonǚ Rìjì》	1
disqualifier	n.	an intentional misuse of the verb "disqualify"—to render unfit or ineligible to compete, enter, join, etc.	被……取消资格者	bèi…qǔxiāo zīgézhě	1
divine	adj.	pertaining to God(s) and/or their celestial abode therefore "the most" wonder-	好极了	hǎo jí le	2

279

		ful, beautiful, superb.			
double en-tendre	n.p.	from the French for "double meaning," i.e., to have two different meanings in the context.	双关语	shuāngguānyǔ	9
double take	n.p.	looking again quickly because one doubts that what one first saw was true or accurate.	一种开始是愣住后来才恍然大悟的反应	yīzhǒng kāishǐ shì lèngzhù hòulái cái huǎngrán dàwù de fǎnyìng	4
doze off	v.p.	to sleep lightly or "nod off" when sitting or standing, that is, when not intending to sleep as in a bed.	打瞌睡	dǎ kēshuì	10
drawl	v.	to say words slowly, especially drawing out vowel sounds.	慢吞吞地说，懒洋洋地说	màntūntūn de shuō, lǎnyāng-yāng de shuō	5
drop dead	v.p.	to suddenly die. Also – adj. so wonderful that one could "die" as in "to die for" or want very much.	猝死	cùsǐ	3
drubbing	n.	corporal punishment; a beating or thrashing.	殴打	ōudǎ	1
dubbing	n.	the act of naming or conferring knight-hood.	命名	mìngmíng	1
economy of space	n.p.	efficient and sparing use of available area (or movement or effort, etc.)	节省空间	jiéshěng kōng-jiān	3
elevate	v.	to move or raise to a higher physical, spiritual, intellectual or political place or level; to promote to greater stature by an increase in rank, status, or office.	提拔，举起	tíba, jǔqǐ	9
Emancipa-tion Procla-mation	p.n.	an announcement of freedom like the document issued by President Abraham Lincoln on January 1, 1863. As the U.S. approached its third year of bloody civil war, this document declared "that all persons held as slaves" within the rebel-lious states "are, and henceforward shall be free."	解放宣言	Jiěfàng xuānyán	8
emboss	v.	to print or decorate so the image is raised from the surface.	作成浮雕，以浮雕装饰	zuò chéng fúdiāo, yǐ fúdiāo	8

				zhuāngshì	
emigration	n.	leaving one country to live in another.	移居出去	yíjū chūqù	1
Empress Dowager	n.	an (elderly) woman who holds (high) rank, office, or position by virtue of being a surviving widow. In China, this term usually refers to Cíxǐ Tàihòu.	豪门贵妇 慈禧太后	háomén guifù Cíxǐ Tàihòu	1
en masse	p.p.	(French) in a group, altogether, as a mass.	全体地	quántǐ de	6
en route	p.p.	Anglicized French phrase meaning "on the way."	在途中	zài túzhōng	2
end up (doing sth.)	v.p.	to conclude or finalize a process with a particular action.	以做某事而结束	yǐ zuò mǒushì ér jiéshù	11
ethnicity	n.	the customs, religion, language, appearance, etc. that characterize a people.	种族	zhǒngzú	1
etiquette	n.	rules or norms for proper behavior under various circumstances or places.	礼仪，礼节	lǐyí, lǐjié	5
exasperation	n.	extreme irritation, annoyance.	恼怒	nǎonù	8
ex-GI	abbr.	20th century slang abbrev. for a U.S. soldier possibly from "General Infantry," "Galvanized Iron, "Government Issue."	战争老兵	zhànzhēng lǎobīng	7
Face Book	n.	previously a book containing pictures of incoming first-year students to facilitate identification, now a web site of the same name or myspace.com where people can register personal information and network.	花名册	huāmíngcè	5
fall to one's knees	v.p.	to drop down to the ground landing on both knees as an act of prayer or gratitude.	跪下	guìxià	11
feces	n.	waste discharged from the bowels, excrement.	屎	shǐ	8
feminist	n.	a term that succeeded "suffragette" to describe those who believe in equal opportunity and rights for women as for men.	女权主义者	nǚquánzhǔyìzhě	1
fervently	adv.	with much warmth or great intensity of spirit, enthusiasm, feeling.	热诚地，热心地	rèchéng de, rèxīn de	11
(the or sb's)		high body temperature caused by disease	退烧	tuìshāo	5

fever has broken		or infection that ceases to climb so that the decrease indicates the patient is recovering.			
flurry	n.	a sudden activity, excitement or commotion like a snow flurry.	阵风	zhènfēng	4
fortify	v.	to enhance with additional ingredients; to strengthen.	加强的	jiāqiáng de	3
fuchsia	n.	a bright purplish red color as is the drooping flower of the same name.	粉红色	fěnhóngsè	7
funky	adj.	slang - having an unsophisticated, odd, quaint, unrefined or earthy character or style though sometimes "hip" or in style or "camp" as a result.	简单的	jiǎndān de	3
furrow	v.	to make a fold or, in this case, wrinkle the area between the eyebrows and/or forehead.	弄绉	nòngzhòu	12
gallop	v.	to run like a horse at full speed.	飞奔	fēibēn	6
get the hang of	v.p.	informal - acquire competence or skill.	得知……窍门	dézhī…qiàomén	3
give a hoot about sth.	v.p.	to care, be concerned or have interest (usually phrased in the negative).	在乎	zàihu	10
go ballistic	v.p.	to (re)act explosively and forcefully like the projectile motion of a bullet or missile.	爆发	bàofā	11
gompa	n.	a Buddhist monastery or temple generally containing a central prayer hall, a Buddha statue, benches for monks or nuns to engage in prayer or meditation as well as attached living accommodation.	寺院	sìyuàn	5
groggy	adj.	not clear-headed as when coming out of unconsciousness or sleep.	头昏眼花的	tóuhūn-yǎnhuā de	5
groomsman	n.	man who attends the groom as his witness to the marriage, usually a brother or friend.	伴郎	bànláng	7
Ha Long	p.n.	a bay in northwestern Vietnam known for its calm water and limestone mountains or karsts that are similar to those in the Lí River near Guìlín, China.	哈浪湾	Hālàng Wān	3
hallucinate	v.	to have sensory experiences unrelated to	使……产	shǐ…	5

282

		actual or real objects, e.g., dreams are "normal" hallucinations associated with sleep whereas drug or fever-induced ones are pathological.	生幻觉	chǎnshēng huànjué	
hard facts	n.p.	since facts are presumed to be true statements, describing them as "hard" suggests they are immutable. Also – being realistic, however difficult, as in "facing the cold truth."	铁的事实	tiě de shìshí	1
Harlem	p.n.	northwestern New York City and site of The New Negro Movement or The Harlem Renaissance when African-American music, dance, literature, and art flourished.	哈莱姆	Hāláimǔ	7
heft	n.	heaviness often measured by placing or balancing sth. in the hand then moving the hand up and down to gauge weight.	重量	zhòngliàng	12
hermit	n.	sb. who lives alone, apart from society (often for religious reasons).	隐士	yǐnshì	1
(when the shit) hits the fan	v.p.	taken literally, it is easy to imagine why the phrase is a metaphor for what happens when those who were previously "kept in the dark" about sth. suddenly discover the truth and are, to say the very least, not happy about the situation.	真相大白所导致的后果	zhēnxiàng-dàbái suǒ dǎozhì de hòuguǒ	12
ho ho ho		the sound of laughter associated with Santa Claus as in the poem, "He had a broad face and a little round belly that shook, when he laughed, like a bowl full of jelly."	ho ho ho !!!	ho ho ho !!!	12
honor one's lineage	v.p.	to respect or carry on one's family (blood) line or name.	尊重家庭传统, 光宗耀祖	zūnzhòng jiātíng chuán-tǒng, guāng-zōng-yàozǔ	11
hood	n.	an attachment to the back collar of a shirt or jacket that can be lifted to cover the head for warmth and/or ("hoodies") style. Also – the front of a car that covers the engine; slang – variously a young man ranging from "wilder" to gangster; "the hood" is short for (ethnic)	兜帽	dōumào	4

		"neighborhood."			
huddle	v.	to crowd or crouch together; to form a close group as players do in an American football game in order to plan strategy.	拥挤	yōngjǐ	9
huff	v.	to audibly puff or breathe out.	吹	chuī	8
hyperglyce-mic	adj.	having too much glucose or sugar in the bloodstream ("hyper" is the slang for "hyperactive" which is to be excessively active).	高糖的, 好动的	gāotáng de, hàodòng de	6
hypnotist	n.	Sigmund Freud, a 19th-century thinker, is considered the "father of psychoanalysis." As a result of his approach to understanding human behavior and the importance of sex, Westernized cultures tend to believe a person's identity consists of a conscious, subconscious, ego, superego, id, etc. Being hypnotized or put into a trancelike state allows access to the "subconscious" self which is often "hidden" from the conscious mind.	施行催眠术的心理学家	shīxíng cuīmiánshù de xīnlǐxuéjiā	1
ignominy	n.	disgrace, dishonor, shame, public contempt.	羞耻, 屈辱	xiūchǐ, qūrǔ	10
immigration	n.	moving into a country after leaving another.	移居进来	yíjū jìnlái	1
immobilize	v.	to stop movement.	使……不动	shǐ… bùdòng	6
in a peremptory tone	p.p.	in a commanding or unconditional way that precludes opposition or counter-argument.	以专横的语气	yǐ zhuānhèng de yǔqì	8
in profile	p.p.	placed or seen so as the outline or side is viewed by the onlooker.	侧面地	cèmiàn de	4
in retrospect	p.p.	different from "hindsight" when new information would have resulted in making a better prediction, this process is to look back and *think about* what happened.	回顾	huígù	1
in the crush of …	p.p.	being within a group formed by many occupying too small a space to avoid bodily contact.	在拥挤的人群中	zài yōngjǐ de rénqún zhōng	7
incisor	n.	one of the two upper or lower front or	门牙	ményá	12

		anterior teeth used primarily for biting or cutting into. See "incisive".			
index finger	n.p.	the first or pointing finger, next to the thumb. When counting with fingers in America, the index finger would be "1," the middle finger "2," etc. so the thumb is "5." If continuing, "6" is the index finger on the other. In China, the thumb is "1," the index finger "2," etc.	食指	shízhǐ	6
indicative (of)	adj.	suggestive of, pointing out/to.	指示的, 象征的, 表示……的	zhǐshì de, xiàngzhēng de, biǎoshì ...de	5
inextricably	adv.	in a way that is so hopelessly intricate, complicated, tangled, or involved that it cannot be undone or avoided.	分不开地，不可避免地	fēnbùkāi de, bùkě-bìmiǎn de	8
Inscrutable Oriental		this phrase has a long history of use, mostly by non-Asians, to describe the(ir) difficulty in reading Asian facial expressions (or the lack thereof). At its worst, it was associated with the "The Insidious Dr. Fu Manchu" character created by novelist Sax Rohmer and visually immortalized in the movies as the personification of the cruel cunning and evil genius that underlies the "Yellow Peril." At its most naïve, it refers to the self-control exercised by Asians who do not "wear their heart on their sleeves" and are less likely to express their feelings in public and who are, therefore, mysterious, not easily understood or seen through.	不可思议的东方人	bùkě-sīyì de dōngfāngrén	9
instant gratification	n.p.	associated with "Generation X" (born 1968-78 or so) whose parents were the "Baby Boomers," their attitude of living for the moment and getting what they want quickly arises from being accustomed to the speed of technology, and the uncertainty of life.	即刻满足	jíkè mǎnzú	6
instinctively	adv.	natural, inborn, innate or unlearned impulse, pattern, or way of doing sth.	本能地	běnnéng de	9

Term	Type	Definition	Chinese	Pinyin	#
inter	v.	to bury a (dead) body in a grave or tomb.	埋葬	máizàng	3
_inter_gration	n.	this word is original to this book and created to suggest journeying between two equally important cultures and not "integration" when different racial groups coexist peacefully as legal and social equals.	融汇	rónghuì	1
internal organ	n.p.	a part of the body occurring beneath the surface such as the heart or liver. Also – "internals" or "innards" usually referring specifically to the bowels or entrails.	内脏器官	nèizàng qìguān	3
intone	v.	to speak or vocalize, in this case in a monotone.	郑重其事地说	zhèngzhòng-qíshì de shuō	12
introspection	n.	observation or examination of one's mental and emotional state; looking within for better understanding of self.	内省	nèixǐng	10
jolly	adj.	cheerful, gay, merry, jovial.	愉快的，高兴的	yúkuài de, gāoxìng de	12
Junior Year Abroad		a program of study that is available to some college students who want to spend all or part of their 3rd year in another country.	去国外大学读三年级的项目	qù guówài dàxué dú sān-niánjí de xiàngmù	4
Kama Sutra		this 2,000 year-old book contains lessons and descriptions for human sexual intercourse hence its name in Sanskrit— "sensuous love" and "formula."	《爱经》	《Àijīng》	1
Kathmandu	p.n.	the capital city of Nepal.	加德满都	Jiādémǎndū	5
kayak	n.	originally a lightweight boat used by Eskimos, now for recreation.	橡皮艇	xiàngpítǐng	3
kick myself/sb.	v.p.	to express regret, be rueful	严厉自责	yánlì-zìzé	5
knock sb. out	v.p.	to hit a person so hard that s/he loses consciousness. Also – n. a "knockout punch" is the blow in boxing that renders the opponent incapable of continuing to fight the match.	打昏	dǎhūn	3
know better	v.p.	to be sufficiently informed so as to make a (more) reasonable decision.	明白	míngbái	3
lady-in-waiting	n.	female attendant to a queen, princess, et al., usually a noblewoman of lower rank	宫女	gōngnǔ	9

		than the one she attends but is not a common servant.			
lament	v.	to feel or express sorrow, regret, rue.	叹惜	tànxī	12
lapse (into)	v.p.	to fall, sink, or return to a previous (lesser) state or standard; to fail to maintain a (higher) state or standard.	陷入	xiànrù	8
lay a hand on sb.	v.p.	to use physical force with the intention of forcing or imposing one's will on another.	动手打人	dòngshǒu dǎrén	1
Lenape Indian	p.n.	a member of a tribe inhabiting an area near the Delaware and Hudson rivers.	德拉瓦族印第安人	Délāwǎzú Yìndì'ānrén	1
live on the hyphen	v.p.	during the 1980s, it became customary (first among the non-White population in the U.S.) to describe their racial or ethnic heritage by placing a hyphen between it and "American." The phrase was popularized in 1994 with the publication of *Life On the Hyphen: The Cuban-American Way* by Gustavo Perez Firmat. By the 2000 census, this practice was formally acknowledged so that people could choose more than one category such that there were 63 possible combinations. Also – "living *in* the hyphen" to indicate overlapping heritages.	生活在双元文化中	shēnghuó zài shuāngyuán wénhuà zhōng	1
Lucky Strike	p.n.	this was a popular brand of American cigarettes.	好彩牌香烟	Hǎocǎipái Xiāngyān	
lull	n.	a temporary period of inactivity or quiet. Also – v. to soothe or induce sleep or rest.	间歇	jiànxiē	12
make-believe	adj.	pretended, fantasized, unreal.	虚构的	xūgòu de	12
mangle	v.	to disfigure, ruin, crush. Also – n. a machine for squeezing excess water from laundry.	碾压	niǎnyā	1
mantra	n.	a word or sound that is recited or sung as an aid to meditation or prayer, now any idea or statement that a person repeats.	颂歌，咒语	sònggē, zhòuyǔ	5

menopausal	adj.	referring to the time when women cease to menstruate, usually between 45-50 years old.	更年期的	gēngniánqī de	1
millennia	n.	plural of "millennium," a period of 1,000 years.	千年	qiānnián	6
minutes	n.	at least two sixteenth of an hour; the official written record of a meeting.	分钟，纪录	fēnzhōng, jìlù	7
miss a beat	v.p.	to respond with hesitation and thus disrupt the established rhythm of a conversation, music, etc., usually expressed in the negative form.	错过一个节拍	cuòguò yīgè jiépāi	5
mod	adj.	from modern, associated with young British style of 1960s, trendy.	现代的，时髦的	xiàndài de, shímáo de	4
mollify	v.	to soften another's attitude or feeling; to placate, appease.	使……安慰	shǐ…ānwèi	3
monastery	n.	a communal residence for persons, e.g., monks, who have taken religious vows and/or are committed to living a secluded life.	修道院	xiūdàoyuàn	5
mutual admiration	n.p.	originally a 1956 song, "mutual admiration society," the phrase now refers to people who express great esteem for each other though sometimes used sarcastically as if there were really no good reason why they should be admired.	相互赞赏，互相了解	xiānghù-zànshǎng, hùxiāng-liǎojiě	5
navel	n.	the residue or scar left on the lower abdomen after severing the umbilical cord.	肚脐	dùqí	4
nostalgia	n.	a desire to return in thought or in fact to a former time in one's life. It is interesting that the song Americans sing with nostalgia at the New Year "Auld Lang Syne," meaning "old long days," is/was one of the best known in China.	乡愁,怀旧之情	xiāngchóu, huáijiù zhī qíng	7
nudist	n.	someone who prefers to be naked, to wear no clothing.	裸体主义者	luǒtǐzhǔyìzhě	1
nurture	n.	upbringing, training, breeding, education. Also – v.	培养	péiyǎng	10
(the) Occident	p.n.	the countries of Europe, Britain, and America.	西方，西方人	Xīfāng, Xīfāngrén	5
off limits	p.p.	area or topic that is not permitted; pro-	禁止进	jìnzhǐ jìnrù,	4

		hibited.	入，界限外	jièxiànwài	
offensive	adj.	of a game player who is aggressively trying to score a point/goal/basket. Together with teammates doing the same, they form the noun "offense." Also – causing displeasure, annoyance, insult, repugnance, disgust.	进攻	jìngōng	2
olfactory	adj	pertaining to the sense of smell.	嗅觉的	xiùjué de	3
one-seater		a vehicle—bicycle, boat, carriage, etc.—with room for one person.	单人座的橡皮艇	dānrén zuò de xiàngpítǐng	3
ontological	adj.	pertaining to metaphysics or the study of being, existence or reality (independent of the physical).	方法论的	fāngfǎlùn de	12
operate on the principle (of)	v.p.	to work, perform or proceed according to a rule.	根据……原理工作	gēnjù … yuánlǐ gōngzuò	3
pack up	v.p.	to arrange (into boxes, vehicles, etc.) things to be carried or moved from one place to another.	收拾	shōushi	11
paddle	v.	using a piece of wood, approximately 5-7 feet long, rounded at one end for holding, flat-sided at the other in the water to propel a small water craft. Shorter versions are used to play ping-pong. Also – n.	划桨	huájiǎng	3
paddy	n.	a field for growing rice.	水稻田	shuǐdàotián	3
parishioner	n.	the people or residents of a religious or civil parish or district.	教区居民	jiàoqū jūmín	10
parochial	adj.	of a limited or narrow scope or outlook; of a parish or church as, e.g., a parochial school.	地方性的，狭小的	dìfāngxìng de, xiáxiǎo de	5
passer-by	n.	someone, usually a stranger, who (coincidentally) walks by.	过路人	guòlùrén	8
perplexed	adj.	to be confused, bewildered, puzzled. Also – v. to perplex, confuse, puzzle, etc.	困惑的	kùnhuò de	12
phalanx	n.	from ancient Greek warfare, now any compact formation of people, animals or things, united for a common purpose.	方阵，密集队人群	fāngzhèn, mìjíduì rénqún	9

289

pinnacle	n.	the highest peak; the pointed or towering top of a formation.	尖峰，高峰，顶点	jiānfēng, gāofēng, dǐngdiǎn	10
play hooky	v.p.	not attend (school) when one should.	逃学	táoxué	1
politically correct	adj.p.	initially, being careful not to offend, especially in speech or writing, those people who are ethnically, religiously, linguistically, economically, or physically different; later, shortened to "p.c." with increasing sarcasm, disapproval and/or criticism of the resultant limitations on one's freedom to speak one's mind regardless of other's (hurt) feelings and/or inhibitions lest one inadvertently offends another.	政治上正确的	zhèngzhì shàng zhèngquè de	10
polyglot	n.	a mix or confusion of several languages.	数种语言的混合	shùzhǒng yǔyán de hùnhé	5
pool	v.	collect or put together (perspectives, viewpoints, opinions, money, etc.)	把观点集中起来	bǎ guāndiǎn jízhōng qǐlái	5
premarital	adj.	preceding marriage.	婚前	hūnqián	11
prioritize	v.	to list or rate in order of preference or precedence.	区分优先次序	qūfēn yōuxiān cìxù	10
pull out of the hat	v.p.	to suddenly or surprisingly produce a result, idea, or plan without prior warning like the stage trick when a performer "magically" lifts a live rabbit out of what seemed to be an empty top hat.	神奇般地给出结果、观点、计划	shénqíbān de gěichū jiéguǒ、guāndiǎn、jìhuà	11
qualifier	n.	sth. that describes, limits or modifies.	限制词	xiànzhìcí	12
quartet	n.	a group of four, often organized to sing or play music.	四个一组	sì gè yī zǔ	2
raucous	adj.	somewhat or seemingly disorderly, boisterous, harsh, strident.	刺耳的	cì'ěr de	2
reassure	v.	to restore confidence; to support, comfort.	使……安心	shǐ…ānxīn	
receptor	n.	that part of an organ that is sensitive to sensory stimuli.	感觉器官	gǎnjué qìguān	3
rectangular	adj.	like a 4-sided geometric figure with 4 right angles.	矩形的	jǔxíng de	3

rectitude	n.	moral virtue; rightness of practice, correctness.	诚实，正直	chéngshí, zhèngzhí	10
reds	n.	the category of wine made from red or dark-skinned grapes.	红酒	hóngjiǔ	3
refrain	n.	recurring phrase or melody in a musical or poetical composition. "To the song's refrain" is to do something like dancing, clapping or marching in time with or to the rhythm of the music. Also – v. to consciously not do something, to abstain.	重复	chóngfù	2
register	v.	to have some effect. Also – to record, take note, apply. Also n. - a book or device to store data.	生效	shēngxiào	3
reinforcement	n.	an additional supply of people, equipment, structural components, etc. to support or bolster a need, purpose, aim.	加强	jiāqiáng	9
renovate	v.	to make new again, restore to good condition.	装修	zhuāngxiū	6
rigor	n.	strict, austere, extreme, harsh, scrupulous.	严格，严峻	yángé, yánjùn	1
ritual	n.	an established or prescribed way of proceeding; a formal ceremony, often religious in nature.	仪式	yíshì	9
rock 'n roll	n.	shortened from "rock and roll" and, more recently, to just "rock," this style of music was popularized in the 1950s by Elvis Presley, Little Richard, and Chuck Berry (whose song, Johnny B. Goode, is "discovered" in the film, Back to the Future) and is characterized by a fast, very noticeable (drum) beat, (loud) electric guitar/piano accompaniment to repetitious phrasing of sound and words.	摇滚乐	yáogǔnyuè	2
rueful	adj.	feeling, expressing, or showing sorrow or regret.	悲伤的，可怜的	bēishāng de, kělián de	4
rule of thumb	n.p.	a general principle based on practical experience (rather than science).	原则	yuánzé	6
rummage	v.	to actively search through a place or receptacle for an object or idea.	到处翻寻，搜出,检查	dàochù fānxún,	9

				sōuchū, jiǎnchá	
sandals	n.	flat, open shoes that generally have straps on top.	凉鞋	liángxié	1
SAT	abbr.	Standard Aptitude Tests in Mathematics or Critical Reading and Writing taken by high school students applying to a college.	美国大学的入学考试	Měiguó dàxué de rùxué kǎoshì	7
savor	v.	to unhurriedly enjoy or appreciate a flavor, usually associated with the sense of taste.	尽情享受	jìnqíng-xiǎngshòu	2
scrutinize	v.	to look at or examine very closely or critically.	仔细检查	zǐxì jiǎnchá	5
sever	v.	to separate (from), to divide, break off, disunite, dissolve (ties) often in a forcible or drastic way.	终止	zhōngzhǐ	10
sexy	adj.	slang - generally or currently attractive, interesting, appealing.	性感的，有趣的	xìnggǎn de, yǒuqù de	4
sheen	n.	surface shine, luster, reflective brightness.	光泽	guāngzé	12
sign on the dotted line	v.p.	to signify legal agreement in that the place on a contract where one's signature is written is usually indicated by a line, possibly appearing as a series of dots which is how early typewriters made a line on the paper.	签字，在虚线上签名	qiānzì, zài xūxiàn shàng qiān-míng	10
skip	v.	to pass to a higher grade, point or place without stopping at the intervening grade, point or place; to omit or not attend. Also – walking fast, lightly leaping, dancing, or advancing by putting one foot forward and then hopping on it once before doing the same with the other.	跳级	tiào jí	1
slide off	v.p.	to go from one place to another in one smooth motion as a snake would slither off a rock to the ground.	滑动	huádòng	5
slump into	v.p.	to drop, fall, bend, or slouch heavily as if weighted down.	陷入，掉入	xiànrù, diàorù	5
slurp	v.	to noisily suck in food or drink.	吃/喝东西时发出	chī /hē dōngxi shí	10

			稀溜溜的声音	fāchū xīliūliū de shēngyīn	
smack of	v.p.	to have a (slight) taste, flavor, touch, or trace of.	带有……味道,有点象	dàiyǒu… wèidao, yǒudiǎn xiàng	10
smorgasbord	n.	originally Swedish, now a style of serving a meal buffet style when a variety of different dishes are placed on a long table and diners serve themselves; a miscellany, mélange, assortment.	大杂烩	dàzáhuì	10
sob	v.	to cry convulsively or loudly with a catching of breath.	哭诉, 哭泣	kūsù, kūqì	9
social elitism	n.p.	the idea or practice that a (small) group of people are more desirable, privileged. See *Social Register*.	社会精英论	shèhuì jīngyīnglùn	1
Social Register		or "Blue Book." Started at the end of the 19th century, this book listed the social "upper crust." Like the *New York Times* wedding announcements, inclusion was limited to the "high society" of "WASPs" to the exclusion of others, including Catholic Whites. Being "dropped" used to be reported in national newspapers!	《社会名流录》	《Shèhuì Míngliú Lù》	1
spike heels	n.p.	women's footwear with the vamp tapering to a point, and high heels, sometimes 3-5 inches long, tapering to a narrow base of less than ½ inch diameter.	女子高跟鞋	nǚzǐ gāogēnxié	1
spiral	n.	a coil or shape formed by connecting circles around a single point but on different planes.	螺旋	luóxuán	6
spoke	n.	one of several bars, rods or rungs radiating from the central hub of a wheel or cylinder.	辐, 辐条	fú, fútiáo	9
Sports Illustrated		since 1964, this magazine has annually featured a "swimsuit" issue that is known for photographs of females wearing swimsuits that have, over the years, needed less and less material to make **!!!**	《体育画报》	《Tǐyù Huàbào》	1
square	v.	to firmly set (the jaw, shoulders, etc.) to	拉长下巴	lācháng xiàba	8

293

		indicate determination and serious intent.			
stark	adj.	unadorned, desolate, utter, extreme, absolute.	完全的	wánquán de	2
stereotypical	adj.	like a standardized and (over) simplified image of one group often held by another based on limited experience.	陈腔滥调的，老套的	chénqiāng làndiào de, lǎotào de	3
stomp	v.	to stamp the foot heavily; to dance by stamping the feet to (fast) music.	踩（脚），重踩	duò (jiǎo), zhòngcǎi,	10
streamer	n.	a long strip of colored crepe paper hung from two high points, entwined around poles, etc. to decorate for a festive occasion.	装饰品	zhuāngshìpǐn	6
stumble over one's words	v.p.	to speak hesitantly, awkwardly or nervously as if trying to walk on uneven ground when the words are like rocks preventing smooth speech.	结结巴巴地说话	jiējiē-bābā de shuō huà	5
stump	v.	to render completely at a loss (for words or response), nonplus, fluster, cause puzzlement. Also – n. the base of a tree after the upper portion has been cut off.	被……难住	bèi … nánzhù	8
supplicating	adj.	in a manner of humble prayer, entreaty, petition.	恳求的	kěnqiú de	5
sustain	v.	to support, bear, hold up.	支撑	zhīchēng	12
sweatshirt	n.	shirt (of heavy cotton knit) originally for athletes to absorb perspiration, now a style of casual clothing.	运动衫	yùndòngshān	4
take in	v.p.	to absorb or grasp the meaning of sth.	领会，理解	lǐnghuì, lǐjiě	4
take shape	v.p.	to become like a certain form; to attain or obtain the character of sth.	以……形式出现	yǐ…xíngshì chūxiàn	10
take to be the case	v.p.	to affirm the truth or accuracy of one's interpretation or assessment of a situation.	接受	jiēshòu	4
taste buds	n.	small fleshy bumps on the tongue which receive sensory stimuli.	味蕾	wèilěi	3
terrace	n.	a raised level or platform area which, when adjoining a building, is usually surfaced with stone, brick, tile, etc.	大街	dàjiē	5

The Wizard of Oz		a (still popular) 1939 musical film about a girl from rural Kansas who, literally and figuratively, finds herself in a magical kingdom, trying to return home and to her "real" self. The theme and characters are often used as metaphors and archetypes for a wide variety of human conditions.	电影《绿野仙踪》	diànyǐng 《Lǜyě xiānzōng》	1
thumb your nose (at)	v.p.	a gesture or sign of disrespect when the thumb is placed on the tip of the nose and the fingers are waved up and down.	对……作蔑视手势	duì…zuò mièshì shǒushì	3
tidy	v.	to make more neat, trim, orderly.	收拾	shōushi	3
time warp	n.p.	in science fiction or "sci fi," the possibility of worm holes, parallel universes, etc. allows for nonlinear space travel because time is bent or warped so one can go from one place/time to another in seconds rather than (light) years.	时间隧道	shíjiān suìdào	6
tin ear	n.p.	incapable of hearing some sounds.	听觉不灵的耳朵	tīngjué bùlíng de ěrduo	8
toot one's horn	v.p.	to tell people how good one is in general or in particular; brag, boast.	炫耀	xuànyào	10
toothless grin	n.p.	smiling broadly so that the lack of teeth is visible.	露齿而笑（露出掉了牙齿的牙床）	lòuchǐ érxiào (lùchū diàole yáchǐ de yáchuáng)	12
tossed salad	n.p.	a food item of loose, raw, green, leafy vegetables, sometimes combined with cooked meat, cheese, etc. which are placed in a large bowl and mixed with a dressing or cold sauce by "tossing" the ingredients u-sing a large spoon or fork in each hand.	拌色拉	bànsèlā	10
traction	n.	adhering or gripping a surface as a good tire does on a road.	摩擦力	mócālì	3
truncate	v.	to cut off a part, apex or end.	切去头端,缩短,截成平面	qiēqù tóuduān, suōduǎn, jiéchéng píngmiàn	11

tug	v.	to pull, drag, or move.	拔（牙齿）	bá (yáchǐ)	12
turn off	v.p.	be no longer interested or attracted.	不感兴趣	bùgǎnxìngqù	5
turquoise	adj.	a blue-green color like that found in the mineral; a semi-precious stone of the same name.	青绿色	qīnglǜsè	3
twirl	v.	to rotate, spin, revolve or whirl rapidly.	快速转动	kuàisù zhuǎndòng	3
upshot	n.	result, outcome, conclusion.	结果，结局	jiéguǒ, jiéjú	12
urinal	n.	a toilet fixture designed for men's (public) bathrooms.	小便池	xiǎobiànchí	4
velveteen	n.	a fabric made of various materials with a short pile that is like velvet but softer and lighter.	绒布	róngbù	7
VHS	abbr.	acronym for Video Home System, the precursor of the CD and DVD for viewing movies.	家用录像系统	jiāyòng lùxiàng xìtǒng	2
Virgo	p.n.	this refers to one of twelve astrological signs of the Western Zodiac. The character of each is supposed to describe personality traits and is associated with one of twelve periods of one solar year.	处女座星座	Chùnǚzuò Xīngzuò	1
visualize	v.	to form a mental image or picture; imagine	使……看得见,将事物放在心里想像	shǐ...kàndejiàn, jiāng shìwù fàngzài xīn lǐ xiǎngxiàng	11
wail	v.	to grieve with prolonged cries or high-pitched sounds.	哭泣	kūqì	11
walk a narrow path	v.p.	from the phrase "the straight and narrow," meaning the morally proper way to behave implying a strict adherence to rules and/or (severe) limitations.	走小路	zǒu xiǎolù	1
Warring States Period		around 221 B.C.E. in China, the Qín managed to overwhelm the Chǔ , Hàn, Qí, Wèi, Yàn, and Zhào states.	战国时期	Zhànguó Shíqī	1
wee	adj.	little, small amount	很少的	hěnshǎo de	7
well up	v.p.	to rise, pool or gather. In this case the tears form and moisten the eyes but not so much as to fall down the face.	(泪如) 泉涌	(lèi rú) quán-yǒng	12

whaddami gonna do?		slurred, slangy, spoken version of "What am I going to do?" as portrayed in comic books.	我该怎么办呢？	Wǒ gāi zěnme bàn ne?	6
wimp	n.	someone who is ineffectual or does not stand firm but easily gives way to others.	懦弱的人，无用的人	nuòruò de rén, wúyòng de rén	12
winery	n.	a place where wine is made.	酿酒厂	niàngjiǔ chǎng	3
wink	v.	to quickly close and open one eye indicating good humor or joke, sometimes as a way to be flirtatious.	眨一眼使眼神	zhǎ yī yǎn shǐ yǎnshén	12
wishy-washy	adj.	watery, that is, lacking substance, character, strength; indecisive; thin and weak.	软弱无力	ruǎnruò-wúlì	10
Year of the Water Horse	p.n.	this refers to one of the possible combinations of twelve animals and five elements that add up to the sixty years of one Chinese cycle. The nature of the animals and elements is supposed to describe personality traits as well as what kind of year to expect.	水马年	Shuǐmǎ'nián	1
zero-sum game	n.p.	a game where the losses and gains are exactly balanced by the gains and losses so that the total of gain and loss is zero and there is a winner only when there is also a loser.	零和游戏	línghé yóuxì	10

CHINESE VOCABULARY

Ài'ěrlányì	爱尔兰裔	愛爾蘭裔	p.n.	Irish descent	1
Àidéhuá Huòěr	爱德华•霍尔	愛德華•霍爾	p.n.	Edward Hall	1
àixīn	爱心	愛心	n.	love, compassion, sympathy	9
Ālābóyǔ	阿拉伯语	阿拉伯語	p.n.	Arabic language	3
Āmǔsītèdān	阿姆斯特丹	阿姆斯特丹	p.n.	Amsterdam	1
Āndámàn	安达曼	安達曼	p.n.	Andaman	2
ānfǔ	安抚	安撫	v.	settle one's mixed feelings	12
ángguì	昂贵	昂貴	adj.	expensive, costly	1
Ānhuī	安徽	安徽	p.n.	Anhui (province)	1
ànnà	按捺	按捺	v.	suppress, restrain	11
Ānnī	安妮	安妮	p.n.	Anne Frank	1
ànshì	暗示	暗示	v.	suggest	2
ānyì	安逸	安逸	adj.	nice and comfortable	11
áo	熬	熬	v.	stick out	11
bá	拔	拔	v.	tug (a tooth)	12
bǎihuògōngsī	百货公司	百货公司	n.	department store	4
Báirén	白人	白人	p.n.	Caucasian, White man or woman	1
bàn	拌	拌	v.	mix in, toss (a salad)	10
Bàng jí le	棒极了	棒極了		Well done!	9
bǎngzi	膀子	膀子	n.	arms	9
bànláng	伴郎	伴郎	n.	groomsman	7
bànniáng	伴娘	伴娘	n.	bridesmaid	7
Bānnítè Bǐ'ēn	班尼特•比恩	班尼特•比恩	p.n.	Bennett Bean	1
bànrìzhì	半日制	半日制	n.	part-time	12
bǎnyā	板鸭	板鸭	n.	pressed duck	8
bànyǎn	扮演	扮演	v.	play a role	9
Bāo Guīyí	包圭漪	包圭漪	p.n.	the Chinese name for Cathy Bao Bean	1
bǎochí	保持	保持	v.	keep, maintain	11
Bàodēng Xuéyuàn	鲍登学院	鮑登學院	p.n.	Bowdoin College	4
bāokuò...zàinèi	包括……在内	包括……在内	v.p.	include sth.	1
bǎolíngqiúguǎn	保龄球馆	保齡球館	n.	bowling alley	2
bǎozhàng	保障	保障	n.	means	9
bèidào'érchí	背道而驰	背道而馳	f.c.w.	run in the opposite direction, run counter to	5
Běiměi	北美	北美	p.n.	North America	9

bēnfù	奔赴	奔赴	v.	be drafted to go (somewhere)	7
bèngbèng-tiàotiào	蹦蹦跳跳	蹦蹦跳跳	f.c.w.	jumping	6
běnnéng	本能	本能	n.	instinct	9
běnqián	本钱	本錢	n.	principal (used to gain or pursue profit)	11
běnshū	本书	本書	n.	this book	1
bènzhuō	笨拙	笨拙	adj.	clunky, clumsy, awkward	1
Bǐ'ěr Kèlíndùn	比尔·克林顿	比爾·克林頓	p.n.	Bill Clinton	7
biànhuàn	变换	變換	v.	switch, alter	2
biānyán	边沿	邊沿	n.	rim	3
biāojì	标记	標記	n.	label	8
biāoqiān	标签	標簽	n.	label, tag	7
biāozhì	标志	標誌	v.	indicate	10
bìbùkěshǎo	必不可少	必不可少	f.c.w.	indispensable, necessary	6
bǐcǐ	彼此	彼此	pron.	one another, each other	9
bìngfēirúcǐ	并非如此	並非如此	f.c.w.	not so	6
bǐrúshuō	比如说	比如說	v.p.	take sth. for example	3
Bókèlì	伯克利	伯克利	p.n.	Berkeley	1
Bókěnpái	勃肯牌	勃肯牌	p.n.	the Birkenstock brand	1
bōnong	拨弄	撥弄	v.	play with sth.	12
bóshì xuéwèi	博士学位	博士學位	n.p.	Ph.D. degree	4
Bōsīdùn	波斯顿	波斯頓	p.n.	Boston	5
bózi	脖子	脖子	n.	neck	8
bùduàn	不断	不斷	adv.	continuously	8
bùjiǎ-sīsuǒ	不假思索	不假思索	f.c.w.	not think deeply	1
bùkě-bìmiǎn	不可避免	不可避免	f.c.w.	inextricable	8
bùkě-sīyì	不可思议	不可思議	f.c.w.	inscrutable	9
bùlǐ	不理	不理	v.	ignore	4
Bùlǔkèlín	布鲁克林	布魯克林	p.n.	Brooklyn	1
bùróng	不容	不容	v.	not approved of	1
bùsùzhīkè	不速之客	不速之客	f.c.w.	uninvited or unexpected caller	5
bùyòngshuō	不用说	不用說	conj.	without saying	7
bùyuē'értóng	不约而同	不約而同	f.c.w.	do the same without prior consultation	2
bùzhī-suǒcuò	不知所措	不知所措	f.c.w.	bewildered	2
cǎinà	采纳	採納	v.	accept, adopt	5
cǎipái	彩排	彩排	v.	rehearse	7
cānguǎn	餐馆	餐館	n.	restaurant	1
cānkǎo	参考	參考	v.	guide	10
cánkù	残酷	殘酷	adj.	heartless	9

cānyù	参与	參與	v.	participate in	11
cānzhuō	餐桌	餐桌	n.	dining table	2
cāozòng	操纵	操縱	v.	operate, handle	11
cèmiàn	侧面	側面	n.	profile, side view	4
céngcéng	层层	層層	adv.	layer upon layer	9
céngjīng	曾经	曾經	adv.	once	12
chànàjiān	刹那间	刹那間	n.	split second	12
chángchūnténg dàxué	常春藤大学	常春藤大學	n.p.	the Ivy League colleges and universities	9
chǎngdì	场地	場地	n.	field, place	2
chángfà	长发	長髮	n.	long hair	1
chángguī	常规	常規	n.	rule of thumb, conventional measure	6
chàngxiāoshū	畅销书	暢銷書	n.	best-seller	1
chāzi	叉子	叉子	n.	fork	1
chéncí-làndiào	陈词滥调	陳詞濫調	f.c.w.	redundant, hackneyed	10
chéngdù	程度	程度	n.	degree, extent	7
chéngfá	惩罚	懲罰	n.	punishment, penalty	10
chénghuáng-chéngkǒng	诚惶诚恐	誠惶誠恐	f.c.w.	upset, with fear and trepidation	3
chéngjiā	成家	成家	v.o.	marry, mate	11
chéngkěn	诚恳	诚恳	adj.	supplicating	5
chéngniánrén	成年人	成年人	n.	adult	10
chéngqún-jiéduì	成群结队	成群結隊	f.c.w.	in crowds	7
chéngshì	城市	城市	n.	city	7
chēngzhīwéi	称之为	稱之為	v.p.	call it…	7
chéngzuò	乘坐	乘坐	v.	embark, take a ride (in a car, ship, etc.)	7
chénshù	陈述	陳述	v.	state, explain	8
chénsī	沉思	沉思	v.	contemplate	10
chībùxiāo	吃不消	吃不消	v (c)	overwhelm, be unable to withstand	3
chīzhīyǐbí	嗤之以鼻	嗤之以鼻	f.c.w.	give a snort of contempt	3
chōngdāng	充当	充當	v.	serve as, act as	7
chóngyǎn	重演	重演	v.	repeat, reenact	9
chuánjiàoshì	传教士	傳教士	n.	missionary	5
chuánshòu	传授	传授	v.	teach	1
chuānsuō	穿梭	穿梭	v.	switch back and forth	10
chuányuán	船员	船員	n.	crew of a ship	3
chuānzhuó	穿着	穿着	n.	the way to be dressed	1
chúchuāng	橱窗	櫥窗	n.	show or display window	8
chūchū-máolú	初出茅庐	初出茅廬	f.c.w.	debutante	1

chúcǐ yǐwài	除此以外	除此以外	p.p.	beyond this, in addition to this	12
chǔnǚ	处女	處女	n.	virgin	4
Chùnǚzuò Xīngzuò	处女座星座	處女座星座	p.n.	Virgo (constellation)	1
chuòchuò-yǒuyú	绰绰有余	綽綽有餘	f.c.w	more than enough	8
chuòhào	绰号	綽號	n.	nickname	1
chǔshì	处世	處世	v.o.	conduct oneself in society	3
chūxué	初学	初學	v.	just begin to learn sth.	3
cì'ěr	刺耳	刺耳	adj.	raucous	2
cíhuì	词汇	詞彙	n.	vocabulary	5
Cíxǐ Tàihòu	慈禧太后	慈禧太后	p.n.	Empress Dowager (1835-1908), ruling over Manchu Qing dynasty in China for 47 years	11
cíxíng	辞行	辭行	v.o.	say good-bye to the host/hostess	5
cōngming-juédǐng	聪明绝顶	聰明絕頂	f.c.w.	extremely smart, bright	12
cóngróng-bùpò	从容不迫	從容不迫	f.c.w.	confidently and without haste	12
cóngwèi	从未	從未	adv.	never	1
cuīmiánshù	催眠术	催眠術	n.	hypnotism	1
cūlǔ	粗鲁	粗魯	adj.	rough, very rude	2
cūshēng-cūqì	粗声粗气	粗聲粗氣	f.c.w.	shout	10
cūsú	粗俗	粗俗	adj.	vulgar, coarse, earthy	5
dàbuliǎo	大不了	大不了	adj.	no big deal, not problematic	10
dàbùxiāngtóng	大不相同	大不相同	f.c.w.	vary greatly	1
dàigōu	代沟	代溝	n.	generation gap	1
dàishù	代数	代數	n.	algebra	8
dàiyǒu	带有	帶有	v.	have	4
dǎkēshuì	打瞌睡	打瞌睡	v.p.	doze off	10
dāla	耷拉	耷拉	v.	hang down	9
dǎlái	打来	打來	v (c)	make (a telephone call)	11
dànánzǐzhǔyì	大男子主义	大男子主義	n.	male chauvinist	3
dāng	当	當	v.	be	2
dāngjí	当即	當即	adv.	at once, right away, immediately	5
dānyōu	担忧	擔憂	n.	worry, anxiety	4
dānzi	单子	單子	n.	list (of items)	12
dàofàng	倒放	倒放	v.p.	be placed upside	1
dàoguà	倒挂	倒掛	v.	be hung upside	8
Dàojiāsīxiǎng	道家思想	道家思想	p.n.	Taoism	4
dǎoyóu	导游	導游	n.	tour guide	3

dǎpò	打破	打破	v (c)	destroy	2
dàtáng jīnglǐ	大堂经理	大堂經理	n.	concierge, hotel manager	1
dàtuǐ	大腿	大腿	n.	thigh	8
dàxiǎn-shēnshǒu	大显身手	大显身手	f.c.w.	pull out of the hat, accomplish	11
dǎxiāo	打消	打消	v (c)	give up	2
dàyǒu bìyì	大有裨益	大有脾益	f.c.w.	be of great benefit	1
dàzáhuì	大杂烩	大雜燴	n.	smorgasbord	10
dǎzuò	打坐	打坐	v.	meditate	4
diāosù	雕塑	雕塑	n.	sculpture	1
dǐbù	底部	底部	n.	base, low level	10
dǐdǎng	抵挡	抵擋	v.	counter the effect of	12
dīdiào	低调	低调	n.	low profile	10
dìdì-dàodào	地地道道	地地道道	r.f.	completely	4
diédié-bùxiū	喋喋不休	喋喋不休	f.c.w.	talk endlessly	9
diēzuò	跌坐	跌坐	v (c)	slump back into	5
dìfāng	地方	地方	n.	local area	5
dǐng	顶	頂	n.	the top of a structure	10
dǐngbù	顶部	頂部	n.	the top part	11
dìngshíde	定时地	定時地	adv.	at regular intervals	3
dísikē	迪斯科	迪斯科	n.	disco	2
dìtújí	地图集	地圖集	n.	atlas	1
diūjìn	丢尽	丢盡	v (c)	lose completely	2
diūliǎn	丢脸	丢臉	v.o.	lose face, be disgraced	5
dìxiàshì	地下室	地下室	n.	basement	11
dì-yī rénchēng	第一人称	第一人稱	n.p.	the first person	1
dòngkǒu	洞口	洞口	n.	hole	3
dòu	逗	逗	v.	provoke (laughter)	2
duàndìng	断定	斷定	v.	conclude, form a judgment	2
duǎnkù	短裤	短褲	n.	shorts	3
duānxiang	端详	端詳	v.	scrutinize carefully	9
duǎnyǔ	短语	短語	n.	phrase	3
duì …gǎnxìngqù	对…..感兴趣	對…..感興趣	p.p.	be interested in sth./sb.	5
duìcǐ	对此	對此	p.p.	pertaining to this	8
duìxiàng	对象	對象	n.	girlfriend/boyfriend, also spouse	11
dúlì	独立	獨立	v.	be independent	8
dúlì-zìzhǔ	独立自主	獨立自主	f.c.w.	independence and self-reliance	10
dùnshī xìngqù	顿失兴趣	頓失興趣	f.c.w.	turn off, lose interest	5
duōyuánhuà	多元化	多元化	adj.	diversified	1

dùqí	肚脐	肚臍	n.	navel	4
dùrì-rúnián	度日如年	度日如年	f.c.w.	spending a day like a year	6
dǔsè	堵塞	堵塞	v.	stop up, block, block up	9
dùshu	度数	度數	n.	degree	3
dúyī-wú'èr	独一无二	獨一無二	f.c.w.	unique	6
érgē	儿歌	兒歌	n.	nursery gamesong	5
èrhuà-méishuō	二话没说	二話沒說	f.c.w.	say nothing	3
ěrpàn	耳畔	耳畔	n.	around one's ears	9
Èrzhàn	二战	二戰	p.n.	World War Two	7
fāfēng	发疯	發瘋	v.o.	go crazy	3
fājiā	发家	發家	v.o.	succeed, get ahead	4
fǎnchā	反差	反差	n.	contrast	2
fànchóu	范畴	範疇	n.	category, domain, range	7
fǎnduì	反对	反對	v.	object	8
fǎnfǎn-fùfù	反反复复	反反覆覆	r.f.	repeatedly	2
fángjiao	房角	房角	n	the corner of the room	3
fàngjìn	放进	放進	v.o.	place in	10
fángshǒu	防守	防守	v.	defend	2
fángzū	房租	房租	n.	rent	4
fāshì	发誓	發誓	v.o.	vow, pledge, swear	5
fàxíng	发型	髮型	n.	hair style	1
Fēiyì	非裔	非裔	p.n.	African descendent	1
fēnbiàn	分辨	分辨	v.	identify, distinguish	7
fènfèn-bùpíng	愤愤不平	憤憤不平	f.c.w.	indignant	2
féngbǔ	缝补	縫補	v.	sew	11
fēngfù-duōcǎi	丰富多彩	豐富多彩	f.c.w.	interesting, rich and colorful	1
fēngtǔ-rénqíng	风土人情	風土人情	f.c.w.	local conditions and customs	5
féngzhì	缝制	縫製	v.	sew	1
fènlì	奋力	奮力	v.	exert oneself to the utmost, do all one can	1
fénmù	坟墓	墳墓	n.	grave, tomb	3
fěnsī	粉丝	粉絲	n.	fans (also, vermicelli made from bean starch)	1
fēnxiào	分校	分校	n.	one of the school campuses	1
Fóxuélǐlùn	佛学理论	佛學理論	p.n.	Buddhism	4
fú	幅	幅	m(n)	used for paintings, cloth, silk, fabric	2
fúbīngyì	服兵役	服兵役	v.p.	serve in military	1
fǔmō	抚摸	撫摸	v.	touch	3

fūsè	肤色	膚色	n.	color of skin	7
fúshì	服侍	服侍	v.	wait upon, attend to	9
fúwùyuán	服务员	服務員	n.	waitress, waiter	1
fùzhū-shíshī	付诸实施	付諸實施	f.c.w.	put into effect	10
fùzhǔxí	副主席	副主席	n.p.	vice chairman	10
gàizi	盖子	蓋子	n.	lid	8
Gǎn'ēn Jié	感恩节	感恩節	p.n.	Thanksgiving	5
gāngà	尴尬	尷尬	adj.	awkward, embarrassed	5
gǎnguān	感官	感官	n.	sensory organ	3
gāogēnxié	高跟鞋	高跟鞋	n.	high-heeled shoes	1
gāojiǎoyǐ	高脚椅	高腳椅	n.	high chair	8
gāoshāo	高烧	高烧	n.	high fever	5
gāoshǒu	高手	高手	n.	master, expert	1
gēcí	歌词	歌詞	n.	words of a song, lyrics	5
gèháng-gèyè	各行各业	各行各業	f.c.w.	all walks of life	7
géhé	隔阂	隔阂	n.	misunderstanding, gap	11
Gělíndá	葛琳达	葛琳達	p.n.	Glinda	1
gēngniánqī	更年期	更年期	n.	menopause	1
gēnshēn-dìgù	根深蒂固	根深蒂固	f.c.w.	deep-rooted	12
gēxīng	歌星	歌星	n.	singing star	2
gōng	供	供	v.	supply	2
gòngchǎn zhǔyì	共产主义	共產主義	n.	communism	1
gōnggong	公公	公公	n.	husband's father, father-in-law	9
gōngjìng	恭敬	恭敬	adj.	respectful	5
gōnglì xuéxiào	公立学校	公立學校	n.p.	public schools	1
gōngnǚ	宫女	宮女	n.	lady-in-waiting	9
gōngtíng	宫廷	宮廷	n.	palace, royal court	9
gōngwéi	恭维	恭維	v.	compliment	3
gòuwù	购物	購物	v.	go shopping	4
gòuzhì	购置	購置	v.	purchase, buy	1
guà	挂	掛	v.	put in	9
guāi	乖	乖	adj.	being well-behaved	8
guǎiwān-mòjiǎo	拐弯抹角	拐彎抹角	f.c.w.	indirectly, in a roundabout way	4
guǎn	管	管	v.	take care of	6
guānchá	观察	觀察	v.	observe	2
guàng	逛	逛	v.	look around shops, stroll	8
guǎnggàopái	广告牌	廣告牌	n.	billboard	4
guānghuī	光辉	光輝	adj.	momentous	11
guāngzé	光泽	光澤	n.	sheen	12

guāngzōng-yàozǔ	光宗耀祖	光宗耀祖	f.c.w.	bring honor to one's ancestors	4
guǎnjiā	管家	管家	n.	housekeeper	12
guǎnjiào	管教	管教	v.	control, teach, or discipline sb.	1
guànlì	惯例	慣例	n.	ritual	9
guānniàn	观念	觀念	n.	icons, concept	12
guǎnyòng	管用	管用	v.	be of use, be effective	12
guì	跪	跪	v.	kneel	11
guīgōngyú	归功于	歸功於	v.p.	owe… to	3
guǐjì	轨迹	軌跡	n.	track, path along which a person goes through his or her life	1
guīlì	瑰丽	瑰麗	adj.	magnificent	7
Guìlín	桂林	桂林	p.n.	Guilin (Guangxi)	1
guòshì	过世	過世	v.o.	die, pass away	1
hǎibào	海报	海報	n.	poster	10
hǎinèiwài	海内外	海内外	n.p.	home and abroad	7
hǎiwān	海湾	海灣	n.	bay	3
Hāláimǔ	哈莱姆	哈萊姆	p.n.	Harlem	7
hǎnjiàn	罕见	罕見	v.	seldom seen	2
hànliú-jiābèi	汗流浃背	汗流浹背	f.c.w.	sweat, perspire	1
Hánzhàn	韩战	韓戰	p.n.	The Korean War	7
hǎobùróngyì	好不容易	好不容易	f.c.w.	after all the trouble	6
háomén guìfù	豪门贵妇	豪門貴婦	n.p.	Empress Dowager	1
háowú-yuànyán	毫无怨言	毫无怨言	f.c.w.	without complaint	9
hé'ěrméng	荷尔蒙	荷爾蒙	n.	hormone	1
hēirén	黑人	黑人	n.	person with black skin	1
hěndà yībùfen	很大一部分	很大一部分	n.p.	a large part of	4
héshang	和尚	和尚	n.	Buddhist monk	5
hézàng	合葬	合葬	v.	be buried together	9
hézi	盒子	盒子	n.	box	3
hóngbāo	红包	紅包	n.	red paper envelope to hold money as a gift	12
hóngluóbo	红萝卜	紅蘿卜	n.	red radish	2
hóngniáng	红娘	紅娘	n.	match-maker	1
hōngtáng-dàxiào	哄堂大笑	哄堂大笑	f.c.w.	the whole room burst into laughter	10
hōngzhà	轰炸	轟炸	v.	bomb	5
huā	花	花	v.	spend time (money)	5
huàchár	话茬儿	話茬兒	n.	thread of conversation	3
huáijiù	怀旧	懷舊	v.o.	remember past times	7

huájìn	划进	划进	v (c)	paddle into	3
huāmíngcè	花名册	花名册	n.	Face Book	5
huàngdòng	晃动	晃動	v.	wave	5
huàngláihuàngqù	晃来晃去	晃來晃去	f.c.w.	move around	6
huāngmiù	荒谬	荒謬	adj.	crazy, ridiculous, absurd, preposterous	11
huǎngrán-dàwù	恍然大悟	恍然大悟	f.c.w.	suddenly see the light	4
huānhū-quèyuè	欢呼雀跃	歡呼雀躍	f.c.w.	galloping joy	6
huànjùhuàshuō	换句话说	換句話說	conj.	in other words	1
Huánqiú Yíngmù	环球影幕	環球影幕		World Screen (a magazine)	4
huànxiǎng	幻想	幻想	n.	fantasy	12
huànyǒu	患有	患有	v.	be afflicted with	3
Huáyì	华裔	華裔	p.n.	Chinese descent	1
huàzhuāng	化妆	化妝	v.	make up	7
hùfūpǐn	护肤品	護膚品	n.	lotion	3
huí	回	回	m (n)	a measure word for sth.	7
huī	挥	揮	v.	wave	9
huībáidìdài	灰白地带	灰白地带	f.c.w.	degrees of difference between "right" and "wrong"	12
huígù	回顾	回顧	v.	review, look back	1
Huīgūniang	灰姑娘	灰姑娘	p.n.	Cinderella	12
huìhé	会合	會合	v.	join, meet	7
huíshǒu	回首	回首	v.o.	look back	1
huīwǔ	挥舞	揮舞	v.	twirl	3
huíyìlù	回忆录	回憶錄	n.	memoir	1
hūlüè	忽略	忽略	v	ignore	11
hūnhòu	婚后	婚後	n.	postnuptial, after marriage	11
hūnqián	婚前	婚前	n.	premarital, before marriage	11
hùnxuè'ér	混血儿	混血兒	n.	hybrid	4
huòduō-huòshǎo	或多或少	或多或少	f.c.w.	more or less	1
huǒji	伙计	伙計	n.	Buster, Mister	5
huǒjī	火鸡	火雞	n.	turkey	5
Huòpǔ Kùkè	霍普•库克	霍普•库克	p.n.	Hope Cooke	1
húxū	胡须	鬍鬚	n.	beard, moustache	1
jì…yòu…	既……又……	既……又……	conj.	both…and…	2
jià	嫁	嫁	v.	(of a woman) marry	11
Jiādémǎndū	加德满都	加德滿都	p.n.	Kathmandu	5
jiālǐ	家里	家裡	n.	at home	8
jiānchí-bùxiè	坚持不懈	堅持不懈	f.c.w.	persistent, unremitting,	12

				persevering	
jiāng	桨	桨	n.	paddle	3
jiāng…lièbiǎo	将……列表	將……列表	p.p.	put sth. on the list	10
jiānjiān	尖尖	尖尖	adj.	pointy-toed	1
jiànshēnfáng	健身房	健身房	n.	aerobics studio	1
jiānyìng	坚硬	堅硬	adj.	hard	1
jiàohǎn	叫喊	叫喊	v.	scream	1
jiāohuàn	交换	交換	v.	exchange	12
jiàohuáng	教皇	教皇	n.	pope	10
jiāohuì	交汇	交匯	v.	intersect	5
jiàomín	教民	教民	n.	parishioner	10
jiàoxùn	教训	教訓	n.	lesson, lecture	8
jiāoyì	交易	交易	n.	transaction	12
jiàozhí	教职	教職	n.	teaching job	1
jiàshì	架势	架勢	n.	posture, appearance	3
jiāyóu zhàn	加油站	加油站	n.p.	gas station	7
jiàyù	驾驭	駕馭	v.	control, master; drive (a cart, horse, etc.)	5
jiāzá	夹杂	夾雜	v.	be mixed up with, be mingled with	5
jiàzhíguān	价值观	價值觀	n.	value system	8
jiāzhòng	加重	加重	v.	beef up, make or become more weighty	10
Jiāzhōu Dàxué	加州大学	加州大學	p.n.	University of California	1
jíduān	极端	極端	adj.	extreme	9
jiěfàng	解放	解放	v.	be free, emancipate	8
jiěgù	解雇	解僱	v.	fire, discharge	1
jiéhé	结合	結合	v.	connect	11
jiěmèi	姐妹	姐妹	n.	sisters	8
jiéshí	结识	結識	v.	get acquainted with sb.	8
jiěshì	解释	解釋	n./v.	interpretation, interpret	1
jiēshì	揭示	揭示	v.	reveal, bring to light	1
jiēshòu	接受	接受	v.	take, accept	11
jiētóu	街头	街头	n.	street corner	12
jiéwěi	结尾	結尾	v.o.	end, wind up	8
jiēxiàlái	接下来	接下來	adj.	then, the following	1
jièyān	戒烟	戒煙	v.o.	give up smoking	1
jièzhùyú	借助于	借助於	v.p.	by the force of, obtain support from	10
jíhuì	集会	集會	n.	assembly, gathering	10
jīhuì	机会	機會	n.	opportunity	5
jìjiào	计较	計較	v.	care about	11

jíkè	即刻	即刻	adv.	at once, immediately	6
jìn	尽	盡	v.	do (one's duty)	9
jīnfà-bìyǎn	金发碧眼	金髮碧眼	f.c.w.	blonde	11
Jīngbàodiǎn	惊爆点	惊爆点		Point Break (a movie)	4
jǐngguān	景观	景觀	n	scene	2
jīnghuāng-shīcuò	惊慌失措	驚慌失措	f.c.w.	losing one's head, seized with panic	11
jīngjì	经济	經濟	n.	finance, economy	9
jīngjìrén	经纪人	經紀人	n.	broker, middleman, agent	1
jīnglì wàngshèng	精力旺盛	精力旺盛	f.c.w.	energizing	7
jìngōng	进攻	进攻	v.	attack	2
jīngshòu-gànliàn	精瘦干练	精瘦干練	f.c.w.	lean but strong	3
jīngsuǐ	精髓	精髓	n.	spirit, essence	11
jīngxì	精细	精細	adj.	fine	2
jìngxuǎn	竞选	竟選	v.	campaign	10
jīngyīng	精英	精英	n.	elite	10
jìnqīn	近亲	近親	n.	immediate family	9
jīnróng	金融	金融	n.	finance	12
jīnsè	金色	金色	n.	gold color	8
jǐnsuǒ	紧锁	緊鎖	v.	furrow	12
jìnǚ	妓女	妓女	n.	prostitute, whore	1
jìnzhí	尽职	盡職	v.o.	fulfill one's duty	9
jīnzìtǎ	金字塔	金字塔	n.	pyramid	10
jīqìrén	机器人	機器人	n.	robot	4
jīròu-fādá	肌肉发达	肌肉發達	f.c.w.	muscular	3
jíshǐ	即使	即使	conj.	even if	1
Jiùjīnshān	旧金山	舊金山	p.n.	San Francisco, CA	11
jiùxiàng	就像	就像	adv.	as if	2
jìxù	继续	繼續	v.	continue	9
jīyīn	基因	基因	n.	gene	11
jìyì-yóuxīn	记忆犹新	記憶猶新	f.c.w.	remain fresh in one's memory	4
jǐyǔ	给予	給与	v.	give, provide	5
jìzǎi	记载	記載	n.	minutes	11
jízhōng-jīnglì	集中精力	集中精力	f.c.w.	concentrate on	12
jù	剧	劇	n.	play	1
jùbèi	具备	具備	v.	furnish, be equipped with	11
juéchá	觉察	覺察	v.	realize, sense, perceive	5
juédìng	决定	決定	v.	determine	10
juésè	角色	角色	n.	role	2
juézhú	角逐	角逐	v.	compete, enter into rivalry	10

				with	
jùhuì	聚会	聚會	n.	party	6
jùjué	拒绝	拒絕	v.	refuse	10
Jūzhùqū	居住区	居住區	n.p.	dwelling district	7
kǎ	卡	卡	v.	get lost, get stuck	6
kāihuái-dàxlào	开怀大笑	開懷大笑	f.c.w.	laugh heartily	2
Kǎisī	凯斯	凱斯	p.n.	shortened form for "Cathy"	6
kāizhàn	开战	開戰	v.o.	battle, fight	3
Kǎlābǐ	卡拉比	卡拉比	p.n.	Krabi	2
kànghéng	抗衡	抗衡	v.	counter the effect of	12
Kāngnàěr Dàxué	康纳尔大学	康納爾大學	p.n.	Cornell University	4
Kānsàsī	堪萨斯	堪薩斯	p.n.	Kansas	1
kànzuò	看作	看作	v.	regard as, consider, look upon as	7
kěchǐ	可耻	可恥	adj.	shameful, disgraceful, ignominious	5
kēmù	科目	科目	n.	school subject	10
kěnqiè	恳切	恳切	adj.	sincere, genuine	5
Kēnǔ Héfēi	柯努•荷菲	柯努•荷菲	p.n.	Keanu Reeves	4
kèzhàn	客栈	客栈	n.	inn	5
Kǒngfūzǐ	孔夫子	孔夫子	p.n	Confucius	1
kù	酷	酷	adj.	cool	5
kuānróng	宽容	寬容	adj.	tolerant, lenient	4
kuānwèi	宽慰	寬慰	v.	be relieved	4
kuàwénhuàde	跨文化的	跨文化的	adj.	cross-cultural	11
kuàyuè	跨越	跨越	v.	cross over	6
kūku-títí	哭哭啼啼	哭哭啼啼	f.c.w.	sob	9
kùnhuò	困惑	困惑	adj.	perplexed, puzzled	12
kuòhào	括号	括號	n.	parentheses	6
kǔwèi	苦味	苦味	n	bitterness	3
kǔxiào	苦笑	苦笑	n.	rueful smile	4
kūzào	枯燥	枯燥	adj.	dry and dull, uninteresting	4
láishì	来世	來世	n.	afterlife	9
lālāduì	拉拉队	拉拉隊	n.	cheer loading squad	1
lángdāng-rùyù	锒铛入狱	鋃鐺入獄	f.c.w.	serve time in jail, be imprisoned	10
lǎobīng	老兵	老兵	n.	veteran	7
lǎolao	姥姥	姥姥	n.	maternal grandmother	2
lǎotào	老套	老套	adj.	stereotypical	3
làoyìn	烙印	烙印	n.	branding, lasting impression	8

lèguān	乐观	樂觀	n.	optimism	12
lèisì	类似	类似	adj.	similar	2
lèngzhù	愣住	愣住	v.	stand in amazement	4
liàng	量	量	n.	quantity, amount	5
liángxié	凉鞋	涼鞋	n.	sandals	1
liángxīn	良心	良心	n.	conscience	10
liǎngyǎn	两眼	兩眼	n.	(two) eyes	8
liǎngzhě	两者	兩者	n.	both	1
liǎngzhě jiēyǒu	两者皆有	兩者皆有	f.c.w.	both	1
liánmǐn	怜悯	憐憫	v.	express sympathy for, have passion for	10
liǎnshàng	脸上	臉上	n.	on the face	6
liǎorúzhǐzhǎng	了如指掌	了如指掌	f.c.w.	know sth. like the palm	4
liáotiān	聊天	聊天	v.o.	chat	8
lièxìng	烈性	烈性	adj.	robust	3
líng	灵	靈	adj.	quick, alert	8
línghé	零和	零和	n.	zero sum	10
língmǐndù	灵敏度	靈敏度	n.	sensitivity	3
lìngrén	令人	令人	v.o.	cause people to..., make one...	4
lìngrén-shēngwèi	令人生畏	令人生畏	f.c.w.	frightening	7
lìngrén-zhènfèn	令人振奋	令人振奮	f.c.w.	exhilarating	7
língtīng	聆听	聆聽	v.	listen respectfully	8
lǐngxián	领衔	領銜	v.o.	star in a movie/play	4
lǐngyǎng	领养	領養	v.	adopt (a child)	10
lìngyǎn-xiāngkàn	另眼相看	另眼相看	f.c.w.	look at sb./sth. with new eyes	3
Lìshā	丽莎	麗莎	p.n.	Lisa	1
lìsuǒnéngjí	力所能及	力所能及	f.c.w.	within one's ability	2
liúlèi	流泪	流淚	v.o.	shed tears	9
liúlù	流露	流露	v.	reveal, show	11
liúyǒu	留有	留有	v.	wear	1
Lǐwéisī	李维斯	李維斯	p.n.	Levi's	4
lǒngtǒng	笼统	籠統	adj.	general	10
lòuchǐ'érxiào	露齿而笑	露齒而笑	f.c.w.	grin	12
luànqībāzāo	乱七八糟	亂七八糟	f.c.w.	be in a mess	6
Lǔdí Jiébǔlín	鲁迪·杰卜林	魯迪·傑卜林	p.n.	Rudyard Kipling	11
lúndào	轮到	輪到	v.	be one's turn	3
lúnhuàn	轮换	輪換	v.	take turns, rotate	6
Luòqí	洛奇	洛奇		Rocky (a movie)	2
luǒtǐ zhǔyì	裸体主义	裸體主義	n.	nudism	1

luóxuán	螺旋	螺旋	n.	spiral	6
lùpái	路牌	路牌	n.	street sign	5
Lǜyěxiānzōng	绿野仙踪	綠野仙蹤		The Wizard of Oz (a movie)	1
lǚyóu-shèngdi	旅游胜地	旅遊勝地	f.c.w.	resort, a place for vacationers	2
Mǎ'ěrkēmǔ X	马尔科姆 X	马尔科姆 X	p.n.	Malcolm X	1
máijìn	埋进	埋進	v.	inter, bury	3
Màikèr Jiékèxùn	迈克尔·杰克逊	邁克爾·傑克遜	p.n.	Michael Jackson	2
májiàng	麻将	麻將	n.	mah-jongg	4
mànbù	漫步	漫步	v.o.	stroll, roam	8
mànbùjīngxīn	漫不经心	漫不經心	f.c.w.	casually	12
máosè-dùnkāi	茅塞顿开	茅塞頓開	f.c.w.	suddenly see the light	3
máoshì	毛式	毛式	n.	the Mao style	7
màoxiǎn	冒险	冒險	v.o.	take a chance	12
méifǎ	没法	沒法	v.	have no way to do sth.	7
Měiguóhuà	美国化	美國化	v.	Americanize	2
Měijí Huárén	美籍华人	美籍華人	p.n.	Chinese-American, Americanized Chinese	1
měimiào	美妙	美妙	adj.	splendid, wonderful	2
měishì	美式	美式	n.	the American style	9
mēngmēngdǒngdǒng	懵懵懂懂	懵懵懂懂	r.f.	groggy	5
Méngtèkèlái'ěr	蒙特克莱尔	蒙特克萊爾	p.n.	Montclair	12
ményá	门牙	門牙	n.	incisor	12
miànjù	面具	面具	n.	mask	7
miànmù-quánfēi	面目全非	面目全非	f.c.w.	beyond recognition, completely changed	10
miàntiáo	面条	麵條	n.	noodles	10
miáoshù	描述	描述	v.	describe	2
miáotou	苗头	苗頭	n.	symptom of a (new) development/trend	2
miǎoxiǎo	渺小	渺小	adj.	insignificant, negligible, paltry	5
miǎozhōng	秒钟	秒鐘	m(n)	second (of time)	10
míliúzhījì	弥留之际	彌留之際	f.c.w.	before dying, at the time of dying	9
mími-hūhu	迷迷糊糊	迷迷糊糊	r.f.	dazed	5
mínglìshuāngshōu	名利双收	名利雙收	f.c.w.	gain both fame and wealth	9
míngliú	名流	名流	n.	elite, person distinguished by society	1
míngpiàn	名片	名片	n.	business card, name card	9

míngshēng	名声	名聲	n.	reputation	4
míngwàng	名望	名望	n.	renown	12
míngyuè	明月	明月	n.	bright moon	2
míngzhì	明智	明智	adj.	brilliant, sagacious, sensible	5
mínyì-cèyàn	民意测验	民意測驗	f.c.w.	poll or survey of public opinion	10
Mínzhǔdǎng	民主党	民主黨	p.n.	Democratic party	1
mócālì	摩擦力	摩擦力	n.	traction	3
mòshēngrén	陌生人	陌生人	n	stranger	7
mósǔn	磨损	磨損	v (c)	wear and tear	3
mótèr	模特儿	模特兒	n.	model	4
móushēng	谋生	謀生	v.o.	earn a living	1
mùdèng-kǒudāi	目瞪口呆	目瞪口呆	f.c.w.	mouth agape with immobilizing fascination	6
mùshī	牧师	牧師	n.	priest	1
mùwū	木屋	木屋	n.	hut	2
mǔyǔ	母语	母語	n.	mother tongue	2
mǔzhǐ	拇指	拇指	n.	thumb	2
nàifán	耐烦	耐煩	adj.	patient	7
nǎinai	奶奶	奶奶	n.	paternal grandmother	2
nǎizhì	乃至	乃至	conj.	even	11
nàmèn	纳闷	納悶	v.	wonder, be puzzled	7
nánnǚ-lǎoshào	男女老少	男女老少	f.c.w.	men, women, old and young	7
nánnǚ-yǒubié	男女有别	男女有別	f.c.w.	differences between men and women	11
nánrěn	难忍	難忍	v.	hard to bear	3
nányǐ-zhìxìn	难以置信	難以置信	f.c.w.	unbelievable, incredible	4
náqǐ	拿起	拿起	v (c)	pick up	12
nèijiù	内疚	內疚	adj.	remorse, compunction, twinge of guilt	9
nèixǐng	内省	內省	v.	introspect	10
niánchū	年初	年初	n.	beginning of the year	1
niàngjiǔchǎng	酿酒厂	釀酒廠	n.	winery	3
niàntou	念头	念头	n.	idea	2
niánzhǎng	年长	年長	adj.	senior	10
Níbó'ěr	尼泊尔	尼泊爾	p.n.	Nepal	5
Níbó'ěryǔ	尼泊尔语	尼泊爾語	p.n.	Nepali	5
Níngbō	宁波	寧波	p.n.	Ningbo (city in Zhejiang Province)	1
Niǔyuē Shì	纽约市	紐約市	p.n.	New York City	5
niúzǎikù	牛仔裤	牛仔褲	n.	jeans	4

nóngnóng	浓浓	濃濃	adj.	(of degree or extent) great, strong	7
nòngqīng	弄清	弄清	v (c)	understand fully	5
nǚ zhǔjué	女主角	女主角	n.p.	female lead	1
nùqì-chōngchōng	怒气冲冲	怒氣沖沖	f.c.w.	as if flushed with rage, as if in a great rage	5
nǚquán zhǔyì	女权主义	女權主義	n.	feminism	1
nǚyōng	女佣	女傭	n.	maid	1
pájìn	爬进	爬進	v (c)	clamber into	3
pāo	抛	抛	v.	leave behind	9
péibàn	陪伴	陪伴	v.	accompany	9
pèidài	佩戴	佩戴	v.	wear (a boutonnière, badge, etc.)	7
piānjiàn	偏见	偏見	n.	stereotype, preconception	10
piāoliú	漂流	漂流	v.	go kayaking	3
pífá bùkān	疲乏不堪	疲乏不堪	f.c.w.	exhausting	7
pǐncháng	品尝	品嘗	v.	taste sample	3
pínghé-wēnróu	平和温柔	平和温柔	f.c.w.	peaceful, gentle	2
píngjiè	凭借	憑借	v.	rely on, use	1
píngmín	平民	平民	n.	common or ordinary people	10
píngtóu-lùnzú	评头论足	評頭論足	f.c.w.	be critical, nit-pick	11
pǐnjiǔ	品酒	品酒	v.	taste wine	3
Pínuòqiū	皮诺丘	皮諾丘	p.n.	Pinocchio	12
pīnxiě	拼写	拼寫	v.	spell	7
pīnyīn	拼音	拼音	n.	spelling	1
píqì	脾气	脾氣	n.	temper	1
póxí	婆媳	婆媳	n.	mother-in-law and daughter-in-law	11
Pǔlínsīdùn	普林斯顿	普林斯頓	p.n.	Princeton	12
pútáojiǔ	葡萄酒	葡萄酒	n.	wine made from grapes	3
pūtiān-gàidì	铺天盖地	鋪天蓋地	f.c.w.	all over the place	4
qiānbēi	谦卑	謙卑	adj.	humble, modest	10
qiānbiàn-wànhuà	千变万化	千變萬化	f.c.w.	ever-changing	5
qiánchéng	虔诚	虔誠	adj.	fervent, sincere	11
qiángdiào	强调	強調	v.	emphasize	11
qiánghuà	强化	強化	n.	reinforcement	9
qiángjiā	强加	強加	v.	impose, force (upon), impose by force	9
qiǎngshǒu	抢手	搶手	adj.	hottest	6
qiánlì	潜力	潛力	n.	potentiality	10
qiānnù	迁怒	遷怒	v.o.	to take one's anger out on sb.	5

qiánsuǒwèiyǒu	前所未有	前所未有	f.c.w.	unprecedented	4
qiánxīn	潜心	潜心	adj.	devotional	5
qiànyì	歉意	歉意	n.	regret	9
qiányìshí	潜意识	潛意識	n.	the subconscious	1
qiānzì	签字	簽字	v.o.	sign on the dotted line, affix one's signature	10
qídǎo	祈祷	祈禱	v.	pray	11
qíngbùzìjīn	情不自禁	情不自禁	f.c.w.	cannot help oneself (doing sth.)	7
qīngchè	清澈	清澈	adj.	crystal-clear	2
qīngchūnqī	青春期	青春期	n.	adolescence, puberty	1
qīngsōng-yōuxián	轻松悠闲	轻松悠闲	f.c.w.	relaxed, carefree, ease	7
qīngsōng-zìrú	轻松自如	輕鬆自如	f.c.w.	with ease	2
qìngxìng	庆幸	慶幸	v.	feel smug	9
qīngyíng-fēiwǔ	轻盈飞舞	輕盈飛舞	f.c.w.	skip	10
qīngyīsè	清一色	清一色	adj.	homogeneous, similar	5
qíngyǒudúzhōng	情有独钟	情有獨鍾	f.c.w.	fixation, focus on sb./sth. with great passion	12
qīnwěn	亲吻	親吻	n.	kiss	9
qìqiú	气球	氣球	n.	balloon	6
qiúhūn	求婚	求婚	v.o.	propose marriage	1
qiúxué	求学	求學	v.o.	pursue one's studies; seek knowledge	5
qǔ	娶	娶	v.	marry (a woman), take a wife	11
quánrìzhì	全日制	全日制	n.	full-time	12
quánshén-guànzhù	全神贯注	全神貫注	f.c.w.	concentrate on sth.	2
quànshuō	劝说	勸說	v.	persuade	10
quánxiào	全校	全校	n.	the whole school	10
qúdào	渠道	渠道	n.	channels, sources	10
quèbǎo	确保	確保	v.	ensure, assure	7
quèqiè	确切	確切	adj.	precise, appropriate	5
quèqiè-búguò	确切不过	確切不過	f.c.w.	precisely	3
qūfēn	区分	區分	v.	distinguish, differentiate	7
qǔjuéyú	取决于	取決於	v.p.	be determined by	3
qún	群	群	m (n)	group (of people)	6
qúnjū	群居	羣居	v.	live in commune	1
qúntǐ	群体	群體	n.	group, community	5
qùshì	去世	去世	v.o.	die, pass away	9
qǔzi	曲子	曲子	n.	song	2
ráoyǒu-xìngzhì	饶有兴致	饒有興致	f.c.w.	be interested in	12
rě	惹	惹	v.	provoke	12

rècháo	热潮	熱潮	n.	crowd-pleasing attention	4
rèlèi-yíngkuàng	热泪盈眶	熱淚盈眶	f.c.w.	tears well up, tearful	12
rènchū	认出	認出	v (c)	recognize	4
rénjì guānxi	人际关系	人際關係	n.p.	human or interpersonal relationships	1
rénjiān	人间	人間	n.	earthly world	2
rènjiào	任教	任教	v.o.	teach	1
rènkě	认可	認可	n.	approval	9
rénnǎo	人脑	人腦	n.	human brain	1
rénshìjiān	人世间	人世間	n.	human world	11
rénzhǒng	人种	人種	n.	ethnicity	2
rèxuè-fènzhàn	热血奋战	熱血奮戰	f.c.w.	fight bravely and with enthusiasm	7
rèzhōng	热衷	熱衷	v.	be loyal to	10
Rìchū Dàjiē	日出大街	日出大街	p.n.	Sunrise Terrace	5
róngbù	绒布	絨布	n.	velveteen	7
róngdexià	容得下	容得下	v.	hold, contain, make room for	11
rónglú	熔炉	熔爐	n.	melting pot	2
róngrǔ-yǔgòng	荣辱与共	榮辱與共	f.c.w.	share honor and disgrace	10
róngshēng	荣升	榮升	v.	elevate	9
róngyù	荣誉	榮譽	n.	reward, honor, credit	10
ruǎnruò-wúlì	软弱无力	軟弱無力	f.c.w.	weak	10
rúcǐ	如此	如此	adv.	in this way	2
Rújiāxuéshuō	儒家学说	儒家學說	p.n.	Confucianism	4
Ruògē	若哥	若哥	p.n.	Rutgers	12
rúyuànyǐcháng	如愿以偿	如願以償	f.c.w.	achieve what one wishes	9
sāhuǎngchéngxìng	撒谎成性	撒謊成性	f.c.w.	chronic liar	12
sāncùn jīnlián	三寸金莲	三寸金蓮	n.	golden lotus	1
sànluò	散落	散落	v.	disperse	3
sānsan-liǎngliǎng	三三两两	三三兩兩	f.c.w.	desolate and scattered	3
sèlā	色拉	色拉	n.	salad	10
shǎguā	傻瓜	傻瓜	n.	the dimwitted	12
shānggǎn	伤感	傷感	adj.	emotional	9
shānghài	伤害	傷害	v.	harm, hurt	2
shàngsī	上司	上司	n.	boss, supervisor	1
shǎnshǎnfāliàng	闪闪发亮	閃閃發亮	f.c.w.	shiny	12
shǎoshùzúqún	少数族群	少數族羣	n.	minority	1
shātān	沙滩	沙灘	n.	sand beach	2
shèjí	涉及	涉及	v.	involve, concern	11
shén	神	神	n.	god	10

shēn	伸	伸	v.	extend	12
shēnbiǎotóngqíng	深表同情	深表同情	f.c.w.	sympathize	12
shēngāo	身高	身高	n.	(a person's) height	11
shēngchēng	声称	聲稱	v.	claim	12
Shèngdàn Lǎorén	圣诞老人	聖誕老人	p.n.	Santa Claus	12
shěngjí	省级	省級	n.	provincial level	9
shēngmíng	声明	聲明	n.	statement	8
shěngqián	省钱	省錢	v.o.	save money, be thrifty	5
shēngqián	生前	生前	n.	before one's death, during one's lifetime	3
shèngrèn	胜任	勝任	v.	be competent in	3
shēngyú	生于	生於	v.p.	be born in	1
shènhuò	甚或	甚或	conj.	even	7
shēnhūxī	深呼吸	深呼吸	n.	deep breath	6
shēnlǜsè	深绿色	深綠色	adj.	dark green	7
shénqí	神奇	神奇	adj.	magical	11
shēnsī-shúlǜ	深思熟虑	深思熟慮	f.c.w.	think deeply and carefully	9
shēnxìn	深信	深信	v.	firmly believe	1
shēnxìn-wúyí	深信无疑	深信無疑	f.c.w.	firmly convinced	11
shénzhì	神志	神志	n.	consciousness, senses, state of mind	5
shèshī	设施	設施	n.	facility	11
shèshìbùshēn	涉世不深	涉世不深	f.c.w.	the immature who have scanty experience of life	12
shǐ	屎	屎	n.	feces, shit	8
shì'érbùjiàn	视而不见	視而不見	f.c.w.	turn a blind eye to, look but (deliberately) not see	8
shíchā	时差	時差	n.	jet lag	5
shīgǔ	尸骨	屍骨	n.	bones of the dead (after all else has decomposed)	3
shíjiānbiǎo	时间表	時間表	n.	schedule, time-table	12
shìjièzhīdiān	世界之颠	世界之巔	n.p.	the top of the world	10
shìjué	视觉	視覺	n.	vision	8
shíkōng	时空	時空	n.	space-time	9
shíqū	时区	時區	n.	time zone	6
shíshàng	时尚	時尚	adj.	in fashion, in vogue	4
shīshén	失神	失神	v.o.	be inattentive, be absent-minded	4
shíshì	实事	實事	n.	work	10
shíshí-zàizài	实实在在	實實在在	r.f.	concretely existing	12
shīwù	失误	失誤	n.	mistake, fault	3
shìxiàng	事项	事項	n.	item, matter	8

shīxíng	施行	施行	v.	apply	1
shìyìhuì	市议会	市議會	n.p.	city council	5
shìyǒu	室友	室友	n.	roommate	1
shízhǐ	食指	食指	n.	index finger, forefinger	6
shīzhí	失职	失職	v.o.	neglect one's duty	2
shǒulǐ	手里	手裡	n.	in one's hand	11
shòupìn	受聘	受聘	v.o.	be employed by	1
shōushi	收拾	收拾	v.	pack up	11
shǒutíbāo	手提包	手提包	n.	purse, pocketbook	9
shòuxīng	寿星	壽星	n.	sb. who celebrates (e.g., his/her birthday)	6
shǒuzhǐ	手指	手指	n.	finger	3
shǔ	数	數	v.	count	6
shuāituì	衰退	衰退	v.	deteriorate	3
shuāngguǎn-qíxià	双管齐下	雙管齊下	f.c.w.	do two things simultaneously	8
shuāngguānyǔ	双关语	雙關語	n.	pun, a play upon words	7
shuāngjiǎo	双脚	雙腳	n	one's two feet	1
shuāngyǔzhě	双语者	雙語者	n.	bilingual	8
shuāxīn	刷新	刷新	v (c)	renovate	6
shūfǎ	书法	書法	n.	calligraphy	5
shuǐdàotián	水稻田	水稻田	n.	rice paddies	3
shuǐlǐ	水里	水裡	n.	in the water	3
Shuǐmǎnián	水马年	水馬年	p.n.	Year of Water Horse	1
Shuìměirén	睡美人	睡美人	p.n.	Sleeping Beauty	12
shuǐní	水泥	水泥	n.	concrete	3
shùncóng	顺从	順從	v.	comply	9
shùnjiān	瞬间	瞬間	n.	in the twinkling of an eye	2
shùnxī-wànbiàn	瞬息万变	瞬息萬變	f.c.w.	take place in a very short period of time	5
shuōcí	说词	說詞	n.	wording	3
shūyú	疏于	疏於	v.	neglect	10
sīlì dàxué	私立大学	私立大學	n.p.	private university	1
sìmiào	寺庙	寺庙	n.	Buddhist temple, monastery of other religions	5
Sītǎndùndǎo	斯坦顿岛	斯坦頓島	p.n.	Staten Island	5
sīwéi	思维	思維	n.	thinking	2
sōngdòng	松动	鬆動	adj.	loose	12
suànchū	算出	算出	v (c)	calculate	6
suànshù	算术	算術	n.	arithmetic	8
suídàliù	随大溜	隨大溜	v.o.	follow the general trend	12

suíshí-suídì	随时随地	隨時隨地	adv.	momentarily	2
suǒjiàn-suǒwén	所见所闻	所見所聞	f.c.w.	what one has seen and heard	8
suǒshuō	所说	所說	n.p.	what one has said	4
suǒzài	所在	所在	n.	location	2
suǒzuò-suǒwéi	所作所为	所作所為	f.c.w.	one's behavior or conduct	4
sùsòng	诉讼	訴訟	v.	file a lawsuit, litigate	10
sùzào	塑造	塑造	v.	shape, mold, portray	8
Tǎfūcí Dàxué	塔夫茨大学	塔夫茨大学	p.n.	Tufts University	1
táijiē	台阶	臺階	n.	step	1
táiqǐ	抬起	抬起	v (c)	look up at	12
tànfǎng	探访	探訪	v.	visit	11
tàng	趟	趟	m (v)	a verbal measure word indicating the frequency of going/coming	8
tàng	烫	烫	v.	iron	11
tángguǒ	糖果	糖果	n.	candy, sweets	3
tánqíng-shuō'ài	谈情说爱	談情說愛	f.c.w.	romantic dating	1
tǎnshuài	坦率	坦率	adj.	blunt, candid, unadorned, frank	4
tànxī	叹惜	嘆惜	v.	lament	12
táokè	逃课	逃課	v.o.	cut class	5
táoqì	淘气	淘氣	adj.	naughty, mischievous	4
táoxué	逃学	逃學	v.o.	play hooky	1
táozuì	陶醉	陶醉	v.	revel in, be intoxicated with	2
tèdì	特地	特地	adv.	for a special purpose	5
téng	腾	騰	v.	make room for	3
tèyì	特意	特意	adv.	for a special purpose, especially	7
tèzhēn	特征	特徵	n.	distinctive character	2
tì	剃	剃	v.	shave	1
tiānhuābǎn	天花板	天花板	n.	ceiling	10
tiánměi	甜美	甜美	adj.	sweet	2
tiānrǎngzhībié	天壤之别	天壤之別	f.c.w.	a world of difference	4
tiánshí	甜食	甜食	n.	dessert	8
tiánwèi	甜味	甜味	n.	sweetness	3
tiàoyuè	跳跃	跳躍	v.	leap	8
tiǎozhàn	挑战	挑戰	n.	challenge	11
tìdài	替代	替代	v.	substitute for, replace, supersede	7
Tínàkè	提纳克	提納克	p.n.	Teaneck	12
tíng	停	停	v.	stop	3

tīngjué	听觉	聽覺	n.	sense of hearing	8
tīngqīng	听清	聽清	v (c)	understand	8
tīngzhòng	听众	聽眾	n.	audience, listener	11
tíshì	提示	提示	n.	clue	12
tònggǎi-qiánfēi	痛改前非	痛改前非	f.c.w.	sincerely mend one's ways	1
tónggān-gòngkǔ	同甘共苦	同甘共苦	f.c.w.	share well-being and woe	10
tōnghūn	通婚	通婚	v.o.	intermarry	1
tòngkǔ bùkān	痛苦不堪	痛苦不堪	f.c.w.	cannot bear the suffering	5
tóngnián	同年	同年	n.	same year	1
tóngnián	童年	童年	n.	childhood	8
tuányuánfàn	团圆饭	團圓飯	n.	family reunion dinner	9
túbù lǚxíng	徒步旅行	徒步旅行	v.p.	backpack, hike with a backpack	2
tǔdūn	土墩	土墩	n.	bump	3
tǔfěi	土匪	土匪	n.	bandit, brigand	1
tuì	退	退	v.	move back	3
tuìchǎng	退场	退場	n.	recessional, formally exit	7
tuīyí	推移	推移	n.	elapse (of time)	12
tūntūn-tǔtǔ	吞吞吐吐	吞吞吐吐	f.c.w.	speak hesitantly	8
tuō'érsuǒ	托儿所	托兒所	n.	day care	8
tuōyǐng'érchū	脱颖而出	脱穎而出	f.c.w.	blossom, develop	1
túxíng	图形	圖形	n.	sketch, drawing	11
tùzi	兔子	兔子	n.	rabbit	2
tūzi	秃子	秃子	n.	a bald person	8
wàichū	外出	外出	v.	go out	7
wàihuì duìhuànlǜ	外汇兑换率	外匯兌換率	n.p.	foreign currency exchange rate	5
wàisūn	外孙	外孫	n.	daughter's son, grandson	4
wāiwāi-niǔniǔ	歪歪扭扭	歪歪扭扭	f.c.w.	careening	6
wàixīngrén	外星人	外星人	n.	creature from outer space	4
wǎncānhuì	晚餐会	晚餐會	n.	dinner party	5
wǎncuò	挽错	挽错	v (c)	take wrongly	7
wàngquè	忘却	忘卻	v.	forget, unlearn	9
wǎngshì	往事	往事	n.	past events	1
wànjīnyóu	万金油	萬金油	n	analgesic balm for muscle soreness, headache, etc.	8
wànshì	万事	萬事	n.	everything	10
wèideshì	为的是	为的是	p.p.	for the purpose of	3
wèijué	味觉	味覺	n.	taste	3
Wēilián	威廉	威廉	p.n.	William	1
wēimiào	微妙	微妙	adj.	subtle	7

wěiwěi-nuònuò	唯唯诺诺	唯唯諾諾	r.f.	wimp	12
wénhuà	文化	文化	n.	culture	1
wénshēn	纹身	紋身	n.	tattoo	1
Wēnsīdùn Luòdé	温斯顿·洛德	温斯顿·洛德	p.n.	Winston Lord	1
wènxīn-wúkuì	问心无愧	問心無愧	f.c.w.	have a clear conscience	9
Wòhǔcánglóng	卧虎藏龙	臥虎藏龍		Crouching Tiger, Hidden Dragon (a movie)	3
wòshì	卧室	臥室	n.	bedroom	6
wǔ	捂	捂	v.	cover up	6
wǔbù	舞步	舞步	n.	dance steps	8
wúfǎ lèibǐ	无法类比	無法類比	f.c.w.	beyond analogy or comparison	8
wúfēi	无非	無非	adv.	simply, only	10
wūguī	乌龟	烏龜	n.	turtle	12
wúlǐ	无礼	無禮	adj.	impolite	2
wúnéng-wéilì	无能为力	無能為力	f.c.w.	powerless, helpless, incapable of action	2
wūpó	巫婆	巫婆	n.	witch	1
wǔshuì	午睡	午睡	n.	nap	6
wúsuǒshìshì	无所事事	無所事事	f.c.w.	do nothing, idle away one's time	12
wúyán	无言	無言	adj.	non-linguistic	2
wūyán	屋檐	屋簷	n.	roof, eaves	1
wūyè	呜咽	嗚咽	v.	moan	6
wúzhī	无知	無知	adj.	ignorant, stupid	5
Xī'ěrwéisītè Shǐtàilóng	西尔维斯特·史泰龙	西尔维斯特·史泰龙	p.n.	Sylvester Stallone	2
xiàba	下巴	下巴	n.	chin, lower jaw	8
xiágǔ	峡谷	峽谷	n.	valley	3
xiàn	馅	餡	n.	stuffing	8
xiànfǎ	宪法	憲法	n.	constitution	10
xiāngchà	相差	相差	v.	differ	6
xiāngdāngyú	相当于	相当于	v.p.	be equivalent of	1
xiǎngfú	享福	享福	v.o.	live in ease and comfort	10
xiānghù	相互	相互	adv.	each other	9
xiāngjiāo	香蕉	香蕉	n.	Banana (refers to an Asian-American who is "yellow" on the outside but "white" on the inside)	1
xiàngjiāoxié	橡胶鞋	橡膠鞋	n.	rubber shoes	3
xiàngpítǐng	橡皮艇	橡皮艇	n.	kayak	3
xiǎngxiàng	想象	想象	v.	imagine	12

xiānnǚ	仙女	仙女	n.	fairy	12
xiānqǐ	掀起	掀起	v.	start, begin to surge	4
xiǎnyǎn	显眼	顯眼	adj.	eye-catching	3
xiànzhìcí	限制词	限制詞	n.	qualifier	12
xiǎobiànchí	小便池	小便池	n.	urinal	4
xiāochú	消除	消除	v.	destroy, terminate	2
Xiǎohǔ	小虎	小虎	p.n.	nickname "Little Tiger"	6
xiàojìng	孝敬	孝敬	v.	be filial and respectful to one's elders	11
xiǎokāng	小康	小康	n.	comparatively well off	3
xiāosǎ	潇洒	瀟灑	adj	casual, natural, informal	5
xiàoshēng	笑声	笑聲	n.	sound of laughter	12
xiǎoshēng	小声	小聲	adj.	in a soft, low voice	12
xiǎoshíhou	小时候	小時候	n.	in one's childhood, when one was young	8
xiàoshùn	孝顺	孝順	v.	filial piety	1
xiàoxīxī	笑嘻嘻	笑嘻嘻	r.f.	grinning, smiling broadly	1
xiàsǐ	吓死	嚇死	v (c)	be horrified	3
Xiàwēiyí	夏威夷	夏威夷	p.n.	Hawaii	4
xiáxiǎo	狭小	狹小	adj.	narrow	5
xiázhǎi	狭窄	狹窄	adj.	contracted, cramped, narrow; limited	1
xiělínlín	血淋淋	血淋淋	adj.	bloody	12
xiézi	鞋子	鞋子	n.	shoe	8
xǐfàshuǐ	洗发水	洗髮水	n.	shampoo	7
Xījīn	锡金	錫金	p.n.	Sikkim	1
xìjùxìng	戏剧性	戲劇性	adj.	dramatic	2
xīliūxīliū	稀溜稀溜	稀溜稀溜	r.f.	slurping	10
xīncháo	新潮	新潮	adj.	mod, trendy	4
xìng'ài dìngxiàng	性爱定向	性爱定向	n.	sexual orientation	1
xìngài	性爱	性愛	n.	love between the sexes, sexual love	1
xìngbié	性别	性別	n.	gender	3
xíngchéng	形成	形成	v.	form	2
xìngfèn	兴奋	興奮	adj.	hypoglycemic	6
xìngfèn de	兴奋地	興奮地	adv.	excitedly	4
xǐngmù	醒目	醒目	adj.	eye-catching	7
xìngqù'àngrán	兴趣盎然	興趣盎然	f.c.w.	have great interest in sth.	12
xìngzhì-bóbó	兴致勃勃	興致勃勃	f.c.w.	take delight in doing a sth.	12
xíngzhī-yǒuxiào	行之有效	行之有效	f.c.w.	act effectively	3
xìnlài	信赖	信賴	v.	trust	12
xīnlǐxuéjiā	心理学家	心理學家	n.	psychologist	1

xīnmǎn-yìzú	心满意足	心滿意足	f.c.w.	be perfectly content or satisfied	6
xīnpíng-qìhé	心平气和	心平氣和	f.c.w.	calm, even-tempered and good-tempered	5
xīnshǎng	欣赏	欣賞	v.	admire	8
xīnshuǐ	薪水	薪水	n.	salary, wage, emolument	1
xīntài	心态	心態	n.	mind set	2
xīnwèi	欣慰	欣慰	adj.	conforming	9
xīnxǐ-ruòkuáng	欣喜若狂	欣喜若狂	f.c.w.	be joyful	11
xìnyǎng	信仰	信仰	n.	belief	2
xìnyù	信誉	信譽	n.	credit	11
Xīnzéxīzhōu	新泽西州	新澤西州	p.n.	New Jersey	1
xiōnghuā	胸花	胸花	n.	boutonnière	7
xiōngmèi	兄妹	兄妹	n.	brother and sister	9
xīshēng	牺牲	犧牲	v.	sacrifice	9
xìshēng-xìyǔ	细声细语	細聲細語	f.c.w.	hushed voice	10
xísú	习俗	習俗	n.	customs, what is customary	5
xiù	秀	秀	n.	show	2
xiūchǐ	羞耻	羞恥	adj.	shameful	9
xiùjué	嗅觉	嗅覺	n.	sense of smell, olfactory	3
xiūyǎng	修养	修養	n.	self-cultivation	4
xīxiào	嬉笑	嬉笑	v.	laugh and play	1
xìxīn	细心	細心	adj.	careful	12
xǐyuè	喜悦	喜悦	n.	joy	11
xū	需	需	v.	need	7
xuānbù	宣布	宣布	v.	announce	8
xuānchēng	宣称	宣稱	v.	announce	8
xuánlǜ	旋律	旋律	n.	rhythm	5
xuānyán	宣言	宣言	n.	proclamation	8
xuànyào	炫耀	炫耀	v.	toot one's horn, show off, flaunt	10
xuèkù	血库	血庫	n.	blood bank	11
xuètǒng	血统	血統	n.	blood lineage	11
xuèxīng-cánbào	血腥残暴	血腥殘暴	f.c.w.	brutal	2
xuéyǐzhìyòng	学以致用	學以致用	f.c.w.	thumb your "knows" (put your knowledge into practice)	3
xūgòu	虚构	虛構	v.	make-believe	12
xùnchì	训斥	訓斥	v.	reproach, accuse	5
xùnsù	迅速	迅速	adj.	rapid	2
xūntáo	熏陶	熏陶	v.	shape, be influenced by	10

xúnwèn	询问	詢問	v.	ask, inquire	8
xùshì	叙事	敘事	v.	narrate	5
xūzhī	须知	須知	n.	notice, announcement	2
yáchǐ	牙齿	牙齒	n.	tooth	12
yáchuáng	牙床	牙床	n.	gum	12
yàgēnr	压根儿	壓根兒	adv.	never, not from the start	4
yǎnchànghuì	演唱会	演唱會	n.	recital	3
yángqiāng-yángdiào	洋腔洋调	洋腔洋調	f.c.w.	foreign accent	5
yànwù	厌恶	厭惡	v.	hate	9
yánxiàzhīyì	言下之意	言下之意	f.c.w.	hidden meaning, between the lines	4
yányòng	沿用	沿用	v.	continue to use (an old method, system, etc.)	5
yáogǔnyuè	摇滚乐	搖滾樂	n.	rock 'n roll music	2
yàome	要么	要麼	conj.	or, either…or…	10
yáowàng	遥望	遙望	v.	look into the distance	2
yáoxiānghūyìng	遥相呼应	遙相呼應	f.c.w.	harmoniously reflect each other	2
yāquè-wúshēng	鸦雀无声	鴉雀無聲	f.c.w.	stunned silence	11
Yàyì	亚裔	亞裔	p.n.	Asian descendent	7
Yàzhōurén	亚洲人	亞洲人	p.n.	Asians	1
yāzi	鸭子	鴨子	n.	duck	2
yì	亿	億	num.	a hundred million	10
yǐ…wéilì	以……为例	以……為例	p.p.	for example	5
yī'nián-dàotóu	一年到头	一年到頭	f.c.w.	throughout the year	9
yī'nián-sìjì	一年四季	一年四季	f.c.w.	all the year round	12
yǐ…wéiróng	以……为荣	以……為榮	p.p.	be proud of	9
yībǐqián	一笔钱	一筆錢	n.p.	a sum of money	4
yīchángtiáo	一长条	一長條	n.p.	a long list	12
yǐcǐ	以此	以此	adv.	so that	7
yīdàduī	一大堆	一大堆	n.p.	a large pile of	12
yīduān	一端	一端	n.	one end, the other side of the world	9
yìguó-tāxiāng	异国他乡	異國他鄉	f.c.w.	foreign country	7
yíhàn	遗憾	遺憾	n.	shame, pity, regret	12
yíjū	移居	移居	v.o.	emigrate	1
yījǔ-yīdòng	一举一动	一舉一動	f.c.w.	body language	7
yīlài	依赖	依賴	v.	rely on, depend on	9
yīlèi	一类	一類	n.	one category	10
yìlùn-fēnfēn	议论纷纷	議論紛紛	f.c.w.	discuss	3
Yìndì'ānrén	印第安人	印第安人	p.n.	(American) Indian	1
yīng'ér	婴儿	嬰兒	n.	baby	9

yìngbì	硬币	硬幣	n.	coin	12
yīngcùn	英寸	英寸	m(n)	(English) inch	1
yìngfu	应付	應付	v.	cope with, handle	12
yīnglǐ	英里	英里	m(n)	mile	1
yíngrào	萦绕	縈繞	v.	linger on	9
yǐngxiǎng	影响	影響	n.	impact	8
yíngyǎngxué	营养学	營養學	n.	nutrition	8
yìngyùn'érshēng	应运而生	應運而生	f.c.w.	emerge	12
yīnjié	音节	音節	n.	syllable	8
yǐnmán	隐瞒	隱瞞	v.	hide	1
yǐnqǐ	引起	引起	v.	cause, give rise to	2
yǐnshì	隐士	隱士	n.	hermit	1
yīrénzuòshì yīréndāng	一人做事 一人当	一人做事 一人當		one is responsible for what one has done	10
yīrú-jìwǎng	一如既往	一如既往	f.c.w.	all the time, for years, just as in the past	11
yìshí	意识	意识	n.	sense, awareness	5
yītā-hútú	一塌糊涂	一塌糊塗	f.c.w.	in an awful or terrible state	6
yíwàng	遗忘	遺忘	v.	forget	9
yìwèi	意味	意味	v.	imply	9
yīxiāng-qíngyuàn	一厢情愿	一廂情願	f.c.w.	one's wishful thinking	12
yīyuán	一员	一員	n.	one of the members	7
yīzé	一则	一則	m (n)	a measure word for an advertisement	4
yǐzhì	以致	以致	conj.	so...that...	1
yǐzhìyú	以至于	以至於	conj.	so...that...	6
yīzǒu-liǎozhī	一走了之	一走了之	f.c.w.	leave	9
yōngbào	拥抱	擁抱	v./n.	hug	9
yòngcí	用辞	用辭	n.	wording	1
yǒngjiǔ	永久	永久	adj.	permanent	3
yònglái	用来	用來	p.p.	for the purpose of doing sth.	3
yònglì-dùnzú	用力顿足	用力頓足	f.c.w.	stomp	10
yòngqián	用钱	用錢	p.p.	by means of money, using money	12
yǒngzhuāng	泳装	泳裝	n.	bathing suit	3
yóu...érdìng	由......而定	由......而定	p.p.	depending on	10
yòuhuòlì	诱惑力	誘惑力	n.	attraction	12
yōumò	幽默	幽默	n.	humor	11
yōumògǎn	幽默感	幽默感	n.	sense of humor	12
yóurènyú	游刃于	游刃于	v.p.	be highly competent in	1

yōuróu-guǎduàn	优柔寡断	優柔寡斷	f.c.w.	indecisive, irresolute, hesitant	10
yǒusuǒ-bùtóng	有所不同	有所不同	f.c.w.	somewhat different	7
Yóutàirén	犹太人	猶太人	p.n.	Jew	1
yóuxì	游戏	游戏	n.	game	10
yōuxiān-cìxù	优先次序	優先次序	f.c.w	priority	10
yóuxíng	游行	游行	n.	parade	1
yǒuxuè-yǒuròu	有血有肉	有血有肉	f.c.w.	true to life	9
yǒuzhāoyīrì	有朝一日	有朝一日	f.c.w.	some day in the future	1
yuànhèn	怨恨	怨恨	n.	hatred, intense dislike	12
yuǎnqīn	远亲	遠親	n.	extended family	9
yǔcǐ-tóngshí	与此同时	與此同時	f.c.w.	at the same time, meanwhile	1
yuèdú	阅读	閱讀	v.	read	1
yuèjiā	越加	越加	adv.	more and more	12
Yuèzhàn	越战	越戰	p.n.	The Vietnam War	7
yúlè	娱乐	娛樂	n.	entertainment	2
yùndòngshān	运动衫	運動衫	n.	sweatshirt	4
yǔnnuò	允诺	允諾	v.	promise, undertake	9
yǔwúlúncì	语无伦次	語無倫次	f.c.w.	speak incoherently	5
zài hěnduō fāngmiàn	在很多方面	在很多方面	p.p.	in many ways	1
zàihu	在乎	在乎	v.	(oft. used in the negative) care about, mind	7
zàishì	在世	在世	v.	exist, be alive	7
zàiwài	在外	在外	p.p.	outside	12
zàiyì	在意	在意	v.	take notice of	10
zànshí	暂时	暫時	n.	temporary	9
zàntóng	赞同	贊同	v.	approve of, agree with	1
zǎoxiān	早先	早先	n.	previous time, before	9
zéguài	责怪	責怪	v.	blame, accuse, remonstrate	2
zēngtiān	增添	增添	v.	facilitate, augment	7
zhà	乍	乍	adv.	at first	4
zhǎ	眨	眨	v.	move (i.e., eyes)	5
zhāgēn	扎根	扎根	v.o.	be rooted in	4
zhāngchéng	章程	章程	n.	bylaws, regulations	10
zhǎngkòng	掌控	掌控	v.	control	12
zhāngláng	蟑螂	蟑螂	n.	cockroach	2
Zhànguó Shíqī	战国时期	戰國時期	p.n.	Warring States Period	1
zhǎngxiàng	长相	長相	n.	looks, appearance	4
zhǎngzhě	长者	長者	n.	elder, senior	1
zhānxīngxué	占星学	占星學	n.	astrology	11

zhànzài	站在	站在	v.	stand at some place	4
zhàogù	照顾	照顧	v.	take care of (a child, a senior, et al.)	12
zhàokàn	照看	照看	v.	take care of	12
zhàomíng	照明	照明	v (c)	lighting, illumination	2
zhě	者	者	n.	person (who does sth.)	1
zhè jiù shì shuō	这就是说	這就是說		that is to say…	7
zhèn'ěr	震耳	震耳	v.o.	(noise) so loud that it shakes one's ears	2
zhēngchǎo	争吵	爭吵	v.	quarrel	1
zhēngdà	睁大	睜大	v (c)	open one's eyes wide	3
zhèngfǔ guānyuán	政府官员	政府官員	n.p.	government official	1
zhěngjiù	拯救	拯救	n.	salvation	10
zhēngróng-suìyuè	峥嵘岁月	峥嵘岁月	f.c.w.	memorable years of one's life	7
zhěngtiān	整天	整天	n.	the whole day	9
zhèngzhí	正直	正直	adj.	honest, upright, fair-minded	10
zhèngzhòng-qíshì	郑重其事	郑重其事	f.c.w.	intone	12
zhènjìng	镇静	鎮靜	adj.	calm	11
zhēnrén-zhēnshì	真人真事	真人真事	f.c.w.	actual person and event	1
zhènshàng	镇上	鎮上	n.	in the town	6
zhènzhǎng	镇长	鎮長	n.	mayor	1
zhènzhèn sònggē	阵阵颂歌	陣陣頌歌	n.p.	chants	5
Zhēnzhūgǎng	珍珠港	珍珠港	p.n.	Pearl Harbor	5
zhèxià	这下	這下	n.	this time	3
zhéxué	哲学	哲學	n.	philosophy	12
zhézhōng	折中	折中	n./v.	compromise	6
zhí	值	值	v.	be worth	6
zhídèngdèng	直瞪瞪	直瞪瞪	adj.	wide-eyed	3
zhìfú	制服	制服	n.	uniform	7
zhìgāo-wúshàng	至高无上	至高無上	f.c.w.	highest	10
zhìhéng	制衡	制衡	v.	balance	10
zhǐkòng	指控	指控	v.	accuse	1
zhìlì	智力	智力	n.	intelligence, intellect	12
zhíqián	值钱	值錢	adj.	valuable, worthwhile	11
zhīsuǒyǐ	之所以	之所以	conj.	the reason why	11
zhǐwàng	指望	指望	v.	bank on, look forward to, pin one's hope on	4
zhǐwàng	指望	指望	v.	expect, pin one's hopes on, hope for	9
zhíxíng zhǎngguān	执行长官	執行長官	n.p.	chief executive officer (CEO)	10

zhízé	职责	職責	n.	duty, obligation	2
zhīzhūwǎng	蜘蛛网	蜘蛛網	n.	spider web	9
zhōngcānguǎn	中餐馆	中餐館	n.	Chinese restaurant	12
zhōnggào	忠告	忠告	n.	advice	4
Zhōngguóchéng	中国城	中國城	p.n.	Chinatown	5
zhōngguóshì	中国式	中國式	adj.	Chinese style	8
zhòngjiǎng	中奖	中獎	v.o.	win the lottery	10
zhòngliàng	重量	重量	n.	heft	12
zhōngqī	中期	中期	n.	middle period	7
zhōngwén xuéxiào	中文学校	中文學校	n.p.	Chinese school	8
zhòngyàoxìng	重要性	重要性	n.	importance, significance	11
zhōngzhǐ	终止	終止	v.	sever, terminate	10
zhōngzú	种族	種族	n.	race (of people)	1
zhǒu	肘	肘	n.	elbow	8
zhōulì dàxué	州立大学	州立大學	n.p.	(public, not private) state university	1
zhuàiguòlái	拽过来	拽过来	v (c)	lift sb. over	3
zhuàngguān	壮观	壯觀	adj.	magnificent	7
zhuāngshìpǐn	装饰品	裝飾品	n.	streamer	6
Zhuāngzǐ	庄子	莊子	p.n.	369-286 B.C.E., Daoist philosopher, Master Zhuāng, also known as Zhuang Zhou	7
zhuānhèng	专横	專横	adj.	peremptory	8
zhuǎnhuàn	转换	轉換	n./v.	transformation/transform	2
zhuànlái-zhuànqù	转来转去	轉來轉去	f.c.w.	twirl	10
zhùfú	祝福	祝福	v.	wish sb. happiness	6
zhuīhuǐ-mòjí	追悔莫及	追悔莫及	f.c.w.	be overcome with regret	5
zhuīxún	追寻	追尋	v.	pursue	7
zhùjìn	住进	住進	v (c)	check in a hotel	5
zhūrú	诸如	諸如	v.	such as	10
zhǔxiū	主修	主修	v.	major in	1
zhúyī	逐一	逐一	adv.	one by one	10
zìháo	自豪	自豪	adj.	proud	8
zīrùn	滋润	滋潤	adj.	moisturizing	3
zīwèi	滋味	滋味	n.	taste, flavor	3
zìwǒ jièshào	自我介绍	自我介紹	f.c.w.	introducing oneself	5
zǐxì	仔细	仔細	adj.	careful	2
zīxún	咨询	諮詢	n.	consultation	5
zìyóu zhǔyì	自由主义	自由主義	n.	liberalism	1
zìyóu-zìzài	自由自在	自由自在	f.c.w.	free	10

zōngjiào	宗教	宗教	n.	religion	10
zōnglǘshù	棕榈树	棕櫚樹	n.	palm	2
zǒujìn	走进	走進	v (c)	walk into	6
zòuyīdùn	揍一顿	揍一顿	v.p.	beat, hit, strike	1
zuìwéi	最为	最為	adv.	the most, extremely	4
zǔjí	祖籍	祖籍	n.	original family home, ancestral home	1
zūnxìng-dàmíng	尊姓大名	尊姓大名	f.c.w.	one's surname and given name	7
zūnzhòng	尊重	尊重	v.	respect	9
zuómo	琢磨	琢磨	v.	think over, ponder	3
zǔxiān	祖先	祖先	n.	ancestors	9